Dissecting the economic, cultural, political, gende engagements with respect to India, this volume succ approaches such as colonialism and intersectionality and provides a firm grounding for analysing the Indian case in a global perspective.

Thomas Faist, Professor of Sociology, Bielefeld University, Germany

This timely volume offers a path-breaking collection of essays on transnationalism with special reference to India and the Indian diaspora. Supported by detailed historical research, both traditional and web-based, each essay interrogates global disjunctures, unequal power structures, gender hierarchies and social and ethnic collisions that underlie the politics of migration, borders, homeland narratives, cosmopolitanism and the changing definitions of the nation state.

Vijay Mishra, Professor of English and Comparative Literature, Murdoch University, Australia

This is an excellent collection of essays that includes the entire gamut of themes relating to Indian transnationalism – from migrant workers (labourers and skilled professionals), implications for culture and identity, political and gender dynamics and global networks – which would appeal to scholars and students of sociology, anthropology, history, geography and diaspora studies.

Brij Maharaj, Professor of Geography, University of KwaZulu-Natal, South Africa

ROUTLEDGE HANDBOOK OF INDIAN TRANSNATIONALISM

This book introduces readers to the many dimensions of historical and contemporary Indian transnationalism and the experiences of migrants and workers to reveal the structures of transnationalism and the ways in which Indian origin groups are affected.

The concept of crossing borders emerges as an important theme, along with the interweaving of life in geographic and web spaces. The authors draw from a variety of archives and intellectual perspectives in order to map the narratives of Indian transnationalism and analyse the interplay of culture and structures within transnational contexts. The topics covered range from the history of transnational networks, activism, identity, gender, politics, labour, policy, performance, literature and more. This collection presents a wide array of issues and debates which will reinvigorate discussions about Indian transnationalism.

This handbook will be an invaluable resource for academics, researchers and students interested in studying South Asia in general and the Indian diaspora in particular.

Ajaya K. Sahoo teaches at the Centre for Study of Indian Diaspora, University of Hyderabad, India. His research interests include the Indian diaspora and transnationalism. He has co-edited the *Routledge Handbook of the Indian Diaspora* (2018), *Indian Transnationalism Online* (2014), *Transnational Migrations: The Indian Diaspora* (2009) and *Tracing an Indian Diaspora: Contexts, Memories, Representations* (2008). He is also the editor of *South Asian Diaspora*, also published by Routledge.

Bandana Purkayastha is Professor of Sociology and Asian American Studies at the University of Connecticut, USA. Her research interests are the intersections of gender/racism/class/age, transnationalism, violence and peace, and human rights. Her recent books are *The Human Rights Enterprise: Political Sociology, State Power, and Social Movements* (2015), *Voices of Internally Displaced Persons in Kenya: A Human Rights Perspective* (2015) and *Human Trafficking* (2018).

ROUTLEDGE HANDBOOK OF INDIAN TRANSNATIONALISM

Edited by Ajaya K. Sahoo and Bandana Purkayastha

Routledge
Taylor & Francis Group
LONDON AND NEW YORK

First published 2020
by Routledge
2 Park Square, Milton Park, Abingdon, Oxon OX14 4RN

and by Routledge
605 Third Avenue, New York, NY 10017

First issued in paperback 2022

Routledge is an imprint of the Taylor & Francis Group, an informa business

© 2020 selection and editorial matter, Ajaya K. Sahoo and Bandana Purkayastha; individual chapters, the contributors

The right of Ajaya K. Sahoo and Bandana Purkayastha to be identified as the authors of the editorial material, and of the authors for their individual chapters, has been asserted in accordance with sections 77 and 78 of the Copyright, Designs and Patents Act 1988.

All rights reserved. No part of this book may be reprinted or reproduced or utilised in any form or by any electronic, mechanical, or other means, now known or hereafter invented, including photocopying and recording, or in any information storage or retrieval system, without permission in writing from the publishers.

Trademark notice: Product or corporate names may be trademarks or registered trademarks, and are used only for identification and explanation without intent to infringe.

Publisher's Note
The publisher has gone to great lengths to ensure the quality of this reprint but points out that some imperfections in the original copies may be apparent.

British Library Cataloguing-in-Publication Data
A catalogue record for this book is available from the British Library

Library of Congress Cataloging-in-Publication Data
Names: Sahoo, Ajaya Kumar, editor. | Purkayastha, Bandana, 1956- editor.
Title: Routledge handbook of Indian transnationalism / edited by Ajaya K. Sahoo and Bandana Purkayastha.
Description: Abingdon, Oxon ; New York, NY : Routledge, 2019. | Includes bibliographic references.
Identifiers: LCCN 2019006463| ISBN 9781138089143 (hardback) | ISBN 9781315109381 (ebook) | ISBN 9781351612906 (ePub)
Subjects: LCSH: East Indians—Foreign countries. | Transnationalism. | East Indians—Migrations. | East Indian diaspora. | India—Emigration and immigration—Social aspects.
Classification: LCC DS432.5 .R675 2019 | DDC 305.8914—dc23
LC record available at https://lccn.loc.gov/2019006463

ISBN: 978-1-03-240134-8 (pbk)
ISBN: 978-1-138-08914-3 (hbk)
ISBN: 978-1-315-10938-1 (ebk)

DOI: 10.4324/9781315109381

Typeset in Times New Roman
by Swales & Willis Ltd, Exeter, Devon, UK

CONTENTS

List of figures — x
List of tables — xi
Notes on contributors — xii
Acknowledgements — xvii
List of abbreviations — xviii

Introduction: Indian transnationalism — 1
Bandana Purkayastha and Ajaya K. Sahoo

PART I
Migrants'/workers' lives — 19

1 Globality in exceptional spaces: service workers in India's transnational economy — 21
 Kiran Mirchandani

2 Skill gap and brain drain for United States: impact of Trump executive order on H1B and India — 31
 Anjali Sahay

3 From students to spouses: gender and labor in Indian transnationalism — 42
 Amy Bhatt

4 Transnationalism and return migration of scientists and engineers from the United States to India — 54
 Meghna Sabharwal and Roli Varma

PART II
On culture and identities 67

5 Translocal puja: the relevance of gift exchange and locality in transnational Guyanese Hindu communities 69
Sinah Theres Kloß

6 Indian music and transnationalism 78
Peter Manuel and Andre Fludd

7 Transnational collaborations by selected contemporary Indian dancers 92
Ketu H. Katrak

8 Revealing the messiness of transnational identities: second-generation South Asians in Canada 104
Kara Somerville

9 Negotiating transnational identity among second-generation Indian residents in Oman 119
Sandhya Rao Mehta

PART III
Political engagement in transnational spaces 131

10 Transnationalism and Indian/American foreign policy 133
Pierre Gottschlich

11 Constructing Hindu identities in France and the United States: a comparative analysis 143
Lise-Hélène Smith and Anjana Narayan

12 Facing strong head winds: Dalit transnational activism today 158
Peter J. Smith

PART IV
Gender and Indian transnationalism 171

13 Experiences of empowerment and constraint: narratives of transnational Indian women entrepreneurs 173
Manashi Ray

14 Indian origin women: organising against apartheid 191
Quraisha Dawood and Mariam Seedat-Khan

15 Workers, families, and households: towards a gendered, raced, and classed understanding of Indian transnationalism in Canada 201
Amrita Hari

16 Is migration a ticket to freedom? exploring sense of freedom among Indian women in Toronto 212
Sutama Ghosh

17 Middling Tamil migrants in Singapore and the translocal village 227
Selvaraj Velayutham

PART V
On historic and contemporary networks in transnational spaces 239

18 The transnational mobility of Indians in the time of the British Empire 241
Sumita Mukherjee

19 Layered cities, shared histories: gold, mobility and urbanity between Dubai and Malabar 253
Nisha Mathew

20 Emergence of Singapore as a pivot for Indian diasporic and transnational networks 266
Jayati Bhattacharya

Glossary 279
Index 281

FIGURES

2.1	H1B visas by country for 2016	36
4.1	Conceptual framework of return migration	61

TABLES

2.1	H1B for India as a percentage of total	35
20.1	Increasing Indian residents in Singapore	271

CONTRIBUTORS

Amy Bhatt is an Associate Professor of Gender and Women's Studies at the University of Maryland, Baltimore County. She is the author of *High-Tech Housewives: Indian IT Workers, Gendered Labor, and Transmigration* (2018) and co-author of *Roots and Reflections: South Asians in the Pacific Northwest* (2013), along with other academic and popular articles about gender, labor and the family. She is the former oral historian for the South Asian Oral History Project and co-chair of the South Asian American Digital Archive's Academic Council.

Jayati Bhattacharya is a lecturer in the South Asian Studies Programme at the National University of Singapore. She has research interests in business history, Indian trade diaspora, connected histories, maritime and overland networks, South-Southeast Asian relations and comparative diasporas. Her publications include *Beyond the Myth: Indian Business Communities in Singapore* (2011), a co-edited volume with Oliver Pye entitled *The Palm Oil Controversy in Southeast Asia: A Transnational Perspective* (2012) for which she has received Reading Committee Accolades Humanities, ICAS Book Prize, 2015, and a co-edited volume with Coonoor Kripalani, *Indian and Chinese Immigrant Communities: Comparative Perspectives* (2015). Some of her recent articles include "Sea of Changes: Shifting Trajectories Across the Bay of Bengal" in *Asian Politics and Policy* (2017) and "Stories from the Margins: Indian Business Communities in the Growth of Colonial Singapore" in *Journal of Southeast Asian Studies* (forthcoming, 2019).

Quraisha Dawood completed her Ph.D. in Sociology and Industrial, Organisational and Labour Studies at the University of KwaZulu-Natal in 2016. She is a member of the RC52, a committee under the International Sociological Association, and director of Write on Q, her company, which assists students with writing skills and editing. Currently she is a lecturer in the Department of Sociology at the University of Pretoria.

Andre Fludd is a Ph.D. candidate in ethnomusicology at the Graduate Center of the City University of New York. His research focuses on North and South Indian classical music, especially in diasporic communities. He is also a student of Hindustani classical vocal music and Carnatic guitar.

Sutama Ghosh is an Associate Professor in the Department of Geography and Environmental Studies at Ryerson University, Toronto. Trained in urban social geography, Dr. Ghosh examines the migration and settlement experiences of immigrant and refugee newcomers in the Canadian urban milieu. Using intersectionality and mixed research methods, Dr. Ghosh has authored several peer-reviewed journal articles and book chapters exploring the interplay of structural-, group- and individual-level factors that lead to various urban inequalities among immigrant families. Dr. Ghosh's current research focuses on the impacts of investment and disinvestments on immigrant families and on migrant resilience.

Pierre Gottschlich is an Assistant Professor in the Department of Political Science at the University of Rostock, Germany. His research focuses on South Asia and the political, socio-economic and cultural effects of transnational migration. He has published two monographs and numerous peer-reviewed research articles on subjects ranging from elections in South Asia to Indian foreign policy. Dr. Gottschlich has co-edited four volumes and is a member of the editorial board of two scientific journals.

Amrita Hari is an Associate Professor in the Institute of Women's and Gender Studies, Carleton University. She is interested in broader questions around global migrations, transnationalisms, diasporic formations and citizenship. Her current research interests lie in examining how gender, race and class are reproduced through migration policies in Canada. Her work is published in peer-reviewed, internationally recognized journals including *Signs*, *Gender, Work & Organization*, *International Migration*, *Refugee*, and the *Journal of South Asian Diaspora*.

Ketu Katrak, born in India, is a Professor in the Drama Department, University of California, Irvine. Katrak specializes in drama, dance, postcolonial literature, performance and feminist theory. She is author of *Contemporary Indian Dance: New Creative Choreography in India and the Diaspora* (2014) and *Politics of the Female Body: Postcolonial Women Writers* (2006), is co-editor with Astad Deboo of "Contemporary Dance in India", *Marg: A Magazine of Indian Arts* (2017), and is co-editor with Dr. Anita Ratnam of *Voyages of the Body and the Soul: Selected Female Icons of India and Beyond* (2014). Katrak is the recipient of a Fulbright Research Award to India, Bunting Fellowship, and was on the Fulbright Senior Specialist roster, 2010–2015.

Sinah Theres Kloß holds a Ph.D. in Social Anthropology from Heidelberg University, Germany. She is a research associate at the Morphomata Center for Advanced Studies, University of Cologne, Germany. Her research interests include migration studies, the anthropology of religion, sensory ethnography, and dress and material culture. Her regional focus is on the Caribbean, especially Guyana and Suriname, but she also specializes in the transcultural flows between India and the Caribbean. Her ethnography *Fabrics of Indianness: The Exchange and Consumption of Clothing in Transnational Guyanese Hindu Communities* (2016) was published with Palgrave Macmillan.

Peter Manuel is an ethnomusicology professor at the CUNY Graduate Center and at John Jay College. He has researched and published extensively on musics of India, the Caribbean and Spain. His most recent book is *Tales, Tunes, and Tassa Drums: Retention and Invention in Indo-Caribbean Music*.

Contributors

Nisha Mathew is Joint Research Fellow at the Middle East Institute and the Asia Research Institute, National University of Singapore. She received her Ph.D. in History from the University of Witwatersrand, Johannesburg, in 2014, where her research explored the methodological possibilities of Indian Ocean studies in the making of a contemporary urban space such as Dubai. She is currently working on her book titled *24 Carat Cities: Gold, Smuggling and Mobility in the Western Indian Ocean*. It tells the story of Dubai's rise to prominence as a 21st-century global city with gold as the protagonist.

Sandhya Rao Mehta is affiliated to the Department of English Language and Literature at Sultan Qaboos University, Oman. She has published widely in the areas of diaspora, with particular focus on the Indian diaspora in the Arabian Gulf and engendering diaspora. She has edited a volume entitled *Exploring Gender in the Literature of the Indian Diaspora* (2015) as well as another entitled *Language and Literature in a Glocal World* (2018), published by Springer. Her major publications include "The Hindu Community in Muscat: Creating Homes in the Diaspora" in the *Journal of Arabian Studies* (2015), "Contesting Victim Narratives: Indian Women Domestic Workers in Oman" in *Migration and Development* (2017), and "Centring Gendered Narratives of the Indian Diaspora", a chapter in *Women in the Indian Diaspora: Historical Narratives and Contemporary Challenges* (2017). She is presently working on a funded university project to write a book on the Indian community in Oman.

Kiran Mirchandani is a Professor at the Ontario Institute for Studies in Education at the University of Toronto. Her research focuses on transnational service work, gendered and racialized processes in workplaces, critical perspectives on organizational learning, criminalization and economic restructuring. She is the author of *Phone Clones: Authenticity Work in the Transnational Service Economy* (2012), co-author of *Criminalizing Race, Criminalizing Poverty: Welfare Fraud Enforcement in Canada* (2007) and co-editor of *The Future of Lifelong Learning and Work: Critical Perspectives* (2008).

Sumita Mukherjee's research focuses on the transnational mobility of South Asians in the Imperial era (nineteenth and twentieth centuries), i.e., the movement of men and women from the Indian subcontinent to other parts of the world and also their return back to India. Much of her attention has been on how travel and the colonial encounter for migrants in Britain has had an effect on social and political identities including race, class, gender and religion. Among her publications are *Nationalism, Education and Migrant Identities: The England-Returned* (2010) and *Indian Suffragettes: Female Identities and Transnational Networks* (2018).

Anjana Narayan is an Associate Professor of Sociology at California State Polytechnic University Pomona. She is the co-author of *Living our Religions: Hindu and Muslim South Asian-American Women Narrate their Experiences* (2009) and the co-editor of *Research Beyond Borders: Multidisciplinary Reflections* (2011). She is currently associated with an international and interdisciplinary collaborative research network to advance the study of lived religions and gender in relation to Hinduism and Islam.

Bandana Purkayastha is Professor of Sociology and Asian American Studies at the University of Connecticut. Her research on the intersections of gender/racism/class/age; transnationalism; violence and peace; and human rights have appeared in ten books and thirty-five articles and chapters since 2000. Her recent books are *The Human Rights Enterprise: Political Sociology, State Power, and Social Movements* (2015); *Voices of Internally Displaced Persons in Kenya:*

A Human Rights Perspective (2015); and *Human Trafficking* (2018). Further details appear at www.sociology.uconn.edu/purkayastha. She has received many local and national awards for scholarship, teaching and community work.

Manashi Ray is an Associate Professor of Sociology at West Virginia State University. Her scholarship explores the intersections of international migration and transnationalism. She uses concepts from migration and transnational studies – including migrant capital, Bourdieu's theory of capital, social ties, transnational spaces, life course perspectives and policies of sending and receiving countries – to understand migratory processes, motives and cross-border mechanisms impacted by technological innovation and globalization. She studies migrant and refugee populations from South and East Asia, asking why and how migrants, non-migrants and refugees engage in migratory movements, adopting a gendered perspective to unravel migratory patterns and settlement experiences.

Meghna Sabharwal is an Associate Professor and Program Head in the Public and Nonprofit Management program in the School of Economic, Political and Policy Sciences at the University of Texas at Dallas. Her research focuses on public human resources management, specifically related to high-skilled migration, diversity, job satisfaction and productivity. She has authored numerous articles for the top public administration journals. She also has two book publications: *Public Personnel Administration* (6th ed.) and *Public Administration in South Asia: India, Bangladesh, and Pakistan* (2013). She is the recipient of several national awards and two National Science Foundation grants to study high-skilled migration patterns.

Anjali Sahay is an Associate Professor of International Relations and Political Science at Gannon University, Erie, PA, USA. Currently she serves as a Commissioner on the Governor's Advisory Commission on Asian Pacific American Affairs (GACAPAA) for 2018–2020. Her book *Indian Diaspora in the United States: Brain Drain or Gain?* is a ground-breaking work that connects economic and political issues to the dimension of migration and the concerns over brain drain. Additionally, she has several book chapters and articles on international migration, diaspora studies and international relations.

Ajaya K. Sahoo teaches at the Centre for Study of Indian Diaspora, University of Hyderabad, India. His research interests include the Indian diaspora and transnationalism. He has co-edited the *Routledge Handbook of the Indian Diaspora* (2018), *Indian Transnationalism Online* (2014), *Transnational Migrations: The Indian Diaspora* (Routledge, 2009) and *Tracing an Indian Diaspora: Contexts, Memories, Representations* (2008). He is editor of the journal *South Asian Diaspora*.

Mariam Seedat-Khan is a senior lecturer in the School of Social Sciences at the University of KwaZulu-Natal, Durban. She is a clinical sociologist as well as the vice-president of the International Sociological Association Research Committee for Clinical Sociology. She is the editor of *Sociology: A South African Perspective*, a text by South African authors for South African scholars.

Lise-Hélène Smith is an Associate Professor of World Literature at California State Polytechnic University, Pomona. Her research interests include exile, hybridity and migration as linked to race and gender in the Southeast Asian diaspora as well as in Francophone and postcolonial literatures. She is the co-editor of *Research Beyond Borders: Multidisciplinary Reflections* (2011).

Peter J. Smith, Ph.D., is Professor Emeritus of Political Science at Athabasca University, Alberta, Canada. His current research interests are in new communications technologies, globalization, religion, trade politics, transnational networks, democracy and citizenship. He is the co-editor with Sabine Dreher of *Religious Activism in the Global Economy: Promoting, Reforming, or Resisting Neoliberal Globalization?* (2016) and co-editor with Katharina Glaab, Claudia Baumgart-Ochse and Elizabeth Smythe of *The Role of Religion in Struggles for Global Justice* (2018).

Kara Somerville is an Associate Professor of Sociology at the University of Saskatchewan. Her broad research area is international migration and transnationalism, with a focus on South Asian migrant families. Recently her work has examined the experiences of second-generation youth in Toronto and the experiences of international students in western Canada. Her findings have been published in both Canadian and international journals.

Roli Varma is Carl Hatch Endowed Professor in the School of Public Administration at the University of New Mexico, Albuquerque. Her research focuses on return migration of Asian scientists and engineers, immigrants in the US science and engineering workforce and women and minorities in information technology education in the US and India. Her research has been supported by the National Science Foundation and the Sloan Foundation. She is the author of *Harbingers of Global Change: India's Techno-Immigrants in the United States* (2007). She served on the Association for Computing Machinery Task Force on Job Migration in 2004–2005.

Selvaraj Velayutham is a senior lecturer in the Department of Sociology at Macquarie University, Australia. His research interests are in international migration, race and ethnic relations, multiculturalism, Tamil cinema and the sociology of everyday life. His research draws on ethnographic and other qualitative research methods to explore issues of identity, social relations and everyday life.

ACKNOWLEDGEMENTS

We would like to thank all the authors for their insightful contributions to this handbook. We deeply appreciate the scholarly effort and work that has gone into this collaborative project. We especially thank the authors for their patience and swift responses to our editorial queries.

We would like to thank Anindita Shome and Sinorita Mazumder (doctoral students at the Centre for the Study of Indian Diaspora, University of Hyderabad) for their editorial help.

At Routledge, our sincere thanks go to Dorothea Schaefter, Senior Editor, Asian Studies, for her very useful and constructive suggestions at various stages during the preparation of this handbook and also to her editorial assistant Alexandra de Brauw for her support and cooperation that made this handbook possible.

Ajaya K. Sahoo
Bandana Purkayastha
5 February 2019

ABBREVIATIONS

AAHOA	Asian-American Hotel Owners Association
ACDA	Anti Caste Discrimination Alliance
AIPAC	American Israel Public Affairs Committee
AJC	American Jewish Committee
BBC	British Broadcasting Corporation
BJP	Bharatiya Janata Party
BPO	Business Process Outsourcing
BRM	Brooklyn Raga Massive
CECA	Comprehensive Economic Cooperation Agreement
CERD	Committee on the Elimination of Racial Discrimination
CII	Confederation of Indian Industry
CMANA	Carnatic Music Association of North America
CMIO	Chinese-Malay-Indian-Others
DGJG	Dubai Gold and Jewellery Group
DNA	Digitally Networked Action
DSF	Dubai Shopping Festival
EADs	Employment Authorisation Documents
EDB	Economic Development Board
ESL	English as a Second Language
FCRA	Foreign Contributions Regulation Act
GJM	Global Justice Movement
GOPIO	Global Organization of People of Indian Origin
GRA	Guyana Revenue Authority
HDB	Housing Development Board
HFB	Hindu Forum of Britain
HIT	Hegemonic Intercultural Theatre
HSS	Hindu Swayamsevak Sangh
IAA	Association of Indians in America
IACPA	India Abroad Centre for Political Action
IAFC	Indian American Friendship Council

Abbreviations

IAFPE	Indian American Forum for Political Education
IASLC	The Indian American Security Leadership Council
ICC	Indian Chamber of Commerce
IDRF	India Development and Relief Fund
IDSN	International Dalit Solidarity Network
IIM	Indian Institute of Management
IITAAS	Indian Institute of Technology Alumni Association Singapore
IIT	Indian Institutes of Technology
ILA	India League of America
IMRC	Indian Muslim Relief Committee
IRB	Institutional Review Board
IRCC	Immigration, Refugees and Citizenship Canada
IT/ITES	Information Technology and Information Technology Enabled Services
IWSA	International Woman Suffrage Alliance
MGNREGA	Mahatma Gandhi National Rural Employment Guarantee Act
MMM	Marwari Mitra Mandal
NAS	National Academy of Sciences
NASSCOM	National Association of Software and Services Companies
NCDHR	National Campaign on Dalit Human Rights
NCIF	National Committee for India's Freedom
NFDW	National Federation of Dalit Women
NHSF	National Hindu Students' Forum
NIH	National Institutes of Health
NRIs	Non-Resident Indians
NSF	National Science Foundation
OCI	Overseas Citizenship of India
OECD	Organisation for Economic Co-operation and Development
OFBJP	Overseas Friends of BJP
OIS	Office of Immigration Statistics
OPT	Optional Practical Training
PIO	Person of Indian Origin
RSS	Rashtriya Swayamsevak Sangh
SAALT	South Asian Americans Leading Together
SEZs	Special Economic Zones
SICCI	Singapore Indian Chamber of Commerce and Industry
SINDA	Singapore Indian Development Association
SMART	Singapore-MIT Alliance for Research and Technology
SPIC-MACAY	Society for the Promotion of Indian Classical Music and Culture amongst Youth
STB	Singapore Tourism Board
STEM	Science, Technology, Engineering and Math
TCS	Tata Consultancy Services
TDB	Trade Development Board
TEs	Transnational Entrepreneurs
TiE	The Indus Entrepreneurs
TRC	Tamils Representative Council
USCIS	United States Citizenship and Immigration Services

Abbreviations

USIBC	U.S-India Business Council
USINPAC	United States India Political Action Committee
USCIS	US Citizen and Immigration Services
VHP	Vishwa Hindu Parishad
WCAR	World Conference against Racism
WSF	World Social Forum

INTRODUCTION
Indian transnationalism

Bandana Purkayastha and Ajaya K. Sahoo

"Transnationalism" has become an integral part of many streams of academic conversations. In some of these conversations, it is a synonym for the older term "international"; in others, it is somewhat more precisely defined and rooted in contemporary globalization. Most of these conversations often start from, and are intended to focus on, movements—e.g., of people, ideas, cultural products, finances, technologies—across political borders. Yet closer analyses of these movements reveal the structural impediments that shape such movements. These structures occur at transnational, regional, national, and local levels, so the movements respond to the intersections of these multiple levels. Focusing on Indians and Indian diasporas, this book offers a critical perspective on some of the problems and prospects of contemporary conversations on transnationalism.

Transnationalism: some contours

Within the social sciences in the Global North, the work by Glick-Schiller *et al.* (1992) is often credited with creating the scholarly stream of conversation about transnationalism related to migrants. Many other conversations were underway, for instance, about transnational public spheres (Gupta and Ferguson 1992), or Castells' thesis about social life that is deterritorialized (1996), or Kearney and Nagengast's discussions of indigenous reconstitution of ethnicity with transnational communities (1989), but Glick-Schiller *et al.* (1992) emerged as a key source that inspired an intensification of the conversation on transnationalism. Another key source in the conversation is attributed to Arjun Appadurai's articles and his book *Modernity at Large* (1996). Appadurai presented a framework that has now been normalized in the transnationalism lexicon: the world of disjunctured flows, that is, the movement of people, finances, technologies, ideas, and cultural flows that create coalescing and divergent "scapes." While the social sciences were not the only incubators of these conversations, we will start with these contours as a way of delineating the debates and divergences that exist within transnationalism conversations.

The trajectories of conversations about transnationalism reflect some of the knowledge hierarchies that have been the subject of many scholarly critiques globally (e.g., Connell 2009, Patel 2006). Conversations about ethnicities (within nation-states) and the possible assimilation of migrants enjoy a long lineage in the Global North, where the concern has been about the efforts of "foreigners" to fit into the new society (Simon and Alexander 1993, Alba and Nee 1997). While intersectionality studies on the same subject (Glenn 2002, 2015, Purkayastha 2010) pointed to the marginalizing structures that prevented migrants from gaining full access to substantive citizenships—i.e., full access to the benefits of political, social, economic, and cultural membership, within white-dominated nation-states—these often remained separate conversation streams. From the 1990s, amidst the new discussion on globalization, the focus on what happens within single nation-states expanded to a recognition that migrants, instead of integrating into the host country only, were also building and maintaining homeland connections. Glick-Schiller *et al.* (1992) pointed out that migrants were no longer confining themselves to life in the destination countries, as the current state of technologies (including easier travel) made it possible to maintain ongoing homeland ties. Other studies, for instance by Alejandro Portes on transnationalism from below (1997) or Peggy Levitt's early work, *The Transnational Villagers* (2001), provided further data on migrants who built lives in more than one country. At the same time, these earlier conversations on migrant transnationalism focused on what *migrants do*; consequently, it diverted the dominant conversation away from studies that traced structural impediments migrants encounter and navigate within and across the multiple contexts.

A wide variety of studies of transnationalism, with very different meanings, emerged over the next decades (for a review, see Vertovec 2009). Amidst the rapid expansion of the term transnational, scholars sought to identify what was transnational and what was international; arguing that the latter should be used to discuss the processes and actions involving states and their agents (see Vertovec 2009 or Faist *et al.* 2013 for more details on this). By 1998, Vertovec suggested some research foci and methodological clusters for understanding transnationalism: he emphasized transnationalism as a social morphology, as a type of consciousness, as a mode of cultural reproduction, as an avenue of capital, as a site of political engagement, and as a reconstruction of "place" or locality. Vertovec also pointed out that many of the processes that are evident within contemporary transnationalism were typical of migration streams in the early 20th century. Turn-of-the-19th-century migrants maintained ties with home via letters and remittances; many returned to their places of origin; and some countries maintained an interest in the fate of their people in the destination countries. What makes contemporary transnationalism different is the pace of these interactions and the formalized ways in which governments and international institutions, such as the human rights organizations, attempt to shape migrant lives (Vertovec 2009).

Among the examples of this expanding stream of work are Levitt (2009), which looks at the ways in which religious institutions, interactions among co-religionists, and ideologies take on a transnational character. More recently, Thomas Faist and his colleagues (2013) have discussed migrant transnationalism, emphasizing three dimensions: transnational ties and practices in various fields that include cross-border transaction of goods, services, capital, ideas, and people; transactions of migrants and other agents that result in social formation in transnational social spaces, including kinship groups; and, at an individual level, a variety of activities including traveling, sending and/or receiving remittances, and exchanging ideas, goods, and services. More recent scholarship on transnationalism discussed the global dimensions of inequality that emerges out of this cross-border migration and transnationalisation and that is starkly different from the mid-19th-and 20th-century conditions of migrations (Faist 2019).

A different focus on transnationalism is evident in feminist literature as well. One stream of this examined transnational activism and the ability of women's groups to forge alliances across nation-states in their attempt to change the international actors such as the UN. Sonia Alvaraz analyzed local movement actors' engagement within transnational activism circuits, especially their ability to navigate power and hierarchy inherent within the circuits of transnational contacts, discussions, transactions, and networks (2000: 32). Many of the UN summits led to activism against violence against women within broader claims for human rights (Ferree and Tripp 2006, Erturk and Purkayastha 2012). At the same time, the condition of female migrants—who already made up a significant share of global migrants—became a visible part of the conversation (e.g., Kofman 2013, Kofman and Raghuram 2005). For instance, studies on transnational female workers (e.g., Guevarra 2009) and transnational mothering (Parennas 2001) began to analyze the structures that affect female migrants in different nation-states. This stream of literature has also made us more conscious of "reading gender" into accounts that describe the male experience but in gender-neutral terms. Gendered transnationalism consequently includes the experiences of both women and men.[1]

A critical point in the global feminist and anti-racist scholarly conversation was the need to question the Global North conceptualization of transnationalism. An equally important objective was to respond to the criticisms of methodological nationalisms inherent in the constant focus on nation-states. In her study of transnationalism reversed, on advocacy around acid violence victims in Bangladesh, Elora Chowdhury (2011) analyzed the entrenched power hierarchies that shape the work of humanitarian organizations, while pointing to the ways in which some of these hierarchies are breached. She emphasized the importance of examining local- to transnational-level interactions in multiple societies instead of focusing on multiple levels in single nation-states. Similarly, in a discussion on intersectionality in a transnational world, Purkayastha (2012) questioned the limits of intersectionality approaches that take the existing structures within the US as the norm for understanding intersecting axes of power in other places. She pointed out that groups could be simultaneously part of the majority in one society and minorities in another depending on the degree to which their lives are organized in tangible geographic and webspaces. Thus transnational, in these formulations, yields far more complex constellations of structures and coalescing and disjunctured layers of power that position people within glocal (local to global), transnational locales.

The focus on complexities of flows across countries as well as the structural barriers that interrupt flows are evident in the work of scholars in the Global South and North.[2] If Appadurai's (1996) description of multiple flows has been normalized to the extent that the author is rarely acknowledged in recent discussions on transnationalism, so too have the arguments of scholars such as Samaddar (1999), who wrote about migration as *cross-border*, instead of cross-international, movements.

The concept of cross-border flows and movements opened up avenues for scholarly discussions on internal and international migration in conversation about transnationalism. The cross-border concept emphasizes that migrants may cross borders, but not always international political borders (Baruah 2003, Yousaf 2018). This approach re-centers the idea that borders and boundaries change as national boundaries are defined or redefined. This approach also highlights internal migrations, including displacement caused by government appropriation of land (Vakulabharanam and Prasad 2017), destruction of natural resources (e.g. Ortiz and Pombo 2014), disasters (e.g. Kristjansdottir and DeTurk 2013), and conflicts (Njiru and Purkayastha 2015). In each of these cases, transnational forces, especially neoliberal structural adjustments, intersect with local forces to shape the lives of a variety of migration streams.[3] Samaddar (2015) has argued that we need to return to 19th- and early 20th-century histories of migration to understand the histories of our times and the ways in which we have begun to take nation-states' borders as the premier units of scholarly analyses and theorization.

This approach re-injects the impact of colonialism that moved people as slaves or indentured workers, within and across nations, while contributing to the rising hunger and desperation among vast numbers of people who then sought to move as a means of survival. Transnationalism today, and the directions of flows of people, technologies, ideas, finances and cultures, include traces of these earlier histories of crossing or being forced to cross borders.

The questions about transnationalism are not simply about getting beyond the structural contexts of discrete nation-states (Purkayastha 2018). Any framework of transnationalism has to recognize the growth of supra-political/economic contexts as well as social life on web-based spaces (Sahoo and De Kruif 2014, Purkayastha 2012, Narayan *et al*. 2011). Both intersect in complicated ways with global and national security regimes (e.g., Collyer and King 2015, Levitan, Kaytaz, and Durukan 2010, Li 2011, Thomas 2014). The emergence of supranational blocks such as the EU or the Mercosur agreement among some Latin American countries (Arcarazo 2015) adds new layers of belonging, as well as new formations of politics and economic functioning. These entities remove some boundaries but add new borders, which are accepted by some and resisted by others (e.g., the Brexit process). Transnationalism occurs not only through nation-states but also through the larger political-economic entities.

Similarly, transnationalism is not only about stable ties, exchanges, and networks across contexts. The spread of neoliberal structures—especially those that lead to footloose production, stateless corporations, and reliance on flexible labo—have generated *repeated* migration, as people move within and across nation-states in search of jobs and other aspects of secure lives. Such industries also create uncertainty and instability in the lives of workers. Wars and armed conflicts and the routinization of large-scale violence lead to displacements of people within and across nation-states (e.g., German 2013, Pandey 2006). Environmental disasters—often human-made and/or the result of deliberate policy—also lead to displacements (e.g., Das Gupta et al. 2010). Das Gupta (2006, 2013), Glenn (2015), and Ortiz and Pombo (2014) have argued that understanding displacements and forced migrations requires analysis of de-territorialization and re-territorialization, which are at the heart of the structural layers that constitute transnationalism. The ideas of borders also can be used fruitfully to understand the structures of inequality—typically discussed in terms of the intersections of race, class, gender, and sexuality—in the Global North, which maintain hierarchies within and across national and transnational contexts. Unstable and interrupted exchanges, as well as networks that are configured during displacements, have become intrinsic to transnationalism.

In sum, these studies indicate that transnationalism emerges through the interactions of multiple contextual layers. The ideas of social morphologies, boundaries and borders, and the development of transnational consciousness and institutions from a global to a local level as well as from the local to global level engendered through activism remain at the core of transnationalism. In addition, as Purkayastha (2005, 2018) pointed out, a key insight of transnationalism is that nation-to-local borders may not always coalesce, nor do transnational to local borders; nonetheless, these partly coalescing or disjunctured borders within global-national-local terrains cumulatively shape today's contexts in which the marginalized and privileged position themselves or are positioned by forces outside their control. Transnational social morphologies, imaginaries, and political action frames emerge from these intersections.

Transnationalism with a focus on India

A brief overview of the scholarship on Indian transnationalism yields additional key themes and emphases that are relevant for understanding transnationalism today. Here "Indian transnationalism" refers broadly to the work that puts the experiences of historical or contemporary

India and Indians at the center. Arguably, a vast literature falls within this category,[4] but the selected few discussed in this section contribute critical insights to contemporary discussions.

In 2010, Madhushree Mukherjee wrote a critical book, *Churchill's Secret War*, which outlined how food was stockpiled in Bengal, for the potential use of British troops fighting in different theaters of World War II. As a result of the food crisis that developed, 4.3 million people died. The book describes the structures inherent to colonialism: the way material resources—in this case, food—were moved out of colonies (or stockpiled) to serve the interests of distant nations. The cross-border movement of material resources, as well as the unequal political-economic conditions that undergird such movement, remain important to understanding transnationalism today.[5] Ranabir Samaddar (2015) has shown how in an earlier period of globalization, the actors,—including nation states, labor brokers, lawyers, employers, money lenders, and banks—were involved in shaping the movement of people across lands and seas. The growth of extractive industries in the colonies to fulfill the needs of the colonial masters' political-economic interests was linked to the growth of indentured labor. Both Mukherjee and Samaddar break away from explanations based on nation-states and point to the intersecting structures of global, national, and local power that shaped colonies. These core ideas are critical for understanding transnationalism today: transnationalism and transnational spaces emanate through historical global political-economic regimes in intersection with national and local power dynamics. These studies emphasize that formal colonialism followed by neoliberal regimes create and recreate structures for extraction of resources and control of the spaces and people from which these resources are extracted.

Another series of influential works focused on Indian indentured labor across British colonies (e.g., Davis 1951, Mahmud 2012, Simatei 2011, Tinker 1977). In their book *Inside Indian Indenture*, Ashwin Desai and Goolam Vahed (2010) quote Bush to describe indenture as "a legally authorised domination which denied them choice as to work, residence or remuneration, and assumed their labor lay in the ownership of some lord, master, employer or custodian" (Bush 2000: 40). The book then examines the harsh conditions in which the laborers attempted to build their lives. In *Calcutta to Caroni* (1974), La Guerre similarly discusses the harsh conditions that structured the movement and settlement of indentured migrants to different parts of the world (see also Tinker 1974, 1977). Under-theorized in general migration studies, the movement of soldiers across the colonial transnational spaces offers another window into looking at migration (Kaur 2011). The India-US migration literature recognizes the movement of the Sikhs from China—where the "British" Army had been moved to quell the Boxer Rebellion—to Canada and ultimately the US (Chandrasekhar 1982, Kaur 2011, Mawani 2012). This migration was possible because these soldiers were able to subvert the tapestry of laws set up through the cooperation of the British and Americans to stop the migration of Indians to places outside British colonies. A few scholars have emphasized the raced/classed/gendered nature of indentured migration. Desai and Vahed (2010), Hiralal (2014), and Seedat-Khan (2012), among others, discuss women's constant vulnerability to sexual assault as both British overseers as well as men within their communities subjected them to sexual harassment and exploitation. But they also point to the earlier vulnerabilities that groups of women faced in their own communities in India that led them to consider migration in order to craft a different kind of survival. These accounts of indentured lives within colonial or neo-colonial regimes also reveal the pattern of international cooperation between powerful nations that facilitated these harsh controls.

The conditions of indenture continue today even though the nomenclature to describe these migrants has changed. Commenting on contemporary migration to the US, with a focus on "temporary workers" Adur (2011) has discussed how employers are well positioned to control workers jobs, residence, and employment conditions and could call on national immigration service agents to control migrant workers who protested. Manohar and Banerjee (2016) further document the status of highly skilled high-tech migrants and their families who are offered few political safeguards while contributing their labor to the US. A different facet of this phenomenon is analyzed by Aneesh (2015), who examined the experiences of call-center workers in India. He raised questions about people who do not move but whose labor and daily lives are subject to the political, social, and economic logics and policies of the distant nation-states, without the benefit of any political safeguards of their rights. Thus, rather than a clear separation of transnational from international, or even a separation between migration and "cyber migration," these historical and contemporary studies show how tapestries of power overlap and transnational spaces and processes are shaped through international co-operation. At the same time, these scholars discuss the intersectional structures that shape the experiences of migrants.

While the work emanating from the Global North typically makes that geographical area the focus of discussions of transnationalism, some scholars focus on South–South political, economic, and cultural exchanges and transactions. In the early decades of the 20th century, many intellectuals, positioned amidst the colonial politics of Europe and America, imagined closer and explicit ties between the Asian civilizations[6] as a way of imagining transnational connections (Bharucha 2006, Inaga 2006, Kaur 2011, Okakura 1903, Tagore 1929).

More recently, scholars have examined South–South ties between countries, with a focus on political, economic, and socio-cultural processes (e.g., Duara 2010, Patel and Uys 2012 on South Africa and India). Diaspora studies offer a range of cases on real and imagined ties to India as a homeland (e.g., Aiyar (2011) on Kenya, Jain (2013) on returnee Indian American second generations, Joseph (1999) on Tanzanian Indians, Crowley (1990) on Trinidad, Hiralal (2015) on South Africa, Tatla and Singh (2008) on the Sikh Diaspora, Gould (2017) on Bengal's Muslim diasporas, Pandurang and Munos (2014) on diasporic subjectivities, Singh and Gatina (2015) on the Australian diaspora). An important stream of the diaspora literature focuses on the circulation of cultures, especially consumption items. Bollywood and the coalescing of Bollywood movies, "Indian fashion," music, dance (e.g., Gopal and Moorti 2008, Khandelwal 2002, Mehta 2015, Ramnarine 2011) and literature make and remake cultural commonalities within diasporas. An important recent collection by Hegde and Sahoo (2017) offers important ways of thinking about contemporary Indian diasporas through migration, remittances, place-making, and cultural constructions. Similarly, the scholarship on women and other excluded groups' activism centers on ties and conflicts between diasporas and within diasporas (Das Gupta 2006, Hiralal 2014, Govinden 2008). The activism by Dalits (e.g., Adur 2011), and queer groups (Adur and Purkayastha 2013) in the US are two examples of such activism. Challenging the boundaries of "Indian," Dalit groups have forged ties with other racialized minority groups at the UN level (Falcón 2016), which points to other complex exchanges and collaborations that constitute transnationalism today.

The literature on Indian transnationalism thus adds significantly to the general discussions on transnationalism. It centers the impact of colonialism and emphasizes the importance of paying attention to the traces of colonialism in contemporary transnationalism. This literature highlights historical and contemporary harsh labor conditions bolstered by shifting terrains of political rights as well as the stratification of rights depending on the social location of different groups of migrants in multiple countries. It draws attention to earlier transnationalism and South–South exchanges, especially in the realm of culture. Most of all, it draws attention to the remaking of culture and collective and individual identities to fit the needs of diasporas buffeted by race/class/gender structures of the host countries. Conflicts within communities based on race/class/gender/religion as well as activism within specific locales and globally emerge as important dynamics of transnationalism.

Introduction

Indian transnationalism in this book

This book presents many aspects of contemporary transnationalism. The first four chapters explore the experiences of migrants and workers with a particular emphasis on the multiple contexts to reveal the structures of transnationalism and how Indian origin groups are affected. The next set of chapters analyze the interplay of culture and structures within transnational contexts, including an emphasis on South–South interactions. Of these five chapters, the last two explore how the political context of rights that migrants and their children can access influences how the second generation weaves diasporic Indian cultures as part of their identity. The next three chapters examine political engagement that maintains dynamism and shifting power hierarchies that constitute the transnational. These chapters examine political engagement through formal political organizations, claims for human rights, and different types of organizing that have emerged in the late 20th and early 21st centuries on geographic and digital spaces. Gendered experiences are the central concern of the next section. Four authors explore women's experiences of transnationalism, moving the discussion beyond home-host country binaries and pointing to fluidity and liminality of the encounters. In contrast, one author focuses on men's experiences and shows how they recreate some of their social positions via virtual transnational villages. The last section presents historic and contemporary transnational networks, highlighting an account that often involves multiple countries and includes strong regional nodes outside the Global North. The concept of crossing borders emerges as an important theme, along with the weaving of life in geographic and web spaces. Colonialism and neoliberalism, in interaction with local processes, remain important structures shaping marginalization and privilege. South–South co-operation, cultural change (including changing faces of religions in response to structures of (restricted) secularism), and fluctuating terrains for claiming political rights substantively are collectively highlighted by the authors in this book.

Part I: Migrants'/workers' lives

In a key chapter on workers in transnational spaces, Kiran Mirchandani discusses workers in India who are part of a transnational economy. Mirchandani discusses how workers, positioned at different levels of these transnational economic spaces, navigate a variety of tenuous relationships with employers while they are denied many political rights because the work is located in special economic zones. She points out that state-sanctioned special economic zones (SEZs) have proliferated in all major urban areas of India. The corporate benefits in these zones include tax holidays, government subsidies, and infrastructure incentives to entice multinational firms. Certain labor laws such as the right to engage in collective action are also suspended inside the zones, with the creation of special information technology/information technology enabled (IT/ITES) zones. She argues that diverse patterns of globality, or the sense of being in the world, are evident among workers in the IT/ITES spaces. For call-center workers, globality involves bridging the gap between their middle-class lifestyles and the need to accept aggression and violence from customers in the Global North as a normal part of their jobs. For low-wage workers, who form a crucial link in the provisioning of the "world-class" infrastructure of these spaces, their sense of globality is about being disposable contract workers who are excluded from the material privileges of their prestigious and affluent settings.

Anjali Sahay considers a different aspect of 21st-century migration to the US. She focuses on highly skilled migrants who are allowed to migrate to the US temporarily on H1B visas. She points out that in today's global interconnected world, the mobility of high-skilled workers plays a vital role in the economy, especially in the knowledge sector. She documents the political rhetoric about "America first" and the impact of new restrictions on the already restrictive work permits given to highly skilled migrants. Historically, the US has gone through many periods of restrictive migration, in tune with highly charged political discourses about too many migrants. The H1B situation is different, since the visa category binds migrants to single employers and allows no political rights or safeguards for their labor contribution. (Their spouses face additional controls as well; Amy Bhatt discusses these in her chapter on women on H4 visas). Sahay discusses the dynamics across countries and shows how additional areas such as students coming for higher education to the US have dropped. She discusses the impact of what she describes as "fractured transnationalism": brain drain from the US and the specter of more jobs being outsourced, probably in zones such as those described by Mirchandani.

Amy Bhatt's chapter focuses on different types of female migrants, with a brief review of caregivers, domestic workers, and female students who migrate to different countries. Her particular focus is the women who are on H4 visas in the US. H4 visas are given to dependents of H1B visa holders. The significant additional restriction on these spouses is they are not allowed to work. Highly educated themselves, the H4 visa holders become subject to two sets of patriarchal structures. Bhatt argues that many of them, irrespective of their own education or aspirations, may have already been subjected to an ideology that they will fulfill the role of supporting the work of the "family wage earner." Then US immigration regimes enforce additional patriarchal norms by restricting spousal work. Bhatt describes how the wives provide intensive service to their children's schools and ethnic communities. These spouses continue to seek opportunities to retrain themselves for potential future jobs. However, the transnational labor regime, which provides the short-term work opportunities to their spouses, make it difficult for non-working spouses to gain additional training within the timeframe allotted to the working spouse. Overall, these regimes rely on the gendered hierarchies as a way of retaining skilled workers.

Meghna Sabharwal and Roli Varma focus on reverse brain drain among scientists and engineers in academia. They examine both the factors that lead to the decisions to leave for India from the US, as well as the post-migration transnational networks. The India-born faculty members occupied full-time positions in Science and Engineering (S&E) at four-year colleges and universities in the US and played an important role in the scientific, technological, and economic growth of the US through their scholarly contributions. But Sabharwal and Varma demonstrate that the US is not a magnet for a one-way process; instead, a large proportion of participants decided to return to India for better economic prospects. Nonetheless, political, social, cultural, and family reasons also contributed to the decision to return. The authors document that return migrants continue to forge collaborations through transnational ties established across various regions around the globe, mainly with Europe and the US. Technology has facilitated an era of rapid technological growth and connectivity, and, they argue, return has a different meaning because of ongoing transnational ties.

Part II: On culture and identities

The idea of translocality, the importance of local place and the social actors who constitute nodes of relationships, is also important to Sinah Theres Kloß's chapter on the Guyanese Hindu traditions of *puja* and gift-giving. Kloß discusses the colonial roots of the Indian presence in Guyana as well as the local borders between Christian Afro-Guyanese and the Hindu-Indian Guyanese. For the latter group, different Hindu traditions have to be managed to create a unified front against the majority Christians. Kloß shows how some of the rituals of *puja*—especially the symbolism of welcoming the deities with gifts of flowers, incense, water, and clothes—are translated into markers of ethnic identity through socially expected gift-giving among Guyanese Hindus. She points out that as another round of migration occurs, some Hindu-Guyanese migrate to the US and continue the practice of exchanging saris or dhotis to mark religious festivals; these gift exchanges serve to maintain links within Guyanese Hindu communities back home. Despite the presence of other Hindus, these rituals serve to cement national and cultural identities with the Guyanese homeland. Other scholars have noted the gaps between Indian and Guyanese Hindu communities. Kloß's chapter highlights some of the underlying factors that create different Hindu scripts for people from different regions and nations as well as an account of the transformation of local cultural practices into transnational and translocal practices.

Peter Manuel and Andre Fludd focus on Indian music and discuss its transnational dimensions. They point out that this cultural form goes far beyond the mere appreciation of Indian classical arts in the West. They discuss a range of socio-cultural dynamics pertaining to the music subcultures of the diverse and increasingly active Indian diasporas, the impact of globalization on music culture in India itself, the formation of music-based "social fields" transcending nation-state boundaries, and the emergence of transnational music networks and scenes involving both classical and commercial popular music. Beginning with a description of earlier historical circuits of influences into and from the Indian subcontinent, they identify the newer forms in different transnational contexts. A type of vernacular music developed in the places where indentured laborers settled. Even as it developed syncretic forms through its intersections with local music, this diasporic music represented a cultural currency to claim and strengthen ethnic bonds. Classical music developed an international presence, first through concerts by a few artists but then in association with the growing presence of a relatively affluent Indian migrant community in countries such as the US. Bollywood music exists between these two genres, popular in form, originally serving an Indian audience, but produced now with an awareness of the diaspora audience. Similarly, *bhangra*, unmoored from its roots in rural Punjab, melds British and American influences into intricate tapestries of transnational music, and some of this music then flows back to the homelands. Manuel and Fludd focus on New York City to highlight the different sites through which these genres of music are popularized and distributed. They point out that the Indian diasporas contain many different types of migrants, from laborers to cosmopolitans, and their distinctive music resonates as nodes of class-cultural identity formation. But the music also constitutes part of a broad, all-encompassing socio-musical field that clearly transcends nation-state boundaries and is characteristically transnational.

Ketu H. Katrak focuses on dance to explore collaborations among dancer-choreographers in the late 20th and 21st centuries. Katrak points out that links between dancers in India and those in the US or Canada have received much scholarly attention. She focuses on a relatively understudied area, global South-to-South collaborations. She examines the collaborations between Astad Deboo and artists in South Korea, and Vikram Iyengar's cultural exchanges with artists in Bangladesh. Katrak describes how the explicit encouragement and funding support from the In Ko Foundation led an internationally prominent dancer like Deboo to explore intercultural dialogue with South Korea. The result was the creation of a dance style and moves that are locally grounded but reach for a global dimension. Katrak emphasizes the difference reflected in this form of transnationalism based on the Global South instead of the Global North: funding and creative leadership foster explicitly global genres of dance. Katrak discusses issues of power and hierarchies as she contrasts the cases of appropriation of non-Western material by groups from the Global North, and their subsequent orientalist representation, with these South–South collaborations. Her discussion of the Indo-German-Bangladeshi collaboration—the co-choreography of Vikram Iyengar and Helena Walmann—emphasizes a similar point. Funded by the German Foundation and supported by Indian and Bangladeshi groups, the piece was subsequently performed in Bangladesh, India, Germany, and Switzerland. Katrak argues that such South–South collaboration produces more respectful interactions, and they are beginning to expand the transnational circuits of dance beyond the hierarchies of North to South collaborations.

Two chapters explore how culture and identity are woven within different political contexts. Both focus on second-generation migrants. The complexity of transnational identities is the subject of Kara Somerville's chapter on second-generation South Asians[7] in Canada. Canada has an official multicultural policy, which recognizes the importance of recognizing diverse cultures instead of expecting migrants to assimilate into one national culture. Somerville argues that, in contrast, the second generation must navigate multicultural America as a *visible minority*, emphasizing the lack of multicultural policies to address everyday racism. In the US they are confronted with continuous processes of incorporation into visions of nationhood, and marginalizations, which make them question their national belonging. This group also must navigate the interplay of this policy with family and co-ethnic community expectations. Participants' religion, skin color, cultural knowledge, language fluency, clothing, accessories, and social networks simultaneously break down and uphold boundaries of belonging. Somerville emphasizes both the fluidity of cultures as well as their embeddedness in structures beyond one nation-state. The boundaries separating one identity from another are porous yet can become rigidly solidified as racial, linguistic, or cultural barriers are erected depending on the political circumstances of their own and their parents' positionality in multiple nation-states. Overall, she argues, members of this group—whether in the US or Canada—develop a transnational consciousness through ongoing cultural reproduction, negotiation, and reconstruction of place as they navigate different social spaces in their host country as well as in India.

Sandhya Rao Mehta explores a similar question in a very different political context. She examines the links between culture and identity among second-generation migrants in Oman. Most of the second-generation Indian residents were born in Oman but are not entitled to any benefits from the state. Mehta examines the way these individuals perceive meanings of home, languages adopted, and choices made about their future. Transnational identity here is not a choice but is the resultant reality of their social situation. Based on interviews and questionnaires with more than 30 individuals born and raised in Oman, this research explores the creation of homes in a transnational context where identity is determined by institutional forces outside the control of individuals. Rao Mehta reflects on the creation of a Gulf-based Indian community whose home becomes more potent in the imagination as its physical presence erodes. Her research suggests that transnational identities among residents in the Gulf are problematized by their inability to reside in the country of their birth while being disconnected to their country of origin, but that such non-belonging, in turn, creates opportunities for the reconceptualization of home within this particular diaspora, which could be termed as creative transnationalism.

Part III: Political engagement in transnational spaces

Pierre Gottschlich focuses on post-1965 Indian migrants in the US. He traces how the arrival of this group—highly educated, high-wage earners—laid the foundation for a more active political involvement and continued attempts to influence U.S. foreign policy. Gottschlich describes political lobbying in the first few decades of the 20th century as the Ghadar party and the India

League of America (ILA) attempted to lobby for US support for Indian independence. Later the ILA and other Indian American anti-colonial voices embarked on a broader transnational political project by lobbying in the United States for the independence of other Asian nations such as Indonesia and Vietnam. The chapter discusses the growth of the religio-political lobbies, including the Hindutva groups, the Sikh lobbies, and the American Muslim associations over the last few decades. From the early 1990s, the Indian American Forum for Political Education (IAFPE) helped create the India Caucus, which marked a new direction in forging political connections between the two countries. Just as a large number of political and economic groups have lobbied to change India's image and standing in the US, the Indian government has created a new category of Overseas Indian citizens to offer Indians in some diasporas formal ways to remain attached to the homeland. Gottschlich draws attention to the role of extra-state actors as the diaspora becomes a source of soft power in the making and shaping a transnational political context.

Lise-Hélène Smith and Anjana Narayan focus on religio-politics in response to the political/cultural rights of minority groups. They focus on the articulation and construction of Hinduism in the United States and France, two countries with distinct migration histories, conceptions of nationhood, and understandings of religion. Since Hinduism does not consist of a uniform set of core elements, they trace whether religious practices and ideologies transcend the specificities of their national and local contexts. They find that despite pronounced national variations, some similar patterns exist across the two contexts. Part of the similarity arises from overt and covert forms of discrimination and de-legitimization that Hindus face. In both countries they attempt to make their religion more compatible with mainstream societies. Smith and Narayan identify an increasingly powerful actor in the affairs of Hindus in diasporas. Emphasizing the need to understand a multi-country transnational circuit, they document the role of American- and British-based Hindu organizations that have emerged as transnational representatives for Hindus across the world, including France. As these organizations influence the politics and structure of multiple host societies, they promote shifts in religious practice and expression based on migrants' experiences in a few host countries in the Global North. The nuclei for particular types of religious practice then shape the contours of the religions across countries, including India. Smith and Narayan's chapter also shows the nexus of politics and culture, a topic explored further in the next section.

Peter J. Smith discusses activism in the context of international advances in human rights, neo-liberal globalization, improved communications, and the growing power of NGOs. He focuses on Dalit transnational movements for human rights, including an activism centering on Dalit women's human rights. Dalit activist groups have used the universalist discourse of human rights—including economic, social, cultural, and women's rights—to gain international recognition and ultimately the abolition of caste and untouchability. Smith unpacks the transnational nature of this activism by documenting the contextual shift from a more socialist, social-justice oriented set of state policies in India after its independence from the UK in 1947, to the enthusiastic adoption of neoliberal policies by the Indian government from the 1990s. He indicates how the migration of Dalits in the 1950s and 1960s established the nucleus for the later activism to gain international attention about their condition. Since that time, and with increasing urgency since the 1990s, amidst the debilitating effects of neo-liberal globalization, Dalit activists in the diaspora and India have made connections with other marginalized peoples, including African Americans, landless workers in Brazil, indigenous peoples, and other groups bearing the stigma of caste wherever they are located: Japan, Africa, and South Asia. They have worked with like-minded groups and solidarity movements in South Asia and Europe and have lobbied the EU, UK, and the United States. Some Dalit activists have been widely recognized for their work through international awards. They have gained international supporters and have created an archive of information on atrocities committed against them so that their treatment does not remain a partially hidden, internal matter of the Indian state. Smith provides crucial insight into the nature of transnational activism: Dalit activists' success at making themselves visible to an international audience, and drawing supporters who have passed resolutions supporting their cause, has been countered by the local resistance from the Indian government and conservative sections of the Indian diaspora. Thus transnationalism can remain fractured and disjunctured, as many theorists suggest.

Part IV: Gender and Indian transnationalism

Manashi Ray examines the experiences of female migrants and returnees who have become entrepreneurs in the US or India. Breaking away from the literature that focuses on males primarily, or the female workers in the lower tier of economies, she documents the presence of female entrepreneurs and the different factors that shape their success. She situates her discussion in a historical moment: recession in the Silicon Valley (US) and the Indian state's actions to maximize "brain gain/circulation/return" migration as a magnet for foreign and diasporic investments in the early 21st century. She analyzes the experience of different types of entrepreneurs. One set migrated to the US for education, married partners whom they met in graduate school, and often worked in corporate America before gravitating to entrepreneurship as an avenue for greater autonomy and self-fulfillment. Another group consists of members of business communities that were expanding into global businesses; these women drew upon "inherited" social, economic, and cultural capital from these networks. In contrast to the women featured in Amy Bhatt's study, these women frequently disputed the ideologies of gendered socialization in their parents' homes. In contrast, they pointed to their own ability to make decisions as they managed their businesses and, as needed, families and networks. The third set of entrepreneurs entered this field from a different position: they became involved in entrepreneurship as a way to deal with difficult personal or family circumstances. Ray illustrates how human, cultural, and class capital function within different types of transnational networking. The women's ability to position themselves within diverse ethnic, national, and transnational networks and flows of capital reinforce inequalities among the entrepreneurs.

Quraisha Dawood and Mariam Seedat-Khan focus on the role of South African Indian women in challenging apartheid and the making of modern South Africa. They point out that despite their entry into a harsh, oppressive, and unequal colonial system via indenture 158 years ago, South African Indian women have played and continue to play a pivotal role in the establishment of a South African Indian community that has survived both indenture and apartheid. Through their multifaceted lived experiences in South Africa since the 1860s, the identity of South African Indian women has been molded by a multiplicity of factors, which include apartheid, indenture, religion, culture, religion, and patriarchy. Ultimately, they have socially constructed a reality that is inclusive of both South African and Indian cultural beliefs and practices. In their discussion of transnationalism, Dawood and Seedat-Khan point out that the political participation of South African Indian women such as Professor Fatima Meer, Frene Ginwala, Amina Cachalia, Dr. Goonam, Ela Gandhi, and Phyllis Naidoo intensified in the 1950s with the struggle against the apartheid regime. Yet their names are mostly invisible in the accounts that focus on men such as Yousuf Dadoo, Dr. Naikar, and (Mahatma) Gandhi. Thus erasures are very much a part of transnational histories and memories. Another key point of the chapter is that under apartheid, it was politically impossible to claim South Africa as a homeland, even though materially and socially this was the reality for South African Indians. But women's anti-apartheid activism broke some of those barriers. Durban-born South African sociologist Professor Fatima Meer epitomized the identity of the South African Indian women while embracing and advocating for all South African women, irrespective of race. As a result, there is a contemporary change in the understanding of India as a homeland; that understanding is replaced by a South African homeland reality.

As many Global North countries have organized their immigration policies to facilitate the migration of highly skilled workers, first males and then females—most of whom were admitted as dependents of male migrants—arrived in the US and Canada. Amrita Hari presents the case of Canada, where government policies restricting the migration of Indians shifted towards encouraging the entry of highly skilled migrants in the 1990s. Much like the situation in the US, Hari points out, female migrants, highly educated themselves, encounter significant barriers to accessing jobs. If they are able to do so, very limited choices in childcare arrangements further limit their career choices. Gendered structures affect them cumulatively: during migration, as they settle, through the jobs they can access given their care responsibilities, to settling into the role of social reproducer while their spouses become the primary earner. Hari, like Bhatt, emphasizes the challenges associated with balancing outside paid work and home-based non-paid caregiving. She links these structural impediments to persistent gendered inequalities among highly educated Indian migrants to Canada.

Sutama Ghosh explores what freedom means to women after migration. She finds that the female participants in her research related the act of being free to a specific geographical space (where) and time (when). When they thought about relative freedom in India, it was tied to being in specific social locations—shaped by social norms defining those positions—in their parents' home or in their marital family homes. This home-centered idea of freedom persisted in their description of Toronto. Ghosh describes that the participant's sense of freedom "outside" was understood in terms of the permissibility to dress in a certain way outside of home, being able to secure (or not) desired employment, and being able to socialize outside the home. But they insisted that this freedom outside was similar to what they had experienced in India, and in some cases they felt more constrained in Canada because of the challenges of daily life, including unfair labor practices that led to their downward mobility. For them the senses of freedom and imprisonment, stability and instability, power and powerlessness exist simultaneously, thereby positioning them both at the center and at the margins, simultaneously, within a transnational habitus.

Unlike the liminality Sutama Ghosh discusses as women's experiences in Canada, Selvaraj Velayutham examines the question by focusing on "middling transnationals," the migrants who occupy middling rather than higher echelon positions in their home and host countries. He focuses on mostly male skilled migrant Tamil workers in Singapore, to examine their ties with home countries. He discusses how middling Tamil migrant workers maintain links with their home village and argues that both social media and budget air travel have revolutionized transnational relations by enabling a real connection with their village. Discussing the key role played by websites dedicated to very specific villages and groups, he argues that social life begins to occur in translocal villages. In a break from social ties that are based on linear communication—phone calls, letters—this particular form of community is based around a translocal village that transcends geographic and web spaces. At the same time, the circuits of duties and obligations to families, and communities, tie these men in specific, assertively constructed ways to transnational lives.

On historic and contemporary networks in transnational spaces

Sumita Mukherjee discusses key areas of transnational mobility during formal British crown control over India, 1858–1947, an era in which ideas of anti-colonialism, nationalism, internationalism, and globalism grew and cohered in different forms. Mukherjee focuses on the migration encounters of middle-class educated Indians, who were allowed to travel more freely during this period. The chartering of the ship *Komagata Maru* in 1914, the subsequent refusal of Canada to allow the passengers to disembark, and the imprisonment of Indians in Japan as they made their return to Calcutta offers one glimpse into this history. Mukherjee explores transnational travel and exchanges amidst patterns of resistance, protest, and collaborations between Indians and the British imperial system. She argues that Indians were turning the gaze back to imperial Britain; this was also the period of thinking about a pan-Asia. She describes the history of Indians' participation in transnational associations and organizations, including in anti-colonial groups, socialist and communist groups, women's groups, and regional associations.

Nisha Mathew describes gold smuggling in the western Indian Ocean that was rampant in the years following decolonization and the end of empire in India. Bombay, Dubai, and Malabar constituted its key nodes, spinning together a regional economy, the spatial and functional limits of which, she argues, exceeded the national economy in India. The chapter draws on the concept of *value* to map the social context driving the mobility of gold between Dubai and Malabar through the changing legal regimes of trade in the 20th century. In restoring a cultural dimension to the economy and a calculative dimension to cultural practices defining the exchange of gold within this geography in the western Indian Ocean, Mathew analyzes the constitution of a particular kind of social space and the different spatial relations reinforcing it. Contesting the territorial economy of the state in India and spilling out of its political borders, this social space, she argues, becomes the basis of Dubai's urban growth and transition from a smuggling capital to the "City of Gold."

Jayati Bhjattacharya draws our attention to a different part of the globe and presents contemporary Indian transnationalism in Singapore. Itself a colony in its early history, Singapore has created itself as a node for the Asia Pacific region and the world. Indian transnational networks have gone through different transformations in Singapore. Bhjattacharya's focus is on Indian celebration of culture, festivities, and sports, which has established a consciousness that is more regional, accommodative, and fluid than a homogenous national identity. She documents that several religious and cultural organizations in different parts of the globe are now quite easily connected with technology. At the same time, Singapore is pushed by globalization flows, market trends, and state-driven policies and initiatives to interact with the diaspora and global citizens. Overall, Bhattacharya links the colonial history to contemporary transnationalism, to the expressions and formation of various interest groups, and to the promotion of this diaspora in the nation's development. Bridging old colonial flows with today's global trends, Singapore remains an important node and platform for linking different interest groups, institutions, and like-minded people in the region, across the world and, for Indians, also back to the homeland.

Notes

1 The scholarship on transgender transnationalism that focuses on the diaspora is still scattered, though the *Journal of South Asian Studies* has published articles related to this subject.
2 Interestingly, many of the scholars who are located in the Global North but offer critical perspectives on structures of race/gender/class/sexuality/religion are immigrants or children of immigrants themselves, for instance, Chowdhury 2011, Guevarra 2009, Glenn 2002, Purkayastha 2010.

3 These forces do not uniformly affect migrants; the impact depends on their relative power to navigate these forces. I have argued elsewhere that migrants exist on a continuum. At one end are the few who can move as they chose, at the other are those who are forced to move or are trafficked, with a majority falling in between. The degrees of violence and structural impediments within and across nation-states they experience rises exponentially as people are forced to migrate (Purkayastha 2018).
4 The vast anti-colonialism literature, including work such as Tagore's reflection on the crisis of Civilization or What is a Nation, fall within this broad categorization.
5 Others have written about the extraction of resources from the African continent by different colonial powers (e.g., Falcón 2016 or Prashad 2007).
6 For an overview of these debates, see Purkayastha 2010.
7 Indian origin South Asians are a subset of this group.

References

Adur, Shweta. 2011. The "Cost" of the American Dream. In Armaline, William, Glasberg, Davita, and Purkayastha, Bandana (eds.), *Human Rights in Our Backyard: Injustice and Resistance in the US*. Philadelphia, PA: University of Pennsylvania Press.

Adur, Shweta and Purkayastha, Bandana. 2013. On the Edges of Belonging: Indian American Dalits, Queers, Guest Workers and Questions of Ethnic Belonging. *Journal of Intercultural Studies*, 34: 418–430.

Aiyar, Sana. 2011. Anticolonial Homelands across the Indian Ocean: The Politics of the Indian Diaspora in Kenya, ca. 1930–1950. *The American Historical Review*, 116: 987–1013.

Alba, Richard and Nee, Victor. 1997. Rethinking Assimilation Theory for a New Era of Immigration. *International Migration Review*, 31: 826–874.

Alvarz, Sonia. 2000. Translating the Global: Effects of Transnational Organizing on Latin American Feminist Discourses and Practices. *Meridians: A Journal of Feminisms, Race, Transnationalism*, 1 (1): 29–67.

Aneesh, A. 2015. *Neutral Accent: How Language, Labour, and Life Became Global*. Durham, NC: Duke University Press.

Appadurai, Arjun. 1996. *Modernity at Large*. Minneapolis, MN: University of Minnesota Press.

Arcarazo, Diego Acosta. 2015. Toward a South American Citizenship? The Development of a New Post-National Form of Membership in the Region. *Journal of International Affairs*, 68: 213–221.

Baruah, Sanjib. 2003. Citizens and Denizens: Ethnicity, Homelands and the Crisis of Displacement in North East India. *Journal of Refugee Studies*, 1: 44–66.

Bharucha, Rustom. 2006. *Another Asia: Rabindranath Tagore and Okakura Tenshin*. Oxford: Oxford University Press.

Bush, Michael L. 2000. *Servitude in Modern Times*. Cambridge: Polity Press.

Castells, Manuel. 1996. *The Rise of the Network Society*. Oxford: Blackwell.

Chandrasekhar, Subramaniam. 1982. *From India to America: Brief History of Immigration, Problems of Discrimination, Admission and Assimilation*. La Jolla, CA: A Population Review Book.

Chowdhury, Elora. 2011. *Transnationalism Reversed: Women Organizing against Gendered Violence in Bangladesh*. New York, NY: SUNY Press.

Collyer, Michael and King, Russell. 2015. Producing Transnational Space: International Migration and the Extra Territorial Reach of State Power. *Progress in Human Geography*, 39 (2): 185–204.

Connell, Raewyn. 2009. *Southern Theory: The Global Dynamics of Knowledge in Social Science*. London: Polity Press.

Crowley, Daniel. 1990. The Remigration of Trinidadian East Indians. In Sanjek, Roger (ed.), *Caribbean Asians: Chinese, Indian and Japanese Experiences in Trinidad and the Dominican Republic*. New York, NY: The Asian/American Center at Queens College, CUNY, 82–95.

Das Gupta, Monisha. 2006. *Unruly Immigrants: Rights, Activism and Transnational South Asian Politics in the United States*. Durham, NC: Duke University Press.

Das Gupta, Monisha. 2013. "Don't Deport Our Daddies": Gendering State Deportation Practices and Immigrant Organizing. *Gender & Society*, 28: 83–109.

Das Gupta, Samir, Siriner, Ismail, and De Partha, Sarathi (eds.). 2010. *Women's Encounter with Disaster*. Kolkata: Frontpage Publications.

Davis, Kingsley. 1951. *The Population of India and Pakistan*. Princeton, NJ: Princeton University Press.
Desai, Ashwin and Vahed, Goolam. 2010. *Inside Indian Indenture: A South African Story 1860–1914*. Capetown: HSRC Press.
Duara, Prasenjit. 2010. Asia Redux: Conceptualizing a Region of Our Times. *The Journal of Asian Studies*, 69 (4): 963–983.
Erturk, Yakin and Purkayastha, Bandana. 2012. Linking Research, Policy and Action: A Look at the Work of the Special Rapporteur on Violence against Women. *Current Sociology*, 60: 20–39.
Faist, Thomas. 2019. *The Transnationalized Social Question: Migration and the Politics of Social Inequalities in the Twenty-First Century*. Oxford: Oxford University Press.
Faist, Thomas, Fauser, Margit, and Reisenauer, Eveline. 2013. *Transnational Migration*. London: Polity Press.
Falcón, Sylvanna. 2016. *Power Interrupted: Antiracist and Feminist Activism inside the United Nations*. Seattle, WA: University of Washington Press.
Ferree, Myra Marx and Tripp, Alili Marie (eds.). 2006. *Global Feminism: Transnational Women's Activism, Organizing, and Human Rights*. New York, NY: New York University Press.
German, Lindsey. 2013. *How a Century of War Changed the Lives of Women*. London: Pluto Press.
Glenn, Evelyn Nakano. 2002. *Unequal Freedoms*. Cambridge, MA: Harvard University Press.
Glenn, Evelyn Nakano. 2015. Settler Colonialism as Structure: A Framework for Comparative Studies of US Race and Gender Formations. *Race and Ethnicity*, 1: 52–72.
Glick-Schiller, Nina, Basch, Linda, and Blanc-Szanton, Cristina (eds.). 1992. *Towards a Transnational Perspective on Migration*. New York, NY: New York Academy of Sciences.
Gopal, Sangita and Moorti, Sujata. 2008. *Global Bollywood: Travels of Hindi Song and Dance*. Minneapolis, MN: University of Minnesota Press.
Gould, William. 2017. Rethinking "Diaspora": Bengal's Muslims and Hidden Migrants. *Ethnic and Racial Studies*, 40 (3): 413–420.
Govinden, Devarakshanam (ed.). 2008. *"Sister Outsiders": The Representation of Identity and Difference in Selected Writings by South African Indian Women*. Leiden: Brill.
Guevarra, Anna. 2009. *Marketing Dreams, Manufacturing Heroes: The Transnational Labor Brokering of Filipino Workers*. New Brunswick, NJ: Rutgers University Press.
Gupta, Akhil and Ferguson, James. 1992. "Beyond Culture": Space, Identity, and the Politics of Difference. *Cultural Anthropology*, 7: 6–23.
Hegde, Radha and Sahoo, Ajaya. 2017. *Routledge Handbook of the Indian Diaspora*. London: Routledge.
Hiralal, Kalpana. 2014. Women and Migration in South Africa: Historical and Literary Perspectives. *South Asian Diaspora*, 6: 65–75.
Inaga, Shigemi. 2006. Tenshin Okakura and Sister Nibedita: On an Intellectual Exchange in Modernizing Asia. Paper delivered at the Japanese Studies Conference: Beyond Borders. Warsaw, 19–21 May 2006.
Jain, Sonali. 2013. For Love or Money: Second-Generation Indian-Americans "Return" to India. *Ethnic and Racial Studies*, 36: 896–914.
Joseph, May. 1999. *Nomadic Identities: The Performance of Citizenship*. Minneapolis, MN: University of Minnesota Press.
Kaur, Raminder. 2011. "Ancient Cosmopolitanism" and the South Asian Diaspora. *South Asian Diaspora*, 3: 197–214.
Kearney, Michael and Nagengast, Carole. 1989. *Anthropological Perspectives on Transnational Communities in Rural California*. Davis, CA: California Institute for Rural Studies.
Khandelwal, Madhulika. 2002. *Becoming American, Being Indian: An Immigrant Community in New York City*. Ithaca, NY: Cornell University Press.
Kofman, Eleanor. 2013. Gendered Labour Migration: Europe and Emblematic Figures. *Journal of Ethnic and Refugee Studies*, 39: 579–600.
Kofman, Elenore and Raghuram, Parvati. 2005. Gender and Skilled Migrants: Into and beyond the Work Place. *Geoforum*, 36 (2): 149–154.
La Guerre, John (ed.). 1974. *Calcutta to Caroni: East Indians of Trinidad*. New York, NY: Longmans.
Levitan, Rachel, Kaytaz, Esra, and Durukan, Oktay. 2010. Unwelcome Guests: The Detention of Refugees in Turkey's "Foreigners' Guesthouses." *Refugee*, 26: 77–90.
Levitt, Peggy. 2001. *The Transnational Villagers*. Berkeley, CA: University of California Press.
Levitt, Peggy. 2009. *God Needs No Passport: Immigrants and the Changing American Landscape*. New York, NY: New Press.

Li, Kwai-Yun. 2011. Deoli Camp: An Oral History of Chinese Indians from 1962 to 1966. University of Toronto (Canada), ProQuest Dissertations Publishing. MR76088.

Mahmud, Tayyab. 2012. Cheaper than a Slave: Indenture Labour, Colonialism and Capitalism. *Whittier Law Review*. Available from: www.columbia.edu/~lnp3/SSRN-id2155088.pdf [accessed on 4 July 2016].

Manohar, Namita and Banerjee, Pallavi. 2016. H-1B Visas. In Huerta, Alvarao, Iglesias-Prieto, Norma, and Brown, Donathan L. (eds.), *People of Color in the United States: Contemporary Issues in Education, Communities, Health, and Immigration*. Vol. 4. ABC-CLIO, 161–168.

Mawani, Renisa. 2012. Specters of Indigeneity in British-Indian Migration, 1914. *Law & Society Review*, 46 (2): 369–403.

Mehta, Brinda. 2015. Inscribing *kala pani* in Ernest Moutoussamy's *A La recherché de L'Inde perdue*. *South Asian Diaspora*, 7 (1): 1–17.

Mukherjee, Madhushree. 2010. *Churchill's Secret War: The British Empire and the Ravaging of India during World War II*. New York, NY: Basic Books.

Narayan, Anjana, Purkayastha, Bandana (and authors in collective). 2009. *Living Our Religions: Hindu and Muslim South Asian Women Narrate Their Experiences*. Stirling, VA: Kumarian Press.

Narayan, Anjana, Purkayastha, Bandana, and Banerji, Sudipto. 2011. Constructing Virtual, Transnational Identities on the Web: The Case of Hindu Student Groups in the US and UK. *Journal of Intercultural Studies*, 32: 495–517.

Njiru, Roseanne and Purkayastha, Bandana. 2015. *Voices of Internally Displaced Persons in Kenya: A Human Rights Perspective*. Kolkata and London: Frontpage Publications.

Okakura, Kakuzo. [1903] 1970. *Ideals of the East with Special Reference to the Art of Japan*. Tokyo: Tuttle & Co.

Ortiz, Laura and Pombo, Dolores. 2014. Introduction: Indigenous Migration in Mexico and Central America. *Latin American Perspectives* (Issue 196), 41 (3): 5–25.

Pandey, Gyanendra. 2006. *Routine Violence: Nations, Fragments, Histories*. Stanford, CA: Stanford University Press.

Pandurang, Mala and Munos, Delphine. 2014. Mapping Diasporic Subjectivities. *South Asian Diasporas*, 6 (1):1–5.

Parennas, Rachel. 2001. *Servants of Globalization*. Stanford, CA: Stanford University Press.

Patel, Sujata. 2006. Beyond Binaries. *Current Sociology*, 54: 381–395.

Patel, Sujata and Uys, Tina (eds.). 2012. *Contemporary India and South Africa: Legacies, Identities, Dilemmas*. London: Routledge.

Portes, Alejandro. 1997. Globalization from Below: The Rise of Transnational Communities. WPTC-98-01. Princeton, NJ: Transnational Communities Programme. Available from: http://maxweber.hunter.cuny.edu/eres/docs/eres/SOC217_PIMENTEL/portes.pdf.

Prashad, Vijay. 2007. *The Darker Nations: A People's History of the Third World*. New York, NY: New Press.

Purkayastha, Bandana. 2005. *Negotiating Ethnicity: Second-Generation South Asian Americans Traverse a Transnational World*. New Brunswick, NJ: Rutgers University Press.

Purkayastha, Bandana. 2010. Interrogating Intersectionality: Contemporary Globalization and Racialized Gendering in the Lives of Highly Educated South Asian Americans and their Children. *Journal of Intercultural Studies*, 31: 55–66.

Purkayastha, Bandana. 2012. Intersectionality in a Transnational World. *Gender & Society*, 26: 55–66.

Purkayastha, Bandana (ed.). 2018. Migration, Migrants and Human Security. *Current Sociology*, 66 (2) (Special Issue & Monograph): 167–191.

Ramnarine, Tina. 2011. Music in Circulation between Diasporic Histories and Modern Media: Exploring Sonic Politics in Two Bollywood Films *Om Shanti Om* and *Dulha Mil Gaya*. *South Asian Diaspora*, 3 (2): 143–158.

Sahoo, Ajaya and De Kruif, Johannes. 2014. *Indian Transnationalism Online: New Perspectives on Diaspora*. London: Ashgate.

Samaddar, Ranabir. 1999. *Marginal Nation: Transborder Migration from Bangladesh to West Bengal*. New Delhi: Sage Publications.

Samaddar, Ranabir. 2015. Returning to the Histories of the Late 19th and Early 20th Century Immigration. *Economic & Political Weekly*, 50 (2): 49–55.

Seedat-Khan, Mariam. 2012. Tracing the Journey of South African Indian Women from 1868. In Patel, Sujata and Uys, Tina (eds.), *Contemporary India and South Africa: Legacies, Identities, Dilemmas*. London: Routledge, 35–48.

Simatei, Peter. 2011. Diasporic Memories and National Histories in East African Asian Writing. *Research in African Literatures*, 42 (3): 56–67.

Simon, Rita and Alexander, Susan H. 1993. *The Ambivalent Welcome: Print Media, Public Opinion and Immigration*. Westport, CT: Praeger.

Singh, Supriya and Gatina, Liliya. 2015. Money Flows Two Ways between Transnational Families in Australia and India. *South Asian Diaspora*, 7 (1): 33–47.

Tagore, Rabindranath. [1910–1930] 1970. Lectures and Addresses. (Selected by Anthony Soares). Madras: Macmillian.

Tatla, Darshan and Singh, G. 2008. *Sikhs in Britain: The Making of a Community*. Delhi: Ajanta Publishers.

Thomas, Dominic. 2014. Fortress Europe: Identity, Race and Surveillance. *International Journal of Francophone Studies*, 17: 445–468.

Tinker, H. 1974. *A New System of Slavery: The Export of Indian Labour Overseas, 1830–1920*. London: Oxford University Press.

Tinker, H. 1977 *The Banyan Tree: Overseas Emigrants from India, Pakistan and Bangladesh*. Oxford: Oxford University Press

Vakulabharanam, Vamsi and Prasad, Purendra. 2017. Babu's Camelot: Amaravati and the Emerging Capitalist Dynamics in "New" Andhra Pradesh. *Economic & Political Weekly*, 52 (2): 69–78.

Vertovec, Steven. 1999. Conceiving and Researching Transnationalism. *Ethnic and Racial Studies*, 22: 445–62.

Vertovec, Steven. 2009. *Transnationalism*. London: Routledge.

Yousaf, Farhan. 2018. Forced Migration, Human Trafficking, and Human Security. *Current Sociology*, 66: 209–225.

PART I

Migrants'/workers' lives

1
GLOBALITY IN EXCEPTIONAL SPACES
Service workers in India's transnational economy[1]

Kiran Mirchandani

Introduction

This chapter focuses on workers who are employed within India's transnational technology sector. Drawing on interviews with a diverse group of workers, I explore the ways in which workers' class positions structure their experiences of globality within zones of exception (Ong 2006) and their sense of themselves in relation to global flows of capital. The creation of special economic zones has been a key feature of India's economic development for decades. Aside from gated residential spaces, securitized shopping malls and exclusive membership based recreational spaces, state-sanctioned special economic zones (SEZs) have proliferated in all major urban areas. In 2005 India passed an Act which stipulates application procedures and corporate benefits related to zones. These include tax holidays, government subsidies and infrastructure incentives to entice multinational firms. Certain labor laws such as the right to engage in collective action are also suspended within zones (Ananthanrayanan 2008, Goldman 2011). Sampat (2010) estimates that by 2010 there were 1046 approved SEZs in India which, despite significant peasant protests and farmer displacements, continue to be depicted as spaces of wealth, development and progress. Of the formally approved SEZs, 60% are in the information technology and information technology-enabled sector (IT/ITES), and zones range in size from as small as six hectares to as large as more than two hundred hectares. This means that there are significant differences between zones, and while some occupy large areas close to old cities and house multiple organizations, others are single-organization zones, developed within existing city spaces. Despite this diversity, while some zones are focused on biotechnology, apparel or gems and a few are multi-product zones, the IT/ITES sector in India dominates the urban landscape of many cities, since close to two-thirds of zones house companies focused on this sector (http://sezindia.nic.in/).

Notwithstanding these differences between special economic zones, much of the literature on exceptional spaces characterizes these sites as bounded systems with internal homogeneity and strong border enforcement, which serves to limit mobility into the zone of those who do not belong. Yet, as ethnographic research on zones has revealed, the building and maintenance of gated communities and special economic zones depends on large numbers of low-wage, precariously employed service and construction workers (Cross 2010) who are part of the group who does not belong and yet are integral to spaces of exception. Despite high fences, the borders of zones are more porous than one would think, because of the constant movement of labor in and out of these spaces. The analysis in this chapter focuses on how special economic zones are themselves microcosms where class discrepancies result in very different experiences of exceptionality for the different groups of workers present.

On exceptional spaces

There has been considerable research on the impact of special economic zones, which have proliferated since the 1960s in many cities around the world. These zones, in countries such as Taiwan, China, the Philippines, Mexico and the Dominican Republic, have historically served as a strategy through which states can attract foreign capital by providing tax havens and corporate incentives to multinational firms. Many countries in Asia, in particular, have embraced zone development. As Sampat notes, by the early 1990s, half of all workers employed in zones lived in Asia (2010). While SEZs were originally focused on manufacturing and assembly, those established in the past two decades have been much more diverse in terms of industry focus. Ong notes that many zones have political and governance structures which are different from the nation within which they exist and that there is significant variation between zones (Ong 2006: 104). In India, some zones house manufacturing and assembly firms in which low-wage workers predominate, while others are occupied by high-tech multinational firms where the country's elite are employed.

Cross traces worker experiences within one of the oldest free-trade zones in India – Visakhapatnam in Andhra Pradesh – through an ethnography of a diamond-processing factory. Rather than a closed or bounded exceptional space, Cross notes that workers within the zone experience labor insecurity, poor working conditions, low wages and little state protection, much like those who are employed in casual, labor-intensive work in other settings. Given their poor wages, workers rely heavily on informal economies to meet their survival needs, and like in many other settings within India, there is an active informal economy within Visakhapatnam. Cross (2010: 369) argues that while "the economic zones being built across India continue to be imagined and conceptualized as unique territorial, juridical and disciplinary spaces by planners, politicians, activists and social scientists . . . in their everyday operation, the continuities and interconnections of these spaces with the wider economy make them decidedly unexceptional".

While this may be true of some larger zones within manufacturing sectors, within-zone diversity is significantly more masked within IT/ITES spaces in India. Corporate "campuses" comprise architectural forms designed to draw attention. Well-manicured lawns surround these glass and marble buildings, which have round-the-clock security. Armed guards in spic and span uniforms posted at imposing gates are not an unusual sight. On the inside, buildings are spotlessly clean and air conditioned. All workers are dressed in Western[2] attire – managers in suits, and housekeepers or security guards in uniforms. All employees and visitors are required to display photo identification. While these transnational spaces may be infrastructure-rich with the look and feel of the most glamorous of Western corporate offices, they are, however, also spaces where labor who occupy a variety of class positions interact. Those employed within spaces of exception in India include not only upper- and middle-class managers, software programmers or call-center workers but also cleaners, caterers, drivers and security guards.

In the analysis below, I explore how IT/ITES sites are exceptional spaces where particular notions of globality are enacted. Globality, as distinguished from globalization, focuses on the practices through which workers conceptualize themselves as existing within the world. I explore the ways in which workers occupying different class positions practice forms of "globality" within spaces of exception.

Globality within exceptional spaces

The term "globality," first used in the mid-80s, can be differentiated from the broader notion of globalization. Schäfer argues that globalization indicates a process of economic, cultural and social expansion across nation states; it has multiple actors, including states, corporations and policies. In contrast, globality is a condition – specifically the "quality of being global." The concept provides an "analytic snapshot of the extent of discrete global processes at a particular point in time" (2007: 8). Brar and Mukherjee note that the notions of globality and globalization are often conceived in relational terms – that is, one causes, or is the effect of, the other – but that it is more useful to use the notion of globality to signal the open, contingent and uneven social relationships in their localized manifestations. Globality, they note, is a "consequence of multiple causes" (2012: 5). These multiple causes bring about a consciousness of the "world as a single social space" in the context of widespread connectivity (Scholte 2002: 15). In the case of Indian housekeepers, for example, the agrarian crisis, state neoliberalism, the predominance of IT/ITES corporations in the urban landscape and the cleaning needs of transnational corporations converge as factors which led to an influx of labor to the city from smaller neighboring towns.

Globality is achieved through a set of practices – it is the "outcome of the conscious and intentional actions of many individual and collective human actors" (Shaw 2000: 17). Others have used the term "critical globality" to refer to practices through which people become "literate in the workings of capitalism and other forms of power" (Weinbaum and Edwards 2000). This focus on literacy, learning, practice, condition and consciousness differentiates globality from more mainstream notions of globalization, which center on description, critique or celebration of worldwide capitalist expansion.

Some theorists note that this "condition of being global" – or globality – is a middle-class orientation – that is, it is a consciousness which serves as cultural capital for the middle classes (O'Bryne and Hensby 2011). However, I argue that "globality" is practiced by all workers who occupy spaces of exception; low-wage workers in fact also cover significant ideological distance in their daily movement between local spaces and spaces of exception. As a result, globality leads to a questioning of the very notion of class, particularly in relation to nation. Weinbaum and Edwards, for example, argue that globality "allows us to signal the historical shift in the constitution of the notion of class, and to understand the ways in which new class formations are precipitated by processes of globalization that disrupt boundaries of nation-states as economic political units in some ways, reconsolidate them in others, and in so doing catalyze new transnational alliances" (2000: 271).

The notion of globality puts at the forefront, rather than in the background, practices through which people occupying distant geographical locations come to see themselves as connected to one another and simultaneously as part of a "world." As the discussion below reveals, the notion of this "world" and conceptions of one's place in it shifts depending on workers' class positions. Exceptional spaces are spaces of mobility, and rather than a fixed position, class is a continually enacted relational construct. Workers understand their place in the world through interactions with one another and in the context of organizational norms and practices. Working within exceptional spaces of free-trade zones involves, I argue, managing the gaps between the pride of working in an exceptional space and the work process which positions workers as subservient in this space.

Methods

This paper is based on field research conducted in India for more than a decade. It draws on interviews with a diverse set of workers employed in transnational firms and focuses on how they develop notions of workplace globality within spaces of exception. Between 2002 and 2010, I interviewed one hundred middle-class workers who were employed as customer-service agents and managers within India's transnational technology sector (Mirchandani 2012). These employees felt privileged to work in secure, clean, professional and Westernized organizational spaces where they received perks such as access to transportation, catering and recreational facilities. Many worked at night, which exacerbated the intensity of the continuous, heavily monitored calls which they received, often from abusive customers. Workers' sense of themselves in relation to the world centered on managing a series of gaps – between customer and local time, between their embodied selves as middle-class Indians and organizational requirements that they practice servitude, and between the pride they felt as workers in an elite space of exception and the work process which was reminiscent of Taylorist factory work. Their sense of being part of a global endeavor involved making sense of hierarchies which structured their interactions: situating them as servers in relation to their clients and employers but simultaneously as people who are served by those required to provide the infrastructure for them to complete their work. In this chapter I provide an account of one worker referred to by the pseudonym Rupa who is typical of those in my sample.

Following the completion of my interviews with call-center workers, I was interested in how such service relations were manifest in global economic relations across class position, so I conducted interviews with drivers, housekeepers and security guards employed within the exceptional spaces of IT/ITES firms. My colleagues (Shruti Tambe and Sanjukta Mukherjee) and I interviewed low-wage service workers employed through contractors at India's transnational firms (Mirchandani et al. 2020). In this chapter, I trace the ways in which the "condition of being global" is interpreted and learned by one housekeeper – Nabanita – who was employed at a large high-tech firm.

Pride and subservience within India's zones of exception

In 2002, a story titled "Housekeepers to the World" appeared on the cover of India's prominent magazine *India Today*. It was about the spectacular growth of the outsourced customer-service labor force in India. The accompanying image was of a fair woman with Anglo-Saxon features and a headset worn over her hoop earrings. While housekeeping work was often associated with caste stigma, poor wages and poverty, this "housekeeper" looked directly into the camera with a confident and professional smile. She was, like many of the call-center workers I interviewed, proud of her work not only because of its contribution to the Indian economy but also because of the prestige associated with living and working within an exceptional space. Such workers are "housekeepers" not because they engage in cleaning but because they are expected to be subservient and manage the emotional "remains" of Western clients – remains which arise due to their anger towards outsourcing or toward poor customer-service protocols. Call-center executives are also housekeepers, because their work is monitored, routinized and relatively low paid – like many engaged in cleaning industries worldwide.

Call-center workers are, however, not the only housekeepers of the world in transnational corporations. Through contractors, companies hire a large round-the-clock cleaning staff who are charged with the task of maintaining extremely high standards of cleanliness, which set the spaces of transnational firms apart. The exclusive nature of the clean space is part of its attraction of these jobs for customer-service employees. Such "geographies of cleanliness" structure zones of exception in many cities around the world (Tomic et al. 2006: 217). In Chile, like in India, shopping malls are examples of spaces of exclusion, which stand for symbols of the county's progress and modernity. Not only are large numbers of cleaning workers deployed to keep such spaces, and the corridors between them, clean but also security guards are hired to make sure that "such spaces are out-of-bounds for both those things and those people that would sully the spaces of purity and cleanliness which are taken to represent the modern Chile" (Tomic et al. 2006: 517). In contrast, poorer neighborhoods in Chile have potholes, garbage scattered on streets, no trash pickup and no organized cleaning; "circulates of modernity through which the middle and upper classes move, by way of contrast, are spotless, for the region's wealthy municipalities spend large sums of money on cleaning so as to keep the appearance of being modern" (Tomic et al. 2006: 522). Tomic et al. summarize, "a network of notes and corridors of asepticism is being carved into the landscape as a way of distinguishing the spaces of modernity from those where the majority of Chileans toil, move and dwell" (2006: 509). A very similar geography of cleanliness exists in many Indian cities, where there are vast discrepancies between hyper-clean spaces of exclusion and the surrounding areas. Yet, while class discrepancies may be masked within zones of exception, they continue to manifest in the diverse of group of service workers employed within these zones.

Housekeepers

Like in Chile, hyper-clean spaces in India require the labor of housekeepers of a very different sort than the ones depicted in the cover story "Housekeepers to the World." Through subcontractors, facilities managers at IT/ITES firms as well as special economic zone administrative officials hire women and men to clean, maintain and provide pantry services. Workers earned on average of about six thousand rupees, or about one-third of the wages of call-center executives. They are hired through contractors and can lose their jobs without notice or be shifted from site to site. Many do not have any formal employment contracts.

While occupying a lower position in terms of status and class than software and customer-service workers, cleaners too, however, see themselves as engaged in different work by virtue of their employment within the exceptional space of a free trade zone. The experiences of Nabanita are exemplary of the housekeepers we interviewed. Hired seven years ago by a contractor and posted at a large transnational call center, Nabanita had started a bachelor of commerce degree but was unable to continue because she failed one subject. Married and living with her mother-in-law, husband and daughter in a one-bedroom home, Nabanita used her income of Rs 7,000 per month to support the family. Her daughter attended an English-medium school. She reported that her husband was an alcoholic with numerous health problems and did not have a regular job. Nabanita worked nine-hour shifts cleaning the pantries and toilets in the nine-floor glass and steel office tower. The male housekeepers at her organization were responsible for the carpets, lobby and cafeterias. She explains that "in 9 hours we do 8 rounds (of cleaning). We do this round after every one hour." Cleaners sign a log as they complete each "round."

When asked to describe the call-center and software employees at the firm, Nabanita notes that "Here (in IT) employees speak to us with warmth . . . when do you come, when do you go, how can you come so early, do you finish domestic work etc. They speak like family members. We also speak with them without any fear." In referring to being spoken to with "warmth" and being able to speak "without fear," Nabanita expresses pride in having a job where she is not required to enact servitude norms which cleaners in many other settings are required to. She attributes these norms as a feature of the work culture "in IT."

Yet Nabanita notes that cleaning staff are also repeatedly told that there should be no complaints about the cleanliness of common areas in the organization. She notes that at times "employees make complaints. Employees leave dirt, papers on the floor, toilets are not properly flushed; water is spilled over the floor then other employees make complaints. If there is no cleanliness then they complain about it." This can have a repercussion on cleaners' jobs, as Nabanita recounts the experiences of one of her colleagues: "Day before yesterday on the third floor here some dirt was left by one woman. There was a complaint about her. INR 200 was deducted from her salary." Nabanita notes that some employees think that maintaining cleanliness is a housekeeper's job rather than a joint responsibility of company employees and housekeepers. Housekeepers receive training not only on chemicals, cleaning practices and schedules but also on protocols on how to speak to employees. Nabanita reports that the trainer

> taught us how to speak to employees and how to keep them happy. . . . We should not be arrogant. Our job is dependent on them. If they are not getting good services from us, if our work is not good then we should tell them softly that we were busy with something that's why we could not do your work. We will do it now.

Such deferential treatment is said to be required because call-center and software employees have high standards of cleanliness. These employees have direct employment relationships with corporations (while cleaners are hired through subcontractors) and comprise the aspiring local Indian elite. Nabanita's notion of her "place in the world" includes the fact that she can legitimately gain entry into prestigious modern organizational spaces associated with the West but can be easily replaced if she does not satisfy the sometimes unreasonable requests of the local Indian elite who are more legitimate participants. Her globality is mediated by the local Indian elite.

Working in a transnational firm as a cleaner is depicted as high-status work by trainers and supervisors who tell workers, Nabanita recounts that,

> We should wear shoes, cut our nails regularly, wear net on our hair, means we should be neat and should not feel less about ourselves. Housekeeping is a good work. We also learn many new things in this. There is nothing bad about it. They told us that while doing housekeeping work we should not be dressed improperly. We should know the importance of this work.

Wearing uniforms and keeping nails trimmed serves to distance housekeeping work done in a global corporation from the caste-stigmatized cleaning work done in local settings.

In these ways, housekeepers like Nabanita are encouraged to develop a sense of pride in their jobs, which, despite the low pay, are deemed important because they occur in space associated with Western (and implicitly superior) levels of cleanliness. Nabanita reports that her trainer said that if housekeepers "do not do our work for 4 days then no one will come here." Indeed, one of the attractions for software and call-center workers of jobs in the sector are the clean and lavish organizational settings. Despite having received an employee award for her work, Nabanita reveals that she has not informed her in-laws, parents, daughter or any other member of her community about the nature of her work. They only know that she works at a large corporation. She says,

> If I am doing this why should I tell others and be a reason for their pain (had tears, remained quiet for some time) . . . my brother will feel bad that his sister is doing this work even after good education. So I do not let them know about my work.

Nabanita reflects that she never thought she would be doing cleaning work but, given that the job allows her to work daytime shifts and support her child, she does not feel she can aspire to higher-status work. While her salary does allow her to pay for her child's English-medium education, it does not allow her to improve her standard of life.

As Tomic et al. (2006) note, cleaners occupy a contradictory position in the global economy. On the one hand, they are engaged in the dirty work of cleaning, and their job requires removing waste generated by others to ensure that the space remains pristine. At the same time, they are key agents in the effort to civilize and modernize an environment. The "condition of being global" for these workers involves being grateful for their escape from unemployment and the ability to work in an air-conditioned space, even though their work remains physically demanding and repetitive. It involves exposure to settings in which they enjoy membership but from which, as permanently transient workers who are contractually employed, they can be removed at any time, and they are required to serve silently. Cleaners at global firms deal with the social stigma that accompanies cleaning work, which is only partially mediated by corporate attempts to professionalize the occupation.

In these ways, while cleaners such as Nabanita may express some pride about working in spaces of exception for global firms, their work is structured so that they continue to feel largely tangential rather than central to the project of globalization. While they are told that they are different from traditional cleaners because of their environment of work and they recognize the exceptionality of this environment, they remain deeply embedded within power structures where they remain subservient to the local middle-class elite. They know that they can be removed from their jobs in an instant, and their globality is significantly structured by the dynamics of pride and subservience which underlies their work.

Call-center workers

Well-educated, English-speaking workers comprise the growing telephone-based customer-service workforce and provide clients in the US, UK and Australia with information on their telephones, banking, credit, insurance, catalogue shopping and airline bookings. As one young woman, Rupa, whose experience was typical of the large number of workers I interviewed, told me, she was proud of working at one of India's large Business Process Outsourcing centers (BPOs) and applied for her current job because she wanted to work with an organization with a "brand name." She has access to a clean workspace, a 24-hour cafeteria, a gymnasium and van transportation to and from work. After her Bachelor of Commerce, she worked as a poorly paid accountant and decided to move from her town to Pune, a nearby IT hub, to seek higher-paid work in a BPO. She received an offer easily, given her convent education and willingness to work at night. Living with friends, she answers service requests about loans by customers in the US.

Rupa has rotating shifts, all at night, so that she can answer calls when her customers in the US are awake. She says that this has a detrimental impact on her body, making it difficult to eat or sleep properly. As a result, it is only on the weekends that she is able to participate in activities with her family or friends. She says, "Saturday, Sunday, yes, you feel like you are here, you are in this world." At the same time, Rupa is grateful to have employment even though she wishes her wage was higher, because with food, housing and occasional contributions to her family in her hometown, she saves very little on her current wage.

Rupa says that on one level, customer-service work is ideal for her because she loves to talk. At the same time, she says,

> speaking eight hours continuously with the same procedure, with the same . . . accent, with the same . . . verbiages, you get pissed off. . . . And even if you are angry, you have to, you know, you have to keep your angriness with you only. You can't show, you have to always keep a smile on your face.

Rupa finds her job difficult not only because of the pace but also because customers are sometimes abusive on calls. She notes,

> ultimately, they ask where you are located because you know, even if you speak in English and even if you try and make the accent with them, but you won't be able to, because we are not born and brought up in U.S. . . . So they ask "where are you located at" so we just answer "in India sir." Then "Oh India!" And sometimes they are very pissed off because the outsourcing is done and they are not getting their . . . work to be done out there.

Rupa's expresses pride in her work with a large "brand name" transnational corporation, but her experience of globality is also shaped by the aggressive customers she interacts with daily. She sees herself as a global worker who can effectively interact with customers and sees herself as a member of India's aspiring global elite. Given that she has to speak continuously and work through the night, she has high expectations of the staff hired to serve her. She says,

> sometimes it gets very difficult in speaking. Sometime, you know . . . if you go for the water, and you don't find the water at place, then you get angry on the people because, the housekeeping people, it's their job to bring the water for us. They have to keep the bottle at our work stations, it's their job. Sometime they don't do their job and because of them, we get pissed off.

In these ways, Rupa expresses frustration that service staff do not always meet her needs, which in turn impacts her ability to do her job. Just as her job is scripted and timed, she expects the appropriate amount of water to be placed at workstations in a timed fashion. Just as her job depends on satisfying customer needs, Rupa believes that housekeepers' jobs depend on satisfying her needs.

Overall, despite the problems she mentions, Rupa plans to continue to work in the BPO sector, and she is planning to complete an MBA by distance education because she wants to become a manager.

Class and the experience of globality within exceptional spaces

Working in exceptional spaces in India for the two workers profiled above is simultaneously an uplifting and degrading process. Through their involvement with multinational companies housed in free-trade zones, workers gain knowledge about customers living in different time zones, about performance and surveillance norms in large, formal firms as well as about notions of time discipline and professionalism. Being part of the world economy is a source of pride, yet workers also report that they experience the social stigma related to the requirement that they have to be permanently subservient to their employers and supervisors. For call-center workers, globality involves bridging the gap between their middle-class lifestyles and the need to accept customer aggression and violence as a normal part of their jobs. Housekeepers' notions of globality are structured by their key role in maintaining exceptional spaces and their sense that they are disposable contract workers, largely excluded from the material privileges of their prestigious and affluent settings. While workers in exceptional spaces are "housekeepers to the world" in different ways, these are spaces within which hierarchies between those who are expected to care and those who can expect to be cared for are perpetually being enacted.

Yet within-zone discrepancies in terms of workers' experiences of their sense of their place in relation to the forces of globalization are stark. Many low-wage service workers feel excluded from the aura of exceptional spaces, despite their presence within these spaces. Notwithstanding the infrastructural novelty of zones of exception, and the requirement that all workers embody the sense of cleanliness and order within zones, disparities within the service workforce relate to the widespread prevalence of forms of labor informalization. While core organizational employees with direct contracts with organizations are often protected by labor laws, a large number of service workers are employed informally. Agarwala (2013) notes that informal workers include those who are self-employed, those employed in informal enterprises and contractually employed workers who work in formal organizations through sub-contractors. Workers not only receive limited or no protection under state labor laws but also have little job security and no recourse if they are fired without cause or paid less than minimum wage. Indeed, zones of exceptions are spaces within which labor subcontracting is rampant, leading to workers with very different levels of employment security working alongside one another.

Globality within exceptional spaces, in this way, is deeply fissured by workers' different employment relationships, which in turn structure notions of security, experiences of sustainable livelihoods and any sense of inclusion in the professed progress which free-trade zones signify. Call-center workers who are employed directly by the organizations where they work see the negotiation of pride and subservience as a part of their work as global service providers. In contrast, low-wage service workers employed through subcontractors see themselves as tangential to the global economy, even though they provide its key infrastructure. Their sense of globality involves confronting the tenuous circumstances of their inclusion within free-trade zones since they experience neither the stability nor the economic advantages which the flow of foreign direct investments into India are assumed to bring.

Notes

1 Both projects discussed in this chapter were funded by the Social Sciences and Humanities Research Council of Canada. An earlier version of this chapter was presented at a workshop on Mobilities and Exceptional Spaces in Asia organized by the Asian Research Institute, National University of Singapore. The project on low-wage service workers was conducted in collaboration with Dr. Shruti Tambe (Savitribai Phule Pune University) and Dr. Sanjukta Mukherjee (DePaul University). For a discussion of complete findings from the two projects discussed in this paper, please see Mirchandani et al. (2020) and Mirchandani 2012.
2 There are a few exceptions where women may wear professional Indian clothing (saris or salwar kameez).

References

Agarwala, R. (2013). *Informal Labor, Formal Politics, and Dignified Discontent in India*. New York: Cambridge University Press.

Ananthanarayanan, S. (2008). New Mechanisms of Imperialism in India: The Special Economic Zones, *Socialism and Democracy*, 22 (1): 35–60.

Brar, B. and Mukherjee, P. (2012). *Facing Globality: Politics of Resistance, Relocation, and Reinvention in India*. Delhi: Oxford University Press India.

Cross, J. (2010). Neoliberalism as Unexceptional: Economic Zones and the Everyday Precariousness of Working Life in South India. *Critique of Anthropology*, 30: 355–373, doi:10.1177/0308275X10372467.

Cross, J. (2014). *Dream Zones: Anticipating Capitalism and Development in India*. London: Pluto Press.

Goldman, M. (2011). Speculative Urbanism and the Making of the Next World City. *International Journal of Urban and Regional Research*, 35: 555–581. doi: 10.1111/j.1468-2427.2010.01001.x.

Mirchandani, K. (2012). *Phone Clones: Authenticity Work in the Transnational Service Economy*. Ithaca, NY: Cornell University Press.

Mirchandani, K., Mukherjee, S., and Tambe, S. (2020). *Standing Out: Service Workers in India's Multinational Technology Sector*. Oxford: Oxford University Press.

O'Bryne, D. J. and Hensby (eds.). (2011). "Globalization: The Global Village," in *Theorizing Global Studies*. Basingstoke: Palgrave Macmillan, 2011.

Ong, A. (2006). *Neoliberalism as Exception: Mutations in Citizenship and Sovereignty*. Durham, NC: Duke University Press.

Sampat, P. (2010). Special Economic Zones in India: Reconfiguring Displacement in a Neoliberal Order? *City & Society*, 22: 166–182. doi: 10.1111/j.1548-744X.2010.01037.

Schäfer, W. (2007). Lean Globality Studies. *Globality Studies Journal*, 7. https://gsj.stonybrook.edu/article/lean-globality-studies/.

Scholte, Jan Aart. (2002, Dec.). What Is Globalization? The Definitional Issue – Again. CSGR Working Paper No. 109/02, Centre for the Study of Globalisation and Regionalisation (CSGR), University of Warwick, Coventry. http://wrap.warwick.ac.uk/2010/1/WRAP_Scholte_wp10902.pdf.

Shaw, M. (2000). *Theory of the Global State: Globality as an Unfinished Revolution*. Cambridge: Cambridge University Press.

Tomic, P., Trumper, R., and Dattwyler, R. H. (2006). Manufacturing Modernity: Cleaning, Dirt, and Neoliberalism in Chile. *Antipode*, 38: 508–529. doi: 10.1111/j.0066-4812.2006.00592.x.

Weinbaum, A. E. and Edwards, B. H. (2000). On Critical Globality. *ARIEL: A Review of International English Literature*, 31 (1): 255–274.

2
SKILL GAP AND BRAIN DRAIN FOR UNITED STATES

Impact of Trump executive order on H1B and India

Anjali Sahay

Introduction

Donald Trump was not an average candidate running for the presidency in the United States, and his election into the White House would mean great changes both economically and politically. With mixed feelings, US's allies and adversaries pondered the policies, which would now be implemented, that candidate Trump had promised over the very heated election campaign. True to his promise, Trump signed various executive orders in January 2017 in the areas of (1) immigration; (2) border security; and (3) interior enforcement. While these were very public and controversial and received great media attention, in April 2017 President Trump hammered away on his "America First" campaign theme (less publicized) and signed an order that would favor American companies for federal contracts and reform the visa program for foreign technical workers. Keeping his promise to the American people: President Trump promised that Buy American, Hire American would be a signature foundation of his administration. With the "Hire American agenda," President Trump was making sure that the immigration system would not be abused to replace hardworking American workers with cheaper foreign labor.

This Executive Order:

(a) calls on the executive branch to fully enforce the laws governing the entry of foreign workers into the U.S. economy, to promote rising wages and more employment. And (b) directs federal agencies to propose reforms to the H-1B program in order shift the program back to its original intent and prevent the displacement of American workers.

(Whitehouse.gov 2017)

"The order was a means to end the 'theft of American prosperity,' which he said had been brought on by low-wage immigrant labor" (Thrush, Wingfield, & Goel 2017).

The H1B program eventually became a focus in the debate over the impact of foreign workers on American economy. President Trump further criticized employers for abusing the program and using it to avoid hiring higher-paid American workers. Thus he promised to revamp its lottery-based selection process. With these reforms underway, many countries, companies, and individuals involved in hiring foreign workers tried to understand the implications of these orders in order to determine their future course of action. And while the US authorities in early January 2018 announced that the Trump administration would not be considering any proposal that would force H1B visa holders to leave the country, "the USCIS has been considering a number of policy and regulatory changes to carry out the President's Buy American, Hire American Executive Order, including a thorough review of employment based visa programs" (Times of India 2018, January 9).

In this paper I will be exploring the impact of this specific executive order, or even its consideration, on H1B visa holders from India as well as its impact on the technology industry and other related industries in the US. The larger question of whether such measures would necessarily lead to more hiring of American workers or lead companies to outsource its tech jobs also will be considered. Lastly, with the Department of Homeland Security considering new regulations that would prevent H1B visa extensions and create a sort of "self-deportation" of hundreds of thousands of Indian tech workers in the US, I explore whether this might potentially lead to a skill gap and a "brain drain" for the US itself.

Migration of knowledge[1] workers and the H1B

In today's global, interconnected world, the mobility of high-skilled workers plays a vital role in the economy, especially in the knowledge sector. These skilled workers make exceptional direct contributions, including breakthrough innovations. "As teachers, policy makers, and entrepreneurs they guide the actions of others. They propel the knowledge frontier and spur economic growth. In this process the mobility of skilled workers, within and across national borders, becomes critical to enhancing productivity" (Ozden 2017). While the 1970s and 1980s were reeling from the trend of worldwide distribution of human capital and its adverse impact on poorer countries in the popular trend known as "brain drain,"

> the migration patterns we see today are the result of a complex tangle of firms and other employers pursuing scarce talent, governments trying to manage these flows through policy, and individuals seeking their best options given the constraints imposed on them. The central outcome, however, is clear: the flows of high-skilled migrants are very concentrated, both within and across national borders.
>
> *(Ozden 2017)*

According to the World Bank, migration flows to OECD (Organization for Economic Cooperation and Development) countries account for less than one-fifth of the world's population, while OECD countries host two-thirds of high-skilled migrants. Among OECD destinations, the distribution is even more skewed. Four English-speaking countries—the US, the United Kingdom, Canada, and Australia—are the chosen destinations for nearly 70 percent of high-skilled migrants to the OECD countries. In fact, the attractiveness of these destination countries has led others, such as France, Germany, and Spain, to increase their policy efforts to attract high-skilled migrants. The US alone hosts close to half of all high-skilled migrants to the OECD. According to the Migration Policy Institute:

> the direct modes of entry to the United States for these workers include employer-sponsored green cards and temporary work visas. In addition, many immigrants join the high-skill workforce indirectly after gaining admission to the United States

through student visas or family reunification visas. The report shows that these immigrants are heavily represented in the medicine, technology, engineering, and science fields, as well as in occupations that have a bearing on national security. Among the high-skilled professionals, the foreign-born are more likely to have an advanced degree than their native counterparts.

(Fix & Kaushal 2006)

Statistics further show that there are stark inequalities in the concentrations of talent that exist across cities and regions within destination countries. Within the US, significant concentrations of high-skilled migrants are found in Boston, New York City, and Seattle as well as many cities in California. Clearly, the presence of leading universities, high-tech firms, and research centers has proved over the decades that the global competition for skills will continue to be an out-migration from developing countries to the developed countries.

H1B visa system

Within the US, the 1960s was a decade of profound change. The Civil Rights Act of 1964 ushered in changes that were to have a profound impact on the life and politics of the country. Not surprising then, the immigration laws of the country also went through an overhaul, changing the criteria for entry into the country from *country of origin*, which favored those who came from European countries, to *skill*, which favored many coming from third-world countries. After the passing of the Immigration and Naturalization Act of 1965, also known as the Hart-Celler Act (which abolished an earlier quota system based on national origin and established a new immigration policy based on reuniting immigrant families and attracting skilled labor to the US), highly skilled immigrants started entering the US from countries in Asia, Africa, and Latin America as opposed to Europe.

This, however, created two problems. For the sending countries, it created the much publicized "brain drain" (Sahay 2009) problem, typical in the third world countries. For the receiving countries, visas granted under the H1 program—originally created in 1952—were handed out too liberally after the 1960s. In the 1980s, Bruce Morrison, a Democratic Congressman from Connecticut, saw problems with temporary visas for workers. He felt that the program allowed entry for too many people who were not vital to the US economy, and he helped to write the Immigration Act of 1990, which created the H1B program. "The intent was clamp down on abuse and open the doors to truly exceptional people through a system when they become Americans and prevent the kind of abuse of the temporary visa system that existed before" (CBS Interactive 2017). Thus from the 1990s, while the US had established the H1B visa as the main gate for skilled workers hired by US companies, in order to avoid any abuse, the United States Senate established quotas for H1B visas on an annual basis.

What is the H1B visa? The H1B is a visa in the United States under the Immigration and Nationality Act, section 101(a) (15)(H) which allows US employers to employ foreign workers in "specialty occupations." The regulations define a "specialty occupation" as requiring theoretical and practical application of a body of highly specialized knowledge in a field of human endeavor including but not limited to biotechnology, chemistry, computing, architecture, engineering, statistics, physical sciences, journalism, medicine and health (doctor, dentists, nurses, physiotherapists, etc.), economics, education, research, law, accounting, business specialties, technical writing, theology, and the arts. The visa requires the attainment of a bachelor's degree or its equivalent as a minimum (with the exception of fashion models, who must be "of distinguished merit and ability"). Likewise the foreign worker must possess at least a bachelor's degree or its equivalent and state licensure, if required to practice in that field. H1B work authorization is strictly limited to employment by the sponsoring employer.

The Immigration Act of 1990 limits to 65,000 the number of foreign nationals who may be issued a visa or otherwise provided H1B status each fiscal year (FY). An additional 20,000 H1Bs are available to foreign nationals holding a master's or higher degree from US universities. In addition, excluded from the ceiling are all H1B non-immigrants who work at (but not necessarily for) universities, non-profit research facilities associated with universities, and government research facilities. "Universities and colleges, non-profits and government research institutions are exempted from the cap. These uncapped employers have accounted for about 10% of H1B visa applications since fiscal 2010" (Ruiz 2017).

H1B and tech companies

In the early 1990s, information technology had hit American firms like a whirlwind, intensifying demand for technical skills and leaving unprepared American workers in the dust. In 1990, the US Congress created the H1B visa program to allow various companies (mostly tech companies) to hire uniquely skilled foreign workers in the relatively rare situations that they could not find American workers to fill specialized roles. H1B visas would be valid for three years and could be renewed for another three years. It would be a visa that eventually became near and dear to the tech community, with many engineers vying for one of the program's 85,000 visas each year (20,000 of which are reserved for advanced degree holders). The program did not hire many workers in the first five years of its creation, only 52,000 workers. However, with the dotcom boom of the 1990s, Silicon Valley's demand for H1B workers increased. Currently, demand for the visa often exceeds the supply—in that case, a lottery system is activated. "Almost 1.8 million H1B visas have been distributed in fiscal years 2001 through 2015, according to a Pew Research Center analysis of government data" (Ruiz 2017). In 2016 there were more than a quarter of a million applications.

"The program provided firms with a ready supply of skilled workers who would accept far lower salaries than Americans. Eight in ten foreign workers hired through this program earn less than similarly skilled Americans" (Broadwater 2017). Furthermore, "Silicon Valley giants began aggressively lobbying for increases in the annual allotment of H1B visas. Google's parent company, Alphabet, shelled out almost $17 million lobbying partly on immigration issues just last year. Microsoft spent nearly $9 million" (Broadwater 2017).

A new study from the National Foundation for American Policy shows that US tech companies are increasingly relying on skilled foreign workers using H1B visas. According this study:

> Four of the 6 U.S. tech companies—Amazon (2,515), Microsoft (1,479), Intel (1,230), and Google (1,213)—were among the top 10 employers for approved H-1B petitions for initial employment in FY 2017. Facebook, with 720 new H-1B initial petitions approved in FY 2017, an increase of 248, or 53%, and Apple, with 673, a 7% increase, were 14th and 15th on the list. Amazon had the second most number of H-1B petitions approved for initial employment in FY 2017, with an increase from 1,416 in FY 2016 to 2,515 in FY 2017, a 78% increase. Amazon's use of H-1Bs reflects its increased growth in the U.S., particularly in research and development.
> *(National Foundation for American Policy 2018)*

On the supply side, India, one of the top recipients of H1B visas, also saw many of its IT services companies increase their lobbying to Congress:

In 2017, India's second-largest IT services company, Infosys, spent $200,000 (Rs1.3 crore) on lobbying the US Congress, four times more than it did in the previous year, data from non-profit Center for Responsive Politics showed. Wipro, the third-largest in the sector, spent $130,000—five-and-a-half times more than a year ago. The country's largest IT company TCS, also increased its spending on lobbying to $110,000 in 2017, up 37%.

(Bhattacharya 2018)

For years the tech community has been lobbying Congress to increase the number of annual visas, which are capped at 85,000. Currently the four top lobbying firms are Microsoft, Google, Facebook, and Amazon.

In the first quarter of 2017 during Trump's presidency, Microsoft lobbied more for immigration and the H-1B visas than any other tech company. . . . Facebook CEO Mark Zuckerberg has been, arguably, the most pro-immigration, pro-amnesty tech leader in the Trump era and before. In two lobbying reports analyzed by Quartz in the first quarter, Facebook argued against Trump's travel ban to protect Americans from terrorism and voiced opposition to any changes in the H-1B visa program, despite widespread reported abuse and displacement to American workers.

(Binder 2017)

H1B and India

While many sending countries have benefited from H1B visas, the lion's share of all H1Bs has gone to India, with China a distant second. Many of these visas were granted to Indian IT companies such as Infosys and Tata Consultancy Services (TCS), which submit tens of thousands of labor condition applications (LCA)—filed by companies seeking to hire someone on an H1B visa—compared to Silicon Valley companies, which submit a few thousand. Looking at federal reports and statistics compiled from Department of Homeland Security, the following table looks at India's percentage of all H1Bs for the last three years.

From this table, it is evident that India earned the lion's share of H1B visas in 2014 and 2015 in percentage, but even with this lion's share in 2016 (see Figure 2.1), the percentage fell to about 40% of all H1B issued in 2016.

Trump executive order on H1B and its impact

President Trump's announcement of H1B reforms came close at the heels of a chaotic time at the White House, as Mr. Trump faced the 100th day of his presidency without much to show for it in the way of legislative accomplishment: his health care overhaul had been defeated; and his two high-profile executive orders cracking down on immigration from predominantly

Table 2.1 H1B for India as a percentage of total (Security n.d.)

Year	H1Bs to India	Total H1Bs	H1B as & of Total
2014	222,241	511,773	43.4
2015	253,377	537,450	47.1
2016	215,462	534,365	40.3

H1B Visas Top 5 Countries in 2016

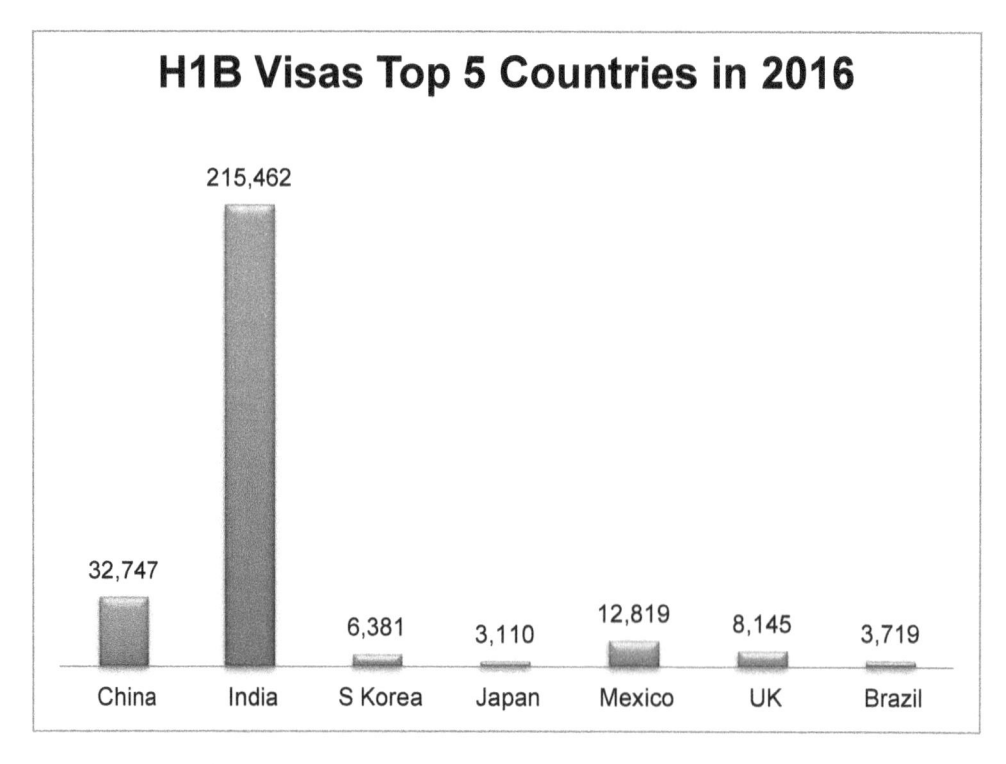

Country	Count
China	32,747
India	215,462
S Korea	6,381
Japan	3,110
Mexico	12,819
UK	8,145
Brazil	3,719

Figure 2.1 H1B visas by country for 2016 (Security n.d.)

Muslim nations had been stymied by the courts. Thus, on April 18, 2017, President Trump signed a "Buy American, Hire American" executive order which sets broad policy intentions directing federal agencies to propose reforms to the H1B visa system. Broadly, the order called for:

i Creating higher wages and employment rates for US workers and protecting their economic interests;
ii Rigorously enforcing and administering the nation's immigration laws;
iii Directing the Department of Homeland Security (DHS), in coordination with other agencies, to advance policies to help ensure H-1B visas are awarded to the most-skilled or highest-paid beneficiaries. (USCIS n.d.)

Currently the H1B visa system allows an extension of three years after an initial three years, making it a total of six years. Eventually, applicants can transition into citizenship (if they choose to) without any federal discernment or regard for regulations or quotas that balance growing job needs of the American population (USCIS n.d.). The H1B reforms advocated by the Trump administration, which have drawn bipartisan support from Congress, would change the lottery system for awarding H1B visas, giving extra preference to the highest-paying jobs—a proposal favored by many in the American technology industry. The order was a means to end the "theft of American prosperity," which President Trump said had been brought on by low-wage immigrant labor. However, the order was met with various reactions from companies in both the US and India (the prime beneficiary of H1B visas).

US Citizenship and Immigration Services (USCIS) was asked to work on a combination of rule-making, policy memoranda, and operational changes to implement the "Buy American, Hire American" executive order. According to the White House, "we are creating and carrying out these initiatives to protect the economic interests of U.S. workers and prevent fraud and abuse within the immigration system" (USCIS n.d.). Clearly this order had a variety of impact on various groups.

Impact on India as sending country

India's leading tech trade group, the National Association of Software and Services Companies (NASSCOM), said Indian companies were being treated unfairly. "We believe that the current campaign to discredit our sector is driven by persistent myths, such as the ideas that H-1B visa holders are 'cheap labor' and 'train their replacements,' neither of which is accurate," the group said in a statement. "Indian IT companies have dramatically reduced their H1B visa filings and foreign nationals are exhibiting reluctance to make the jump to a US company due to the Trump administration's hardline anti-immigration stance" (Economic Times 2018). The "Trump administration has also made the process of extension of H-1B visas more difficult" (Times of India 2018). Previously, the H1B was given for three years with an easy extension for another three years. One of the clearest impacts was a fall in visa applications by 50% in 2017 (Economic Times 2018).

Furthermore, as the US tightened its regulations around the filing and handling of the H1B visas, many overseas workers headed to other countries such as Canada, Germany, and Australia, which are making it easier for international students to stay in the country after they graduate and to become part of the workforce. At the same time, the US is throwing more hurdles in the path of technology companies looking for high-skilled foreign talent. According to Immigration, Refugees and Citizenship Canada (IRCC), "Indian IT workers made up more than 35% of the 4,400 professionals seeking a Canadian visa under the country's Global Skill Strategy program" (Immigration, Refugees and Citizenship Canada n.d.).

One of the most notable impacts on tightened H1Bs has been a sharp decline in the number of studies visa (F1 visa) applications to the US. "The number of F-1 visas issued to foreign students seeking to attend college and other types of academic institutions in the United States decreased by 17% in the year that ended September 30, 2017. . . . The biggest decline in visa approvals in 2017 was seen among students from Asian countries, particularly those from China and India which typically account for the largest number of F-1 visas" (Kavilanz 2018). According to the State Department, Indians accounted for the largest drop—from 65,257 in 2016 to 47,302 in 2017. Also, uncertainties relating to optional practical training (OPT) offered at the end of the studies, which enable students to find a work visa and sponsor, further lead to a declining interest in pursuing higher education in the US.

Many university administrators have expressed concern that the current administration's "America First" mantra is causing international students a great deal of anxiety and fear. "The Wall Street Journal, which first reported the new state department data on Monday, attributed the overall fall to stricter admissibility rules mandated by the Trump administration, which required consular officials to ensure students planned to return to their home countries after finishing their studies" (Raj 2018).

Those already in the country are also fearful of hate crimes such the Kansas man who fatally shot an Indian-born engineer after angrily confronting him about his immigration status. The shooter yelled "get out of my country" before firing the shots that killed the engineer, Srinivas Kuchibhotla (from India), and wounding two others" (Stevens 2018).

According to a recent report called 'Communities on Fire' by the Washington, DC-based group South Asian Americans Leading Together (SAALT), hate crimes against Indian Americans and other South Asian Americans surged 45% from November 8, 2016, to November 7, 2017. The group recorded 302 incidents during that period, 213 of them being direct physical or verbal assaults.

(Janmohamed 2018)

These hate crimes have further added to the problem of H1B restrictions.

Lastly, plans to rescind an Obama-era rule[2] that allows spouses of thousands of H1B visa holders to work in the US were also underway under President Trump. Prior to the Obama administration's change, H4 holders (spouses of H1B visa holders) had not been allowed to earn an income or have a Social Security Number, especially the spouses of legal foreign workers, mainly tech workers from India and China, to obtain their own work visas (Murphy 2018). Many spouses, mostly women, have also come forward to report instances of domestic violence exacerbated by their inability to acquire a bank account, an independent income, and a right to work. And even though the Department of Justice and the Department of Homeland Security plans to defer the rollout of this proposal, it has sowed panic and chaos amongst those affected. This, along with all the restrictions and hurdles with H1B, has led to a largely "unwelcome sign" for most Indians in the Unites States.

Impact on US-based companies

With the new executive order taking effect, many US outsourcing firms would also now be under greater scrutiny. According to the USCIS, these companies would now have to provide more information about H1B workers' employment to ensure that the workers are doing what they were hired for (Policy Memorandum n.d.). Companies would also have to provide specific work assignments, including dates and locations, to verify the "employer–employee" relationship between the company applying for an H1B and its visa recipient. In the memorandum, "USCIS acknowledges that third-party arrangements may be a legitimate and frequently used business model. . . . Scenarios involving a third-party worksite generally make it more difficult to assess whether the petitioner has established that the beneficiary will actually be employed in a specialty occupation or that the requisite employer–employee relationship will exist" (Policy Memorandum n.d.: 3). Some staffing agencies seek hard-to-get H1B visas for high-skilled workers, only to contract the workers out to other companies. "There's nothing inherently illegal about contracting out visa recipients, but the workers are supposed to maintain a relationship with their employers, among other requirements" (O'Brien 2018).

Richard Burke, CEO of Envoy, a company that helps US companies process visa applications, reveals the scale of how the new visa crackdowns are affecting companies and prospective employees alike: many US companies "rely on foreign talent to fill the biggest skills gaps in the US, which is primarily in the STEM areas: engineering, software development and data science." He further adds that the new visa regulations have impacted 85% of employers in their hiring, have delayed projects, and about 22% of employers have relocated work overseas over the last two years (Short 2018).

Another question in the mix is whether these visa restrictions impact innovations, especially for start-up companies. Small companies cannot afford to pay high salaries and are already struggling to attract talent in a tight market. Startups already have a tough time accessing the current lottery system because their small number of visa applications are dwarfed by the high volume filled by bigger firms. Punit Soni, the chief executive of Learning Motors, a six-person company in Silicon Valley that is trying to apply artificial intelligence to health care, states that a visa system that favors the highest-paid workers will steer immigrants only to already successful big companies like Google or Microsoft (Thrush, Wingfield, & Goel 2017).

Skill gap in the United States and reverse brain drain

For decades, the United States has attracted the best and the brightest to its shores, with generation after generation contributing to the American successes in start-ups, innovation, research, or simply filling jobs in STEM fields. Those immigrants, usually found at the high end of the job market, are given the H1B visa in specialty occupations because there has been a decline in the number of Americans filling these jobs. Demographics has a large part to play in this debate. Many Americans are not choosing to be employed in the tech industry. "This decline is due to aging-population demographics, and this trend will intensify in the years ahead. In addition, middle-class jobs are increasingly requiring higher skill levels. The skills gap in the U.S. is substantial" (Kaplan 2017).

However, with the Trump Administration's slogan "Make America Great Again" the "Buy American, Hire American" executive order, and an overhauling of the immigration system especially in the hiring practices prevalent over decades, this migration trend is now reversing. With stricter laws for H1B visas, many highly educated foreign-born entrepreneurs and workers in the US have started looking at alternatives to the obstacle-strewn path to US citizenship. "Hardships for foreign entrepreneurs in the United States have increased as of late, thanks to the heightened vetting of H-1B visas, Trump's Muslim ban and an increasingly hostile stance toward immigration" (Sheng 2018). Students coming to study in the US are now looking at alternative destinations or choosing the return option, more freely than they did in the past. This possibly is leading to America's own brain drain, as foreign students and workers from India, China, and elsewhere who used to stay are now returning to their home countries to start businesses. This is alarming because it will adversely impact US innovation. While reverse brain drain and return migration were already established trends, a tightening of immigration laws has accelerated these trends further.

Conclusion

The looming question of the fate of the H1B visa under the administration of US president Donald Trump still hangs in the air, and it is a question to which many around the world are anxious to get an answer. While it is important to close some of the loopholes in the H1B visa program, current actions have led to various unintended consequences, which may prove detrimental to the US. This paper highlights some of these consequences, as summarized below:

i   a decline in H1B visa applications from India-based IT companies;
ii a decline in visa applications for foreign students opting to study in the US (mostly from India and China);
iii an increase in Indian and Chinese students shopping for alternate destinations other than the US, such as Canada, Germany, and Australia;
iv an increase in the out-movement of entrepreneurs and workers from the US to new destinations;
v   a decrease in the hiring of foreign workers by US-based companies (mostly coming from India, as India gets the lion's share of all H1Bs);
vi more hurdles on the processing and extending the H1B visa;

vii a rescinding of the Obama order that allowed H4 dependent visa holders to work; and
viii an increased sense of fear among Indian-American immigrant communities related to job security, processing of paperwork, and hate crimes against them.

Finally, the classic argument in favor of hiring immigrants. Are tech workers from India really stealing American jobs? Can we compare the skill set of workers coming in under an already established system designed to hire the best and the brightest with the skill set of an average American citizen? Should there be no immigrants to fill these jobs, especially in the STEM fields, do we have enough qualified Americans to fill these jobs, given the skill gap that does exist in the US? These questions need to be raised; after all, the average immigrant family in high-end jobs contributes much to the US economy through taxes, innovation, and start-up businesses, to name a few.

As a prediction, should stricter rules and associated with the H1B, actually be applied, we may end up seeing jobs exported or outsourced to where talent meets requirements as opposed to blanket hiring of citizens. Meanwhile, as we see tech hubs emerging in so-called third-world countries such as India, China, and Singapore, to name a few, we may actually be witnessing a whole new reverse brain drain out of the US to these new destinations. After all, worker mobility is always in the direction of better opportunities, ease of paperwork, jobs, and social security.

Notes

1 In his introduction, Binod Khadria (1999) explains in detail the use of the term "knowledge workers" as a preferred alternative to "brain." The term "knowledge worker" was coined by the management guru, economist, and futurologist Peter Drucker in 1960 (Drucker 1997). Majumdar (1997) provides a comprehensive description of this classification as follows: "Knowledge workers are those who have been successfully educated and/or trained to reach the higher levels of proficiency in some or other branch of knowledge—intellectual or applied.
2 The Obama administration implemented the rule known as H4 EAD, or employment authorization documents, in 2015, in part to help deal with a massive backlog of H1B visa holders from India and China waiting for green cards. Some estimates put the backlog at more than 1 million.

References

CBS Interactive (2017, August 13). *How H-1B visas have been abused since the beginning.* Retrieved June 19, 2018, from https://www.cbsnews.com/news/how-h-1b-visas-have-been-abused-since-the-beginning/.

Bhattacharya, A. (2018, March 9). *Fearing Trump's visa stance, Indian IT firms are spending top dollar on lobbying.* Retrieved from https://qz.com/1223460/fearing-donald-trumps-h-1b-visa-stance-indian-it-firms-splurge-on-lobbying/.

Binder, J. (2017, May 2). *4 tech companies lobbying for H-1B.* Retrieved from https://www.breitbart.com/texas/2017/05/02/4-tech-companies-lobbying-h-1b/.

Broadwater, T. (2017, August 23). *Silicon Valley is using H-1B visas to crowd out American minorities.* Retrieved from https://www.stltoday.com/opinion/columnists/silicon-valley-is-using-h--b-visas-to-crowd/article_2c3ac63c-360a-5c79-88b2-729d8673aa28.html.

Druker, P. F. ([1959]1997). *Landmarks of Tomorrow.* New York: Harper.

Fix, M., & Kaushal, N. (2006, July). *The Contributions of High-Skilled Immigrants.* Retrieved from Migration Policy Institute: https://www.migrationpolicy.org/research/contributions-high-skilled-immigrants.

Immigration, Refugees and Citizenship Canada. (n.d.). Retrieved from https://www.canada.ca/en/immigration-refugees-citizenship.html.

Economic Times (2018, April 3). *Indian companies have dramatically reduced H1B visa filing, reports US daily.* Retrieved from: https://economictimes.indiatimes.com/nri/visa-and-immigration/indian-companies-dramatically-reduced-h1b-visa-filing-us-daily/articleshow/63592908.cms.

Janmohamed, Z. (2018, March 11). *How Indian-Americans are becoming more vocal with their reporting of hate crimes*. Retrieved from Economic Times: https://economictimes.indiatimes.com/nri/visa-and-immigration/how-indian-americans-are-becoming-more-vocal-with-their-reporting-of-hate-crimes/articleshow/63248907.cms.

Kaplan, R. (2017, April 12). *America Has to Close the Workforce Skills Gap*. Retrieved from Bloomberg: https://www.bloomberg.com/view/articles/2017-04-12/america-has-to-close-the-workforce-skills-gap.

Kavilanz, P. (2018, March 14). *Sharp Drop in International Student Visas Worries Some US Colleges*. Retrieved from CNN: https://money.cnn.com/2018/03/12/news/economy/international-student-visa-college/index.html.

Khadria, B. (1999). *The Migration of Knowledge Workers: Second Generation Effects of India's Brain Drain*. Thousand Oaks, CA: Sage Publications.

Majumdar, T. (1997). *Economics of Indian Education*. New Delhi: Jawaharlal University Press.

Murphy, B. (2018, February 1). *Spouses of Indian and Chinese tech workers could be stripped of right to work in U.S*. Retrieved from Chicago Tribune: http://www.chicagotribune.com/business/ct-biz-h1b-visa-spouses-20180201-story.html.

National Foundation for American Policy (2018). *Policy Brief*: https://nfap.com/wp-content/uploads/2018/04/H-1B-Visas-By-The-Number-FY-2017.NFAP-Policy-Brief.April-2018.pdf.

O'Brien, S. A. (2018, February 23). *Trump administration cracks down H-1B visa abuse*. Retrieved February 28, 2018, from CNN: http://money.cnn.com/2018/02/23/technology/h1b-visa-abuse/index.html.

Ozden, C. (2017, May 31). *Global Talent Flows: Causes and Consequences of High-Skilled Migration*. Retrieved from www.worldbank.org: http://blogs.worldbank.org/developmenttalk/global-talent-flows-causes-and-consequences-high-skilled-migration.

Policy Memorandum. (n.d.). Retrieved from USCIS: https://www.uscis.gov/sites/default/files/USCIS/Laws/Memoranda/2018/2018-02-22-PM-602-0157-Contracts-and-Itineraries-Requirements-for-H-1B.pdf.

Raj, Y. (2018, March 12). *28% drop in US student visas to Indians in 2017*. Retrieved from Hindustan Times: https://www.hindustantimes.com/world-news/28-drop-in-us-student-visas-to-indians-in-2017/story-JUyHy3S9GGSygk7rTr7UZM.html.

Ruiz, N. G. (2017, May 3). *H1B Visa Programme: Some Key Facts*. Retrieved January 17, 2018, from Livemiint.com: https://www.livemint.com/Politics/UfEr2sY1vYQvuggRf5Y1UK/US-H1B-visa-programme-some-key-facts.html.

Sahay, A. (2009). *Indian Diaspora in the United States: Brain Drain or Gain*. Lanham, MD: Lexington Books.

Security, Dept. of Homeland (n.d.). *Yearbook of Immigration Statistics 2016*. Retrieved from https://www.dhs.gov/immigration-statistics/yearbook/2016.

Sheng, E. (2018, April 9). *Silicon Valley is fighting a brain-drain war with Trump that it may lose*. Retrieved from cnbc: https://www.cnbc.com/2018/04/09/trumps-war-on-immigration-causing-silicon-valley-brain-drain.html.

Short, E. (2018, March 5). *How are US companies coping with Trump's H-1B visa crackdown?* Retrieved from Silicon Republic: https://www.siliconrepublic.com/careers/h1b-visa-envoy-richard-burke.

Stevens, M. (2018, May 5). *Kansas Man Who Fatally Shot Indian Immigrant Gets Life in Prison*. Retrieved from New York Times: https://www.nytimes.com/2018/05/05/us/adam-purinton-sentenced-kansas-shooting.html.

Thrush, G., Wingfield, N., & Goel, V. (2017, April 18). *Trump Signs Order That Could Lead to Curbs on Foreign Workers*. Retrieved from New York Times: https://www.nytimes.com/2017/04/18/us/politics/executive-order-hire-buy-american-h1b-visa-trump.html.

Times of India (2018, January 9). *Relief for Indian techies, US says no change in H-1B extension policy*. Retrieved January 20, 2018, from: https://timesofindia.indiatimes.com/business/international-business/relief-for-indian-techies-us-says-no-change-in-h-1b-extension-policy/articleshow/62426660.cms.

Times of India (2018, February 24). *US tightens H-1B visa rules, Indians to be hit*. Retrieved from: https://timesofindia.indiatimes.com/india/us-tightens-h-1b-visa-rules-indians-to-be-hit/articleshow/63050944.cms.

USCIS (n.d.). *Buy American, Hire American: Putting American Workers First*. Retrieved from: https://www.uscis.gov/legal-resources/buy-american-hire-american-putting-american-workers-first.

Whitehouse.gov (2017, April 18). *President Trump Promotes "Buy American and Hire American."* Retrieved January 15, 2018, from: https://www.whitehouse.gov/briefings-statements/president-trump-promotes-buy-american-hire-american/

3
FROM STUDENTS TO SPOUSES
Gender and labor in Indian transnationalism

Amy Bhatt

This chapter explores how gender shapes Indian labor transmigration. While there has been a larger proportion of men emigrating out of India for work historically, women are a vital component of transmigration as workers and spouses. Women make up half of all international migrants, but there are gender differences in the motivations, channels, and limitations that characterize their movement. Family formation and household duties influence the career paths that women choose and are highly indicative of women's ability to work outside of the home or the country. While Indian women overwhelmingly migrate as part of marriage or family reunification policies, work opportunities also create new pathways for women's global movement (Mishra 2015, 73). The line between the categories of worker and wife is blurred through the invaluable labor that women perform within transnational Indian households, even though it often is not recognized as labor.

In order to examine the role that gender plays in transnational labor migration, I start by reviewing literature on women who move abroad as students and through "women-led" labor channels, such as domestic work and nursing. These circuits have paved avenues for Indian women to move between India, Australia, the Gulf countries, Europe, and North America. I examine also women's roles as global information technology (IT) workers who travel on assignments abroad or for new positions. In the second part of this essay, I focus on IT migration between India and the United States to consider how family reunification and women's unpaid labor in the household supports Indian transnationalism and community formation more broadly.

Migration and gendered employment

While there has been substantial scholarship on Indian men's migration for educational opportunities, women's stories are often missing or seen as exceptional (Amrith 2011; Baas 2010; Gollerkeri and Chhabra 2016; Hune and Nomura 2003). Some notable historical accounts of women traveling overseas for schooling *have* been well documented. Pandita Ramabai and Anandibai Joshee, perhaps among the earliest documented Indian woman travelers, came to the United States in the 1880s (Chakravarti 2014). Caroline Wells Healey Dall compiled Joshee's life stories and her travel abroad in a biography in 1888. Dall relates how Joshee set sail from Calcutta on her own in 1883 to travel to New York City, purportedly making her the first unconverted, high-caste woman from India to undertake such a journey. Joshee came to the United States to study medicine and enrolled at the Women's Medical College of Philadelphia. She graduated in 1886 and is considered the first Indian woman to receive a graduate degree in the United States (Dall 1888).

Her cousin, Pandita Ramabai, also sought medical training overseas after working as a social reformer in India. She traveled to Britain to start her studies, along with her young daughter, Manorama Bai. She eventually went on to the United States to join Joshee. While there, she translated textbooks and gave lectures around the country on the status of women in India. Ramabai's daughter would eventually follow in her footsteps, both by studying in England and the United States and by becoming a missionary and social reformer.

While fewer in number, Indian women began to move as students as well, enrolling in U.S. universities and colleges, often as undergraduates as well as graduate students. There is a long history of Indian migration for education. When the British controlled most of the Indian subcontinent, many Indians used the relationship to migrate to the United Kingdom or other colonies to pursue education and training. In the United States, Ross Bassett (2016) has shown that the U.S. government and institutions, such as the Massachusetts Institute of Technology, helped mostly elite Indians come abroad for higher education starting from the 1880s. On the Indian side, Sandipan Deb (2004) recounts the role that key institutions have played in facilitating Indian student migration, particularly the Indian Institutes of Technology (IITs). The networks created by IIT alumni helped Indians move abroad and establish themselves overseas. However, immigration restrictions in the United States, such as the Chinese Exclusion Acts of 1882 and subsequent legislation, severely limited Indians from immigrating. Moreover, vice laws that prohibited the migration of unmarried foreign women cut into the numbers of women who could travel abroad to study.

After the immigration policies in the United States changed in the 1960s, Indians began migrating in even greater numbers to pursue education abroad. In the late 2010s, Indians made up the second largest group of international students to come to the United States, though women still only comprised of about 27 percent of international students (Sondhi 2015). Debalina Dutta (2016) and Roli Varma and Deepak Kapur (2015) have shown that women, even when they have studied abroad, are not necessarily relieved of the gendered expectations to return to India to marry and start families. However, time abroad can open up avenues of employment after marriage. Thus, women's transnational migration as students plays an important role in their desire and ability to pursue economic opportunities in the future.

Domestic work abroad

Beyond migration for education, there are certain sectors in which Indian women have been the primary drivers of migration. In particular, Indian women's migration for work in the caring or reproductive industries has created networks between India and places such as the Gulf countries of the Middle East, the United States, and Canada. Two major fields account for these women-led migrations: domestic work and nursing.

Indian migration to the Middle East has a long history, as S. Irudaya Rajan and K. C. Zachariah (2013) have explored in their historical account. However, with the expansion and rising wealth of oil-rich nations of the region, there has been a voracious need for foreign labor (Azhar 2016). Since 1973, Indians have flowed to the region in ever-greater numbers. In some countries such as the United Arab Emirates and Qatar, Indians make up between 23–30 percent of the population and are predominantly concentrated in semi-skilled or unskilled labor (Pethiyagoda 2017). Women who migrate to the region tend to find employment as domestic workers. The history of women's migration for work to the region is complicated; as Praveena Kodoth (2016) has pointed out, the 1983 Indian Emigration Act has created new hardships for women who are permitted by the Indian state to migrate as domestic workers. The act requires close scrutiny of women who seek to go abroad but does little to protect women who might find themselves in exploitative conditions.

Even though Indian domestic workers are predominant in Kuwait and the United Arab Emirates, they are undercounted or, in some cases, omitted from official tallys of migrants to the region, which adds to their vulnerability (Pethiyagoda 2017, 90). The International Labor Organization estimates that there are more than 2.1 million foreign domestic workers in the region, and a great many of them come from India (ILO 2013). The *kalafa* system in Kuwait, for instance, requires that workers must have a fixed sponsor/employer while in the country, which makes it difficult for workers to find work in a different household or industry (Jarallah 2009). Moreover, as Pardis Mahdavi (2013) has argued, women's vulnerability as domestic workers also leads some to enter into sex work or to be trafficked to other regions without their consent.

At the same time, the terms of Indian migration to Gulf countries are highly regulated and do not offer easy opportunities for permanent affiliation through residency or citizenship, even though some Indians have worked and lived in the region for decades (Vora 2013). Nonetheless, for some Indian women workers, as Attiya Ahmed's (2017) study shows, migration abroad offers a break from the past and allows women to develop a new sense of self away from established kinship networks. The journey and settlement (even if only temporary) in a new land with different customs and cultures can produce unexpected effects, such as greater numbers of Indian Christian or Hindu women converting to Islam.

Nursing and caring labor

In contrast to domestic worker migration, nursing and skilled caregiving employment opportunities have afforded Indian women the chance to explore new pathways abroad that can lead to long-term affiliations in host nations and drive family reunification. Sujani Reddy's (2015) historical account of the evolution of the nursing profession in India traces the complex factors that led Indian-trained nurses to emigrate to the United States. Showcasing the ways in which women were far from passive or dependent migrants, Reddy argues that women actively sought out nursing education and training to improve their global mobility. As "women in the lead," these women have become symbolic of the opportunities and institutional access that come with migration out of India (Reddy 2015, 5).

At the same time, there are stigmas tied to caste and religion associated with nursing that persist in India and the diaspora. Seen as "unclean" or polluting work by Hindu majorities, the field is heavily dominated by Indian Christian women. With its long association with British Empire-era missionaries, nursing continues to be seen as work performed by those who occupy the longer rungs of the Indian social order (Reddy 2015). Despite these stigmas, Irene Hardill and Sandra MacDonald (2000) and Sonali Johnson, Judith Green, and Jill Maben (2014) have shown also that while nursing has long been woman-dominated around the world, certain caregiving labor shortages in places such as the United Kingdom, Canada, the Middle East, and the United States have spurred a new wave of young women to enter nursing, with the hope of migrating out. Marie Percot's (2006) study of Keralite nurses in Gulf countries specifically points to the desire that nurses have to gain financial independence but shows also that they seek greater autonomy away from gender- and family-based restrictions. Leaving India for work becomes one such avenue for achieving those goals.

In most cases, Indian nurses are women who migrate on their own or before their spouses or other family members. As a result, they do not easily fit into the stereotypical model minority narratives that are grounded in the idea of the heterosexual nuclear family driven by male employment. As Miriam Sheba George's (2005) ethnography of South Indian nurses shows, many women are the catalyst for family reunification even as they face derision because they are the primary or sole breadwinners who are seen as displacing traditional gender and social norms. Nonetheless, caregiving professions still hold considerable draw for young women seeking to venture out of India and to create transnational links.

Global IT workers

Though in fewer numbers than Indian men who migrate for work, Indian women also make up a significant portion of the world's global flow of information technology workers. As Parvati Raghuram (2004) and Namrata Gupta (2007) have argued, IT work has increasingly been viewed as ideal work for women. Gupta refers to this trend as the "feminization of science," led partly by parents encouraging their daughters to pursue STEM fields to increase their marriageability. Debalina Dutta's (2016) study of Indian women engineering students reveals that the decision to study engineering or pursue science is highly shaped by parents' rather than by individual student desires. Moreover, for Indian women who face enormous pressure to marry, working in the STEM fields fits within gendered and cultural assumptions associated with appropriate work–life balance (Radhakrishnan 2009).

Family pressures can work to keep women from advancing within IT firms also, as women are less likely to move abroad for short-term assignments or take on roles that would demand more working hours because of their domestic responsibilities. As a result, Indian women with degrees in information technology, software development, and computer science are more likely to remain in India in lower-tier IT jobs, even though the work they do is often transnational in scope. As Reimara Valk and Vasanthi Srinivasan (2011) and Carol Upadhya and A.R. Vasavi (2006) have shown in their studies of women IT workers in Bangalore, gender is a major determinant in what kinds of career pathways are available to workers. Moreover, women tend to be concentrated in certain fields such as quality control, testing, and support, which are seen as auxiliary or second-tier to male-dominated aspects of software development, such as back-end coding, architecture, and design.

When women do progress in the IT field, they are valued for the "soft skills" they possess in addition to their technical prowess (Ghosh and Chanda 2015; Adya 2008). They still must adhere to gendered codes, even while demonstrating "flexible aspirations" or positioning themselves as modern, global subjects who retain traditional values tied to Indian domesticity (Vijayakumar 2013). Even when they do have the chance to migrate, Smitha Radhakrishnan (2009) argues that ideas about the "new Indian woman," or appropriate demonstrations of femininity and domesticity, still shape how Indian women view work and their identities, particularly when they are living abroad and away from family and kinship networks. Moreover, women IT workers in the United States often consider their time abroad as way to gain valuable work skills but also to enjoy freedom away from their family and social networks in India, even though they face family pressures to marry and start families (Bhatt 2018). Beyond gendered and cultural expectations, women still face restrictive immigration policies in their host countries as global IT workers, as Sareeta Amrute's (2016) research on Indian IT workers in Germany suggests.

Family reunification and gendered labor

While education and employment opportunities have been two major avenues for Indian women's labor migration, another unrecognized stream of transnational gendered labor comes through family reunification policies. Globally, the ability to form a family has been recognized as a fundamental human right since the United Nations' 1948 Declaration on Human Rights. The United Nations' International Covenant on Economic, Social and Cultural Rights goes further and notes that the family is the "the natural and fundamental group unit of society" (United Nations 1966). From these international legal codifications, family reunification has been viewed as a key component of transnational migration.

In the Gulf countries, family reunification can be harder to achieve because of restrictive immigration and citizenship policies that preclude many Indians from permanent settlement (Vora 2013). In Western nations such Canada, the United States, the United Kingdom, and Australia, family reunification has been a major driver of women's migration through spousal and extended family sponsorship. While Indians had historically flowed to the United Kingdom, particularly in the post-Independence period when they were heavily recruited as laborers, the Commonwealth Immigrants Act 1962 and Immigration Act 1971 severely limited new entrants. However, family members of already-resident immigrants were allowed to settle in the country.

In the same time period that the United Kingdom was curtailing Indian immigration, policy changes in the United States and Canada made migration to North America more appealing. As Kerry Abrams (2013) has traced, the United States has held contradictory views on family reunification as part of changing immigration policies historically. On one hand, European immigrants were granted relatively unrestricted immigration rights through the mid-19th century. In the same period, Chinese and other Asian migrants were encouraged to come to the United States to help meet the needs of the nation's burgeoning rail, fishing, and timber industries (Bhatt and Iyer 2013). On the other hand, with rising backlash against these "unassimilable" immigrants, the Chinese Exclusion Acts of 1882 and the immigration acts of the early 20th century that created the "Asiatic Barred Zones" worked to limit new Asians and specifically sought to curtail women's migration (Takaki 1989; Lee 2015). The impulse behind these measures was to encourage laborers to go back to home countries to marry and settle, rather than remain in the United States long term (Sohoni 2007).

Temporary worker programs

After a more than half a century of restrictions on Asian migration, approximately 12,000 Indian immigrants were living in the United States by 1960. The passage of the Immigration and Nationality Act of 1965, also known as the Hart-Celler Act, radically expanded that population and changed the country's immigration system. Previously, country-based quotas were used to limit the flows of new immigrants, but under the 1965 Act, new categories were created that gave preference to immigrants with skills needed in the United States' quickly growing economy. It also enshrined the right to family reunification as fundamental to immigration policy and opened the door to new waves of migrants. Indians began to flow to the United States to pursue educational and work opportunities and quickly began sponsoring family members to join them abroad.

The Immigration Act of 1990 further expanded opportunities for worker- and family-based migration with the creation the H-1B visa program. The H-1B program is an employment-based visa system that encourages the temporary migration of workers in the technology, education, health-care, and finance fields. Since its inception, Indians have dominated the visa program: nearly 70 percent of all H-1Bs go to Indian nationals, and 85 percent go to men (Bhatt 2018). Even though it is considered a temporary and "non-immigrant" visa, the program allows employers to sponsor workers for permanent residency, which makes it a very appealing pathway to residency, and even citizenship, for foreign workers. This program has contributed to the large numbers of Indians now living in the United States. As of 2015, 2.4 million Indian immigrants lived in the United States, making them the second-largest immigrant group after Mexicans.

Worker-based programs have expanded the Indian population, as have family reunification policies. While family reunification programs in the United States have allowed permanent residents and naturalized citizens to sponsor family members (often on immigrant visas intended for settlement), the H-1B program allows temporary workers to also bring over immediate family members through the H-4 visa. This visa has been used by H-1B workers to sponsor spouses and children (under 21 years old) to accompany them to the United States. The holders of this visa historically have been unable to work, as it is considered a "dependent" visa. However, changes to the program made under President Obama's administration in 2015 allowed qualified H-4 visa holders, who were filing for permanent residency, to receive "employment authorization documents" (EAD), which are temporary work permits. That right to work has been challenged since Donald Trump took office as president in 2017. For many professionally trained Indian women, H-4 work authorization offers a much-coveted way to find employment in the United States, and about 100,000 EADs have been granted so far. Even with the EAD, H-4 visa holders face many challenges in the job market, and their authorization to work is still tied to their spouse's H-1B visa. In practical terms, this means that if the H-1B-holding spouse loses his work visa, the H-4 visa holder would also lose her ability to work as well.

As a result, the H-1B program has created a new category of housewives who are either forbidden or restricted in their ability to work. By inviting spouses of temporary workers to migrate, while limiting their ability to work, immigration policies create a surplus of migrants whose unpaid or underpaid labor is subsumed by the household or other sectors. Scholarship on South Asian immigrant communities has illustrated the key role that women play in providing free or low-cost labor to family or ethnic-specific businesses (Dhingra 2012; Hewamanne 2012), in helping with acculturation (Nayar, Hocking and Giddings 2012), in building and supporting community institutions (Manohar 2013), and by caring for the family and households (Bhalla 2008). In the next section, I explore how women's gendered labor in the household also helps maintain a transnational system of professional IT labor.

Transnational housewives

Since 2008 I have conducted more than one-hundred interviews with H-1B and H-4 visa holders who live, work, and move between India and the United States. Considering that the H-1B program is so heavily used by young men to work abroad, there are considerably fewer women who come as IT workers. However, women make up nearly half of the H-1B program as dependents and are impacted by the policies that govern the visa program.

There are advantages and disadvantages to migration through the H-1B program. On one hand, H-1B workers can bring their families to the United States immediately, whereas green card holders face a waiting period before their immediate relatives can immigrate. On the other hand, the work restrictions that spouses face on the H-4 dependent visa can be a hindrance to the family unit. Many H-4 visa holders have high levels of education, often in engineering or

STEM fields, and hope that they will be able to work abroad after getting married to an H-1B worker. However, there is no guarantee that spouses will be able to find a company to sponsor them after they migrate, and many are stuck on the dependent spousal visa until the family can successfully gain permanent residency.

In my study, many H-1B men asserted that they wanted a bride who had the potential to work, but they also admitted that having their wives at home was a sign that they are capable of providing financially for the family unit on their own. This sentiment is echoed in India, as Carol Upadhya and A.R. Vasavi (2006) report in their study of IT workers who prefer wives who will leave formal employment after marriage. More recently, the 2016 Centre for the Study of Developing Societies and Konrad Adenauer Stiftung (CSDS-KAS 2017) survey of Indian youth revealed that even as the Indian economy and workforce becomes more globalized, younger generations of Indian men hold highly patriarchal attitudes about marriage and family life. The CSDS-KAS study found that 51 percent of participants believed that women should be obedient to their husbands, and 41 percent thought that women should not work after marriage (CSDS-KAS 2017).

In the case of H-1B/H-4 visa holders, women are therefore conscripted into the role of the "transnational housewife" (Bhatt 2018). I use this term to highlight the social and caregiving roles played by women in the home that allow men to be ideal global employees. My use of the term *housewife* is derived from Marxist feminist understandings of the unpaid and gendered work done in the household to produce workers who are able to meet the needs of late capitalism. As Gillian Hewitson argues, this non-waged work is an "essential component of the development of future citizens, workers, and taxpayers" (2003, 266). However, much of this work is systematically devalued and characterized as an extension of women's "natural" roles as caretakers rather than as foundational to capitalism itself. Maria Mies (1986) famously argued that this rendering of women's work as "non-economic" positions women (and their labor) below men economically and socially. By dividing labor according to gender roles, men are able to accumulate capital in their roles as "breadwinners," who are free to sell their labor precisely because women, as housewives, are not free to do the same. Among H-1B families, this division of labor is functionally enacted through immigration policies that obscure the true cost of labor power.

Since most H-1B workers migrate as single young men, they tend to save on expenses by living with roommates and learn how to manage cooking and cleaning on their own. However, after marriage, the combined retreat of women from the workforce along with migration amplifies the reproductive roles that women play at home. This shift from paid employment to the home, and the corresponding losses in financial independence and career security, has been characterized as "de-skilling" (Man 2004) "cumulative disadvantage" (Purkayastha 2005) or "re-domestication" (Yeoh and Willis 2005). Parvati Raghuram (2004) argues that women's exit from the labor market "do[es] not arise out of the particularities of women per se, but out of social norms that limit women's mobility and social expectations around their contribution to and responsibility for undertaking unpaid reproductive labor within the household" (170). Even when H-1B visa holders' spouses are able to work, the burdens of household labor do not shift significantly. Women's workloads are often multiplied when they work outside of the home, particularly if they have children.

However, H-4 visa holders' social reproductive work benefits individual families, as well as communities in the host country. As "custodians of culture," transmigrant women play a pivotal role in ethnic-specific organizations and often take on the task of transmitting cultural norms and values to future generations. At the household level, the gendered labor that women provide allows transmigrants to maintain connections to family, friends, and networks in India, while also creating homes abroad. In their roles as transnational housewives, Indian women host informal social gatherings for other transmigrants as well as for religious and cultural celebrations, maintain relationships with dispersed relatives, and engage in informal sector work such as cooking, sewing, childcare, or teaching arts, language, music, and dance. This emphasis on social reproduction grows out of traditional assumptions about gender roles and household labor but also operates as a vital form of cultural maintenance and transmission for migrants who may engage in multiple moves or have to recreate communities in new settings (Kõu and Bailey 2017; Mallapragada 2017).

Professional volunteers

Beyond the unpaid but economically valuable work that women provide in their homes and communities, H-4 visa holders offer their unpaid labor to companies, businesses, and educational institutions. As part of "intensive mothering" (Hays 1996), transmigrant women devote considerable time, money, and personal resources toward parenting children. As they take on the role of household managers, transmigrant women also are expected to act as key conduits for their children's educational success, particularly when they are restricted from building their own careers or pursuing personal development. While volunteering for schools may be an extension of their social and gendered roles as mothers, Indian women also take on culturally specific tasks in their children's schools. Recounting efforts to establish an "Asian Parents Link," one of my study respondents noted that she became involved in her child's school as way to use her skills in communications and program management, even though she could not formally work. As result, she worked to help translate school documents into a variety of Asian languages and to find opportunities to better incorporate parents with limited English-language skills into school governance.

As H-4 visa holders wait for their families to move through the immigration process or to find an employer to sponsor an H-1B visa on their behalf, others turn to certification or degree-seeking programs to maintain and build new skills. Many women look to further their education, despite often being highly educated already, in order to bolster their resumes and rejoin the job market. As my study shows, women sought degrees and certifications in areas ranging from business administration, social media, program management, and coding languages such as C++ and JavaScript. Others moved out of technical fields to pursue degrees in nonprofit management, preschool education, and many other fields. While women were serious about these programs, they also viewed them as a way to demonstrate that they were able to compete in the U.S. job market.

The disconnection that H-4 visa holders experience from the formal job market has costs. Feminist sociologist Pamela Stone (2007) has argued that when women take a break from the labor market for family or other reasons, they face substantial challenges with re-entry. H-4 visa holders are doubly disadvantaged as immigrant women, as employers are reluctant to start a new immigration process to hire them. Generally, women who are employed before exiting the labor market are more likely to re-enter and find work more quickly than women who have not worked previously (Berger and Waldfogel 2004). Women who do not have substantive previous work experience have a much harder time finding work after employment gaps. Among the H-4 visa holders in my study, most did not work in the United States, even though they may have worked in India before migrating. Many of these women were also limited in their employment prospects because of family obligations or because their husband's jobs were prioritized over their own ability to work. Moreover, the majority of H-4 visa holders had been educated in India and found it difficult to have their degrees recognized in the United States, so they found themselves competing with U.S.-educated graduates who were more desirable as employees (Arbeit and Warren 2013).

Women on the H-4 visa still desired opportunities to put their skills to work, even if they could not be formally employed. By volunteering for smaller companies or taking on unpaid internships, H-4 visa holders sought to show that they had useful talents. They hoped to demonstrate that they could manage a project from beginning to end or to gain some experiences that could be translated to a resume line item. In one case, Radmila (name changed for anonymity) had a degree in computer science and had been working in Chennai. After getting married, she moved to join her husband in Seattle. Initially on a H-4 visa, she pursued an accounting degree and became a certified public accountant. However, because of her visa status, she had difficulty finding an employer who was willing to sponsor a work visa for her. Eventually she was able to work as a volunteer accountant while waiting either for her husband's H-1B to be converted to a green card or to find an employer willing to apply for a worker visa on her behalf.

While volunteering offers women a way to stay connected to the job market, it can also take advantage of women's labor and is not as valuable as paid employment. Another H-4 visa holder, Revati, spent substantial time seeking unpaid work. She was unable to find a formal internship but eventually offered her time to a local company just to have the chance to stay engaged. She recalls, "I worked at the organization for two projects. The last project which I did was design[ing] curriculum for new people and also did all their visa processing and everything." Even though her work was more of a full-time job than a volunteer experience, she was resigned to her exploitation: "Yeah, that is the way it is though. They can just ask you to do anything and you will do it because you want the experience." As Ann Vogel and Iain Lang (2006) have argued, many facing a "crisis of work" have been driven to accept unpaid or underpaid work in the name of gaining experience and to stand out in a crowded job market. Thus H-4 visa holders are often willing to work without economic gain because they anticipate a future pay-off. Without a doubt, companies benefit from this source of free labor, as they are willing to give women the chance to work without any of the guarantees or benefits that come from employment.

Anchors and displacements

In addition to the labor they provide to local companies and institutions, transmigrant women also act as an anchoring force for the global IT industry. As H-1B workers become integrated into the work teams and environments of their host companies, they become expensive to replace. Companies have an incentive to maintain a stable workforce in the highly competitive IT industry, which is often characterized as having a skilled labor shortage. Since the H-1B is an employer-sponsored visa, it becomes very difficult for workers to move to another company that is willing to sponsor a visa on their behalf. Therefore the "temporary" worker program can actually work to stabilize technology workforces, while also providing an easily retractable flow of labor when needed. Moreover, H-1B workers are less likely to seek employment or move back to India if they have dependents at home, making them more likely to stay with their employers.

In the contemporary moment, the transnational Indian family must also navigate new terrain as future settlement or migration has been thrown into question by changing immigration policies in the United States. While some H-1B families ultimately decide to return to India after living abroad, others wait until they are able to receive citizenship or decide to permanently live in their host countries. Others go back for periods of time but then choose to return to the United States or elsewhere for new opportunities. Others do not have such choices: some are forced to return if they lose their jobs or something happens to the primary visa holder. There are also intergenerational issues as some children of H-1B workers are beginning to "age out" of family reunification programs after turning 21 years old. They must either apply for a foreign student visa or potentially return back to India despite having lived in the United States for long periods, or nearly all, of their lives. In that sense, the transnational housewife must also be prepared to coordinate and oversee the relocation of the family, as well as plan for the future needs of any children in H-1B families. In that sense, the gendered labor of the transnational housewife becomes essential to both maintaining equilibrium in the global IT industry, even when the individual family may be thrown into imbalance and must start over in a new location.

Conclusion

The H-1B and H-4 visa program allows temporary workers to migrate abroad with their immediate family; however, the visa restrictions that accompany family reunification inscribe a patriarchal household that presumes men are breadwinners, while women are homemakers. The work that women provide at home and in their communities sustains transmigrant households and also allows men to dedicate themselves to their jobs. The dependency enforced on transmigrant spouses makes it difficult for them to participate in the public economic sphere, and most find themselves laden with domestic responsibilities and reproductive work. Women's unpaid and voluntary labor, however, is not economically neutral and works to sustain transmigrant households. Many participate in entrepreneurial self-development with the hope of moving into the formal workforce, while others embrace their roles as transnational housewives whose labor makes capitalist divisions of labor possible. Even while reinforcing women's roles as caretakers and non-earning members of the family unit, the unpaid labor of transnational housewives subsidizes the wages of Indian guest workers and supports a system of transmigration globally.

References

Abrams, Kerry. "What Makes the Family Special?" *University of Chicago Law Review* 80, no. 1 (2013): 7–28.
Adya, Monica. "Women at Work: Differences in IT Career Experiences and Perceptions between South Asian and American Women." *Human Resource Management* 47, no. 3 (2008): 601.
Ahmed, Attiya. *Everyday Conversions: Islam, Domestic Work, and South Asian Migrant Women in Kuwait*. Durham, NC: Duke University Press, 2017.
Amrith, Sunil. *Migration and Diaspora in Modern Asia*. Cambridge: Cambridge University Press, 2011.
Amrute, Sareeta. *Encoding Race, Encoding Class: Indian IT Workers in Berlin*. Durham, NC: Duke University Press, 2016.
Arbeit, Caren, and John Robert Warren. "Labor Market Penalties for Foreign Degrees Among College Educated Immigrants." *Social Science Research* 42 (2013): 852–871.
Azhar, Muhammad. "Indian Migrant Workers in GCC Countries." *Diaspora Studies* 9, no. 2 (2016): 100.
Baas, Michiel. *Imagined Mobility: Migration and Transnationalism among Indian Students in Australia*. New York, NY: Anthem Press, 2010.
Bassett, Ross. *The Technological Indian*. Cambridge, MA: Harvard University Press, 2016.
Berger, Lawrence, and Jane Waldfogel. "Maternity Leave and the Employment of New Mothers in the United States," *Journal of Population Economics* 17, no. 2 (2004): 331–349.
Bhalla, Vibha. "'Couch Potatoes and Super-Women': Gender, Migration, and the Emerging Discourse on Housework among Asian Indian Immigrants." *Journal of American Ethnic History* 27, no. 4 (2008): 71–99.
Bhatt, Amy. *High-Tech Housewives: Indian IT Workers, Gendered Labor and Transmigration*. Seattle, WA: University of Washington Press, 2018.

Bhatt, Amy, and Nalini Iyer, *Roots and Reflections: South Asians in the Pacific Northwest*. Seattle, WA: University of Washington Press, 2013.

Centre for the Study of Developing Societies–Konrad Adeneur Stiftung. "Key Highlights from the CSDS-KAS Report 'Attitudes, Anxieties and Aspirations of India's Youth: Changing Patterns.'" New Delhi: CSDS-KAS, April 3, 2017. Accessed July 24, 2017, www.kas.de/wf/en/33.48472.

Chakravarti, Uma. *Rewriting History: The Life and Times of Pandita Ramabai*. Delhi: Zubaan, 2014.

Dall, Caroline Wells Healey. *The Life of Dr. Anandabai Joshee: A Kinswoman of the Pundita Ramabai*. Boston, MA: Roberts Brothers, 1888.

Deb, Sandipan. *The IITians: The Story of a Remarkable Indian Institution and How its Alumni are Reshaping the World*. New York, NY: Viking, 2004.

Dhingra, Pawan. *Life Behind the Lobby: Indian American Motel Owners and the American Dream*. Stanford, CA: Stanford University Press, 2012.

Dutta, Debalina. "Negotiations of Cultural Identities by Indian Women Engineering Students in US Engineering Programmes." *Journal of Intercultural Communication Research* 45, no. 3 (2016): 177–195.

George, Sheba Mariam. *When Women Come First: Gender and Class in Transnational Migration*. Berkeley, CA: University of California Press, 2005.

Ghosh, Sudeshna, and Rupa Chanda. "International Mobility of Skilled Women" in *India Migration Report: Gender and Migration*, edited by S. Irudaya Rajan. London: Routledge, 2015.

Gollerkeri, Gurucharan and Natasha Chhabra. *Taking India to the World*. Oxford: Oxford University Press, 2016.

Gupta, Namrata. "Indian Women in Doctoral Education in Science and Engineering: A Study of Informal Milieu at the Reputed Indian Institutes of Technology." *Science, Technology and Human Values* 32, no. 5 (2007): 511.

Hardill, Irene, and Sandra MacDonald. "Skilled International Migration: The Experience of Nurses in the UK." *Regional Studies* 34, no. 7 (2000): 681–692.

Hays, Sharon. *The Cultural Contradictions of Motherhood*. New Haven, CT: Yale University Press, 1996.

Hewamanne, Sandya. "Threading Meaningful Lives: Respectability, Home Businesses and Identity Negotiations among Newly Immigrant South Asian Women." *Identities* 19, no. 3 (2012): 320–338.

Hewitson, Gillian. "Domestic Labor and Gender Identity: Are All Women Careers?" in *Toward a Feminist Philosophy of Economics*, edited by Drucilla K. Barker and Edith Kuiper, 266–284. New York, NY: Routledge, 2003.

Hune, Shirley, and Gail Nomura. "What Happened to the Women? Chinese and Indian Male Migration to the United States in Global Perspective" in *Asian/Pacific Islander American Women: A Historical Anthology*, edited by Shirley Hune and Gail Nomura, 58–74. New York, NY: New York University Press, 2003.

International Labor Organization. *Domestic Workers across the World: Global and Regional Statistics and the Extent of Legal Protection*. Geneva: ILO Office, 2013.

Jarallah, Yara. "Domestic Labor in the Gulf Countries." *Journal of Immigrant & Refugee Studies* 7, no. 1 (2009): 3–15.

Johnson, Sonali, Judith Green, and Jill Maben. "A Suitable Job?: A Qualitative Study of Becoming a Nurse in the Context of a Globalizing Profession in India." *International Journal of Nursing Studies* 51 (2014): 734–743.

Kodoth, Praveena. "Structural Violence against Migrant Domestic Workers and Survival in the Middle East: The Effects of Indian Emigration Policy." *Journal of Interdisciplinary Economics* 28, no. 1 (2016): 83–106.

Kõu, Anu, and Ajay Bailey. "'Some People Expect Women Should Always be Dependent': Indian Women's Experiences as Highly Skilled Migrants." *Geoforum* 85 (2017): 178–186.

Lee, Erika. *The Making of Asian America: A History*. New York, NY: Simon and Schuster, 2015.

Mahdavi, Pardis. "Gender, Labour and the Law: The Nexus of Domestic Work, Human Trafficking and the Informal Economy in the United Arab Emirates." *Global Networks* 13, no. 4 (2013): 425–440.

Mallapragada, Madhavi. "Immigrant Activism: Narratives of the 'H-4 Life' by Indian Women on YouTube." *Communication, Culture & Critique* 10, no. 1 (2017): 76–92.

Man, Guida. "Gender, Work and Migration: Deskilling Chinese Immigrant Women in Canada." *Women's Studies International Forum* 27 (2004): 135–148.

Manohar, Namita N. "Support Networks, Ethnic Spaces, and Fictive Kin: Indian Immigrant Women Constructing Community in the United States." *AAPI Nexus* 11, no. 1/2 (2013): 25–55.

Mies, Maria. *Patriarchy and Accumulation on a World Scale: Women in the International Division of Labour*. Atlantic Highlands, NJ: Zed Books, 1986.

Mishra, Renuka. "Vulnerability of Women in International Marriage Migration" in *India Migration Report: Gender and Migration*, edited by S. Irudaya Rajan. London: Routledge, 2015.

Nayar, Shoba, Clare Hocking, and Lynne Giddings. "Using Occupation to Navigate Cultural Spaces: Indian Immigrant Women Settling in New Zealand." *Journal of Occupational Science* 19, no. 1 (2012): 62–75.

Percot, Marie. "Indian Nurses in the Gulf: Two Generations of Female Emigration." *South Asia Research* 26, no. 1 (2006): 41–62.

Pethiyagoda, Kadira. "Supporting Indian Workers in the Gulf: What Delhi Can Do." Washington, D.C.: The Brookings Institute. November 21, 2017.

Purkayastha, Bandana. "Skilled Migration and Cumulative Disadvantage: The Case of Highly Qualified Asian Indian Immigrant Women in the US." *Geoforum* 36, no. 2 (2005): 181–196.

Radhakrishnan, Smitha. "Professional Women, Good Families: Respectable Femininity and the Cultural Politics of a 'New' India." *Qualitative Sociology* 32 (2009): 195–212.

Raghuram, Parvati. "Migration, Gender, and the IT Sector: Intersecting Debates." *Women's Studies International Forum* 27, no. 2 (2004): 163–176.

Rajan, S. Irudaya, and K. C. Zachariah. *Indian Migrants to the Gulf: The Kerala Experience*. New York, NY: Columbia University Press, 2013.

Reddy, Sujani. *Nursing & Empire: Gendered Labor and Migration from India to the United States*. Chapel Hill, NC: University of North Carolina Press, 2015.

Sohoni, Deenesh. "Unsuitable Suitors: Anti-Miscegenation Laws, Naturalization Laws, and the Construction of Asian Identities." *Law and Society Review* 41, no. 3 (2007): 587–618.

Sondhi, Gunjan. "Indian International Students: A Gender Perspective" in *India Migration Report 2015: Gender and Migration*, edited by S. Irudaya Rajan, 104–119. London: Routledge, 2015.

Stone, Pamela. *Opting Out? Why Women Really Quit Careers and Head Home*. Berkeley, CA: University of California Press, 2007.

Takaki, Ronald. *Strangers from a Different Shore: A History of Asian Americans*. Boston, MA: Little, Brown and Company, 1989.

United Nations General Assembly, "International Covenant on Economic, Social and Cultural Rights," December 16, 1966, www.ohchr.org/EN/ProfessionalInterest/Pages/CESCR.aspx.

Upadhya, Carol, and A. R. Vasavi. "Work, Culture and Sociality in the Indian Information Technology (IT) Industry: A Sociological Study." Final report submitted to Indo-Dutch Programme for Alternatives in Development, 2006. Available at: http://silk.arachnis.com/anthro/NIAS-IDPAD%20IT%20Study%20Final%20Report.pdf. Accessed March 23, 2018.

Valk, Reimara, and Vasanthi Srinivasan. "Work–Family Balance of Indian Women Software Professionals: A Qualitative Study." *IIMB Management Review* 23 (2011): 39–50.

Varma, Roli and Deepak Kapur. "Decoding Femininity in Computer Science in India." *Communications of the ACM* 58, no. 5 (2015): 56–62.

Vijayakumar, Gowri. "'I'll be like water': Gender, Class, and Flexible Aspirations at the Edge of India's Knowledge Economy." *Gender & Society* 27, no. 6 (December 2013): 777–798.

Vogel, Ann, and Iain Lang. "Working in the Age of Flexibility: The 'Crisis of Work' and the Meaning of Volunteering," paper presented at the American Sociological Association 101st Annual Conference. Montreal, Canada, 2006.

Vora, Neha. *Impossible Citizens: Dubai's Indian Diaspora*. Durham, NC: Duke University Press, 2013.

Yeoh, Brenda, and Katie Willis. "Singaporeans in China: Transnational Women Elites and the Negotiation of Gendered Identities," *Geoforum* 36, no. 2 (2005): 211–222.

4
TRANSNATIONALISM AND RETURN MIGRATION OF SCIENTISTS AND ENGINEERS FROM THE UNITED STATES TO INDIA

Meghna Sabharwal and Roli Varma

Introduction

In 2015, more than half of all science and engineering (S&E) degree holders in the U.S. were from Asia, of which one-fifth (21%) belonged to India, followed by China (10%). However, China held the lead for S&E doctorate degrees (22.4%), followed by India at 16.2% (National Science Board 2018). This large proportion of foreign-born scientists and engineers in the U.S. shows that this nation is heavily dependent on their expertise and the scientific and technical capital amassed by foreign-born workers. Studies have shown the contributions made by foreign-born academics to the scientific output of the U.S. (Levin & Stephan 1999; Stephan & Levin 2001; Corley & Sabharwal 2007; No & Walsh 2010). They are filing patents, receiving grant funding, and publishing articles at a much higher rate than native-born faculty (Broad 2004; Corley & Sabharwal 2007).

Migration of people from developing nations to developed economies has often been considered a one-way phenomenon (Sabharwal & Varma 2017). The notion that one would return after studying and working in the U.S. to India was unheard of – given that migrants establish social, cultural, and economic ties in the host country. However, during the economic recession, a wave of mainstream newspaper articles in India highlighted return migration – challenging the attractiveness of living and working in the U.S. A few scholars examined this phenomenon and termed it as "reverse brain drain" (Mayr & Peri 2008; Wadhwa 2009). Meanwhile, the National Science Foundation (NSF) and the National Academy of Sciences (NAS) are addressing how the U.S. can maintain its international lead in S&E. Retaining the talent of foreign-born in S&E is an area of increasing concern in the U.S.

This paper sheds light on an understudied but important area of reverse migration among Indian academic scientists and engineers. It examines a group of scientists and engineers who, after receiving a PhD from the U.S. and working in the host country, decided to return to India, their country of origin. The returnees, having built networks in both countries, are considered circular transnational migrants – people who have circulated from their country of birth to another country and back to their home country – and they continue to participate in social and economic relationships in both countries though they reside in one country. Basically, they have ties to countries other than their country of birth. This paper specifically examines their reasons for return and how they continue their social networks beyond Indian boundaries. The paper is based on a qualitative study conducted with 83 scientists and engineers who returned to India to take a faculty position, which is detailed in the methodology section.

Literature review

Return migration of scientists and engineers is an understudied area. It is challenging to pinpoint the exact reason for return; this concept was classified by King (2000) in several ways: occasional return, seasonal return, temporary return, permanent return, return due to retirement, return due to failure to assimilate in the host country, return due to problems with acculturation in the destination country, and return to innovate and serve as change agents — a trend more commonly referred to as circular migration. Several economic models and theories attempt to explain return migration. One of them is the *immigration market model* (Borjas 1989). The model suggests that migrants decide to emigrate to a host country in the hopes of amassing wealth and thus are "wealth maximizers." In the case of Indian migrants it was argued that this was perhaps the most prevalent reason for individuals to leave India for the U.S. (Bhagwati 2003). The *circular migration theory* posits a great variety of movement, usually short term, repetitive, or cyclical in nature but having in common the lack of any declared intention of a permanent or long-lasting change of residence (Zelinsky 1971). These theories analyzed return migration from an economic standpoint; none have examined the concept from a social, cultural, and political standpoint, therefore failing to provide a complete picture of the phenomenon of return migration. Additionally, these theories do not incorporate the impact of personal and work attributes on decisions of migrants to return to their country of origin.

With the advent of globalization and the rapid development of transportation and communication systems, scholars have focused their attention on transnational migration, in which "immigrants forge and sustain simultaneous multi-stranded social relations that link together their societies of origin and settlement" (Schiller, Basch & Blanc 1995, p. 48). This framework signifies how migrants maintain, sustain, and forge relationships in more than one country. Thus the transnational framework is a fluid concept, and return migration is not limited to a geographic or political border; rather, the exchange of ideas happens irrespective of spatially bounded territories (Appadurai 1991; Levitt & Jaworsky 2007; Ley & Kobayashi 2005). This model goes beyond circular migration theory, which requires physical mobility of migrants in contrast to transnational migration.

Transnationalism also includes ties of people, networks, and organizations across borders (Faist 2000). Saxenian (2006) found Chinese, Indian, Israeli, and Taiwanese engineers used their transnational social ties in their home country to make investment and migration decisions. Further, since transnational social networks are becoming formalized (Patterson 2006), governments are realizing that expatriates do not have to physically return in order to contribute to economic growth – a growing trend among New Zealand migrants (Larner 2007). A study among UK migrants to Canada found that lifestyle was the most important factor when determining initial migration, but family ties and relationships remained crucial in an individual's decision to return, while transnational social ties with businesses and governments did not appear as important in determining return (Harvey 2011).

Returnees are of great importance, as their decision to return strengthens loyalty and a sense of nationalism in a global world. Making sense of the experiences of return migrants serves as a powerful lens for understanding how these individuals redefine their relationships, particularly within the institutional, societal, and transnational contexts. It is proposed that the decision to return is mostly value driven rather than economic (Waldorf 1995; Razum, et al. 2005). While there are several reasons for leaving a place (push factors) and moving into a place (pull factors) that may influence individuals' decision to return, we examine key push and pull dimensions highlighted in the scholarly literature.

Economic factors

Most literature on transnational migrants focuses on economic factors as stimuli for return migration. Return tends to signify push factors in the country in which the migrant is living, such as economic downturn or unemployment, or pull factors from the country of origin, such as economic development and higher wages. Though the U.S. has been offering better economic conditions, namely high wages and a higher standard of living compared to developing countries to attract migrants, many Asian countries, including China, India, South Korea, and Taiwan, have seen spectacular economic growth in the last two decades. Governments of these countries are devising policies to attract their graduates back from the U.S. (and elsewhere) by creating newer economic opportunities for their returnees and the nation (Saxenian 2002). The Taiwanese government established the National Youth Council in the early 1970s to track migrants in a database, advertise jobs overseas, and provide travel subsidies and job placement to returnees. The National Science Council and Ministry of Education in Taiwan have been recruiting migrants as professors and visiting lecturers for the country's growing universities. In 2009, China launched the Thousand Talents Programme that aims to offer top scientists grants of one million yuan (about $146,000) along with generous lab funding (Engardio 2009). India, in contrast, has not been as aggressive as other Asian countries, but its booming economy (7% GDP growth rate in 2016) has become rather attractive to migrants living abroad (Wadhwa 2009). In 1991, India opened its doors to foreign investment in a series of economic reforms leading to economic liberalization, privatization, deregulation, increased foreign trade, and remittances (Aneesh 2006). It is trying to emerge as a "soft power," a term introduced by Nye (1990), by relying on information technology (IT) and other emerging technologies. The University Grant Commission, a government body that accredits and funds institutions of higher education in India, reported receiving hundreds of applications from PhDs of Indian origin for faculty positions (Chronicle of Higher Education 2009).

Most economic theories, however, have not examined return migration from the social, cultural and political standpoints and are thus limited. Since some immigrants do return to their home countries, differences in their behavior are a consequence of the different economic, social, and political situations they face in the host and home countries. Changes in global economies have given rise to a new form of migration that crosses borders, termed "flexible citizenship," a label made popular by Ong (1999). According to her, an understanding of the political, economic, and social factors is central to transnational migration.

Political factors

Political pushes behind return may range from limitations initiated by the host country (for example, non-renewal of visas from a given country), or even expulsion, to less direct restrictions, for example, on possibilities for changing jobs, bringing one's family, or enjoying other citizenship benefits. Examples of political pull factors are policies to encourage and facilitate return on the part of the home country, such as tax benefits, social assistance, and housing grants (King 2000). Foreign-born faculty on temporary H-1B visas express the greatest fears about job security (Sabharwal 2011), making them the most likely group to return to their home country. In the U.S., the stay rates for temporary residents working in S&E fields decreased by 10% in just four years, from 91% in 2003 to 81% in 2007 (Finn 2010). Faculty members on temporary visas are most vulnerable and likely to leave within the first five years of being in the country (Gupta 2004). Furthermore, young males dominate the temporary visa category. Their spouses hold H-4 visas, which allow them to stay in the U.S. as dependents of H-1B visa holders; however, it does not allow them to work, even though they may be qualified to work in specialty occupations. This adds to the frustration, since spouses are unable to use their education and training in the U.S. (Varma & Rogers 2004) – a phenomenon recently termed as "brain waste" (Ozden 2006). Back home, female spouses can have a job and be independent.

To be able to stay permanently in the U.S., foreign nationals have to acquire LPR (legal permanent residence), adding to additional hurdles confronted by foreign-born scientists and engineers. Citizens of Indian and Chinese origin experience the longest delays in the processing of their permanent residency. An estimate suggests that there are more than a half-million skilled individuals waiting to get permanent residency in the U.S. (Wadhwa 2009). The massive backlog in acquiring permanent residency may be adding to the frustration faced by scientists and engineers. Challenges with acquiring LPR status can serve as deterrents for scientists and engineers who would like to stay in the U.S.

Social/cultural/family factors

Social motives for return may involve the push factors of racism or xenophobia or challenges assimilating in the host country (King 2000). Other push factors can be societal barriers such as stereotyping and prejudice and internal barriers such as lack of mentoring, biased rating and testing systems, lack of access to networks, counterproductive behavior by colleagues, and a working climate leading to isolation (Wu 1997; Fletcher 2000; Varma 2002, 2004, 2006). The related pull factors may be homesickness or the prospect of enhanced status when one has returned, for example, through being able to launch a business venture, build a new house, or contribute to the community (King 2000). Close family ties and cultural loss experienced by immigrants in the U.S. can play an important role in the decision to return to their home country (Chacko 2007; Haour-Knipe & Davies 2008). Strong cultural values serve as "pull" factors for return migrants who might feel culturally alienated in the U.S. Return migration may also involve family or life-cycle factors such as finding a spouse, having one's children educated "at home" in their native language, extended family networks, parental ties, or retirement. Migrants may return home to look after aging or ailing parents (King 2000). Studies, however, have not established a link between family and immigration factors.

Methodology

Primary data were acquired through in-depth interviews of 83 return migrants in 2013. The returnees were academics who have doctoral degrees in science or engineering disciplines from a U.S. institution of higher education and had worked in the U.S. before deciding to return to their home country, India. The returnees held academic jobs in well-known institutions in India and had at least five years of post-return experience. We used the technique of in-depth interviews, as they provide the best methodological medium to uncover the attitudes, beliefs, and experiences (Erickson 1986) of return migrants. We were interested in meanings (tacit and explicit), beliefs, actions, and ideologies embedded in practice, particularly the interpretations of return migrants within a social context (Miles & Huberman 1994; Lincoln & Guba 1985).

The study was interpretive in nature, as it involved a process of deliberative inquiry with the goal of progressive problem-solving (Patton 2002).

The interviewees were employed at 14 institutions of higher education across seven Indian states with a good distribution of geographic locations. The sample was obtained by creating a master list of all U.S. trained PhDs who were teaching at well-known institutions of higher education in India. The list was created by combing through institutional websites and downloading resumes of individuals with a PhD in an S&E discipline from a university in the U.S. and a minimum of five years of work experience in the U.S. The returnees should have also worked in India for a minimum of five years to qualify for the study. A random stratified sample by geographic location was created, and emails were sent requesting participation in the study. We followed the Institutional Review Board (IRB) guidelines to conduct the research, to maintain the anonymity of the returnees. The names of the returnees and their institutions, therefore, are not revealed in the study. A semi-structured interview protocol was used to interview the returnees on a host of questions ranging from their decision to come to the U.S. to their decision to return to India, their research and teaching experiences both in the U.S. and India, and their engagement in international collaboration. Interviews ranged anywhere from an hour to two hours, and all interviews were recorded purely for transcription purposes.

The analysis was conducted in NVivo 10 software, and the responses were individually coded by two student workers who were trained prior to the research. The majority (75%) of the returnees were employed at public institutions in India, while the remaining worked at private institutions. Close to half of the sample (44.2%) were younger than 40 years of age, while 30% of them ranged between 40 and 49 years, close to one-fifth ranged from 50 to 59 years, and 6.5% were 60 years and beyond. A large proportion of the returnees were assistant professors (46%), about one-third were full professors (32%), and approximately one-fifth were associate professors (22%). More than half of the returnees (55%) were employed in engineering departments –aerospace, civil, computer, electrical, environmental, or mechanical – while the remaining worked in biology, chemistry, and physics departments. Almost all of them were married (96%), and about three-fourths (73%) had children. In the U.S., a large majority of the returnees (82%) had been on temporary visas, and the remaining had a permanent residency card, including one who was a U.S. citizen. On average, these returnees had spent 9.5 years in the U.S. before they decided to return and had been in India for an average of 9.3 years post-return. On average, these returnees had spent more than 13 years in academia. An overwhelming majority of them were male (84%) in the sample, thus the analyses are not broken down by gender.

Findings

The returnees were questioned about their decision to move back to India. The question elicited an interesting mix of primary reasons, which are grouped into four major themes: economic and career prospects in India; political factors, namely immigration challenges in the U.S.; social and cultural identity; and family obligations.

Economic factors: career prospects in India

Close to half (44%) of the returnees chose to return based on better economic and career prospects in India. The potential for research funding and compelling job offers from premier research institutions in India were attractive for most returnees. The job market in the U.S. was still recovering from the 2008 economic crash, and tenure-track jobs were hard to come by for some. Additionally, the research environment and the entire system of pursuing grants had become too competitive in the U.S. for most returnees. The promise of guaranteed funds and research grants in India served as a great attraction for several returnees.

Returnees also felt that the research environment and available funding in India promoted risk taking, while in the U.S. one could not take risks, else they would not be able to fund their research and students, run labs, and conduct experiments. The ability to take risk in the U.S. is very low, owing to the competitive nature of the research funding. The research environment in India has drastically changed since the economic liberalization in the 1990s that opened India to the forces of globalization. However, the majority of India's growth has occurred in the last 10–15 years; India has made huge investments in higher education, starting and expanding several research institutions, building infrastructure, and attracting the best personnel. Additionally, faculty in the U.S. are under constant pressure to raise funds to conduct and sustain their research agenda. The returnees felt that in the U.S. they had been constantly working towards applying for funds from a limited number of federal agencies (e.g., NSF & NIH), whose budgets were always under the threat of shrinking. This left the faculty less time for teaching and working on innovative ideas. However, the returnees did recognize that the U.S. was the hub for cutting-edge research and that the critical mass available to them was lacking in India. The advantage of being a researcher and faculty in India was that they were not under incessant pressure to seek funding streams. Funding for graduate students, research labs, and conference travel is assured by universities in India. As one of the returnees indicated:

> It is a much more cut throat environment [U.S.]. Which means that a certain class of ideas cannot be tested, they are just too risky. [India] is a place where you can do that as well as test the more . . . newer stuff, which requires our attention, which is more current in the world. So I think that the birth of ideas you see coming out of India is higher than the U.S., given of course that you are starting with a smaller base.

The ability to take risk also allowed for scholars in India to conduct theoretical research driven by curiosity rather than research that is industry driven and designed to result in patents. Given that theoretical research and funding associated with it is diminishing in the U.S., the Indian research environment appeared conducive to those who work on issues related to basic sciences. Furthermore, job security and the allure of tenure was promising for several returnees. The salary structure is also competitive; while the returnees indicated that comparing U.S. salaries to those in India is like comparing apples to oranges, the cost of living is lower in India.

Political factors: immigration problems in the U.S.

More than one-quarter (26%) of returnees cited immigration problems as a reason to return to India. A vast majority had been on an H-1B or employer visa, which is temporary in nature and is initially issued for three years, extendable for another three years. If one's immigration card, popularly known as green card, is not filed during the six-year period and one's I-140 petition (i.e., labor certification) not approved, the individual must return to their country of origin. When the study was conducted in 2013, dependents of H1-B visa holders were not allowed to work in the U.S.; in 2015, however, then-President Barack Obama passed an executive order that allowed select H-4 visa holders to seek employment in the U.S. As a result, more than 100,000 dependent spouses received work permits in the first three years (Natarajan, 2017). Prior to 2015, most spouses of H1-B visa holders who were on H-4 visa status could not work in the U.S. legally. This added to the frustrations of several returnees whose spouses, despite their qualifications, could not work in the country.

Furthermore, foreign workers are restricted to working with the employer who files the H1-B visa, i.e., they are not free to change jobs. As one returnee noted: "Because I was H-1B I could not apply to certain jobs." If returnees on H-1B visa quit their job or are terminated from the job, they must secure a change of status from the immigration authorities, find another employer to sponsor them, or exit the U.S. It should be noted that when the study was conducted, there was little grace period for foreign workers on an H1-B visa to stay in the U.S. without a sponsoring employer. One returnee expressed his frustration: "I used to look at listings of jobs, but industry did not want non-citizens to apply." The paperwork and wait time involved in getting a work visa can be additional irritants for these workers. Families of H1-B visa holders wishing to see their children and relatives have to apply for a tourist visa, which was often given for six months at a time. Parents who visit the U.S. need to purchase travel insurance, which is often not accepted by several health care providers in the U.S. and is a major challenge for aging parents.

Social and cultural factors: identity and patriotism

One-fifth (20%) of the returnees went back to India due to strong cultural affinity and a deep sense of patriotism for the country. Several returnees wanted to raise children in India, wanting to expose their children to the Indian heritage and education system. These returnees felt that they had to be close to their cultural roots; their social and cultural identities were deeply entrenched in their country of origin, India. In a few cases, the spouses of the returnees did not want to live in the U.S. and wanted to return home to India to be close to family.

National pride and a desire to give back to the country of origin also were reflected in a small percentage of responses (6%). These returnees showed an uncritical affection to India, their country of birth. They took pride in India and idealized its social and cultural environment, despite numerous problems which made them migrate in the first place. This was especially true of returnees who had been in the U.S. only for a short time period and who had achieved only some acculturation. As one returnee noted: "I think there was this desire to return, to do something for the country, to do something to contribute, I think there was a feeling that Indian society has done a lot to make me get where I am, in my studies, etc." To some it was a way to give back to their country and contribute to the development of science in India.

Family factors

One-tenth of the returnees identified family obligations and responsibilities as a reason to return to India. It is a common expectation in India for the male child to take care of ailing and aging parents. As one returnee indicated:

> My father fell quite ill in 2007. Initially the plan was to come to India for a short period of time that would allow us to resolve the financial issues, but then he passed away and by that time we had settled down in India.

The decision to return is not easy, but for some the norms and cultures that surround family caretaking responsibilities dictate these decisions. Nevertheless, not all of the returnees lived with their parents post-return. While most returnees lived and worked away from parents and family, several indicated a sense of security that emanated from being geographically close

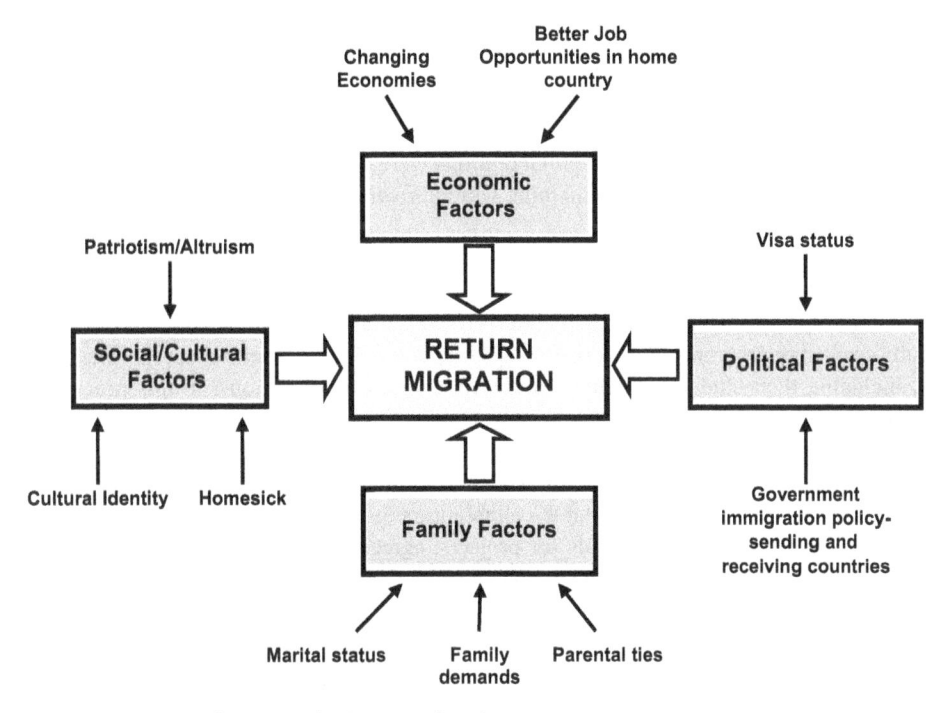

Figure 4.1 Conceptual framework of return migration

to their parents. The returnees felt that they could be a short plane ride away in an emergency situation, which is not the case when they were in the U.S. (it can take 36 hours of travel time from the U.S. to India). One of the returnees returned to India despite his wife's discontentment with the decision.

Conceptual framework

Based on the findings, we developed a conceptual framework of return migration which is depicted in Figure 1. The framework advances the current literature on return migration by including economic, political, social/cultural, and family factors and not solely relying on economic reasons for return. This approach is multidimensional rather than unidimensional and is thus holistic in its application of studying return migration. In a world where boundaries are becoming fluid and migration is anything but one-way, an inclusive structure to study return migration becomes imperative. This framework can be tested empirically in the future by researchers employing larger data samples.

Post-return transnationalism

Returnees in this study brought with them a wealth of ideas, connections, and networks that they had built during their time studying and working in the U.S. These connections were not just with U.S.-born faculty but also with researchers from various countries around the globe (Sabharwal & Varma, 2018). Returnees thus not only sought to use their scientific and technical know-how to continue past collaborations but also forged new ones with peers in India and beyond. A majority (61%) of the returnees reported some form of international collaboration. On average, they had 2.4 international collaborative projects. It is interesting to note that there was a general willingness to build international collaborations among those who were not involved in one at the time of interview. Interestingly, of the returnees who collaborated internationally, a greater number of collaborations were with researchers in Europe (37%) as compared to the U.S. (24%); the remaining had international projects with the countries outside Europe and North America.

Returnees performed two sets of activities in international collaboration. Majority ways in which returnees collaborated included through grants, research projects, publishing papers, and laboratory work (67%); the remainder (33%) collaborated via student, post-doc, and faculty-exchange programs and workshops. While collaborating internationally, these returnees, including their students, traveled to the collaborators' institutions. In this process they built working partnerships with institutions outside of India. Most importantly, they set up a network of communication and exchange so that their students and they could work outside India. These collaborative activities were carried out despite numerous challenges which returnees faced, namely finding suitable collaborators, geographical distance between returnees and collaborators, securing funds for projects, agreeing on common scientific activities, and bureaucratic limitations. As one returnee explained:

> In the U.S., they have high end technology whereas here we have to develop more cost effective or what is called more frugal work. I cannot try to repeat what is happening in the U.S. but definitely we have a scope to learn from there and they have opportunities to learn from us, the way we do our experiments.

Another said: "I started exchange program between my university here [India] and there [U.S.]. Under this program faculty and students exchange visits."

It should be noted that not all international research projects were formal, with funding, organizational support, task structure, and a well-established relationship wherein a set project is completed. Some returnees discussed informal international collaborative relationships with colleagues and institutions, although the terms upon which these informal relationships were based were not entirely certain. It appeared that informal collaboration involved general communication and an active attempt to remain open to the potential for a new collaborative project. Returnees continued the exchange of ideas both formally and informally.

An element characterizing the transnationalism of returned scientists and engineers is their temporary mobility for work outside their country of birth. Such travel is a transnational activity, as it solidifies ties with other countries on the one hand and revitalizes transnational identities that span borders on the other hand. It reflects the extent to which they belong to scientific work spaces that go beyond national borders. Most returnees (74%) were able to travel outside India for work, including for a sabbatical, without any issue, although the availability of funding and the frequency of travel varied. As one said, "In the past four years, I have never had to say I cannot go to an international conference because I do not have money." Not only there was a support for faculty to travel abroad; students were also encouraged to have international exposure. As one returnee said, "We have amazing travel funds. Government of India has set up special funds for students to travel abroad for conferences." Travel for the remaining returnees was restricted because of a lack of funding, a limit by their institution on how often they could travel, or other obligations such as lack of time and familial issues. Even most of this latter group acknowledged that the quality of conferences is better outside of India and that there are more networking opportunities available at international conferences. Returnees who traveled abroad typically went once a year, though some went once every few years, and a few of them a couple of times a year.

Most of these returnees were traveling outside of India to work on collaborative projects or to attend conferences. A few stated they went abroad to give talks or presentations at a workshop or in a university. A few returnees who did not travel abroad stated that they send their students to present their own work so that they could take advantage of the opportunity. As one said, "I made it a policy to make it possible for my students to travel abroad instead of me." The areas to which the returnees traveled varied. It appeared mostly to be somewhere in Europe, followed by the U.S., or a combination of both. Their travel was consistent with their earlier statements that they had more collaborative projects with European countries than with the U.S. One returnee declared, "I went to Germany, then Netherlands, then France, then Malaysia. Too much travel over the past last year."

Since faculty's international mobility for a longer time period is an important aspect of transnationalism (as it expands their research and teaching profile and also creates professional development initiatives), we explored whether returnees would consider a visiting faculty position in the U.S. Many returnees (49%) stated that they would consider a position in the U.S. at the time of the interview, while another 29% said they would consider a position in the future, but not in the near future due to various reasons. These returnees discussed their commitments to the projects in India and the potential for disruption in their children's education which hindered their ability to travel for extended period of time. The remaining returnees were not open to taking a position in the U.S., mostly because they had already had one in the past; thus, they preferred to go elsewhere or favored Europe because it was easier to get a visa to Europe than to the U.S. There was general agreement that going outside India for a longer time period would expand their horizons to a greater degree, in addition to allowing them to meet potential collaborators. As one said, "It would be good for your own intellectual development, to keep a little bit of an open perspective, to get experience from various places." Sabbaticals (generally given once after six years) were seen as the best way to visit the U.S. or other countries.

Conclusion

This study has developed a theoretical framework for understanding factors that lead to reverse brain drain among scientists and engineers in academia. Additionally, this chapter also provided information on how return migrants maintain transnational connections post-return. India-born faculty members occupy a major proportion of the full-time positions in S&E at four-year colleges and universities in the U.S. These faculty members play an important role in the scientific, technological, and economic growth of this nation through their scholarly contributions. Losing them in the form of reverse migration can add to the challenges faced by the scientific enterprise in the U.S. Yet there is little scholarly work on return migration from developed to developing countries. It is mostly because immigration to the U.S. is viewed as a one-way process, where the immigrants come with the intention to permanently settle in the country, a process referred as "brain drain." Recently there is a growing concern about an increase in return migration rates among foreign-born scientists and engineers from the U.S. to India, a phenomenon termed as return migration/reverse migration/reverse brain drain. However, existing studies on return migration tend to be statistical, based on the U.S. Census, U.S. Immigration and Naturalization Services (INS), and other quantitative data rather than on the returnees' situation and experiences.

This study has expanded existing models of return migration, which overwhelmingly focus on the economic impacts and do not include political, cultural, social, and family factors that contribute to the phenomenon of reverse brain drain. Future research can take the framework provided here and test it with larger samples of data to ensure external validity and generalizability. While this is not the goal of a qualitative study, the findings on post-return transnationalism show that the framework of return migration ought to expand to take transnationalism into account. Future research can expand the framework presented here by incorporating transnationalism.

Despite the fact that a large proportion of participants decided to return to India due to better economic prospects, political, social, cultural, and family reasons also contribute to the decision to return among academic scientists and engineers. The decision to return to one's home country after years of living, studying, and working in a host country is a complex phenomenon, one that is anything but linear (Sabharwal & Varma 2016, 2017). In fact, research suggests that the highest odds for return are among those who are strongly transnational (Carling & Pettersen 2014). It is evident through this study that return migrants continue to forge collaborations through transnational ties established across various regions around the globe, mainly with Europe and the U.S. Their return was not a result of failure of assimilation in the U.S. or due to retirement but can be considered what Cerase (1974, p. 251) has characterized as a "return of innovation" – as being "prepared to make use of all the means and new skills [returnees] have acquired during their migratory experiences." Return migrants in this study can be labeled as "cosmopolitan" (Bozeman & Corley 2004) in their approach to collaboration, i.e., they have cultivated ties and advanced their networks beyond India and the U.S. to Europe and other Asian countries. Technology has certainly made this transformation possible and has facilitated the idea of virtual borders. In an era of rapid technological growth and connectivity, return has a different meaning – despite the fact that borders do not seem to matter much for conducting scientific work, they do have a deeper social, cultural, and political significance.

Acknowledgments

The author(s) disclosed receipt of the following financial support for the research, authorship, and/or publication of this article: This research was supported by grants from the National Science Foundation (1230091, 1229990, 1655366 and 1655322).

References

Aneesh, A. (2006). *Virtual migration: The programming of globalization.* Durham, NC: Duke University Press.
Appadurai, A. (1991). Global ethnospaces: Notes and queries for a transnational anthropology. In R. Fox (ed.), *Recapturing anthropology* (pp. 48–65). Santa Fe, NM: School of American Research Press.
Bhagwati, J.N. (2003). Borders beyond control. *Foreign Affairs*, 82, 98–104.
Borjas, G.J. (1989). Economic theory and international migration. *International migration review*, 23 (3), 457–485.
Bozeman, B. & Corley, E. (2004). Scientists' collaboration strategies: Implications for scientific and technical human capital. *Research Policy*, 33 (4), 599–616.
Broad, J.W. (2004, May 3). U.S. is losing its dominance in the sciences. *New York Times*, p.1.
Carling, J. & Pettersen, S.V. (2014). Return migration intentions in the integration–transnationalism matrix. *Migration*, 52 (6), 13–30.
Cerase, F.P. (1974). Expectations and reality: A case study of return migration from the United States to Southern Italy. *International Migration Review*, 8 (2), 245–262.
Chronicle of Higher Education. (2009, May 28). Recession prompts foreign academics to seek jobs at Indian universities.
Chacko, E. (2007). From brain drain to brain gain: Reverse migration to Bangalore and Hyderabad, India's globalizing high tech cities. *GeoJournal*, 68 (2), 131–140.

Corley, E. & Sabharwal, M. (2007). Foreign-born academic scientists and engineers: Producing more and getting less than their U.S.-born peers? *Research in Higher Education*, 48 (8), 909–940.

Engardio, P. (2009, November 19). China's reverse brain drain. *Business Week*, 26.

Erickson, F. (1986). Qualitative methods in research on teaching. In M. Wittrock (ed.), *Handbook of research on teaching* (pp. 119–161). New York, NY: Macmillan.

Faist, T. (2000), *The volume and dynamics of international migration and transnational social spaces*. Oxford: Clarendon Press.

Finn, M.G. (2010). *Stay rates of foreign doctorate recipients from U.S. universities, 2007*. Oak Ridge, TN: Oak Ridge Institute for Science and Education.

Fletcher, A.M. (2000, March 4). Asian Americans coping with success. *The Washington Post*, p. A03.

Gupta, D. (2004). *The careers and return migration of foreign-born in United States PhDs*. PhD dissertation, University of California-Berkeley, Digital Dissertations database, Publication No. AAT 3165392.

Harvey, W.S. (2011). Immigration and emigration decisions among highly skilled British expatriates in Vancouver. In Nicolopoulou, K., Karata, M., & Tatli, A. (eds.), *Global knowledge work: Diversity and relational perspectives* (pp. 33–56). Cheltemham, UK: Edward Elgar.

Haour-Knipe, M. & Davies, A. (2008). *Return migration of nurses*. Geneva: International Centre on Nurse Migration.

King, R. (2000). Generalizations from the history of return migration. In B. Ghosh (ed.), *Return migration: Journey of hope or despair?* (pp. 7–55). Geneva: International Organization for Migration and the United Nations.

Larner, W. (2007). Expatriate experts and globalizing governmentalities: The New Zealand diaspora strategy. *Transactions of the Institute of British Geographers*, 32 (3), 331–345.

Levin, S. & Stephan, P. (1999). Are the foreign born a source of strength for US science? *Science*, 285 (5431), 1213–1214.

Levitt, P. & Jaworsky, B. (2007). Transnational migration studies: Past developments and future trends. *Annual Review of Sociology*, 33, 129–156.

Ley, D. & Kobayashi, A. (2005). Back to Hong Kong: Return migration or transnational sojourn? *Global Networks*, 5 (2), 111–127.

Lincoln, Y. & Guba, E.G. (1985). *Naturalistic inquiry*. Beverly Hills, CA: Sage Publications.

Mayr, K. & Peri, G. (2008). *Return migration as a channel of brain gain*. Cambridge: National Bureau of Economic Research, Working Paper no. 14039.

Miles, M.B. & Huberman, A.M. (1994). *Qualitative data analysis: An expanded sourcebook*. Thousand Oaks, CA: Sage Publications.

Natarajan, N. (2017). More than 100,000 H4 dependent spouses in the US got work permits in the last 3 years. *Firstpost*. Retrieved April 4, 2018 from: https://www.firstpost.com/world/more-than-100000-h4-dependent-spouses-got-work-permits-in-the-last-3-years-4234273.html.

National Science Board. (2018). *Science and engineering indicators*. Arlington, VA: National Science Foundation.

No, Y. & Walsh, J.P. (2010). The importance of foreign-born talent for US innovation. *Nature Biotechnology*, 28 (3), 289–291.

Nye, J. (1990). *Bound to lead: The changing nature of American power*. New York, NY: Basic Books.

Ong, A. (1999). *Flexible citizenship: The cultural logics of transnationality*. Durham, NC: Duke University Press.

Ozden, C. (2006). Educated migrants: Is there brain waste? In C. Ozden & M. Schiff (eds.), *International migration, remittances, and the brain drain* (pp. 227–244). New York, NY: World Bank and Palgrave Macmillan.

Patterson, R. (2006). Transnationalism: Diaspora–homeland development. *Social Forces*, 84 (4), 1891–1907.

Patton, M.Q. (2002). *Qualitative research and evaluation methods*. Thousand Oaks, CA: Sage Publications.

Razum, O., Sahin-Hodoglugil, N., & Polit, K. (2005). Health, wealth or family ties? Why Turkish work migrants return from Germany. *Journal of Ethnic and Migration Studies*, 31 (4), 719–739.

Sabharwal, M. (2011). High-skilled immigrants: How satisfied are foreign-born scientists and engineers employed at American universities? *Review of Public Personnel Administration*, 31 (2), 143–170.

Sabharwal, M. & Varma, R. (2016). Return migration to India: Decision-making among academic engineers and scientists. *International Migration*, 54 (4), 177–190.

Sabharwal, M. & Varma, R. (2017). Grass is greener on the other side: Return migration of Indian engineers and scientists in academia. *Bulletin of Science, Technology and Society*, 37 (1), 34–44.

Sabharwal, M. & Varma, R. (2018, December). International collaboration: Experiences of Indian scientists and engineers after returning from the United States. *Perspectives on Global Development and Technology*, 17 (5–6), 593–613.

Saxenian, A.L (2002). Transnational communities and the evolution of global production networks: The cases of Taiwan, China and India. *Industry & Innovation*, 9 (3), 183–202.

Saxenian, A.L (2006). *International mobility of engineers and the rise of entrepreneurship in the periphery*. Research Paper No. 2006/142. United Nations University.

Schiller, N., Basch, L., & Blanc, C. (1995). From immigration to transmigrant: Theorizing transnational migration. *Anthropological Quarterly*, 68 (1), 48–63.

Stephan, P.E. & Levin, S.G. (2001). Exceptional contributions to US science by the foreign-born and foreign-educated. *Population Research and Policy Review*, 20, 59–79.

Varma, R. (2002). High-tech coolies: Asian immigrants in US science and engineering workforce. *Science as Culture*, 11 (3), 337–361.

Varma, R. (2004). Asian Americans: Achievements mask challenges. *Asian Journal of Social Science*, 32 (2), 290–307.

Varma, R. (2006). *Harbingers of global change: India's techno-immigrants*. Lanham, MD: Lexington Books.

Varma, R. & Rogers, E.M. (2004). Indian cyber workers in the United States. *Economic and Political Weekly*, 39, 5645–5652.

Wadhwa, V. (2009). A reverse brain drain. *Issues in Science and Technology*, 25 (3), 45–52.

Waldorf, B. (1995). Determinants of international return migration intentions. *The Professional Geographer*, 47 (2), 125–36.

Wu, D.T.L. (1997). *Asian Pacific Americans in the workplace (Critical perspectives on Asian Pacific Americans)*. Walnut Creek, CA: Altamira Press.

Zelinsky, W. (1971). The hypothesis of the mobility transition. *Geographical Review*, 61 (2), 219–249.

PART II

On culture and identities

5
TRANSLOCAL PUJA
The relevance of gift exchange and locality in transnational Guyanese Hindu communities

Sinah Theres Kloß

Introduction

When Guyanese Hindus conduct *puja*—the ritual veneration of deities—saris, dhotis, or five yards of cloth are offered to a deity. While this practice of offering clothing is common in Guyana, it is conceived as challenging in diasporic communities. Increasing numbers of textile offerings and textile *prasadam*—auspicious leftovers—in the diaspora have influenced the development of transnational pujas. This chapter discusses how Hindu pujas transform and maintain the Guyanese transnational community and raises the question: how do transnational pujas continue to be influenced by local contexts and through their being situated in specific localities? To analyze these aspects, a brief overview of the development of Hinduism and the definition of Indianness in contemporary Guyana is provided first, then we look at specific pujas and their transformation into transnational and translocal practices.

Guyanese Indianness, Hinduism, and puja

In Guyana, ethnic identities impact all aspects of social, cultural, and political life, often leading to conflict. The different ethnic groups defined today are Indian, African, *Chinee* (Chinese), *Potogee* (Portuguese), Amerindian (Indigenous), and European/White. According to the latest census in 2012, 'Indian' and 'African' form the two biggest groups with 39.8 per cent of the population categorized as 'Indian' and an 'African' percentage of 29.3 (Bureau of Statistics 2012).[1] Both African and Indian are emic terms used in Guyana to denote people, cultural practices, objects, religions, and political parties. As ethnic groups and concepts such as Indianness or Africanness are always social constructions that are (re-)created and defined by social actors, discourse, and cultural practices, it has to be highlighted that Guyanese Indianness is constructed in the context of othering processes and largely in opposition to Guyanese Africanness (Williams 1991; Garner 2008; Ramey 2011). Defined in relation to each other, the African and Indian ethnic groups thus form constitutive others in Guyana today (Premdas 1992, 1994; Cross 1980; Hall 2000; Hinds 2011). Ethnic identities are usually expressed through the idea of shared cultural heritage and social practices but also through the notion of common descent. Guyanese Indians commonly refer to themselves as descendants of Indian indentured laborers, who were shipped to the Caribbean to work on sugar plantations during colonial rule from then

British India between 1838 and 1917 (Nath 1950; Tinker 1993; Bisnauth 2000). Also drawing on the idea of common descent as essential to ethnic identity, Guyanese Africans refer to enslaved Africans as their ancestors, who were forced to the Caribbean prior to the system of indentureship.[2]

Ethnic identification extends not only to people and groups but also to religions and religious denominations. While Christianity is primarily associated with African, Mixed, and Portuguese groups, Hinduism and Islam are perceived to be Indian religions. Peter van der Veer and Steven Vertovec label Hinduism as an 'ethnic religion' in the Caribbean that consolidates Indian ethnic identity (van der Veer and Vertovec 1991). According to the latest national census, 64 per cent of the Guyanese population is Christian, 24.8 per cent is Hindu, and 6.8 per cent is Muslim (Bureau of Statistics 2012). Hinduism has been a minority religion since the arrival of the first indentured laborers in Guyana, and its percentage has been declining from the middle of the twentieth century, for example from 35 per cent to 24.8 per cent between 1991 and 2012. Although this decline seems to support the often-pronounced claims that a large number of Hindus have been converting to Christianity, the role of migration to North America also must be taken into consideration; emigration numbers have been particularly high among the Guyanese Indian group since the late 1980s (Plaza 2004; Roopnarine 2005).

Conversion has always been a topic of great concern to Guyanese Hindus and continues to be addressed in Hindu ceremonies and everyday discourse. Elsewhere I discuss how this perceived 'threat of conversion' continues to foster a constant need within the Hindu community to justify and defend Hindu practices and beliefs (Kloß 2016, 2017a, forthcoming). This discourse is influenced by the history and development of Hinduism in Guyana, which has been transformed by processes of proselytization, stigmatization, and inferiorization. Hindus were usually declared to be 'heathen', 'uncivilized', and 'backward'—hence subordinate to 'civilized' Christians—in the predominantly Christian society. This has significantly affected the development of different Hindu traditions in Guyana and has even resulted in internal contestations of the groups' social status. The Guyanese Hindu community does not form a homogeneous group; there exist various strands and subgroups of Hinduism. The three most important ones in contemporary society are: the Sanatan (short for Sanatan Dharm), the Madras, and the Arya Samaj traditions. The Sanatan tradition is the mainstream Hindu tradition, which consolidated as a 'Great' or Sanskritic Hindu tradition in Guyana over the course of the twentieth century (Younger 2004, 2009; Kloß 2017b). This consolidation was fostered by various social actors, for instance *pandits* (priests), who sought to implement a local Hindu orthodoxy by excluding particular rites associated with 'popular Hinduism' (Vertovec 1994; Younger 2004; Harms 2010; McNeal 2010, 2011). Rituals excluded were, for example, the practices of 'life sacrifice' (animal sacrifice) or 'manifestations' of deities during healing rituals (Jayawardena 1966). These rituals did not disappear but were sustained and conducted in secret. They were and often continue to be described as 'backward' and 'demonic' in Caribbean societies (McNeal 2005).

Sanatanists believe in a pantheon of Sanskritic deities, for instance Krishna, Shiva, Hanuman, or Lakshmi. The epics *Ramayana* and *Mahabharata* are the core scriptures referenced during ceremonies and in general religious discourse.[3] On Sundays, so-called services are conducted in *mandirs* (temples), which are congregational and sometimes conducted by members of a mandir committee. This is due to the growing 'lack of pandits' in the Guyanese countryside, resulting from the massive emigration of Guyanese to North America. Sunday services as well as *parbs* (public religious functions) are directed at the general community. Combined with household-oriented, semi-public functions, such as *Hanuman Jhandi, Durga Paath*, and *Ganga Puja*, they form the core of contemporary Sanatan practices.[4] The popular but stigmatized practices that were excluded from mainstream Sanatan practices consolidated in what Guyanese Hindus commonly refer to as the Madras tradition or *Kali-Mai Puja* (Mother Kali's Puja). The development of this tradition took place in various phases of revitalization over the course of the twentieth century. The revitalizations were often initiated by specific socio-economic conditions that caused periods of 'hardship', such as economic crises or epidemics (Kloß 2017b). Today, three different 'ways' of the Madras tradition can be identified in Guyana: the English, the Tamil, and the Vegetarian ways. These ways have been evolving particularly since the 1970s, and the English way is currently the most prominent, considering its numbers of *koiloos* (temples) and attendees during Sunday services. 'English' and 'Tamil' are classifications that indicate the languages spoken during worship by the *pujaris* (ritual practitioners) and by deities during their manifestations. Less commonly named as a distinct way is the Vegetarian way, in which animal sacrifice is prohibited and limes and nutmeg serve as substitutional offerings. Contestations of authority, leadership, and social status within the Madras community and especially among the pujaris have massively influenced the development of these specific subgroups.

Puja and transnational gift exchange

As described in the last section, the Sanatan and Madras traditions are constructed in opposition to each other; hence are based on othering processes. Guyanese Hindus usually emphasize the differences between the traditions. However, when paying close attention to the outline and concept of puja and services, both traditions reveal similarities in terms of purpose and structure. In all pujas a ritual practitioner and the hosts of the ceremony revere the major deities in a prescribed sequence. Deities are invited as guests and are offered gifts, which are handed to them in a practice called *charhaway*. Charhaway is a core aspect of any puja conducted by Guyanese Hindus. It refers to the practice of giving a gift to a deity as well as the deity's acceptance of the gift. Charhaway includes kneeling and bowing in front of the deity's *murti* (manifestation or representation of a deity; divine statue), circling the gift three times in front of the murti, and placing the offered gift on the altar next to the murti (Kloß 2016). The devotee touches the murti's feet after having made the offering, and in return receives blessings and auspicious energies. The gift remains on the altar throughout the ritual proceedings and is only collected when the puja is concluding. Either the ritual practitioner collects the offerings for personal or institutional use, as is often the case with regard to gifts of clothing, for example, or distributes them among the people in the congregation.

Pujas remain a significant means of recreating Guyanese Indian and Hindu ethnic identity. They (re-)establish groups such as religious communities and families even in the context of migration. Commonly, family members who have migrated to North America continue to contribute to pujas such as the annual Hanuman Jhandi, which are often conducted by family members residing in Guyana. Contributions from migrants vary from monetary support to the sending of ritual paraphernalia or Indian clothing (Kloß 2016). In the context of the extensive outward migration of Guyanese to North America, puja facilitates an important means to performatively reconstruct relationships and to establish continuity. It is an intricate aspect of Guyanese Hindu migration and thus is constitutive of Guyanese transnationalism and Guyanese transnational social spaces. Guyanese migration to North America is often a transnational migration—a migration that results in connections and movements across national borders and that facilitates practices that cannot develop in either of the different localities (Glick-Schiller et al. 1995). The different generations of Guyanese migrants are involved to varying degrees in the maintenance of these transnational social spaces. Particularly first-generation migrants in the diaspora maintain their transnational ties with relatives in Guyana on a long-term basis. Pujas may become transnational practices in this context, which means that they create new social phenomena that develop through the interconnectedness of the contributors and their density of communication and exchange practices (Faist 2001; Pries 2001).

Gift exchange is part of maintaining these transnational relationships as well as a part of puja. For example, Guyanese Hindus in the U.S. continue to give clothes to family members at 'home' in Guyana, a practice that is common within families who live in the same region but who face difficulties when family members are dispersed. Guyanese as well as other Caribbean communities have established means through which migrants in North America may provide material support for and continue long-distance gift-giving practices with family members and friends at home. As letters and parcels sent with the national postal services usually do not reach the addressee, Guyanese either hand small parcels to a person who will be traveling home soon or ship large barrels to their relatives with specialized shipping companies. Barrels are containers with a volume of approximately 400 liters, which migrants fill with consumer goods such as food items, textiles, or electronic items (Plaza 2014; Kloß 2018). The recipients of barrels distribute the contents primarily among family members, but sometimes neighbors and friends receive a share as well (Kloß 2016, 2018). As is always the case in gift exchange, social hierarchy is negotiated in this context: the social status of a gift-giver rises in relation to the receiver of the gift (Mauss 1966; Parry 1986). The receiver's status is only reconstituted when he or she reciprocates the gift immediately or at a later point in time. Family members in Guyana usually reciprocate by sending small parcels filled with local food items, such as fried fish or pickled fruit.

Transnational gift exchange in Guyanese Hindu communities takes place on various levels. For example, clothes are exchanged not only among family members and friends but also within religious communities and between humans and deities. As discussed earlier, gift exchange between devotees and deities is part of the practice of charhaway. Charhaway thus visualizes, materializes, and recreates the relationship between human and deity.[5] Charhawayed items become the possession of the deity, who consumes them, at least partially. Through this partial consumption, the items are turned into *prasadam* (auspicious leftovers). At the end of a puja, prasadam is shared among the people in the congregation. Particularly food prasadam, the most prominent form of prasadam in Guyana, is distributed in equal shares to every person in the audience. Textile prasadam, in contrast, can only be given to a single person due to its material condition. It serves as a special kind of prasadam handed to an especially 'deserving' person. Its particularity as prasadam is emphasized by the fact that Guyanese Hindus consider textiles to have a specific capacity to store divine blessings and substances, which transfer to the next consumer.

Textiles have become a very prominent category of charhaway and hence also of prasadam in Guyana and the Guyanese diaspora. In North America, the amount of charhaway items and consequently prasadam has increased significantly due to the greater availability of reasonably priced items and the increasing purchasing power of a number of Guyanese. When conducting and hosting pujas in the Guyanese diaspora, devotees commonly strive to charhaway not only a single sari or dhoti to a particular Hindu deity but also commonly give pieces of clothing and jewelry to every deity. As murti clothing is usually only changed twice a year in mandirs and koiloos, an excess of charhawayed clothing is created, which murtis cannot wear. Because they have become the deity's possession and are imbued with divine and auspicious essences, they cannot be disposed of and require special treatment. Particularly in the Guyanese Madras tradition, the practice has developed to collect these surplus charhaway saris and dhotis and to barrel them to Guyana. They are distributed to 'deserving' members in the affiliated temple communities, who often wear them as temple clothing for Sunday services, or they are used as decorations for altars and buildings.

The most decorative and 'richest' garments are reserved to be worn exclusively by the murtis in Guyana. North American barrel-senders enclose lists or instruct on the phone as to which sari is meant to be worn by which deity. Although usually the color of a piece of clothing already restricts its use to a specific deity, barrel-senders give very specific directions.[6] These demands seem to be indicative of the creation and enactment of superior status by the barrel-sending party vis-à-vis the barrel-receiving party, an aspect addressed by general gift-exchange theory. While indeed these requests may at first sound authoritative and inferiorizing with regard to the receiving community, I argue that they are part of a transnational puja and a transnational practice of charhaway: the surplus saris have been charhawayed in the North American temple during puja and have become the possession of the respective deity. They are not shared as prasadam with the community in North America but instead are shared with the community in Guyana, deemed as more 'deserving'. The affiliated temple at home, in this context, is not only the place where people have a greater need for these items but also is generally considered to be the place where more authentic puja can be conducted. The rituals and practices of charhaway and of sharing prasadam are hence extended, both temporally and spatially, across national borders. Murtis are considered to be manifestations of a deity, for example a Durga murti in the U.S. and a Durga murti in Guyana are manifestations of the same deity. In this context the instructions concerning the question of which sari belongs to which deity, as pronounced by the barrel-senders, cannot be considered as an authoritative means of creating superior status within the Hindu community. They are indeed expressions of a concern that the charhawayed sari, owned by a deity, will continue to be directed and used by the same deity. Pujaris and other temple members hence regard it as their obligation to ensure the continuity of the transnational charhaway practice and prevent any kind of disruption or possible ritual failure.

Locality and puja

As mentioned earlier, puja in both the Sanatan and Madras traditions is similar in its objective—to honor the deities and receive merit—but varies with regard to how it is conducted. Particularly the role of place, locality, and physicality/materiality takes on a different meaning. In the Sanatan tradition, puja is conducted either in mandirs or at temporary constructed ritual sites outside a family's house. A pandit sits next to the altar, where, amongst other things, the murtis and the *hawan kund* (site of the ritual fire) have been placed. The family who conducts and 'sponsors' the puja sits next to him, headed by the *jajman* (main host), who is usually the male head of the household. All contributors are registered through a ritual called 'sankalp' at the beginning of puja, in which the contributors' Hindu names are used, the so-called 'right names' based on *patra* (Hindu astrology). Family members who cannot be present receive merit as long as their names have been registered by the pandit. This allows for the inclusion of people who may be absent because of sickness, work, or migration but who have contributed financially or materially to the puja. During these pujas, all deities are placed on the same altar, where they are revered as essentially one (Kloß 2016). This is generally the case in Sanatan mandirs. In this case the veneration of the different deities does not require a lot of movement, and the sequence of veneration is visualized only when ritual practices are directed at the murtis or framed pictures of the different deities. Visibly different is puja in the Madras tradition, which takes place in so-called Kali temples or koiloos. In Guyana, these consist of a large compound with a number of small buildings, each housing one to four deities.

These buildings are often numbered, indicating the correct order of worship, on the basis of which devotees enter to pray. The official veneration, conducted by pujaris, requires physical movement from building to building.

Although not irrelevant in Sanatan pujas, space as well as bodily and physical movements have an important meaning in the Guyanese Madras tradition. According to some Guyanese Sanatanists, the relevance of physicality and movement in the Madras tradition supports their claims that 'Madrassis' are 'more physical people', opposing them to the allegedly more spiritual Sanatanists. They use this difference as a mode of othering and inferiorization in contestations and negotiations of Hindu authority and leadership. As mentioned earlier, religious communities of the Madras tradition are the primary groups in which the communal practice of barrel-sending has been established, particularly within religious communities of the so-called English way. The tradition's continuous marginalization in Guyanese society and its stigmatization by Sanatan Hindus has fostered the need to consolidate and create a particularly strong group identity, influencing this development of uniting and maintaining group identity through charhaway even in the context of migration.

In the context of the transnationalization of charhaway, the role of physical space and materiality leads to an additional perspective on Madrassi puja: the continued relevance of locality in transnational social spaces. While transnational social spaces are often discussed as free-floating spaces in which physical space has become irrelevant, indeed transnational social spaces and networks are always constructed by social actors. Social actors are embedded in specific environments, both social and geographical, hence transnational migrants, although highly mobile, always act in specific places and are influenced through these localities and by being located (Guarnizo and Smith 1998; Brickell and Datta 2011; Verne 2012; Greiner and Sakdapolrak 2013). Generally, place and locality remain important influences in the formation and maintenance of highly mobile, transnational communities and families, an aspect which the concept of translocality emphasizes. Translocality can be defined as a 'form of "grounded transnationalism"—space where deterritorialized networks of transnational social relations take shape through migrant agencies' (Brickell and Datta 2011: 3). It refers to 'sets of multidirectional and overlapping networks, constituted by migration, in which the exchange of resources, practices and ideas links and at the same time transforms particular places' (Greiner 2010: 137). It thus becomes of relevance when considering the transnationalization of gift exchange, puja, and charhaway.

Material gifts are never free-floating objects that cross time and space in unrestricted ways and without any hindrances. Due to their materiality and the situatedness of the social actors who give, receive, and return gifts, notions of place and locality continue to be of relevance when analyzing the practice of exchanging gifts in transnational social spaces. Transnational gift exchange is affected by place, national borders, and other actor-related aspects such as citizenship. Material objects that travel between and connect the various nodes of transnational networks cross national borders and are impacted by, for example, transportation and customs regulations. For instance, Guyanese Hindus of the Madras tradition have been struggling with the Guyanese government over the past years, particularly the Guyana Revenue Authority (GRA), to be granted duty-free concessions to import surplus charhaway saris free of charge from the North American temples to be distributed in the various Guyanese temple communities. They have formed corporations and organizations that would allow the communities to be granted tax exemptions for the import of these excess puja *sarjam* (ritual paraphernalia). According to some pujaris, however, changed national regulations, internal administrative inconsistencies, and contestations of leadership within the Madras communities have prevented the renewal of duty-free licenses since 2009 (Kloß 2016).[7]

Particularly in the context of migration, the materiality of gifts becomes especially relevant. It may intensify feelings of closeness to and intimacy with the absent gift-giver on the one hand, but may also create feelings of loneliness and distance on the other hand. Beyond having symbolic meaning, especially gifts of clothing facilitate tactile touch between giver and receiver (Kloß 2016, 2018). Most Guyanese Hindus consider textiles to be structures in which substances and essences of, for example, former users are dwelling. Material gift exchange facilitated by barrels thus often remains the only way for transnational families to stay in touch, as visits to Guyana may be rare due to the high costs of traveling or may be impossible at all because of the sometimes illegal status of migrants. As not only people but also places may be imbued in textiles, they also become a means of accessing distant places and of being transformed. This transfer of essences and substances through transnational gift exchange highlights the role of locality, physicality, and the embeddedness of social actors in transnational social spaces.

Conclusion

Puja, with its intricate practice of charhaway, may become not only an international but furthermore a transnational and translocal ritual. As all socio-cultural practices are situated and embedded in specific locales, so are practices of gift exchange. In transnational pujas the role of locality and even nations remain of relevance, as has been illustrated for example by (legal) restrictions in the different nodes of the transnational Guyanese network. These specific kinds and modes of puja, particularly the combination of charhaway and barrel-sending, cannot exist in either of the localities. They are a product of continued communication and exchange in transnational social spaces, transforming and influencing the different locales and social actors involved over time. They are a specific kind of puja that can be labeled as translocal and that influence other practices of puja and hence the various traditions of Guyanese Hinduism. For example, followers of the Madras tradition sometimes label their translocal pujas as particularly moral, sustainable, and charitable, opposing it to (Sanatan) communities who do not barrel excess puja sarjam and prasadam to Guyana. On this ground they sometimes claim higher social status in relation to Sanatan Hindus, challenging socio-religious hierarchies in both Guyana and the Guyanese diaspora.

Notes

1 Mixed: 19.9%; Amerindian: 10.5%; Chinese: 0.2%; Portuguese: 0.3%; White: 0.1% (Bureau of Statistics 2012: 4).
2 'Indian' is sometimes also substituted with 'East Indian'. The term 'East Indian' was invented in the first half of the twentieth century, to refer to an identity linked to the experience of indentureship and to distinguish the groups that—from the perspective of the colonizer—could otherwise be subsumed under the label Indian (Seecharan 1993). It sought to differentiate the (East) Indian from the indigenous group, which henceforth came to be labeled as 'Amerindian'. It has to be noted that the label 'East Indian' created an opposition between East Indians and the West Indies, the colonial term for the Caribbean. It thus situated Indians ideologically 'outside' or as other to the Caribbean (Segal 2006).
3 This is similar to the Trinidadian context, as described for example by Sherry-Ann Singh (2012).
4 The influence of the Arya Samaj movement has to be taken into consideration when discussing the development of Hinduism in Guyana. It has been discussed in detail by Steven Vertovec, for example, who considers the Arya Samaj as a 'chief catalyst for the institutionalization of a unitary, standardized Brahmanic Hinduism' (1994: 136) in the Caribbean. Arya Samaj missionaries initiated the movement in then British Guiana in the 1920s (Seecharan 1993, 2011).
5 It has to be noted that charhaway is not the same as the notion of *daan* or *dana*, commonly referred to in the context of Hindu gift-giving in India (Parry 1986: 460).

6 In Guyanese Hinduism, specific colors are linked to the different deities: Dharti Ma (green), Suruj (white), Shiva (blue, lilac), Ganga (yellow), Katerie (black), Hanuman (red), Krishna (blue, green), Ganesha (apricot), Kali (yellow, red), Lakshmi (pink), Svarsattie (white), Durga (yellow).
7 The annual amount of puja sarjam imported prior to 2009 sometimes filled up to six barrels. According to some pujaris, the GRA assumed that instead of sharing the items charitably, ritual practitioners would instead sell them, which would require them to pay taxes. The heated debate concerning duty-free concessions of puja sarjam is linked to the Hindu community's charges against the government's alleged favoritism towards Christians. Hindus often claim that Christian groups are favored, for instance in legal documents which decree that the import of Christian altar bread and wine is deemed as duty free.

References

Bisnauth, Dale A. 2000. *The Settlement of Indians in Guyana, 1890–1930*. London: Peepal Tree Press.
Brickell, Katherine, and Ayona Datta. 2011. 'Introduction: Translocal Geographies'. In *Translocal Geographies: Spaces, Places, Connections*, edited by Katherine Brickell and Ayona Datta, 3–20. Farnham, Burlington, VT: Ashgate.
Bureau of Statistics. 2012. 'Population and Housing Census'. Accessed January 27, 2017. http://www.statisticsguyana.gov.gy/census.html.
Cross, Malcolm. (1972) 1980. *The East Indians of Guyana and Trinidad*. New ed., reprint. MRG report 13. London.
Faist, Thomas. 2001. 'Developing Transnational Social Spaces: The Turkish-German Example'. In *New Transnational Social Spaces: International Migration and Transnational Companies in the Early Twenty-first Century*, edited by Ludger Pries, 36–72. London: Routledge. 36–72.
Garner, Steve. 2008. *Guyana 1838–1985: Ethnicity, Class and Gender*. Kingston, Jamaica: Ian Randle.
Glick-Schiller, Nina, Linda Basch, and Cristina Szanton-Blanc. 1995. 'From Immigrant to Transmigrant: Theorizing Transnational Migration'. *Anthropological Quarterly* 68 (1): 48–65.
Greiner, Clemens. 2010. 'Patterns of Translocality: Migration, Livelihoods and Identities in Northwest Namibia'. *Sociologus* 2: 131–61.
Greiner, Clemens, and Patrick Sakdapolrak. 2013. 'Translocality: Concepts, Applications and Emerging Research Perspectives'. *Geography Compass* 7 (5): 373–84. doi:10.1111/gec3.12048.
Guarnizo, Luis, and Michael P. Smith. 1998. 'The Locations of Transnationalism'. In *Transnationalism from Below*, edited by Michael P. Smith and Luis Guarnizo, 3–34. Comparative Urban and Community Research v. 6. New Brunswick, NJ: Transaction Publishers.
Hall, Stuart. 2000. 'Cultural Identity and Diaspora'. In *Diaspora and Visual Culture: Representing Africans and Jews*, edited by Nicholas Mirzoeff, 21–33. London, New York: Routledge.
Harms, Arne. 2010. 'Happy Mothers, Proud Sons: Hybridity, Possession, and a Heterotopy among Guyanese Hindus'. In *Transfer and Spaces*, edited by Axel Michaels, 107–24. Ritual Dynamics and the Science of Ritual. Wiesbaden: Harrassowitz.
Hinds, David. 2011. *Ethno-Politics and Power Sharing in Guyana: History and Discourse*. Washington, DC: New Academia Publishing.
Jayawardena, Chandra. 1966. 'Religious Belief and Social Change: Aspects of the Development of Hinduism in British Guiana'. *Comparative Studies in Society and History: CSSH; An International Quarterly* 8 (2): 211–40.
Kloß, Sinah Theres. 2016. *Fabrics of Indianness: The Exchange and Consumption of Clothing in Transnational Guyanese Hindu Communities*. London, New York: Palgrave Macmillan.
Kloß, Sinah Theres. 2017a. 'Contesting "Gifts from Jesus": Conversion, Charity, and the Distribution of Used Clothing in Guyana'. *Social Sciences and Missions* 30 (3): 346–65. doi:10.1163/18748945-03003003.
Kloß, Sinah Theres. 2017b. 'Manifesting Kali's Power: Guyanese Hinduism and the Revitalisation of the "Madras Tradition"'. *Journal of Eastern Caribbean Studies* 41 (1): 83–110.
Kloß, Sinah Theres. 2018. 'Staying in Touch: Used Clothes and the Role of Materiality in Transnational Guyanese Gift Exchange'. In *Reshaping Glocal Dynamics of the Caribbean: Relaciones y Desconexiones—Relations et Déconnexions—Relations and Disconnections*, edited by Anja Bandau, Anne Brüske, and Natascha Ueckmann. Heidelberg: Heidelberg University Press.
Kloß, Sinah Theres. forthcoming. 'Giving and Development: Ethno-Religious Identities and "Holistic Development" in Guyana'. In *Faith Based Organizations: Boundary Agencies in Development Discourses and Practice*, edited by Andreas Heuser and Jens Köhrsen.

Mauss, Marcel. 1966. *The Gift: Forms and Functions of Exchange in Archaic Societies*. London: Cohen & West.
McNeal, Keith E. 2005. 'Doing the Mother's Caribbean Work. On *Shakti* and Society in Contemporary Trinidad'. In *Encountering Kālī: In the Margins, at the Center, in the West*, edited by R. Fell McDermott and J. J. Kripal, 223–48. Delhi: Motilal Banarsidass.
McNeal, Keith E. 2010. 'Pantheons as Mythistorical Archives: Pantheonization and Remodeled Iconographies in Two Southern Caribbean Possession Religions'. In *Activating the Past: History and Memory in the Black Atlantic World*, edited by Andrew H. Apter, 172–226. Newcastle upon Tyne: Cambridge Scholars Publ.
McNeal, Keith E. 2011. *Trance and Modernity in the Southern Caribbean: African and Hindu Popular Religions in Trinidad and Tobago*. New World Diasporas. Gainesville, FL: University Press of Florida.
Nath, Dwarka. 1950. *A History of Indians in British Guiana*. London, New York, NY: Nelson.
Parry, Jonathan. 1986. 'The Gift, the Indian Gift and the "Indian Gift"'. *Man* 21 (3): 453–73.
Plaza, Dwaine E. 2004. 'Disaggregating the Indo- and African-Caribbean Migration and Settlement Experience in Canada'. *Canadian Journal of Latin American and Caribbean Studies* 29 (57/58): 241–66.
Plaza, Dwaine. 2014. 'Barrels of Love. A Study of the Soft Goods Remittance Practices of Transnational Jamaican Households'. In *Caribbean Food Cultures: Culinary Practices and Consumption in the Caribbean and Its Diasporas*, edited by Wiebke Beushausen, Anne Brüske, Ana-Sofia Commichau, Patrick Helber, and Sinah Kloß. 227–55. Postcolonial Studies 18. Bielefeld: transcript.
Premdas, Ralph R. 1992. *Ethnic Conflict and Development: The Case of Guyana*. Geneva: United Nations Research Institute for Social Development.
Premdas, Ralph R. 1994. 'Problems and Opportunities for Political Reconciliation in a Multi-Ethnic State: The Case of Guyana'. In *The East Indian Odyssey: Dilemmas of a Migrant People*, edited by Mahin Gosine, 59–64. New York, NY: Windsor Press.
Pries, Ludger, ed. 2001. *New Transnational Social Spaces: International Migration and Transnational Companies in the Early Twenty-First Century*. London: Routledge.
Ramey, Steven. 2011. 'Hindu Minorities and the Limits of Hindu Inclusiveness: Sindhi and Indo-Caribbean Hindu Communities in Atlanta'. *International Journal of Hindu Studies* 15 (2): 209–39.
Roopnarine, L. 2005. 'Indo-Caribbean Intra-Island Migration: Not So Marginalized!' *Social and Economic Studies* 54 (2): 107–36.
Seecharan, Clem. 1993. *India and the Shaping of the Indo-Guyanese Imagination, 1890s–1920s*. Leeds: Peepal Tree.
Seecharan, Clem. 2011. 'India's Awakening and the Imagination of the "East Indian Nation" in British Guiana'. In *India and the Diasporic Imagination = L'Inde et l'imagination diasporique*, edited by Rita Christian, Judith Misrahi-Barak, and Khaleel Torabully, 33–52. Collection 'Horizons anglophones'; Série PoCoPages. Montpellier: Presses universitaires de la Méditerranée.
Segal, Daniel A. 2006. 'Circulation, Transpositions, and the Travails of "Creole"'. *American Ethnologist* 33 (4): 579–81.
Singh, Sherry-Ann. 2012. *The Ramayana Tradition and Socio-Religious Change in Trinidad, 1917–1990*. Kingston, Miami: Ian Randle.
Tinker, Hugh. 1993. *A New System of Slavery: The Export of Indian Labour Overseas 1830–1920*. 2nd ed. London: Hansib.
van der Veer, Peter, and Steven Vertovec. 1991. 'Brahmanism Abroad: On Caribbean Hinduism as an Ethnic Religion'. *Ethnology* 30 (2): 149–66.
Verne, Julia. 2012. *Living Translocality: Space, Culture and Economy in Contemporary Swahili Trade*. Erdkundliches Wissen 150. Stuttgart: Franz Steiner (Zugl. Bayreuth, Univ., Diss., 2010).
Vertovec, Steven. 1994. '"Official" and "Popular" Hinduism in Diaspora: Historical and Contemporary Trends in Surinam, Trinidad and Guyana'. *Contributions to Indian Sociology* 28 (1): 123–47.
Williams, Brackette F. 1991. *Stains on My Name, War in My Veins: Guyana and the Politics of Cultural Struggle*. Durham, NC: Duke University Press.
Younger, Paul. 2004. 'Guyana Hinduism'. *Religious Studies and Theology* 23 (1): 35–54.
Younger, Paul. 2009. *New Homelands: Hindu Communities in Mauritius, Guyana, Trinidad, South Africa Fiji and East Africa*. New York, Oxford: Oxford University Press.

6
INDIAN MUSIC AND TRANSNATIONALISM

Peter Manuel and Andre Fludd

Along with cuisine, music has certainly been India's most prominent and celebrated cultural export, and the ongoing presence of visiting and resident classical Indian performers throughout the developed world has done much to establish recognition and appreciation of the richness of Indian culture as a whole. Indeed, the international popularity of musicians such as sitarist Ravi Shankar or *qawwāli* singer Nusrat Fateh Ali Khan has not only offset associations of South Asia with poverty and backwardness but also stands in contrast to the relative lack of international (as well as domestic) interest in the traditional musics of other "old high cultures" such as those of China and Japan. However, the transnational dimensions of Indian music culture go far beyond the mere appreciation of Indian fine arts in the West. Instead, they would include a range of socio-cultural dynamics pertaining to, among other things, the music subcultures of the diverse and increasingly active Indian diasporas, the impact of globalization on music culture in India itself, the formation of music-based "social fields" transcending nation-state boundaries, and the emergence of quintessentially transnational music networks and scenes involving both classical and commercial popular musics. This essay surveys the principal contours of these dynamics and concludes with a more focused look (written primarily by Fludd) at their presence in a particular diasporic node, that of the greater New York City area.

International connections prior to independence

Until the twentieth century, the music culture of the Indian subcontinent was in many ways a geographically bounded entity, its physical domains delimited by the surrounding mountains, deserts, jungles, and oceans. In the first millennium of the common era, a "Sanskrit cosmopolis" provided a layer of literary, aesthetic, and ideological homogeneity among elites throughout the region (Pollock 2006). By the end of this era, Sanskrit musicological treatises were acknowledging the rise of regional (*desi*) art musics which had replaced the extinct music system described in well-circulated, hoary texts—especially the *Natya-Shāstra* of several centuries earlier. From the eleventh century, Muslim invaders—primarily Persianized ethnic Turks—established dynasties in North India with strong cultural links to Persia. The Persian language became the medium of official discourse and Islamicate poetry and prose, and North

Indian court music adapted various Persian instruments, modes, meters, and other features, though invariably domesticating them in the process. A certain sort of cosmopolitan ecumenicism prevailed in Mughal court culture, with performing troupes of diverse local, Persian, and Central Asian origins and musical treatises routinely enumerating Persian rough equivalences of Indian *rāgs* (modes). However, while Persian poetry (especially the *ghazal*) was actively cultivated through the mid-nineteenth century, by the mid-seventeenth century Persian music itself was out of vogue, and Indo-Muslim rulers had been long since won over to local rather than imported fine arts. Further, if North Indian music had incorporated, in its way, many elements from Persian music, the influence does not appear to have been mutual, as Indian music had little significant presence or influence outside the subcontinent.

British colonial rule brought a new set of foreign influences to bear on the region's music culture, although these had relatively little impact on music per se and did not precipitate any widespread introduction of Indian music to audiences in the West (see, however, Farrell 1997). Nineteenth-century British military and administrative personnel amused themselves with *nāch* (courtesan dance) troupes, a few civil servants published informative studies of Indian music, and from the 1930s Theosophist Annie Besant and others successfully campaigned with middle-class Brahman reformers to wrest South Indian temple dance out of the hands of its traditional *devadāsi* courtesan performers and reinvent it in a sanitized form, as "bharatanatyam."

From the 1840s, certain sectors of Indian music culture were in fact exported to distant shores, albeit in a quite limited and distinctive context. Responding to demand for cheap labor in remote outposts of the Empire, the British established programs in which Indians were induced to work abroad as indentured laborers. Until the cessation of the program in 1917, more than a million Indians came to settle in Mauritius, Fiji, South Africa, and Caribbean sites—primarily British Guiana (now Guyana), Trinidad, and Dutch Guiana (now Suriname). Most hailed from the Bhojpuri region (straddling present-day Bihar and Uttar Pradesh) and brought with them the rustic folksongs of that impoverished and backward region, along with smatterings of other North Indian music genres.

If diasporic transnationalism would imply a state of constant contact and flows of people between ancestral and new homelands, the indentured labor diasporas would serve as antithetically distinct forms of displacements. Once the ships of laborers stopped coming in 1917, these diasporic communities found themselves cut off from the Indian homeland and from each other, even as they remained proud of their ethnicity and determined to perpetuate their religion and cultural practices. Hence they took the form of isolated transplant diasporas, whose music cultures came to comprise combinations of marginal survivals (such as vernal Bhojpuri-style *chowtāl* singing), creolized entities (such as Trinidadian chutney and chutney-soca), and various genres which evolved along Indian lines but were quite distinct from anything in India itself. In the latter category would fall the Trinidadian and Guyanese genre of "local classical music," a thoroughly idiosyncratic idiom reinvented out of the fragments of knowledge of Hindustani music brought by a few immigrants (Manuel 1998, 2000). Even more vital today is the Trinidadian style of *tāssa* drumming, which derived originally from North Indian sources but evolved into a considerably more rich and sophisticated art form, now indispensable at Hindu weddings in Trinidad and its secondary diaspora sites (Manuel 2015). New forms of contacts between Indo-Caribbeans and "India people" have been facilitated by the internet and personal interactions (especially in secondary diasporic sites such as New York City), but in many ways the Indo-Caribbean, Indo-Fijian, and Indian communities have become too distinct for their relationships to become genuinely transnational.

The transnationalization of Indian classical music

A different sort of internationalization of Indian music occurred from the 1960s with the popularization of Indian (and especially North Indian, or Hindustani) classical music in the West and elsewhere. By far the most important figure in this development was sitarist Ravi Shankar (1920–2012), who, from the late 1950s, undertook a personal mission to bring Hindustani music to the concert halls of the developed world (primarily the West, but also Japan and Australia). Shankar was uniquely qualified for this challenge, since, aside from being a brilliant sitarist, he was fluent in English and French, had acquired a cosmopolitan sophistication from his adolescent years spent in Paris, and was gregarious and engaging by nature. Shankar, with his accompanists, toured indefatigably for decades, serving as India's energetic musical ambassador while remaining level-headed about the trendy and superficial nature of much of the new Western countercultural interest in Indian music and religion (see Shankar 1999: 202–03). This faddish level of engagement—spurred by such events as Shankar's 1967 performance at the Monterey Pop Festival and George Harrison's sitar excursions—was neither deep nor durable, but it helped lay the foundation for a more serious and sustained Western appreciation of Indian fine arts.

In Shankar's wake, a steady stream of North and South Indian performers has continued to tour the West. Many have taken up permanent or temporary residence in order to teach, founding such institutions as the Ali Akbar College of Music (from 1967) near San Francisco. Several have found full- or part-time employment teaching in Western colleges and universities, such as UCLA or Wesleyan University. Many base themselves abroad while returning to India to concertize. Meanwhile, many Westerners—certainly some thousands over the decades—have studied Indian music and dance in India itself, and several have achieved professional levels of competence. Like Indian fine-arts students, such enthusiasts, regardless of their level of skill, form the core of the relatively informed, if quantitatively modest, Western audiences that Indian performers may encounter on their tours. For various reasons, North Indian music has enjoyed greater popularity among Westerners than has South Indian (Carnatic, Karnatak) music; the latter has less flamboyant displays of virtuosity, it is more imbued with Hindu devotion, and its performers—feeling relatively secure and satisfied with the enthusiastic (primarily Brahman) patronage extant in South India—may have felt less motivated or obliged to travel than their Hindustani counterparts (see Krishnan 2013: 361–90). However, the relatively standardized and systematic pedagogy and performance format of South Indian *bharatanatyam* dance have contributed to its attracting considerably more foreign students than the Northern classical dance, *kathak*. Meanwhile, Western ethnomusicologists—better funded than their Indian counterparts—have generated much solid scholarship on Indian fine arts, even if their findings are typically published in the West and not easily available in India itself.

Since the 1980s, the internationalization of Indian classical music has come to be sustained, in at least as substantial a way, by the growth of non-resident Indian (NRI) communities and their own interest in and cultivation of fine arts. This development has been particularly conspicuous in the realm of South Indian music and dance. In North America, by the early 1980s the South Indian immigrant communities had attained a critical mass of relatively affluent, primarily Brahman professionals who were committed to the patronage and performance of South Indian music and dance, and to transmitting those arts to their children. Music clubs have proliferated, hosting tours of South Indian artists (most of whom themselves have been educated, cosmopolitan Brahmans quite at ease with Western travel). Music festivals began to be held, the most extensive of which has been in Cleveland, Ohio, otherwise an undistinguished rust-belt city. The Cleveland Thyagaraja Festival, started in 1978, has evolved into a major event on the Carnatic music calendar, attracting hundreds of enthusiasts from around North America and featuring dozens of top performers from India every year.

A concurrent development has been the entrenchment of pedagogy in North America, as the immigrant community has come to comprise many competent performers—male and female, professional or amateur—who teach privately or in temples or modest institutions, enabling thousands of second- and third-generation young people to study and reach advanced levels in music and dance. Many of these students attain fully professional levels and receive as good training as they could in Chennai or elsewhere in India. Some occasionally visit India for grooming with a master, or—increasingly—they take lessons from an Indian guru via Skype. The activities of such a scene, in the New York area, will be commented on further in this essay.

NRI activity has had mixed sorts of impact upon music and dance scenes in India itself. These contradictory effects have been particularly conspicuous in Chennai's *bharatanatyam* scene, where, as Shanti Pillai (2002) has discussed, local connoisseurs are likely to regard NRI interventions with ambivalence. Competitive NRIs, by virtue of their affluence, are able to flood venues with vanity performances of their daughters, whether talented or not, while effectively driving up prices for music and dance classes in Chennai. Inflationary pressures even extend to newspaper coverage, as through direct or indirect favors to journalists NRIs are often able to solicit favorable (and much-prized) reviews. Meanwhile while local critics complain that the NRI performers typically lack the knowledge of Telugu and Tamil that is necessary for sensitive depiction of song lyrics.

Commercial popular music and dance

Despite the much-deserved prominence and renown of Indian classical music and dance, it need scarcely be pointed out that these worthy art forms—like classical arts everywhere—command the attention of only a small fraction of the general public, whose tastes overwhelmingly incline toward more accessible forms of lighter entertainment, especially commercial popular music. India is, of course, host to a thriving popular music industry whose size is commensurate with the subcontinent's vast population. Since the 1930s, most—but not all—of this music has been embedded in commercial cinema, including the vast Hindi-language ("Bollywood") film industry in Mumbai, as well as regional-language movies which themselves tend to follow general stylistic trends of the Bollywood scene. Meanwhile, since the cassette revolution of the 1980s (followed by digital formats), non-film regional popular music styles have also flourished, often incorporating elements of local traditional music styles as well as language (Manuel 1993).

Mainstream Hindi film music, as established and produced in the decades following Independence, evolved as an eclectic hybrid, typically combining some Western instruments and ensemble practices with distinctively Indian vocal style, modes, instruments, and, of course, language and lyric themes. Until the last decade, the films themselves were clearly produced for Indian—rather than foreign—audiences, and their improbable plots, glittery sets, and themes of Indian mythology and domestic melodramas attracted almost no interest among Western audiences. However, appropriately dubbed or subtitled, Hindi films, with their lively song-and-dance scenes and their fantasy worlds of cabarets and mansions, did come to be enjoyed by many millions of viewers in Africa, the Middle East, the Soviet Union, and other seemingly unlikely locales (see, e.g., Lipkov and Mathew 1994). This global dimension of Indian cinema would be better characterized as "international" rather than transnational, as it involved no particular presence of Indians themselves, nor any particular flows of content or personnel back to India itself. It did, however, spawn a few distinctive hybrid music genres, especially Indonesian *dangdut*, which combines Indian-style rhythms and instrumental idioms with international pop and rock sounds.

A different sort of internationalization of Indian popular music developed in tandem with the growth of diasporic South Asian (including Pakistani) communities abroad. The earliest, and perhaps still most vibrant, such scene has been that of immigrant, primarily Punjabi, communities in Great Britain, who were attaining sizeable numbers by the 1950s. The Punjab—and especially the Indian Punjab—had since the 1960s been host to one of South Asia's most lively regional popular music scenes, flourishing independently of mainstream Hindi film music. The cassette boom of the 1980s, which precipitated the flourishing of regional pop music genres, further nourished Punjabi music, even as sectarian violence crippled the live entertainment scene (not to mention other aspects of life) in the Indian Punjab. Meanwhile, since the 1960s, a remarkable vogue of amateur social and stage dancing had emerged, in the form of "bhangra" troupes—often based at colleges or other institutions—who performed vigorous and festive choreographies as creative reinventions of the region's folk dances.

By this time the Punjabi immigrant communities in British cities such as London and Birmingham had attained a size, self-confidence, and hybrid ethnic identity that enabled and inspired its younger generation to create their own popular music and social dance scene as a uniquely Indo-British parallel to counterparts in India. While bearing obvious links to the latter, the UK *bhangra* scene was centered around social dance more than stage dance groups, and it featured songs with short, light lyrics (often of the "Hey, let's dance" variety) in accordance with the fact that many of its enthusiasts were second-generation immigrants who no longer spoke much Punjabi. Punjabi music in India, by contrast, tends to be highly text-driven, with lyrics about love, social themes, or machismo. Accordingly, the audiences for the two sister genres were in many ways distinct, with 1980s UK groups like Heera and Alaap having little visibility in India. Some UK *bhangra* also incorporated rhythms of contemporary reggae, reflecting the community's social interactions with West Indian immigrants. Another manifestation of this interaction was the music of second-generation Punjabi Steve Kapur, who, under the sobriquet Apache Indian, enjoyed some popularity as a dance-hall reggae artist, with clever lyrics and album covers playfully juxtaposing his South Asian ethnicity and West Indian orientations in a sense of postmodern *jouissance*. In their self-conscious hybridity and creative vitality, both Kapur and the UK *bhangra* scene—which spread to other Punjabi outposts in the West—attracted the interest of several academics (e.g., Banerji and Baumann 1990, Banerji 1988, Maira 1998, Zuberi 2001).

While in many ways idiosyncratically Western, the UK *bhangra* scene was in some respects transnational, especially insofar as it became part of what could be seen as a larger Punjabi popular music network. People of Punjabi origin—both Indian and Pakistani—constitute the largest South Asian regional diasporic group, with many sizeable communities in Europe and North America. Although divided by religion (either Muslim, Sikh, or Hindu) and national origin, Punjabis are at least potentially united by a shared language and expressive culture. Moreover, unlike the Bhojpuri labor diaspora long since cut off from contact with the region of its origin, the Punjabi diaspora communities have retained many links with South Asia, via chain migrations, family visits, and, increasingly, a popular-music culture that, whether via the internet or touring musicians, comfortably traverses international boundaries (except, to a considerable extent, those between India and Pakistan). Even differences of religion and national origin that might divide Pakistani and Indian Punjabis can be to a considerable extent overshadowed by the vogue of Punjabi popular songs celebrating the identity of Jats, the dominant caste in the Punjab, encompassing members of all three religions. Whether or not foreign-born Punjabis retain fluency in the Punjabi language, many avidly cultivate an interest and pride in maintaining Punjabi identity, especially Jat values of machismo, hard work, hard play, and a love of dancing (Mooney 2011, 2013, Gera Roy 2015).

Accordingly, the manifestations of this transnational music culture are to be found both in the diaspora as well as South Asia itself. A city such as Vancouver may contain many Canadian-born Punjabis who speak only English and have no particular interest in being Punjabi. However, it will also host several thousand people of Punjabi origin who maintain links with relatives in South Asia and who enthusiastically and proudly cultivate their identity as Punjabis (and most typically, as Jats). Music may in fact be the most prominent element in such an identity, such that enthusiasts, whether fluent in Punjabi or not, may dance *bhangra* at weddings and parties and use the internet to keep abreast of new songs and videos, whether produced in India or elsewhere. Meanwhile, in the Punjab itself, many people retain links with relatives abroad and may have traveled there themselves. Music videos reflect and reinforce this perspective, easily juxtaposing scenes of proud Jats driving tractors with those of compatriots cavorting in some picturesque European locale. Production credits at the end of videos typically feature individuals based everywhere from Patiala, India, to Portland, Oregon (see Gera Roy 2009, 2010, 2015; Schreffler 2012).

Given Punjab's relatively long history of emigration, the international connections have come to extend beyond the landowning Jats even to the Chamars, a caste of untouchables, or *dalits*, who number more than three million in the Indian Punjab. Chamars have historically been subjected to the same sorts of oppression and discrimination as have *dalits* elsewhere in India. In recent generations, however, many have escaped the tyranny of village Jats by urbanizing, acquiring education, availing themselves of government affirmative-action-type opportunities, and moving into the working and lower-middle classes. In recent decades, many have also emigrated, establishing communities throughout the West (including non-Anglophone countries such as Spain and Italy). Remittances from such emigrants have heavily subsidized the independent Chamar-based religious institutions venerating the sixteenth-century saint Ravidas, which have sprung up throughout the Indian Punjab as well as abroad wherever critical masses of emigrant Chamars exist. Since around 2008, Chamars have also cultivated their own popular-music movement, asserting their caste pride and their defiance of Jat exploitation. As production credits in their videos indicate, funding from expatriate communities has played a significant role in this musical movement, and Chamars proudly foreground their own community members who drive Hummers and wear fashionable clothes, both in India and abroad (see Gera Singh 2015, Lum 2014, Singh 2017).

It should be kept in mind that such internationalism is by no means universal among Indian regional popular-music cultures. Bollywood dance scenes may routinely depict fashionable global locales, showing the lovers dancing through Dutch tulip fields and Parisian parks (Bhattacharya 2009), but most Indian regions have not generated such substantial emigrant communities as has the Punjab. Thus, for example, both the Bhojpuri and Braj regions of North India have fostered their own lively popular-music scenes, centered around music videos (disseminated on VCD discs, the internet, and USB sticks). However, these videos have their own thematic conventions, which almost never feature scenes outside of India (see, e.g., Manuel 2014).

A case study: the greater New York City region

A useful perspective on transnational dimensions of Indian music culture may be obtained through a closer, albeit still cursory, look at a particular representative global city, namely

New York City and its surroundings. This tri-state region, comprising nearby environs of New York, New Jersey, and Connecticut, is now home to at least 800,000 persons of South Asian origin (primarily Indians, but also Pakistanis, Bangladeshis, and Indo-Caribbeans). Over the decades the area has also evolved into a hub of activity for South Asian performing arts.

In accordance with changing American immigration policies, New York's South Asian community emerged decades later than counterparts in the urban United Kingdom. Whereas the Luce-Celler Act of 1946 had allowed entry to only one hundred Indian immigrants per year, the Immigration and Nationality Act of 1965 opened doors to Indian immigration by removing national-origin quotas and giving preference to highly educated, skilled workers. Subsequently, the New York region's South Asian population came to be the largest in the US, comprising a high proportion of Indians of upper- and middle-class backgrounds. As compared to the Canadian, UK, and even prior US South Asian diasporas, which historically have been predominantly from the Punjab, the New York-area diaspora is regionally diverse, including, for example, many Gujaratis and Tamils.

Indian classical music in the metropolis

Indian classical music got off to a somewhat later start in the New York region than on the west coast of the US, where Ravi Shankar had founded the (short-lived) Kinnara School of Music in Los Angeles in 1967 and his brother-in-law opened the still-extant Ali Akbar Khan College of Music in the San Francisco Bay Area in 1967. Through the 1980s the New York area hosted only a few skilled resident performers and teachers, along with a lower stratum of sitarists and accompanists, typically of ordinary proficiency, who played in the windows of the row of Indian (primarily Bangladeshi-owned) restaurants on 6th St. in the East Village. A visiting Indian soloist might well have to fly tabla-player Shyam Kane from the West Coast in order to have an accompanist for his or her concert. Audiences for classical music grew slowly, as from 1985 the non-profit World Music Institute, directed by Robert Browning, came to regularly include visiting Indian musicians and dancers in its numerous concerts. North Indian performers considerably outnumbered South Indians in these events, and audiences might comprise roughly equal numbers of Anglo-Americans and South Asians.

By the early 1990s, however, the area's South Asian population had reached a critical mass that enabled it to set up its own networks of both private and quasi-institutional teaching contexts and concerts, whether in theaters or private homes. Audiences and students in these contexts soon came to feature more PIO's (persons of Indian origin) than Anglo-Americans, and the South Indian music scene, especially in New Jersey, came to be particularly lively, with hundreds of second-generation children (especially girls) learning to competently sing *kritis* and dance *bharatanatyam*. (Quite a few, meanwhile, have also taken up Western classical music, sometimes attaining impressive virtuosity.) Since that decade the growing population of upwardly mobile Indian Americans has also founded a substantial number of non-profit arts organizations, which are too numerous and diverse to be accurately counted. These would include at least two dozen organizations specifically dedicated to classical music/dance and at least fifty other organizations that intermittently sponsor Indian arts programs. These organizations have played an important role in maintaining interest in Indian culture broadly, and a few such local exemplars may be mentioned here in order to illustrate general trends in their form.

The Carnatic Music Association of North American (CMANA), founded in 1976, is a non-profit organization based in New Jersey. CMANA caters primarily to the highly discerning and dedicated local South Indian community; audiences at its events are almost entirely Indian, in contrast, for example, to those at North Indian concerts in New York City. CMANA concerts are often longer than those in the City, and they feature both established artists as well as daughters and protégées of local Indians.

Chhandayan, founded by an enterprising Bengali tabla player, is an organization devoted primarily to Hindustani music, offering private and group lessons as well as small lecture-demonstrations, talks, and performances in its Manhattan facility. Most of the students are Indians. Chhandayan is perhaps best known for its Annual All-Night Concert, featuring top-level visiting artists and affording listeners otherwise scarce opportunities to hear morning *rāgs*.

Also in midtown Manhattan is another organization, Navatman Inc., dedicated primarily to *bharatanatyam* and *kathak* dance, along with lessons in Hindustani and Carnatic music; most students are of Indian origin. Navatman also houses a respected *bharatanatyam* dance troupe (Navatman Dance) and a chorus, the Navatman Music Collective, which performs choral versions of Carnatic songs and occasionally *ghazals* and Bollywood numbers. Navatman also curates a weeklong summer concert series called "Drive East." As might be expected, the concerts and classes sponsored by the organizations serve as sites for lively social interactions as well as arts showcases.

There are also organizations that combine classical music with other genres. One unique entity is Brooklyn Raga Massive (BRM), consisting of a loose collective of artists of diverse musical backgrounds, including skilled performers of Indian music as well as Western classical or jazz musicians who dabble in Indian music. Around two-thirds are Indian. This aesthetic diversity and originality are showcased in weekly concerts that have included concepts such as "Women's Raga Massive" (an all-female ensemble), "Raga Cubana" (synthesizing Indian classical music and Cuban music), and "Coltrane Raga Tribute," a mix of jazz and Indian classical music. Every weekly performance—usually on Thursday evenings, at one venue or another—is followed by an open jam session featuring the performing ensemble.

Organizations that attempt to rely solely on concerts in order to sustain themselves tend to be more ephemeral and financially unstable. Overall, audiences in New Jersey are more Indian-dominated than those in the City, where organizations may deliberately target non-Indian audiences. Meanwhile, audiences and students have come to include many Indian visitors or migrants who had not formerly been able or inclined to pursue music in India itself. Classes are tailored according to demand. Hence vocal classes—which need not involve the purchase and maintenance of instruments—outnumber students of *vina* and *mrdangam* classes, although skilled performers of these instruments do teach privately. Girls far outnumber boys among students, and students of Carnatic music and dance seem to outnumber those of North Indian music and *kathak*, perhaps because the latter's pedagogy and performance styles are less structured. It would be incorrect, for example, to regard Carnatic music as "easier" than Hindustani music, but a Carnatic student of limited talent can make considerable headway learning pre-composed *kritis* by rote, whereas a student of Hindustani music must soon develop skill at improvisation in order to make any progress (except, perhaps, in tabla, with its substantial repertoire of compositions). Carnatic music has a well-established curriculum that makes it particularly suitable for large groups of children (gifted or not). New Jersey's South Indians—and perhaps especially the Brahmans therein—have shown themselves to be to be particularly ardent supporters of the fine arts, with the *arangetram* performance of Carnatic music or *bharatanatyam* serving as a common rite of passage for teenage girls. Some critics, however, disparage the competitive spirit with which some parents promote their daughters, including, as mentioned above, the effects these efforts have on the arts scene in Chennai itself.

As is typical of fine arts programs anywhere, most students do not go on to become professional or even semi-professional performers, especially given the high career ambitions of so many American NRI families (Saran, 2015). It is not unusual for a concert to feature, for example, an outstanding young female Carnatic vocalist who, the program notes mention, is also a neurosurgeon, or an attorney. Nonetheless, the area does host a handful of Indian Americans—usually of middle-class rather than artisan backgrounds—who manage to make careers for themselves as performing artists and teachers, perhaps mixing teaching with performing various forms of either traditional or "fusion" music.

Non-profit organizations of course are not the only spaces that bring the Indian community together, or that present music. Many Hindu temples such as New Jersey's Chinmaya Vrindavan also regularly sponsor both music and dance. WKCR 89.9 FM NY, Columbia University's radio station, also has long offered weekly Indian classical music programing as well as a twenty-four-hour Indian music festival titled Raga's Live Festival, which BRM helps to coordinate.

Universities and regional musics

Universities constitute another arena in which Indian arts have been flourishing, but in quite a different manner. Although very few American colleges offer any instruction in Indian classical arts, some student-run organizations either focus on them or work with non-profits to bring the arts onto campus. For example, the Society for the Promotion of Indian Classical Music and Culture Amongst Youth (SPIC-MACAY) is an international non-profit that is well known for partnering with colleges to promote Indian classical music. Nonetheless, popular genres are by far the most liked by student organizations, and some neo-folk genres, mostly *bhangra* and *garba*, are also common. On campuses, the number of student organizations as well as their demographics differs dramatically based on the school's general population. The largest state university in New Jersey, Rutgers New Brunswick (RU), has roughly twenty different South Asian organizations, roughly half of which are devoted to music or dance.

Regardless of how many student groups a school has, the South Asian population tends to make its presence known through largely popular or neo-folk music and dance performances. Though these college-based groups remain predominantly South Asian, it is not uncommon for a few non-South Asians to join, especially in the case of dance teams. Student organizations regularly host events in which they present original choreography that draws heavily from Bollywood, *bhangra*, and American popular music and dance. These performances often involve months of rehearsals, and for students who remain part of an organization throughout their undergraduate career, "Bollywood music and dance" can effectively constitute a sort of second major. The better dance teams (such as New York University's Pandemonium, or University of Texas's Nach Baliye, and University of Michigan's Manzil) compete for bragging rights in Indian dance competitions throughout the US, some of which are highlighted on local South Asian channels such as AVS TV. When these students get married some years after completing college, it is often the old dance team that reconvenes to perform for the wedding.

Having amateur dance performances at a wedding is almost obligatory, even if only for the social media representation. Moreover, as social media have grown along with the ease of recording high quality video, wedding performances have become even more visible. There are organizations that offer wedding performance services, but even if they are used, there will still likely be a dance performance by a few close friends or family members. Women tend to predominate among the dancers in such routines, while men often enact comedic roles.

Another South Asian university phenomenon is *a cappella* (unaccompanied vocal) music. Like dance teams, *a cappella* groups come out of university clubs and blend Bollywood and American genres into original arrangements. Some of the groups, such as University of

Pennsylvania's Penn Masala (whose innovative arrangements are accessible on YouTube), are very popular, but overall *a cappella* has not been nearly as widespread as dance.

Meanwhile, there is a great abundance of young South Asian DJs, whose "instruments" are the laptop or turntable rather than *vina* or sitar. There are many South Asian young men (and a few women, such as New York's DJ Rekha) who work semi-professionally as DJs, especially in high school and college. They often perform at university events and weddings, specializing in playing and remixing current music from Bollywood, *bhangra*, and the US hit parade. Some of these DJs offer their services for *garba* events, but might on occasion run out of *garba* tunes and resort to *bhangra* mid-dance. In addition to family and college parties there is also a club scene for Indian DJs. The New York area hosts several nightclubs that present weekly events such as "Desi Saturdays" for South Asians, and there are also a few hookah lounges and nightclubs that cater to South Asians. The campus and club scenes offer much of the same style of music, but within clubs, reggae, Latin American, and electronic music are more regularly included in remixes (see Maira 1998, 2002, Kvetko 2003).

Holidays and Festivals

The holidays of Navaratri, Diwali, Holi, and Indian Independence Day attract considerable attention in the South Asian diaspora. As with the popularity of *bhangra* in the Canadian and UK diasporas, these Indian holidays to some degree transcend their original regional or religious associations and may be attended by diverse members of the South Asian community, as well as handfuls of non-South Asians, including friends or spouses of South Asians.

The Hindu festival of Navaratri is celebrated in the autumn for nine nights in praise of the goddess Durga. Diwali, the festival of lights, is also a fall festival and is traditionally observed by many Jains and Buddhists as well as Hindus. These two holidays, sometimes combined and advertised as Navaratri/Diwali for events, are celebrated with food and performances by both non-profit organizations, temples, and college clubs. Another popular activity during this time is *garba*, a Gujarati genre of collective dance and music celebrated during Navaratri nights. New Jersey has a large Gujarati population, and every year there are many venues for *rās-garba*. In Jersey City, for example, during Navarati the Indian-dominated neighborhood known to locals as "Indian Square" is blocked off for live music and all-night *garba* dancing. The event is free, and vendors line the sidewalks with food, beverages, and *dandiyas* (sticks used for *rās-garba* dancing). Many other cities in the state, such as Somerset, offer indoor ticketed *garba* dances, and college organizations do their best to stagger their *garba* events as to not lose audiences to competing events.

Holi is celebrated with particular enthusiasm in the New York area. Holi celebrations, with their customary spraying of colored water and powder, happen in parks and public areas in cities throughout New York City and urban New Jersey as well as on some college campuses. Festivities may also be accompanied by dance and music, whether enlivened by a single dhol player, a more extensive stage group, or choreographed dance team cavorting to familiar favorites such as "Hori Khele Raghuveera," "Do Me a Favour Let's Play Holi." However, the largest Holi (or "Phagwa") celebrations are those in Queens' Richmond Hill neighborhood, where many thousands of Indo-Caribbeans (Guyanese, Trinidadians, and some Surinamese) throng to spray powder, dance to *tāssa* drumming, and sing *chowtāl* (the aforementioned rowdy Doab-derived genre, sung mostly by temple groups, in which antiphonal groups of singers negotiate Braj Bhasha verses through lively and complex rhythmic modulations [see Manuel 2009].)

Both Indian Independence (August 15th), and Pakistani Independence (August 14th) are celebrated with parades in New York City. The Indian parade tends to be much larger and generally attracts more famous South Asian celebrities. Many of the floats include DJs and/or dancers, and the parade ends at a stage, where there will be a few speeches followed by many performances. This is a context in which distinctions between classical, folk, and popular are irrelevant, and the day tends to be dominated by fusion-type dances. Folk drumming and dancing also enliven New York City's Sikh Day Parade, which invariably features floats dedicated to the memory of Sant Bhindranwale and the Khalistan cause; as might be imagined, Punjabi Hindus would be unlikely to join such an event.

High school in the South Asian diaspora

I (Fludd) may draw on my own recollections to give some sense of the South Asian cultural atmosphere in a high school in the aforementioned New York suburb of Jersey City. Though I am not of South Asian descent, my upbringing in this community was greatly informed and enriched by engagement with South Asian culture. My high school experiences in particular are characteristic of many individuals in the local South Asian diaspora. Demographically, Jersey City (pop. ca. 280,000) is one the most South Asian cities in the region, and Dickinson High School (DHS) is located on the same street as "Indian Square." As such, about twenty percent of the DHS student population is South Asian—especially Gujaratis, Indian and Pakistani Punjabis, and smaller proportions of other Indians. Only a few members of my South Asian cohort were born in the US, and the majority immigrated between the ages of three and ten. Mornings and lunch periods were often spent listening to the latest Bollywood songs and discussing movies and gossip. About once a month we went to the local theater, often to see Bollywood movies and enjoy snacks of samosas as well as popcorn. Like much of the South Asian diaspora, Bollywood music and culture served within DHS as a unifier of pan-South Asian identity, but each regional group still proudly maintained and displayed its own identity. For example, the Punjabis kept the rest of us up to date with the latest *bhangra* music, while the Gujaratis showed us how to dance *rās-garba* during Navratri season. For their part, the Pakistani students jokingly conceded that Lollywood, Pakistan's Bollywood equivalent, only produced a few good songs a year.

In many ways DHS, with some three thousand students, functioned like a small college. Each student chose a major, and there was even a diverse array of student organizations. The Pakistani Student Organization, for example, organized an annual dinner party for the Muslim holiday Eid-al-Adha, featuring Pakistani food and dancing to mostly Bollywood music. The other groups organized similar events. Once a year the school held a multicultural festival, which put all the different cultural organizations on display. Multicultural Day was the only exception to the uniform policy, when students were encouraged to dress in their best cultural attire. Each of the student groups put on a dance performance, and afterward there was a barbecue along with regional food from each organization. There was always fierce competition between the different South Asian groups during the performance portion of Multicultural Day. And, just as is the case with university organizations, students carefully remixed music and created elaborate original dances. Often the Punjabi performances were the most popular due to superior music selection and highly acrobatic dances.

Concluding perspectives

One of the most striking features of Indian diasporas is the sheer range of types they comprise, from the Indo-Caribbean and Indo-Fijian isolated transplant labor diasporas, to the more recent peregrinations of upper-class cosmopolitans who move easily between subcontinental and Western sites and affiliations. In all these communities, musical practices, whether dividing or uniting people, may provide particularly tangible indications of cultural orientations, and indeed may even constitute sites where such orientations are enacted, formed, and rearticulated. A comprehensive perspective would, of course, include the second- or third-generation POI immigrant who, for whatever reasons, has no interest in maintaining any South Asian identity and who regards Bollywood and its music as risible kitsch. More common, however, is for POIs to situate themselves in what Levitt and Glick-Schiller (2004), drawing on Bourdieu, call a "social field," in which, in this case, individuals can position themselves, in various ways, in various contexts, and to varying degrees, in networks of affiliation to a transnational Indianness.

As suggested above, perhaps the most tenuous and least transnational constituents of this social field would be the Indo-Caribbeans, most of whom retain a strong sense of ethnic pride while long having lost contact with the ancestral Bhojpuri-region homeland. Some of them enjoy Bollywood music and respect the pandits who can return from India with fresh *bhajans*. However, as mentioned, they have also cultivated their own forms of Indian music, whether nineteenth-century transplants like *chowtāl*, distinctively local but thoroughly Indian entities like *tāssa* or local-classical music, or hybrids like chutney-soca. Ultimately, such POIs have created their own local forms of Indianness, in which contemporary subcontinental connections are relatively unimportant. And while Indo-Caribbeans and NRIs may occasionally rub shoulders in New York, on the whole the two communities have relatively little interaction with each other, socially or musically. Musical practices are again an important affiliation symbol; some Indo-Caribbeans feel that despite having lost their ability to speak Hindi, they are nevertheless more active in maintaining folk traditions like *chowtāl* than are the "India people," who, they feel, are more interested in making money than in cultivating such rustic arts (see Manuel 1997–1998, 2015).

More characteristically transnational are the more recent waves of immigrants, for whom music may constitute a particularly salient reflection and component of identity formation. In forming social fields, of course, music can divide as well as unite, with, for example, diasporic Gujaratis and Punjabis gravitating toward their respective *garba* and *bhangra* dances and North and South Indian classical music fans preferring their own regional styles. While such constituencies might naturally be represented as discrete shaded regions in a Venn diagram, they would also have to be seen as constituting parts of a broad, all-encompassing socio-musical field that clearly transcends nation-state boundaries, in ways that are characteristically transnational. Hence, for example, the Cleveland Thyagaraja Festival that is as substantial and respected as any music conference in South India; the America-born teenager of Tamil parents who can get as good a classical music training from a local guru—perhaps supplemented by occasional Skype lessons with a pandit in India—as she could get in India itself; the Indo-Guyanese *pujāri*—descendent of Tamil villagers who migrated in the 1850s—in a New York "Madrasi" Mariamman temple who seeks to improve his repertoire of chants and songs by finding relevant South Indian clips on YouTube (Jackson 2016); and quite often, the American-born, broken-Hindi-speaking twenty-something-year-old, whose family is split between, say, Birmingham and Delhi and who attends family weddings in both sites, merrily participating in lively Bollywood dance routines with the same repertoire of songs and moves. All these individuals may move freely in and out of different social fields which align them variously toward either incorporation and assimilation in the new homeland, or, alternately, some form of transnational Indianness. Music—even more than language and religion—may often constitute the single most important entity in representing and actively forming such transnational social identities.

References

Banerji, Sabita. 1988. "Ghazals to Bhangra in Great Britain." *Popular Music* 7(2): 203–13.
Banerji, Sabita, and Gerd Baumann. 1990. "Bhangra 1984–8: Fusion and Professionalization in a Genre of South Asian Dance Music." In *Black Music in Britain: Essays on the Afro-Asian Contribution to Popular Music*, ed. Paul Oliver. Milton Keynes: Open University.
Bhattacharya, Nilanjana. 2009. "Popular Hindi Film Song Sequences Set in the Indian Diaspora and the Negotiating of Indian Identity." *Asian Music* 40(1): 53–82.
Farrell, Gerry. 1997. *Indian Music and the West*. Oxford: Clarendon Press, and New York, NY: Oxford University Press.
Gera Roy, Angela. 2009. "Black, White and Brown on the Dance Floor: The New Meanings of Panjabiyat in the Twenty-first Century." In *The Ashgate Research Companion to Popular Musicology*. Burlington, VT: Ashgate.
Gera Roy, Angela. 2010. *Bhangra Moves from Ludhiana to London and Beyond*. Aldershot: Ashgate.
Gera Roy, Angela. 2015. "Becoming Men in the Global Village: Young Sikhs Reenacting Bhangra Masculinities." In *Young Sikhs In a Global World: Negotiating Traditions, Identities and Authorities*, ed. Knut Jacobsen and Kristina Myrvold, 167–87. London and Burlington: Ashgate.
Jackson, Stephanie. 2016. "From Stigma to Shakti: The Politics of Indo-Guyanese Women's Trance and the Transformative Potentials of Ecstatic Goddess Worship in New York City." In *Indo-Caribbean Feminist Thought: Genealogies, Theories, Enactments*, ed. Gabrielle Jamela Hosein and Lisa Outar, 301–20. New York, NY: Palgrave MacMillan.
Krishnan, T.M. 2013. *A Southern Music: Exploring the Karnatik Tradition*. Noida: HarperCollins India.
Kvetko, Peter. 2003. "When the East is in the House: The Emergence of Dance Club Culture among Indian-Americans." *Sagar* XII: 1–18.
Levitt, Peggy, and Nina Glick-Schiller. 2004. "Conceptualizing Simultaneity: A Transnational Social Field Perspective on Society." *International Migration Review* 38(3): 1002–39.
Lipkov, Alexander, and Thomas J. Mathew. 1994. "India's Bollywood in Russia." *India International Centre Quarterly* 21(2/3): 185–94.
Lum, Kathryn. 2014. "Manufacturing Self-Respect: Stigma, Pride and Cultural Juggling among Dalit Youth in Spain." In *New Multicultural Identities in Europe: Religion and Ethnicity in Secular Societies*, ed. Erkan Toğuşlu, Johan Leman, and İsmail Mesut Sezgin, 95–118. Leuven: Leuven University Press.
Maira, Sunaina. 1998. "Desis Reprazent: Bhangra Remix and Hip-Hop in New York City." *Postcolonial Studies* 1(3): 357–70.
Maira, Sunaina. 2002. *Desis in the House: Indian American Youth Culture in New York City*. Philadelphia, PA: Temple University Press.
Manuel, Peter. 1993. *Cassette Culture: Popular Music and Technology in North India*. Chicago, IL: University of Chicago Press, 1993.
Manuel, Peter. 1998. "Chutney and Indo-Trinidadian Cultural Identity." *Popular Music* 17(1): 21–43.
Manuel, Peter. 1997–1998. "Music, Identity, and Images of India in the Indo-Caribbean Diaspora." *Asian Music* 29(1): 17–36.
Manuel, Peter. 2000. *East Indian Music in the West Indies: Tan-Singing, Chutney, and the Making of Indo-Caribbean Culture*. Philadelphia, PA: Temple University Press.
Manuel, Peter. 2009. "Transnational Chowtal: Bhojpuri Folksong from North India to the Caribbean, Fiji, and Beyond." *Asian Music* 40(2): 1–32.
Manuel, Peter. 2014. "The Regional North Indian Popular Music Industry in 2014: From Cassette Culture to Cyberculture." *Popular Music* 33(3): 389–412.
Manuel, Peter. 2015. *Tales, Tunes, and Tassa Drums: Retention and Invention in Indo-Caribbean Music*. Urbana, IL: University of Illinois Press.
Mooney, Nicola. 2011. *Rural Nostalgias and Transnational Dreams: Identity and Modernity among Jat Sikhs*. Toronto: University of Toronto Press.

Mooney, Nicola. 2013. "Dancing in Diaspora Space: Bhangra, Caste, and Gender among Jat Sikhs." In *Sikh Diaspora: Theory, Agency, and Experience*, ed. Michael Hawley, 279–318. Leiden: Koninklijke Brill.

Pillai, Shanti. 2002. "Rethinking Global Indian Dance Through Local Eyes: The Contemporary Bharatanatyam Scene in Chennai." *Dance Research Journal* 34(2): 14–29.

Pollock, Sheldon. 2006. *The Language of the Gods in the World of Men: Sanskrit, Culture, and Power in Premodern India*. Berkeley and Los Angeles, CA: University of California Press.

Saran, Rupam. 2015. *Navigating Model Minority Stereotypes: Asian Indian Youth in South Asian Diaspora*. New York, NY: Routledge.

Schreffler, Gibb. 2012. "Migration Shaping Media: Punjabi Popular Music in Global Historical Perspective." *Popular Music and Society* 35(5): 333–58.

Shankar, Ravi. 1999. *Raga Mala: An Autobiography*. New York, NY: Welcome Rain.

Singh, Santosh. 2017. "The Caste Question and Songs of Protest in Punjab." *Economic and Political Weekly* 52(34).

Zuberi, Irfan. 2001. *Sounds English: Transnational Popular Music*. Urbana and Chicago, IL: University of Illinois Press.

7
TRANSNATIONAL COLLABORATIONS BY SELECTED CONTEMPORARY INDIAN DANCERS

Ketu H. Katrak

Transnationalism in the 21st century operates in economic, geopolitical, and artistic areas among others. In this essay I analyze collaborations among dancer-choreographers belonging to different geographical regions unfolding in contemporary times—late 20th and into the 21st century. Intercultural links such as between dancers in India and those in the US or Canada, namely global South to global North connections, receive more critical attention than the global South to South collaborations that I propose to discuss here. I explore this arena by focusing on two contemporary Indian dancers, namely Astad Deboo's contemporary collaborations with artists in South Korea, and Vikram Iyengar's South–South cultural exchanges between India and Bangladesh. Their work enables me to address questions and concerns such as what such artistic endeavors bring to both sides of the South–South artistic exchanges; what artists and audiences gain and learn from such intercultural linkages; and the significant realities of funding and producing such work across national boundaries.

In contemporary times, there are new and different power dynamics than those which existed in the early 20th century—between Indian and Western dancers, such as Uday Shankar's work with Anna Pavlova—when Asia was still very much under the shadow of stereotypical Orientalist views that influenced unequal power relations between artists. The period of the post-1980s, with the impacts of globalization and the internet on daily lives and aesthetic engagements of dancers, musicians, and scholars, enables innovative dialogues on a more equal playing field among artists than in earlier periods, along with new challenges.

Astad Deboo's name is synonymous with the genre of Contemporary Indian Dance; indeed, he is recognized as a pioneer of this style, recipient of the Sangeet Natak Akademi Award in 1996, a Padma Shri in 2007 from the Government of India. Previously I have engaged with the nearly four-decade career of his contemporary choreography, marked significantly with *rasa*, in my book entitled *Contemporary Indian Dance: New Creative Choreography in India and the Diaspora* (Katrak 2014). However, in that book I explored Deboo's different solo and group dance located within India, using masks or puppets, or his choreography for the deaf community, or with Manipur's martial arts *thang-ta* practitioners as well as with *pungcholam*, i.e., drum-dancers. Deboo has danced across India and in nearly 70 countries world-wide. His work is described as poetry in motion. In this essay I analyze Deboo's explorations and collaborations across India's national boundaries, and although he has worked with artists in Europe and the US, I focus on his work within the global South, in particular his artistic exchanges with the InKo Centre in Korea.

Deboo's collaboration with Korean artists was facilitated by an important individual, namely, Rathi Jafer, Director of the InKo Centre based in Chennai.[1] This is an arts and culture initiative supported by Chennai industrialist T. Srinivasan. InKo Centre undertakes different projects such as working with children, organizing ceramics camps, and holding writer's workshops. For prominent artists such as Deboo, they provide funding for a 3-month residency in Korea to develop a project and to conduct research on its theme and form, providing enough time for this phase before its presentation. Rathi Jafer comments that this

> research phase is an important aspect of all collaborations that we undertake so that there is sufficient time built in to the project for artists to share and respectfully absorb each other's artistic vocabularies. We do strongly believe that if this phase is missed out or too rushed, the resultant outcome is at best a hurried fusion with no real attempt to find, however fleetingly that 'shared space' that lies at the heart of any effective collaborative enterprise.
>
> *(Jafer 2018)*

Such objectives create an effective working environment where artists crossing national and artistic boundaries have enough time and opportunity to explore similarities and differences in their styles, techniques, and aesthetic approaches. "The mandate" as explained by Jafer is

> to meaningfully deepen and strengthen the intercultural dialogues between India and South Korea . . . to promote an inter-cultural dialogue that drawing on the rich traditions of both India and Korea, will look at the global dimension of such a dialogue while showcasing the local and national characteristics that underpin such exchange.
>
> *(Jafer 2018)*

In this articulation of interculturalism, Jafer indicates that through artists themselves exploring their traditional movements styles, they would reach for a "global dimension"; in other words, first honoring the local, and then moving from that base to the global. This is a noteworthy difference from usual intercultural exchanges that are mounted by prominent Western dancers and theater directors who borrow, appropriate, and in other ways work with or exploit traditional arts. This top-down approach exerts power asymmetrically, since usually, the Western artist or scholar is equipped with funding and other professional support, though with varying degrees of expertise in the traditional arts. In contrast, Jafer advocates intercultural exchanges that are enabled between and among artists of different cultures who come to such experiences with respect and willingness to share, learn, and even transform certain traditional forms of movement or music in the interest of creating new illuminations for artists and spectators.[2]

In order to situate this kind of exemplary collaborative process fostered by the InKo Centre, it is important to recognize a body of scholarship on interculturalism from the 1990s into the present with prominent Western players such as the British Peter Brook or the American Richard Schechner and, at an earlier time, Polish Jerzy Grotowski.[3] In such cultural exchanges, power is expressed not only via funding but also is exerted via colonial(ist) and Oriental(ist) attitudes to traditional cultures of South and Southeast Asia. Such hierarchical transactions in recent memory (not even going back to the beginning of the 20th century), include Peter

Brooks' adaptation/version of *The Mahabharata*. In the words of India's highly respected theater scholar, Rustom Bharucha:

> Peter Brooks' *Mahabharata* exemplifies one of the most blatant (and accomplished) appropriations of Indian culture in recent years. Very different in tone from the Raj revivals, it nonetheless suggests the bad old days of the British Raj, not in its direct allusions to colonial history—the *Mahabharata*, after all, deals with our "ancient" past, our "authentic" record of traditional Hindu culture. For Brooks' Vyasa, it is nothing less than "the poetical history of mankind." Within such a grandiose span of time, where does the Raj fit? Not thematically or chronologically, I would argue, but through the very enterprise of the work itself: its appropriation and reordering of non-western material within an orientalist framework of thought and action, which has been specifically designed for the international market.
>
> *(Bharucha 1993: 68)*

Bharucha has also engaged in critical exchanges with US-based theater scholar Richard Schechner, who was one of the early academically based proponents of Western artists and scholars who borrowed from traditional arts such as India's *kathakali* and brought those techniques into the classroom for American students.[4] Schechner is also well known for his "creation" of the "rasa boxes," an exercise that he evolved from *The Natyasastra*'s delineation of the *navarasas* (the nine primary emotions). What is missing in such endeavors is the vast history behind traditional forms and immersion in them as required by serious students and practitioners in their study and performance of these styles. Rather, hegemonic Western attitudes enter, often with arrogance, and borrow freely, at best decontextualizing the techniques and at worst making a mockery of traditional arts' intentions and purposes.

Another US-based theater artist, Robert Wilson, appropriated Chinese traditional material for consumption by westerners, even making these ancient cultures, which feel inaccessible to unknowledgeable viewers, marketable and appealing to a global audience. These are critiqued in Daphne Lei's path-breaking essay, "Interruption, Intervention, Interculturalism" (2011). Lei coins the acronym HIT that stands for "hegemonic intercultural theatre." She describes HIT as "a specific artistic genre and state of mind that combines First World capital and brainpower with Third World raw material and labor, and Western classical texts with Eastern performance traditions. Well-known practitioners of HIT include Peter Brook, Ariane Mnouchkine, and Richard Schechner, as well as their Eastern counterparts Suzuli Tadashi of Japan, the Contemporary Legend Theater of Taiwan, and to a certain extent, Ong Keng Sen of Singapore" (Lei 2011).

The India-Korea collaboration

Deboo performed as a dancer-actor in a theater project entitled *Hamlet Avataar*, directed by the prominent theater personality Hyoung-Taek Limb, well respected in Korea and beyond and Artistic Director of Seoul Factory. This unique creative work adapts Shakespeare's original play, with Indian and Korean dance, music, theater vocabularies, and the "avatar" as an underlying concept. In my phone interview with Astad, he described the process of how such a collaboration began and then was brought to fruition. Hyoung-Taek Limb had seen Astad perform with the Manipuri drummers (another of Astad's creative collaborations) and invited him to be part of the residency on the Hamlet project. Astad agreed and noted that he had a very positive experience and that indeed "it was a joy" to work with Limb. Deboo comments:

Being asked to be a part of Hamlet_Avataar project brings a new dimension to my work. It is a theatre production where I have been asked to act as well as be a cochoreographer. This, as well as the opportunity to have an exchange with the Korean theatre director Hyoung Taek Limb who is so multi-talented as well as such a dynamic force in the field of contemporary Korean Theatre, promises to be a very exciting creative and learning experience.

(InKo Centre "Hamlet_Avataar")

Hamlet Avataar brings together different cultural frameworks in its very subject and key participants that includes *Hamlet*, by English Renaissance playwright Shakespeare, the Indian dancer Deboo, the singer Parvati Baul, and a Korean director, Limb. Shakespeare's drama received a Korean interpretation as a musical, as indeed Shakespeare's text is richly available for adaptation and transposition in different contexts and regions of the world.[5] Director Limb describes Hamlet as a man "educated to be a thinker, but who becomes a man of action, motivated by the dark force of revenge" when he finds out about his father's murder (InKo Centre "Hamlet_Avataar"). Hamlet decides, remarks Limb, to "be a clown who can play the fictional truth. He now will live in the shape of his 'Avataar' Hamlet." As in any adaptation, Limb draws on contemporary concepts that resonate from Shakespeare's play, such as "dislocation, discord, disillusionment, collapse of family, betrayal." Limb aims to have his audience imagine and discover "our real avatar" not simply the superficial pursuit of money and power. He comments: "Hamlet Avataar is an exploration . . . a journey . . . seeking sublimation through Indian spiritual culture as well as its music and dance fused with Korean art forms."

Deboo portrayed Hamlet's father's ghost as well as the master of the play-makers within *Hamlet*, and another artist from India, Parvathy Baul, took on the role of Ophelia. Together these artists brought their own innovative energies into their portrayal of traditional dance and music styles such as *Kathak* danced by Deboo and the *baul* style of singing by Parvathy, one of a few women practitioners of this style of singing. They created a synergy of *kathak bols* and *baul* syllables, along with sounds and vocabularies on stage that made the production, in Jafer's words, "visually and aurally rich" (Jafer 2018). Parvathy Baul remarks that this was the first time that she "discovered the Korean artists and the Korean Tradition of theatre, music and dance. I was very touched to find similarities between the voice work of Pansori and the Baul tradition" (InKo Centre "Hamlet_Avataar"). She continues:

> In working with Seoul Factory, I discovered the way Korean contemporary theatre and dance practitioners are working for a new language through the universal story of "Hamlet" and the "crazy wisdom" within it. This language relates a lot to the ancient Asian philosophies and practices. As a Baul practitioner, I was discovering a new way to relate to others present in the group and to the story of Hamlet. . . . I even received a name from the Korean performers, "Pa-sem!" Sem means "teacher," and they could not pronounce my name, "Parvathy," so they shortened the name they gave me to "Pa-Sem! I was very impressed to see the Korean youth taking interest in Indian traditions.
>
> *(InKo Centre "Hamlet_Avataar")*

Baul's positive responses to the working methods of artists of Indian and Korean traditions demonstrate that this was a successful collaboration:

> The work process we had to go through for this performance was even more interesting as we discovered each other's individual style, practice and methodology. . . . With

this work, I had to find a new way to relate as a Baul performer, to bridge the gap between us, sometimes to "let go," to be able to connect. This "letting go" can happen when the artists and the group have found a way to have trust in each other and mutual respect for the work. I experienced throughout the work process when we were together for a week in August. I am looking forward to working a longer term in October, where we will have a greater possibility to discover each other through the story of Hamlet Avatar.

Hamlet Avataar premiered in India at The Hindu Theater Festival in August 2015; in October 2016 it was performed in Bengalaru and Chennai as well as presented at the Seoul Performing Arts Festival in Korea in October 2015, where Astad noted in my interview with him that he featured in 12 performances.

The 2017 music project entitled *Same-Same but Different* was spearheaded by a well-known Korean music group, *Noreum Machi*, with Artistic Director Juhongman. This group is well known for combining "traditional instrumentation with contemporary soundscapes" (Jafer 2018), though it mainly uses a variety of drums. Their project's aim to foster collaborations with musicians from across the world leads the music ensemble to select a country and its musicians to work with such as Japan, or Germany. When they were interested in India, Deboo worked through Jafer to bring three Indian musicians—a mridangam player, C. Manjunath (who has also played in productions of Akram Khan, based in London), and two Carnatic musicians, a female singer and a flute player, Praveen D. Rao and Varijashree. The Indian musicians were to collaborate with jazz music.

This production's young director was using Deboo as a dancer, but this collaboration was not as harmonious as the one on Hamlet, remarked Astad in my interview with him, and especially since Deboo had provided the Indian musicians. When Deboo was put in a position of taking "dictates" from the director without discussion or a collaborative spirit that is at the heart of these ventures, Rathi Jafer had to intervene. She reminded the director that artists have to work together, take input, have discussions, and come to agreements even as the director may structure and put the final presentation together. Eventually the performance was a success. Jafer's remarks are particularly positive about Astad's "superbly controlled, graceful movements [that] were a fantastic counterpoint to the rising crescendo of the percussion, the lilt of the gayageum, the mellifluous notes of the flute and the sonorous vocals" (Jafer 2018). This production had its premiere on October 20 at the National Theater in Korea and at Sarang, the Festival of India in Korea on October 21. The show will most likely tour India in 2019/2020.

Deboo performed a solo entitled, *Liminal* on October 25 at Jeju Stone Park, "a recent creation, a gallery and huge showcase of Korean art, architecture and design, a vast outdoor garden and sculpture park . . . on Jeju Island," as noted by Dr. Maynard Kirkpatrick (based in British Columbia) in a highly positive and lyrical review of Deboo's performance titled, "Late October on Jeju Island in South Korea."[6] Deboo's performance began on "a sunny afternoon" in this "unique and challenging setting for any dancer," comments Dr. Kirkpatrick, "and a challenge that Astad Deboo has succeeded beautifully in overcoming many times in his stellar international dance career." Deboo used the indoor and outdoor space creatively, "mounting the lip of a vast round pool of water flat to the horizon . . . as the skirt of his white costume absorbed the water and he invoked the spirit of the water with an anointing gesture." Next, with his feet and hands wet, Deboo "descended the steps from the caldera fountain" and enticed the audience to follow him "past a potters' field of large upturned earthen pots in symmetrical rows shimmering in the late afternoon sun as he and the nearby fields of Pampas grass waved everyone to the next performance venue . . . the opening to the great exhibition hall of the Stone Park." Now, with the sun tilting and casting elongated shadows on the stones, Deboo

> danced his tribute to all those modern-day stone-shapers who laboured to create and animate the park from Jeju's abundant inert stone. He danced the stones to life by casting his shadow on each, summoning life from the cold flat brown Herculean torsos, as each embraced the setting sun.

Another one of Deboo's South–South collaborations includes his work with Hong Kong Theatre Director Danny Yung, the Artistic director of Zuni Icosacherdron. Yung has been following Astad's career since the 1980s. Most recently he involved Astad in a 2016 theater work. Astad noted (in my March 2018 interview) that "it is amazing what this group does. Over 25 years, this theater director, a big name, an educator" has accomplished many projects. Astad worked as a facilitator for deaf groups in Hong Kong with another Hong Kong-based group, Mok Chin. Astad has a noteworthy track record of working with the deaf in Kolkata, in Chennai, and elsewhere, teaching the dancers his particular style of choreography with slow, minimalist movements, balancing poses and rigorous technique always underpinned by affect and emotion drawing from the Indian tradition of the *navarasas*. Astad noted an alternative dance company in Hong Kong entitled Y Space, which receives regional support and funds from different cultural groups, even the municipality of the area where they work.

Deboo's collaborative spirit welcomes working with theatre directors and dancers as well as with musicians and visual artists. Previously, in 2007, he collaborated in Japan with Japanese musician Keiko Harada, a well-known composer. Astad noted that the two connected very well as artists. Keiko Harada has also worked with Taiwanese dancer-choreographers, and currently his music is being performed in Europe. Astad also noted a residency program with Tokyo Wonder Site, though this is much more in the visual arts with a renowned Japanese theater director.

Deboo comments (interview 2018) that the main difference in collaborations within India from the ones between Indian artists such as himself with Korean artists is that, apart from good funding, the entire process of work is very methodical and professional. Each person is assigned a task, whether in production or in technology. The team works very hard. For instance, Astad notes that even the *Hamlet* rehearsals felt like performances, with the diligent work put in by the creative and design team. Working in Korea, Astad was impressed with the precision of following set times for rehearsals and other highly professional ways of working together so that it was a joy for him to be part of such a team.

Collaborative ventures within India most often suffer from lack of funding, yet Deboo notes (interview 2018) that it is creditable that so much creative work is produced; however, the process, he adds, is "harrowing." The people with whom one works are not always dedicated, since they regard the work as "just a project." They very often are not open about giving input. Deboo recognizes that there are different levels of satisfaction for all involved in the collaboration—such as his dancing with the Dhrupad singers, with Dadi Padamjee's puppetry, most recently with *rudra* veena player Mohi Bahaud-din Dagar, also working in the *Dhrupad* style. "It is more than the camaraderie between Bahaud-din and me," remarks Astad. "The rapport helps in more ways than one. Despite the diversity in the thought process, approach, and genre, the singular purpose comes through clearly in the work." Deboo has always been fond of *drupad* and remarked to Chitra Swaminathan of *The Hindu*: "like my dance, drupad is vigorous one moment and meditative the next" (Swaminathan 2018). Deboo continues:

This made my collaboration earlier with the Gundecha Brothers exciting. Like the way they unravel the many layers of their music, slowly and steadily, I too invest a lot of thought into every move and gesture. I like the dance to grow on me and the audience at its own pace.

(Interview 2018)

Overall, Astad enjoys collaborations, even though the process is challenging because it varies with different artists and locations.

Deboo's creative choreography with Manipuri *pung-cholam* and *thang-ta* artists, although located within the national boundary of India, is noteworthy because Manipur's distance from the major metropolitan cities of Delhi, Bombay, Chennai, Kolkata renders it marginal in terms of the power-brokers of Indian dance and arts residing in the capital, Delhi, and other cities. Manipur is also a conflict-ridden region, with struggles between the agents of the Indian State such as police and military and the local Manipuri people often struggling for their land.

The India-Bangladesh collaboration

Vikram Iyengar, based in Kolkata, is trained in *kathak* along with being an innovative creative dancer, choreographer, theater director, and researcher who co-founded The Renan Performance Collective, which brings together movement from classical Indian and other dance styles, along with "drama and design, creating an experience of total theater" (Iyengar "Biography"). Iyengar developed The Pickle Factory in 2013/2014, a valuable artistic venture which aims to be a "venue to curate, catalyse, and promote dance and movement practice and discourse in a changing Indian context" (Iyengar "Management and Curation"). Iyengar's many productions include dancers and actors, working across the boundaries of "stage and film, dance and theater explorations, and performance collaborations" (Iyengar "Biography"). One such cultural exchange that I discuss below includes Iyengar as co-choreographer on Helena Waldmann's piece *Made in Bangladesh*, a multi-media work that used movement, video, and photographs with an original musical score. This project was co-funded by the German Federal Cultural Foundation with the Goethe Institute of Bangladesh along with the Bangladeshi organization Shadhona.

The inspiration for this show came to German director and dance-maker Helena Waldmann as news of the 2013 Rana Plaza, an eight-story building in Dhaka, Bangladesh, where garment workers toiled collapsed because of violation of safety regulations. The factory building's crumbling structure that crashed, killing over 1100 workers, caught the world's attention and outrage. Waldmann created a dance-theater work as choreographer along with Vikram Iyengar, whom she invited to be co-choreographer for *Made in Bangladesh*. In an interview, Iyengar states forthrightly: "Gone are the days of 'I know more than you,' an inherent characteristic in the old school East-West exchanges." In this cultural exchange, as noted by Vanini Belarmino in interviewing Iyengar, this artist, draws out "striking realities between the sweatshops of the garment industry and that of the artistic practice" (Belarmino 2015). This is an unusual comparison between the risky economic existence of garment workers and dancers despite important differences of class background among the working-class garment-makers and mostly middle-class dancers. Although both professions in the creative or economic industries endure capitalism's goal of products that are marketable and profitable, factory workers endure harsher working conditions than dancers.

The choreography illuminated "the drudgery of factory work," as Ashna Chowdhury remarks in a review in *Dhaka Tribune* when the work premiered in January 2015. Chowdhury admits that "the entire show proved to be an exercise in capacity to sit with discomfort and unease" reflected in "frenetic rhythms" of dance movements, "and precision of music, magnified by the relentless drill of sewing machine needles" (Chowdhury 2015). The piece reflected "the sterile, dignity-stripping, numbers-driven repetitive culture of the industry." The reviewer positively responds to "automated posturing" as "haunting and tragic." She records the intensity of being "immersed in the chaotic ambient sounds of the Rana Plaza collapse, followed by a grinding halt—backlit by the infamous image of two people huddled in an embrace as the building crushed them and the air out of their lungs." One dancer then stares straight at the audience as if conveying reproach to a global capitalist system that relies on cheap labor in countries such as Bangladesh to produce garments for westerners.

Manjulika Rahman's review vividly describes how the piece opens with video footage of the garment factory, as live dancers enter silently:

> with only their legs illuminated as their feet use *tatkars* (the stamped rhythmic footwork of *kathak*) to echo the rhythm of a sewing machine. The background sound is a propulsive click accompanied by the metallic sounds of a sewing machine's pin hitting its rotating wheel. White lines of oversized threads and needles appear on the background screen. The silhouettes of the dancers' bodies are visible, but the focus is on their moving, working body parts.
>
> *(Rahman 2016)*

As the dancers are called by name, they join an assembly line as photos of garment workers are shown on the screen with quotes by them. "As the dancers perform together, they form a rectangular squadron that moves like an efficient automaton." The dancer-workers have to meet near impossible targets of "100 products per hour, 1000 products per day," a goal reflected in their fast-paced, mechanical movements. Accompanying this hard work, the screen displays numbers—a Bangladeshi worker earns "0.28 euros in comparison to profits made in the German market (445 euros) during the performance up to that point (21 minutes)." Such evidence points out the common reality of cheap labor; however, the affect with which this comes across is not in the arena of dry statistics but, rather, through the living, breathing bodies of the dancers on stage representing the workers, literally working their fingers to the bone, a cliché that is starkly true for garment makers. A male dancer steps forward to enact a wordless reminder of our responsibility in this tragedy as he interacts with an iconic photograph (from the building collapse) of a man covered in dust and blood, tenderly embracing a woman who leans backward as the fatal weight of the concrete kills them both. The sounds recreate the panic of the emergency with sirens blaring and shouts of rescuers and victims via the "dancers' tatkars that sound like the muted pounding of trapped victims."

In the second section, the scene changes to the same dancers, now dressed in Western clothes, in a dance studio taking dictates from an authoritative director informing them of "the meager conditions under which the dancers might be hired for a production: two months rehearsal without pay, 45 euros per show." These artists are competing as if "their skills and bodies (are) in a trading market, where only the dancers with the optimum skills will be 'bought' by sponsors to perform for the show." The final section brings together the "characters" played by the same dancers in both sections. Rahman (2016) is critical of the "othering," once again, of the brown-skinned over the white-skinned dancers since the risks that the two groups "share" are vastly different. Once again, the economic power differential prevents a level playing field. Rahman does acknowledge Iyengar's work on the project but contends that Waldmann, although she draws attention to the heartlessness that underlies neoliberal capitalism, "is not as reflexive about the racial and economic hierarchy that underlies projects where the funding sources and the 'framers'—directors and producers—are from a 'developed' nation.... Made in Bangladesh is framed from the outside, for a European audience, and does not provide enough depth of perspective for a non-European, Bangladeshi viewer." Syed Jamil Ahmed expressed a similar critique about the show that centers "the global center of cultural production in Europe, which continues to marginalize the postcolony" (Ahmed 2016).

Waldmann interviewed many factory workers for her project and was initially shocked to hear that "they are happy to be leading independent lives." But Waldmann realized that like young people anywhere in the world, they desire their own income. Plus, for them to be factory workers "is still better than living in the countryside with no water or basic amenities" (Chowdhury 2015). Of course one must add that Western corporations that employ these workers should ensure that they are not subjected to labor in decrepit buildings and under inhumane working conditions (such as no bathroom breaks). These garment workers also face "various forms of risk on a daily basis," remarks Rahman (2016), such as "difficult commutes on public transport, sexual harassment and exploitation that can cause them to lose their jobs and even their lives."

However, for Iyengar, the cultural exchange experience of working with Waldmann entailed translating the visions of both Waldmann, as choreographer, and Iyengar as co-choreographer, onto the bodies of the Bangladeshi *kathak* dancers. "Our roles were clearly defined" comments Iyengar (Belarmino 2015). "Her role was very much the larger picture, the scenario, the kind of spacing and image she wanted to create on stage, while mine was very much the actual creation and development of movement material in response to and contributing to these impulses." The collaborative work enabled Iyengar, as he remarks in the same interview, to "grow as a choreographer, artist, teacher, creative partner and collaborator and take all this back with me to my work with others and my company in Calcutta." Iyengar acknowledged that along with differences of opinion, this was "an equal and easy" collaboration when both choreographers listened carefully, were willing to debate and try out various movements and concepts to arrive at decisions about what would work, though these were fluid and could change. Both collaborators allowed enough time to this process rather than pinning down a decisive movement or affect. Rather, the improvisation used to create material involved a very different method than the imparting of dance movements or items in traditional settings in India or Bangladesh, where the choreography is set. Such a process resonates with what I discussed above with Deboo's experience of working as an equal with his Korean collaborators and in Jafer's delineation of the process that allows ample time for creative synergy among artists from different cultures to evolve.

What attracted Iyengar to this work was the opportunity to draw upon *kathak* in new ways. As he remarks:

> I am actively searching for inspirations and impulses from the outside—from those who may not be from the Kathak world—which can trigger new discoveries and ways of perceiving the form.... I have always been interested in playing with Kathak. I have never held it sacred in a reverential manner that doesn't allow a full openness of mind and am very happy to break it up and reconstruct it, exploring different ideas and impulses.
>
> *(Belarmino 2015)*

For Waldmann, the staccato rhythms of *kathak* evoked "the rapid needle of a sewing machine... I have deconstructed Kathak for this show, taken out its lyrical aspects and the bells on the feet.... I am using the footwork and arm work as a tool to talk about exploitation" (Johari 2015).

Iyengar's role included working with the Bangladeshi dancers in honing their *kathak* technique as well as getting them to be comfortable with this different process of working through improvisation and changes even as he incorporated *kathak*'s vocabulary of footwork, *mudras* (hand gestures), and *chakars* (circles). Iyengar had to remain attentive to Waldmann's ideas and the affect or mood that was to be conveyed. In this regard, Iyengar remarks that the lyrical aspects of *kathak* were less suited to this production than the more vigorous ones. However, this itself involved a process of discovery. Iyengar's work was instrumental also in serving as a translator not only linguistically from Bengali, spoken by him and the Bangladeshi dancers, but also "in terms of intent," since this process of choreographic creation was so different from what the dancers were used to. Iyengar wanted them to understand this new method so that they could participate in the creative process and decision-making, a kind of democratic inclusion that is not often practiced in the teaching of traditional Indian dance. Iyengar also realized that his "off-stage and on-stage role . . . a good dramaturgical choice" evolved through the rehearsal process as he communicated Waldmann's vision to the dancers.

Iyengar's own approach to *kathak* even when working with his own Company is characterized by openness and inclusion of different viewpoints and approaches shared by dancers that he describes (Belarmino 2015) as "a no-holds-barred approach." Working on *Made in Bangladesh* took this approach "to another level," he remarks, "because I was working with a person who brought in a fresh perspective." Hence he could adopt Waldmann's open approach, but the challenge was in getting the twelve Bangladeshi dancers who came from different backgrounds and experiences to feel comfortable with this method that was initially foreign to them; they were not used to working as an ensemble. In their traditional training, they followed a pre-set approach in choreography and in music as determined by the teacher. Iyengar, unlike them, was familiar with an "unfixed, exploratory" mode, but for the dancers "this open space where nothing is fixed—no script, no music, no movement . . . nothing was an approach which was extremely difficult for them to come to terms with. They were constantly trying to learn and fix things."

In this context, it was highly important to give them time to imbibe a method new to their training. Iyengar learned from Waldmann that by giving them time, something may "emerge." He describes the process in a lyrical and astutely useful manner. By giving dancers time

> to repeat something, to go beyond a fatigue point until a sort of sub-conscious, liminal space takes over, which you could never have imagined: the process of abstracting elements of dance to a great degree, where they become completely metaphorical not representative, interpretative or decorative, and the ability to convey a clear narrative and make a political point without telling any sort of linear story.
>
> *(Belarmino 2015)*

Another challenge resided in the fact that Bangladesh is an Islamic nation, though Iyengar found it "more Bengali than Islamic" (Belarmino 2015), which he felt comfortable with. Nonetheless, contact between men and women is more restricted than what Iyengar is used to in India.

Iyengar (Belarmino 2015) echoes Deboo's comment about appreciating "a certain kind of professionalism in every sphere" in his work with Waldmann, "something that sadly does not exist in India," he comments, though he adds that dancers themselves are disciplined but do not find the same "in the larger community or infrastructure surrounding the dance world." At the same time, Iyengar acknowledges that India compared to Bangladesh is "far better equipped in terms of infrastructure. The quality of training we have access to, the diversity of influences and approaches (national and international) we engage with. This does not automatically translate into better dancers—though it should!" The experience overall was productive for Iyengar, who gained professional insights such as "delegation of job responsibilities, and production management." He also realized that for Waldmann and her German team, it was not easy to work "in chaotic conditions—something that Bangladesh has surfeit of!"

When asked about audience responses to *Made in Bangladesh* when performed in Germany and Switzerland and then India and Bangladesh, Iyengar notes that European audiences engaged with the work's socio-political theme of the sub-standard work conditions faced by garment-factory assembly-line laborers along with a fascination with *kathak*. However, in the very spaces where Waldmann found inspiration for this work, Iyengar was doubtful about how much of the political message came across. Audiences were more interested in the quality of the dancers, the technical details, and the innovations, departing from *kathak*.

In conclusion, although artistic exchanges in our contemporary times have evolved since the era of overt inequities between Western and other dancers, challenges of dialogue and respectful interaction as well as of unequal funding realities even within the global South, such as between India and South Korea or between India and Bangladesh as analyzed here, remain. Nonetheless, both Astad Deboo and Vikram Iyengar, profiled here, invite collaborations that inspire provocative re-thinking of issues, methods, and choreography that bring new illuminations into their own artistic journeys as well as to their audiences.

Notes

1 I am grateful to Astad Deboo for putting me in touch with Rathi Jafer. I am also thankful for Deboo's time in sharing his collaborative work experiences with me via a phone interview in March 2018.
2 There is a body of scholarship on interculturalism. See Bharucha 1993, 2000; Pavis 2006; Knowles and Mundel 2009; and Fischer-Lichte et al. 2014.
3 See, among other publications, Schechner 1990, 2014. Schechner is also Editor of *The Drama Review*, an influential journal of theater studies. Jerzy Grotowski's influential book is entitled *Towards A Poor Theater* (1968, reissued by Routledge, 2002).
4 See Bharucha and Schechner 1984 for exchanges between Bharucha and Schechner: "A Reply to Rustom Bharucha" and "A Reply to Richard Schechner." Bharucha remarks: "If my article 'A Collision of Cultures: Some Western Interpretations of the Indian Theater' (Bharucha, 1984) were as 'reductive, incomplete, and inaccurate' as Schechner claims, I fail to see why he should respond to it with so much passion and rancor."
5 Shakespeare plays are adapted in different parts of the world, where they are transposed into the context of that culture—such as in India, South Africa, and Romania, among other areas. Several Shakespeare plays—*Macbeth, Merchant of Venice, Hamlet, Cymbeline*—have been translated into regional languages in India and performed. For more information, see Trivedi ("Shakespeare in India") and Yadev 2014. Scholarly material on Shakespeare adaptations is vast. See Clement 2013 and Al-Shetawi 2013. For Canadian adaptations, see "Canadian Adaptations" 2007.
6 I thank Astad Deboo for sharing this review with me via email.

References

Ahmed, Syed Jamil. 2016, Fall. "Review of *Made in Bangladesh*." *Asian Theater Journal* 33:2, 499–503.
Al-Shetawi, Mahmoud F. 2013. "Arabic Adaptations of Shakespeare and Postcolonial Theory." *Critical Survey*, Special Issue: Creating Shakespeare, 25:3, 4–28. Accessed April 15, 2018.
Belarmino, Vanini. 2015, July 15. "Made in Bangladesh": Importing and Exporting the Fabric of Kathak. Interview with Vikram Iyengar. https://culture360.asef.org/magazine/made-bangladesh-importing-and-exporting-fabric-kathak-interview-vikram-iyengar/.
Bharucha, Rustom. 1993. *Theatre and the World: Performance and the Politics of Culture*. London: Routledge.

Bharucha, Rustom. 2000. *The Politics of Cultural Practice: Thinking through Theatre in an Age of Globalization*. London: Athlone Press.

Bharucha, Rustom, and Schechner, Richard. Autumn 1984. "A Reply to Rustom Bharucha." *Asian Theater Journal*, 1:2, 245–253. Bharucha's response, "A Reply to Richard Schechner" is in the same *Asian Theater Journal* 1:2, 254–260.

"Canadian Adaptations." 2007, August. http://www.canadianshakespeares.ca/main.cfm. Accessed April 15, 2018.

Chowdhury, Ashna. 2015, January 27. "Thoughts on Helena Waldmann's Made in Bangladesh," *Dhaka Tribune*.

Clement, Jennifer. 2013. *Beyond Shakespeare: Early Modern Adaptation Studies and Its Potential*. Wiley Online Library. https://doi.org/10.1111/lic3.12080. Accessed April 15, 2018.

Fischer-Lichte, Erika, Jost, Torsten, and Jain, Saskya Iris, eds. 2014. *The Politics of Interweaving Performance Cultures: Beyond Postcolonialism*. New York and London: Routledge.

Grotowski, Jerzy. 2002. *Towards A Poor Theater*. New York: Routledge.

InKo Centre. "Hamlet_Avataar." http://www.inkocentre.org/hamlet_avataar.html. Accessed May 1, 2018.

Iyengar, Vikram. "Biography." https://vikramiyengar.in/biography/. Accessed May 2, 2018.

Iyengar, Vikram. "Management and Curation." https://vikramiyengar.in/management-and-curation/. Accessed May 2, 2018.

Jafer, Rathi. 2018, March 19. Email from Director of InKo Center, based in Chennai, to Katrak.

Johari, Aarefa. 2015, January 16. "Through Kathak, a German Choreographer Tells the Story of Bangladesh's Exploited Garment Workers." https://scroll.in/article/700726/through-kathak-a-german-choreographer-tells-the-story-of-bangladeshs-exploited-garment-workers.

Katrak, Ketu H. 2014. *Contemporary Indian Dance: New Creative Choreography in India and the Diaspora*. Basingstoke: Palgrave Macmillan.

Knowles, Ric, and Mundel, Ingrid, eds. 2009. "'Ethnic,' Multicultural, and Intercultural Theatre." Special Issue of *Critical Perspectives on Canadian Theatre in English*, 14. Toronto: Playwrights Canada Press.

Lei, Daphne P. 2011, December. "Interruption, Intervention, Interculturalism: Robert Wilson's HIT Productions in Taiwan." *Theatre Journal* 63:4, 571–586.

Pavis, Patrice, ed. 2006, Spring. *The Intercultural Performance Reader*. London: Routledge.

Rahman, Manjulika. 2016, Spring. "Capitalism and Corporealities: Helena Waldmann's Made in Bangladesh." *The Drama Review* 60:1, 150–156.

Schechner, Richard. 1990. *By Means of Performance: Intercultural Studies of Theatre and Ritual*. Cambridge: Cambridge University Press.

Schechner, Richard. 2014. *Performance Theory*. London: Routledge.

Swaminathan, Chitra. 2018, April 12. "Astad Deboo Never Fails to Surprise." *The Hindu*.

Trivedi, Poonam. "Shakespeare in India: Introduction." http://globalshakespeares.mit.edu/india/#. Accessed April 15, 2018.

Yadev, Mukesh. 2014, September. "Domesticating Shakespeare: A Study of Indian Adaptation of Shakespeare in Popular Culture." *European Journal of English Language and Literature Studies* 2:3, 48–58. http://www.eajournals.org/keywords/popular-culture-indian-cinema-shakespearean-adaptations-bollywood/. Accessed April 15, 2018.

8
REVEALING THE MESSINESS OF TRANSNATIONAL IDENTITIES
Second-generation South Asians in Canada

Kara Somerville

Introduction

Migration literature increasingly recognizes that the migratory journey cannot be fully understood by only studying migration experiences in the receiving society. People migrate for a variety of reasons, yet many maintain meaningful emotional, social, economic, and political ties to their country of origin. A transnational perspective suggests that migrants are forging and maintaining meaningful and varied relationships across national borders. In other words, literature from this transnational lens suggests that migrants remain embedded in the countries of origin and settlement simultaneously (Basch et al., 1994). These transnational attachments alter the experiences of assimilation and belonging among migrants. It is a little less evident, however, what happens among the second-generation children of these immigrants.

This chapter is based on in-depth interviews with the Canadian-born children of South Asian[1] immigrants. I explore the ways their lives are being enacted across borders and how these border crossings, both physical and imagined, shape their sense of belonging in both Canada and South Asia. I argue that the lives of these young people are shaped by growing up in Canada but also by growing up embedded in the "transnational social field" (Levitt and Glick-Schiller, 2004) created through the cross-border ties of themselves and their immigrant parents. As a result, their sense of belonging in any given social location cannot be fully understood without exploring the multiple social locations in which they live their lives. For the majority of my participants, these social locations occur in both Canada and India. They must grapple with feeling included and excluded, too Indian and too Canadian. This boils down to shifting identities and belongings based on changing transnational social contexts. Where they are, who they are with, what language they are speaking and how well they are speaking it collectively transform the identities of participants. These social processes take place across borders and highlight the saliency of transnational social fields in understanding the boundaries of belonging for second-generation South Asians. I argue that there is not a stable pattern of identity empowerment, or a consistent feeling of marginalization; it is *both* a journey of flexible inclusion and a journey of obstinate exclusion. Transnational flows continually reshape boundaries of belonging for the second-generation youth in this study, making belonging fractional and context specific.

Context

South Asians in Canada

Canada attracts approximately 250,000 immigrants annually. Most new immigrants in this "mass immigration policy" (Reitz, 2012) were admitted under the economic category, which is based on Canada's points system[2] and as a result are highly educated and skilled. The source country of these immigrants is varied; however, most are from Asian countries. As a result, the visible minority population in Canada is approximately 22 percent and steadily growing. Despite the importance of understanding countries of origin, and their specific local and national contexts, much of the academic literature in Canada focuses on South Asians, as opposed to specific countries of origin (see Ashutosh, 2008). As a result, there is limited transnational research on an exclusively Indian population in Canada. In order to provide a comprehensive literature review, this chapter focuses on the broader South Asian population, which includes individuals from India, Sri Lanka, Pakistan, Nepal, and Bangladesh, as is common in the literature (see Chilvers and Walton-Roberts, 2014; Patel, 2006; Purkayastha, 2005; Zaidi et al., 2014). South Asian is the largest visible minority group in Canada, accounting for roughly one-quarter of the total visible minority population. Approximately two-thirds of South Asians in Canada reported East Indian[3] ethnic ancestry (Statistics Canada, 2017).

Second-generation South Asians in Canada

Many of these immigrants have children who were born in Canada. In 2016, 37.5 percent of the total population of Canadian children were first or second-generation immigrants. Currently 17.7 percent of the Canadian population is second generation (Statistics Canada, 2017). Projections suggest that if current immigration trends continue, the population of children born in Canada to two foreign-born parents will significantly increase to between 1.3 million and 2.0 million children in 2036 (Statistics Canada, 2016).

These second-generation migrant communities in Canada are mostly residing in large metropolitan areas; Toronto, Vancouver, and Montréal are home to almost half of the second-generation population in Canada (Statistics Canada, 2017). These second-generation South Asians in Canada are highly educated and relatively young. Researchers in both Canada and the United States have noted the high educational achievement of second-generation Asians (Abada and Tenkorang, 2009; Boyd, 2002; 2008; Boyd and Grieco, 1998; Reitz et al., 2011; Somerville and Robinson, 2016), who are outperforming the mainstream population and are therefore labeled a "model minority" (Asher, 2002; Bhattacharya, 2000; Rahman and Witenstein, 2014; Shankar, 2008). Several key factors have been identified in explaining the educational success among second-generation South Asians, including parental education levels and aspirations, cultural factors, city of residence, and ethnic capital (Picot and Hou, 2011; Reitz et al., 2011). Despite this model minority label, some studies indicate that second-generation South Asians face challenges of social adaptation, particularly regarding their cultural belonging and experiences of cultural conflict (Saran, 2009).

The visible minority second generation in Canada are considerably younger than their non-visible-minority counterparts. The median age for all visible minority groups in the second generation in Canada is 13.6 years, compared with a median age of 43.4 years for the second generation who are not visible minorities. Among the South Asian population, the median age in Canada is slightly lower at 12.2 years (Statistics Canada, 2011). Their youth is important when studying integration and transnational experiences; many of the second-generation South Asians are too young to have completed their education, entered the labour force, gotten married, or had children. As a result, what we know about this new group of second-generation South Asians is limited, and some conclusions may therefore be premature.

Multiculturalism

Canada has an official policy of multiculturalism. Although there are many criticisms of this policy (see Banting and Kymlicka, 2010; Vertovec, 2001), it has become part of Canada's national identity: "*Being* multicultural has become closely intertwined with what it means to *be* Canadian" (Amarasingam et al., 2016: 120), and research is growing on the ways in which multiculturalism shapes the identities and lived experiences of second-generation migrants in Canada (Ali, 2008; Amarasingam et al., 2016). Some researchers argue that Canada's policy of multiculturalism makes it a unique research site because of the ways multiculturalism becomes a form of identity politics (Sriskandarajah, 2008); however, others argue that the differences between American and Canadian integration are more of an illusion than a reality (Reitz and Breton, 1994), and some researchers conclude that the myths of multiculturalism will lead visible minority second-generation youth to feel marginalized and disappointed (Ali, 2008). Researchers are grappling with how society and the state respond to visible minority groups in Canada and whether the promotion of diversity and protection of minority rights is facilitating their integration and sense of belonging. Some argue that second-generation Canadians, including South Asians, are more likely to feel socially excluded in Canada (Reitz and Banerjee, 2007; Sano et al., 2015; Wu et al., 2012) and develop a reactive ethnicity (Rumbaut, 2008; Sano et al., 2015); others argue that second-generation Canadians have a "strong sense of national allegiance, belonging and civic identity as Canadians" (Hebert et al., 2008: 63).

Research suggests that minorities in Canada negotiate multiculturalism in complex ways and that they are cognizant of the important role it plays in their identity construction, informing both their national and transnational identities (Sriskandarajah, 2008); Canadian multiculturalism has become unbounded (Sriskandarajah, 2008; Walton-Roberts, 2011). In a study of second-generation Tamil-Canadians in Toronto, Sriskandarajah (2008) argues that these youth express their hybridity through a process of appropriation, reinterpretation, and navigation of multiculturalism, so their "Canadian" identity is not in juxtaposition to their "Tamil" identity. Multiculturalism may therefore have a role to play in fueling transnationalism, but transnationalism may also be viewed as challenging contemporary forms of multiculturalism (Wong and Satzewich, 2006: 1).

Literature

Transnationalism

The following literature review focuses on North American studies and is not limited to an exclusively Canadian context. This is a direct result of the small body of literature in Canada that explores issues of transnationalism among South Asian Canadians (see Bhat and Sahoo, 2003; Chilvers and Walton-Roberts, 2014; Patel, 2006; Somerville, 2013; Srinivasan, 2018; Walton-Roberts, 2001, 2003) and the even smaller body of work that focuses exclusively on the transnational practices of their Canadian-born children (see O'Neill, 2015; Samuel, 2010; Somerville, 2008, 2009; Sriskandarajah, 2008; Zaidi et al., 2014). A growing number of international researchers, however, are exploring how second-generation experiences are shaped by transnationalism (see Reynolds and Zontini, 2016), especially among migrant communities in the United States (Levitt, 2009; Levitt and Waters, 2002; Purkayastha, 2005). The United States context is relevant, although not completely transferable, to the Canadian context. Given the importance of factors relating to the receiving society's policies, and the context of reception for immigrants and racialized people, generalizations should be made with caution. Nevertheless, there are many similarities within the Canadian and American research findings on transnationalism, and similar central themes have been identified in the literature. The following review is therefore based on North American literature in order to summarize the major findings relating to transnationalism among second-generation South Asians.

There is a debate in the literature as to whether the second generation is transnational or whether transnationalism is simply a first-generation phenomenon. Some scholars argue that transnationalism may be important for the first generation but that evidence suggests it does not remain salient for their children (Kasinitz et al., 2002; Portes, 2001; Rumbaut, 2002). Others argue that transnational ties continue into the second generation but that the magnitude and meanings are less clear (Basch et al., 1994; Kibria, 2009; Levitt, 2009; Levitt and Glick-Schiller, 2004; Purkayastha, 2005; Reynolds and Zontini, 2014, 2016; Somerville, 2009; Sriskandarajah, 2008). Researchers are gaining a shared understanding that "transnational parents do not necessarily produce transnational children" (Levitt et al., 2014: 18).

Studies on the transnational lives of second-generation South Asians revolves around two main themes: identity formation and intergenerational tensions with immigrant parents. Research focusing on second-generation South Asian transnationalism tends to be qualitative in nature and examine the challenges these young people experience with competing cultural and religious values from their sending and receiving societies. This chapter focuses on the theme of identity formation and belonging.

Transnational identity formation

In general, South Asian immigrants and their children have been economically successful and achieve high levels of education. Nevertheless, many studies indicate that they face challenges of social adaptation, particularly in regards to their cultural belonging, experiences of cultural conflict, and identity formation. There is debate about whether being part of two cultures and two nation-states causes intergenerational struggles, clashes, and stress for the second generation (Saran, 2009; Zaidi et al., 2014) or whether they fairly effortlessly modify and merge their multiple spatial and cultural contexts (Hebert et al., 2008). In a study of second-generation youth in Calgary, Winnipeg, and Toronto, Hebert et al. (2008: 75) conclude that "there is no evidence here of alienation or exclusion. Instead these youth have embraced difference as the new normal". Regardless of how much difficulty is experienced, researchers seem to agree that the second generation carve a new path to balance competing messages, cultures, opportunities, and constraints.

The children of immigrants are being raised and socialized in the cultural rules and institutions of the countries where they were born and reside, but also of the countries from which their families originate (Levitt et al., 2014). As a result, there are a myriad of identity options available that the second generation can mobilize if they wish. There are many powerful social factors that inform expressions of identity among second-generation transnational youth. Specifically, these include religion (Byng, 2017; Levitt and Jaworsky, 2007; Purkayastha, 2010; Saran, 2009), citizenship (Colombo and Rebughini, 2012), culture (Das Gupta, 1997), and racialization (Purkayastha, 2005; Sano et al., 2015). Second-generation migrants construct identities by negotiating challenging intersecting processes (Saran, 2009). In other words, hyphenation is not a simple process of putting two parts together (Colombo and Rebughini, 2012; Das Gupta, 1997; Levitt, 2009; Purkayastha, 2005); hyphenation involves multiple layers which "diverge, intersect, coalesce and clash" (Purkayastha, 2005: 172). Research also suggests that these ebb and flow over the life-course (Levitt, 2002). There are specific life-course events, such as marriage and the birth of children, that trigger transnational belonging and links to a parental homeland, which intensify transnational identities (Somerville, 2009: 41). In addition, research suggests homeland trips can alter the identities of second-generation South Asians (Bolognani, 2014; DeHanas, 2013; Maira, 2002).

The second generation identify with multiple national and/or ethnic identities simultaneously. The interesting part of this process is not simply the identities they are selecting, but how their transnational social field influences their identification processes. Although there are a multitude of identity options within the diaspora, researchers argue that there are powerful social processes limiting the ability of the second generation to independently navigate these options. According to Finn (2008: 16), "in contrast to theories of diaspora that describe multiple *belongings*; narratives of identity and linguistic acts of identification often focus on situations of exclusion". In other words, many second-generation migrants find that they are barred from claiming membership or belonging within certain identities. These young people may develop an oppositional or reactive identity (Saran, 2009; Purkayastha, 2005). As a result, some recent researchers have argued for the need to focus on identity processes rather than identity outcomes (Colombo and Rebughini, 2012; Reynolds and Zontini, 2016; Shankar, 2008; Somerville, 2008); shifting the lens to analyze "ways the second-generation are transnationally 'doing ethnicity' and less about the actual ethnicities that they do" (Somerville, 2008: 22). This provides more opportunity to understand the ways migrants negotiate identities, exclusions, and belongings. Colombo and Rebughini (2012: 135) summarize the available identity options by stating that "it is less useful to think of people as having ethnic, national or hyphenated identities and more useful to think of people as active agents able to use different forms of identification ... in relation to different contexts". This paper will help us understand the ways in which second-generation identities are multi-faceted and constructed via physical and imagined mobility across borders.

Methods

This paper is based on in-depth interviews with 30 second-generation South Asians living in Toronto, Ontario, Canada. All participants had parents who immigrated to Canada from a South Asian country, but recruitment methods did not require them to personally identify as "South Asian". Toronto was chosen for the research because the majority of South Asians in Canada reside there. Among the South Asian Canadian population, the top three source countries are India, Pakistan, and Sri Lanka. Participants were recruited from the core countries of India, Pakistan, Sri Lanka, and Bangladesh. Recruitment for participants was done through a free local classifieds website and some snowball sampling. The interviews were audio-recorded with the informed consent of participants, then transcribed verbatim by the author. Analysis of the interview data was done inductively to identify patterns.

More than two-thirds (69%) of the sample had parents who immigrated from India, followed by Sri Lanka, Pakistan and Bangladesh. Almost three-quarters of the sample (73%) is currently enrolled in university, with the remaining (27%) having completed their post-secondary degrees. South Asian youth are considerably more educated than the native-born Canadian population, so a highly educated sample is to be expected. Out of the 30 individuals interviewed for this study, 13 are men and 17 are women. No gender differences were found regarding processes of identity formation.[4] Participants' ages ranged from 18 to 35, with a median age of 20 years and an average age of 22. Half of the sample identified their religion as Hinduism, with seven participants personally identifying as Muslim, three as Christian, and two as Sikh. Three participants were raised in religious households but indicated no religious affiliation.[5] Given the sample size, generalizations should be made with caution. In the following sections, pseudonyms have been used to ensure anonymity.

Findings: negotiated belonging in a transnational social field

The current study illustrates the complexities of shifting transnational identities. I argue that there is not a simple or stable pattern of identity empowerment, or a consistent feeling of marginalization among this sample of second-generation South Asians. In other words, it is *both* a journey of flexible inclusion and a journey of obstinate exclusion. Identity production cannot be determined by quantifying the number of participants who feel included or excluded at any given time; it can only be understood through the ways both processes simultaneously interact within any one individual and among different individuals in various social spaces.

Furthermore, second-generation South Asian youth in Canada are developing, negotiating, and creatively coming to terms with their identities as they navigate boundaries of belonging within both South Asia and Canada. Second-generation South Asians in this study use ways of being and ways of belonging (Levitt and Glick-Schiller, 2004) within a transnational social field to articulate their identities and embeddedness in more than one nation-state. Although these young people were born and raised in Canada, they are being socialized within a transnational social space made up of family, friends, and relatives in both South Asia and Canada. This transnational journey profoundly influences their self-identities and their notions of inclusion. Revealing the messiness of transnational identity construction, without trying to classify or simplify it, is a contribution of this chapter.

Understanding belonging through physical border flows

This process of identity negotiation is accentuated when the second-generation migrants in this study physically travel across the borders of Canada and India, Sri Lanka, or Pakistan. These physical movements not only shape boundaries of belonging while in their parents' country of origin but also inform their sense of nationhood when they return to Canada. As a result, the process is constantly in flux, and there is an unavoidable and continuous reconstruction of boundaries. Previous research has suggested that family visits to the homeland can lead to feelings of displacement, as close friends and family treat second-generation migrants as foreigners (Reynolds and Zontini, 2016: 385), suggesting that transnational kinship relationships and family dynamics can profoundly shape how migrants view themselves. The current findings lend further support to this argument.

When asked how they self-identify, the following phrases were used by some of the participants: Indian-Canadian, Indian and Canadian, Canadian with Indian background, South Asian,

Sri Lankan Tamil, Canadian, Tamil-Canadian, Sri Lankan, South Asian Canadian, a mix, Indo-Canadian, hybrid, Sri Lankan born in Canada. What do these labels tell us about identity processes? I argue that they tell us very little. Hidden behind these simplified responses is a complex series of negotiations based on religion, skin colour, language, cultural values, and customs that are constructed within and across national borders. These social forces result in transnational boundary negotiations. As participants physically flow across borders, their identities are continually renegotiated. Devi, a 27-year-old female whose parents migrated from India, articulated the fluidity of her identities and how she presents herself differently in Canada and in India:

> I would say I'm Indian, but it's weird. Right now I would say I'm Indian but when I went to India I would tell people when I was asked that I was Canadian but that was because they knew there was something different about me and that I really wasn't from some other part of India, I was actually from another country. Indo-Canadian, but that is not a term that is used really, and I would say I feel more Indian here because that is just how I have grown up, but when I was there I just felt a connection to being Canadian.
>
> *(Devi, 27-year-old female, India)*

Ajay, a 30-year-old whose parents migrated from India, shared similar experiences of renegotiating his identity based on his physical location and the reactions he receives in different social spaces:

> I mean this is something I am just gonna say. When I'm in Canada and someone asks me what are you I'll obviously say Indian because we all assume we are Canadian. But when I'm in India I always tell people I'm Canadian, even though they can clearly see I'm of Indian origin. Because once you tell them you're Indian they'll ask you where in India are you from, and then it'll make you realize you're actually not Indian, you are Indian in the context of when you are in Canada or in North America, because that is how you identify yourself in that context that we are all Canadian. So it is a very interesting thought process.
>
> *(Ajay, 30 year old male, India)*

Devi and Ajay's self-identities are shaped by the assumptions of others in various, and at times competing, social spaces. These identities are rooted in markers of otherness, such as their skin colour, accent, or local knowledge. Processes of racialization remain salient as these second-generation migrants negotiate their transnational social locations and shifting racialized contexts. Realizing when he is in India that he is "actually not Indian", despite always feeling Indian in Canada (because of his skin colour), had a profound impact on Ajay's shifting self-concept. Similarly, Devi's statement that people knew there was "something different" about her illustrates the ways ethnic boundaries are constructed transnationally, based on a process of othering.

We see similar experiences among other participants. Having others' perceptions and interactions reveal which identity options are closed off, thus implying that participants must renegotiate more fluid self-identities, was a common sentiment. For example, when asked if she feels like she belongs when she visits India, Aarushi, a 30-year-old female whose parents migrated from India, answered:

No, that is a great question. No, I don't because I don't speak fluently, but yet I look like the people from there. So, I've had people come up to me and talk to me and I struggle to speak back and it's like "What is wrong with her?" "Why do you talk like that?" And then you travel to different parts of India and you don't speak the language there at all, but you speak the main language Hindi fluently and it is like, "Where are you from? Why don't you speak?" You don't fit in there either. But then going back to India is almost like going home because I have been there since I was a little kid. So, it feels like home but I still don't fit in.

(Aarushi, 30-year-old female, India)

Aarushi indicates that India "feels like home", but she simultaneously feels she does not belong there, partially because she feels her Indian-ness is challenged owing to her lack of language knowledge or fluency. Interestingly, although Aarushi states that she does not "fit in" in India, she also indicates that she does not feel a sense of belonging in Canada and therefore selects a primarily Indian identity, but with qualifiers: "I am Indian I would say, but I would always say I'm born here . . . I think there are times that I do struggle with [where I belong]". For Aarushi, these struggles are the result of processes of othering, which reveal the social significance of her language and accent. The second generation thus might be experiencing obstacles to integration that lead them to feel like outsiders who are not included in the national imaginary of Canada or in the national imaginary of their parents' country of origin.

The struggle Aarushi describes was a common theme throughout the narratives. The second generation is managing complex and at times contradictory identifications as they physically move between two or more nation-states, languages, cultures, and religions. For example, when asked if she feels like she belongs in India, 19-year-old Fatima revealed her inner struggles with her identity, which are shaped partly by her experiences as a Muslim woman:

Yeah . . . not, I guess . . . umm. . . . That is kinda a tricky question [laughs]. In one way I felt like I did belong [in India], in some ways even more than I belong in Canada, but then sometimes I would just feel very different . . . Very, very different. Like I would think this is not my . . . like I belong in Canada. I guess it depended on the situation and the timing, and where exactly I was in India. I would say that because I wear a hijab, when I was in India a lot of people wear it too, so it didn't feel like different compared to when I am in Toronto and it is always a minority situation; like it isn't everyone who wears a hijab obviously.

(Fatima, 19-year-old female, India)

Fatima's consciousness that she belongs in both countries, yet also in neither country, speaks to her location within the transnational social field. She is exposed to an almost constant flow of identity options and exclusions that make her identity process one which necessitates an ongoing conscious connection to various social spaces. This awareness of multiple connections does not always lead to a sense of belonging in both nation-states. Some of the second-generation migrants fiercely felt a sense of exclusion and non-belonging. Nevertheless, this exclusion did not lead them on a linear pathway to either a solid reactive ethnicity or a fiercely nationalistic identity; in contrast, it led them on a similar journey of fluid self-discovery. This is illustrated through a conversation with Braj, a 34-year-old male whose parents were born in India. I asked Braj if he felt a sense of belonging in India during his regular visits to the country:

Absolutely not. I don't really know how to verbalize that. . . . I told my parents when we were in India that I needed to speak with them in English to remind myself that they are still mom and dad, and not a bunch of locals, because they seemed to blend in with the locals so much from my perspective. I explained to my mom that I'm sitting there kinda bored and reading a book at my uncle's, and said I feel all alone in a foreign country, and my mom went postal on me! She was mad!

(Braj, 34-year-old male, India)

When asked if he therefore felt he belonged in Canada, Braj expressed uncertainty:

Ummmm, I don't know. I don't know. Because of my looking different, because of my heritage, because of my upbringing. I feel like I belong more in Canada when I am in India. As strange as this may sound, I remember when I was in Kerala and there would be like Caucasian tourists or people backpacking, and I actually did the head nod at the Caucasian tourists, but when you're here [in Canada] you do the head nod with the brown guys. It's kinda like the brown guy head nod and everyone kinda understands the acknowledgement, but I found myself doing that there. I ahhh honestly don't know.

(Braj, 34-year-old male, India)

Each visit to India appears to shift participants' sense of belonging in India, but it also clearly informs their sense of belonging in Canada. As a result, understanding identity construction in one social location cannot be complete without also understanding how it is influenced by simultaneous reconstructions of identity in other social locations. The second-generation Indians' identity formation and re-formations cannot be interpreted in isolation from the transnational social field in which they are being raised. The young people in this sample constructed their identities through a process in which they negotiate their sense of belonging through constantly changing and sometimes competing sentiments: on the one hand, they experience differentiation in which ethnic boundaries are firmly upheld; on the other hand, they experience a sense of similarity in which boundaries become blurred and porous.

Understanding imagined belonging

Despite the importance participants placed on physical movements shaping their identity processes, many participants also discussed how their identities were being contested and renegotiated regardless of whether they were making physical trips to India, Sri Lanka, Pakistan, or Bangladesh. For some second-generation individuals, the relationships their parents maintain with their country of origin are so strong that they transform the lives of their Canadian-born children, even within the borders of Canada. Participants commented on the ways their transnational identities are shaped by their parents' culture, relationships, and religious beliefs which are flowing across borders and changing the ways the second generation define what it means to be Canadian, or Indian, or Pakistani, etc. The transnational flows therefore reshape boundaries of belonging for the second-generation youth in this study.

By virtue of being raised in a transnational social field, these young people were involved in ongoing processes of inclusion and exclusion which shaped their sense of imagined belonging to South Asian countries and to Canada. Even within the borders of Canada they surround themselves with different groups of people, from different national and cultural contexts, and they subsequently express fluid and changing transnational identities. Sabeena, an 18-year-old whose parents emigrated from India, was clearly grappling with choosing one identity. When I asked about her identity, Sabeena hesitated:

> I would say I'm a Canadian who . . . ummm . . . but I am from . . . well . . . I am from India. . . . I wouldn't say my parents are from India because I have been exposed so much. Like I would say my background is Indian but I was born in Canada. Even though I was born in Canada I am totally Indian.
>
> *(Sabeena, 18-year-old female, India)*

This confusion over one's sense of place was repeatedly expressed by participants in this study. It would be difficult and futile to try to classify Sabeena based on her descriptions of her identity. It is far more valuable to try to understand the ways her "exposure" to India become incorporated into her identity negotiations as she navigates her sense of belonging.

Having many possibilities of transnational inclusion can be complicated. When asked if he struggles with his identity, Roshan replied:

> Yes sometimes I'll say I'm Canadian and sometimes I'll say I'm Tamil. When I'm around my family and stuff I'd say I'm more Tamil, and many of my friends are South Asian as well, so I'd say I'm Tamil, but if I'm at school or something I'd say Canadian.
>
> *(Roshan, 19-year-old male, Sri Lanka).*

These constant shufflings and reshufflings of identities were a seamless process for some of the participants; for others, it left them feeling inadequate, and therefore they expressed reluctance to admit they were wavering in their identities. Among these participants there were feelings of awkwardness, embarrassment, and self-blame for what they interpreted as uncertainty and confusion. For example, when Harshan was asked if he ever struggles with where he belongs, he answered "No. . . . Yeah, okay, if you want me to be 100% honest with you . . . it depends like where I live" (Harshan, 19-year-old male, Sri Lanka). Harshan is constructing his identities out of multiple and intersecting affiliations and marginalizations as he moves across and between national borders.

Braj described his multiple and fluid identities as a result of the self-consciousness he feels when he senses boundaries being erected around him. Braj feels dislocated and excluded in both Canada and his parents' country of origin, which had a profound impact on his identity experiences.

> I'm not Indian enough for the Indian community, I never have been, I never will be. I learned that as a little boy that I would never be Indian enough for the Indian community. . . . But at the same time [in Canada] I am self-conscious. I am a loner, and if I have to go to a social event, I am the only Indian guy there, and I am self-conscious because of that. But at the same time, if I had to go to an Indian function I am more self-conscious.
>
> *(Braj, 34-year-old male, India)*

This expression of self-consciousness is a way of describing the feeling generated by ethnic boundaries that are constructed around the second generation based on their citizenship, race, language, culture, or other markers of social distinction and otherness. Some participants expressed these boundaries as sources of angst and confusion; others identified them more as reminders of the need to shift their identity. In other words, for some of the participants the creation of a boundary during social interaction simply acted as a stimulus to switch out that identity for another one that was more encompassing, less rigid, or more socially acceptable given their current social location. For others it led to a sense of confusion and exclusion that they struggled to overcome. These second-generation youth are therefore helping us to appreciate the ways that transnational social fields reveal both the identity mobilizations of marginalized groups and the identity mobilizations of those included in various ethnic or national imaginaries.

Conclusion

The second generation in this study are balancing their South Asian-ness with their Canadian-ness as they navigate transnational social fields made up of fluid identity markers and cultural resources. In doing so they are confronted with continuous processes of incorporation into visions of nationhood and national marginalization which make them question their belonging. The boundaries separating one identity from another are porous yet can be rigidly solidified as racial, linguistic, or cultural differences are accentuated. Participants' religion, skin colour, cultural knowledge, language fluency, and social networks break down and simultaneously uphold boundaries of belonging. This is not a tidy or linear process.

Findings from this study echo Saran's (2009: 56) argument that the identity formation of second-generation South Asians "cannot be interpreted in isolation of their parents' pre-immigration and post-immigration cultural, social, and economic experiences". Their parents' countries of origin and settlement form a crucial part of their transnational social field, which informs their own sense of belonging and incorporation in both sending and receiving societies. This study builds off existing studies of the transnational lives of second-generation South Asians. Firstly, it lends support to scholars who contend that the second generation may be important transnational actors in both their physical movements and their imagined belongings. Secondly, I argue that social locations can powerfully transform notions of belonging, as they are negotiated and re-enacted physically and symbolically across borders. I therefore find further evidence to support Colombo and Rebughini's (2012: 96) argument that "belonging emerges as a blurred and mobile location" in which identities are constantly being shifted, rearranged, and renegotiated as the second generation is immersed and omitted from various transnational social spaces.

In our globalized world, and with the growing presence of the children of immigrants in Canada, it is increasingly relevant and important to understand the ways these young people are incorporating into Canadian society, (including their sense of belonging. As the second generation experiences the erection of social boundaries, we need to further explore how their situated transnational experiences shape their identities and belongings in multiple nation-states, so we can be better prepared to facilitate their inclusion. It appears, based on findings from this research, that second-generation South Asians in Canada manage to engage in transnational identity processes even when they do not migrate and do not physically move across borders. At the same time, there must be an acknowledgement of the importance of place, as many second-generation youths do physically travel across borders and consequently renegotiate their belonging in multiple social spaces. Clearly, both physical and imagined transnational belonging impact ethnic identities; and we see the creation of a deterritorialized social identity. Future research needs to reflect upon the ways in which geographic and social spaces are being reconfigured by the second generation.

Whether the second generation will continue to maintain transnational connections as they move through the life course is difficult to predict, and the extent to which Canada can meet the needs of these transnational youth remains uncertain. We need continued and increased research on the South Asian diaspora across generations in Canada before conclusions can be drawn with any precision. Future research on South Asians in Canada will clarify the relationship between transnationalism and belonging within a multicultural setting. Nevertheless, existing research, including this chapter, suggests that second-generation South Asians are part of a growing transnational community in Canada. They develop a transnational consciousness, ongoing cultural reproduction, and a continual negotiation and reconstruction of place as they navigate different social spaces in Canada, as well as in India, Pakistan, Bangladesh, and Sri Lanka. This chapter therefore contributes to the small body of literature on transnational second-generation South Asians in Canada. It also contributes to the literature on the relationships between transnationalism and multiculturalism. I find that these youth navigate their belonging in a multicultural city through physical and imagined border crossings, which contribute to both their inclusion as Canadians, and also their sense of being outside the national imaginary. This contradiction is not fully reconciled but, instead, is constantly renegotiated as they also grapple with their inclusion as an Indian, Pakistani, Bangladeshi, or Sri Lankan. Therefore, the second generation navigate and negotiate multiculturalism in unique ways, providing opportunities for locating their sense of place within the nation-building efforts of both Canada and their parents' country of origin.

Finally, this chapter contributes to the emergent literature on transnational social locations and boundary reconstructions among second-generation youth by underscoring the messiness of identity processes and the ways in which multiple belongings can be fused, fractional and context specific. Enduring homeland involvements remind us that local experiences in Canada are connected to how one feels and experiences belonging in South Asia; feeling embedded in Sri Lanka is equally connected to one's national identity in Canada; and so on. What this suggests is that understanding where and how identities are constructed requires widening our analytical lens. Instead of trying to organize and classify identity outcomes, this chapter reveals the untidiness and complexity of belonging for a group of second-generation South Asians in Canada.

Notes

1 South Asia refers primarily to immigrants from India, Pakistan, Bangladesh, Sri Lanka, and Nepal. It is a term that has been used by the community itself and by the Government of Canada's national census. For a broader discussion of the label "South Asian", see Ashutosh (2008) and Chilvers and Walton-Roberts (2014).
2 Canada's points system is a skill-based immigrant selection, in which immigrants are admitted on the basis of transferable human capital characteristics such as education, employment experiences, and knowledge of Canada's official languages.
3 Depending on the data sources and preferences, Canadian researchers use a variety of terms to refer to individuals with origins in India: Indian, East Indian, or Indo-Canadian. Generally, "Indian" is used when referring specifically to people from India and when referencing people's self-identities and connections to their country of origin; "East Indian" is used to distinguish this group from Canada's Indigenous community; "Indo-Canadian" is used for persons of Indian origin who have Canadian citizenship or to reflect the personal merging of identities among individuals who identify themselves as both Indian and Canadian.
4 Gender differences were found regarding other topics in the larger study, such as social regulations and dating/marriage expectations.
5 I did not detect any religious differences in identity processes. This could be a limitation of the study size, as there were not large enough samples from each religious group to draw meaningful comparisons.

References

Abada, Teresa, and Eric Y. Tenkorang (2009). "Pursuit of university education among the children of immigrants in Canada: The roles of parental human capital and social capital". *Journal of Youth Studies* 12(2): 185–207.

Ali, Mehrunnisa Ahmad (2008). "Second-generation youth's belief in the myth of Canadian multiculturalism". *Canadian Ethnic Studies* 40(2): 89–107.

Amarasingam, Amarnath, Gayathri Naganathan, and Jennifer Hyndman (2016). "Canadian multiculturalism as banal nationalism: Understanding everyday meanings among Sri Lankan Tamils in Toronto". *Canadian Ethnic Studies* 48(2): 119–141.

Asher, Nina (2002). "Class acts: Indian American high school students negotiate professional and ethnic identities". *Urban Education* 37(2): 267–295.

Ashutosh, Ishan (2008). "From the census to the city: Representing South Asians in Canada and Toronto". *Diaspora: A Journal of Transnational Studies* 17(2), Summer: 130–148.

Banting, Keith, and Will Kymlicka (2010). "Canadian multiculturalism: Global anxieties and local debates". *British Journal of Canadian Studies* 23(1): 43–72.

Basch, Linda, Nina Glick-Schiller, and Cristina Szanton Blanc (1994). *Nations unbound: Transnational projects, postcolonial predicaments and deterritorialized nation-states*. London: Gordon and Breach Science Publishers.

Bhat, C., and Ajaya K. Sahoo (2003). "Diaspora to transnational networks: The case of Indians in Canada". In Sushma J. Varma and Radhika Seshan (eds.), *Fractured identity: The Indian diaspora in Canada* (pp. 141–167). New Delhi: Rawat Publications.

Bhattacharya, Gauri (2000). "Adjustment of South Asian immigrant children to schools in the United States". *Adolescence* 35(137): 77–85.

Bolognani, Marta (2014). "Visits to the country of origin: How second-generation British Pakistanis shape transnational identity and maintain power asymmetries". *Global Networks* 14(1):103–120.

Boyd, Monica (2002). "Educational attainments of immigrant offspring: Success or segmented assimilation?". *International Migration Review* 36(4):1037–1060.

Boyd, Monica (2008). "Variations in socioeconomic outcomes of second-generation young adults". *Canadian Diversity* 6(2): 20–24.

Boyd, Monica, and Elizabeth Grieco (1998). "Triumphant transitions: Socioeconomic achievements of the second generation in Canada". *International Migration Review* 32(3): 853–876.

Byng, Michelle (2017). "Transnationalism among second-generation Muslim Americans: Being and belonging in their transnational social field". *Social Sciences* 6:131.

Chilvers, Simon, and Margaret Walton-Roberts (2014). "Introduction: Deconstructing the (re)construction of South Asian identities in Canada". *Diaspora: A Journal of Transnational Studies* 17(2), Summer 2008 (published in 2014): 121–129.

Colombo, Enzo, and Paola Rebughini (2012). *Children of immigrants in a globalized world: A generational experience*. Houndmills, Basingstoke: Palgrave Macmillan.

Das Gupta, Monisha (1997). "What is Indian about you? A gendered transnational approach to ethnicity". *Gender and Society* 11: 572–596.

DeHanas, Daniel, N. (2013). "Of hajj and home: Roots visits to Mecca and Bangladesh in everyday belonging". *Ethnicities* 13(4): 457–474.

Finn, Rachel L. (2008). "South Asian? American? Confused?: Categories of identification for young women of South Asian descent". In Anand Singh (ed.), *Youth and Migration* (pp. 11–21). Delhi: Kamla-Raj Enterprises.

Hebert, Yvonne, Lori Wilkinson, Mehrunnisa Ahmad Ali, and Temitope Oriola (2008). "New modes of becoming in transcultural glocal spaces: Second-generation youth in Calgary, Winnipeg and Toronto". *Canadian Ethnic Studies* 40(2): 61–87.

Kasinitz, Philip, Mary C. Waters, John H. Mollenkopf, and Merih Anil (2002). "Transnationalism and the children of immigrants in contemporary New York". In Peggy Levitt and Mary C. Waters (eds.), *The changing face of home: The transnational lives of the second generation* (pp. 96–122). New York, NY: Russell Sage Foundation.

Kibria, Nazli (2009). "'Marry into a good family': Transnational reproduction and intergenerational relations in Bangladeshi American families". In Nancy Foner (ed.), *Across generations: Immigrant families in America* (pp. 98–113). New York, NY: New York University Press.

Levitt, Peggy (2002). "The ties that change: Relations to the ancestral home over the life cycle". In Peggy Levitt and Mary C. Waters (eds.), *The changing face of home: The transnational lives of the second generation* (pp.123–144). New York, NY: Russell Sage Foundation.

Levitt, Peggy (2009) "Routes and roots: Understanding the lives of the second generation transnationally". *Journal of Ethnic and Migration Studies* 35(7): 1225–1242.

Levitt, Peggy, and Mary C. Waters (2002). *The changing face of home: The transnational lives of the second generation*. New York, NY: Russell Sage Foundation.

Levitt, Peggy, and Nina Glick-Schiller (2004). "Conceptualizing simultaneity: A transnational social field perspective on society". *International Migration Review* 38(3): 1002–1039.

Levitt, Peggy, and Nadya Jaworsky (2007). "Transnational migration studies: Past developments and future trends". *Annual Review of Sociology* 33: 129–156.

Levitt, Peggy, Kristen Lucken, and Melissa Barnett (2014). "Beyond home and return: Negotiating religious identity across time and space through the prism of the American experience". In Russell King, Anastasia Christou, and Peggy Levitt (eds.), *Links to the diasporic homeland: Second generation and the ancestral 'return' mobilities* (pp. 17–32). London: Routledge.

Maira, Sunaina (2002). *Desis in the house: Indian American youth culture in New York City*. Philadelphia, PA: Temple University Press.

O'Neill, Tom (2015). "In the path of heroes: Second-generation Tamil-Canadians after the LTTE". *Identities* 22(1): 124–139.

Patel, Dhiru (2006). "The maple-neem nexus: Transnational links of South Asian Canadians". In Vic Satzewich and Lloyd Wong (eds.), *Transnational identities and practices in Canada* (pp. 151–163). Vancouver: University of British Columbia Press.

Picot, Garnett, and Feng Hou (2011). "Preparing for success in Canada and the United States: The determinants of educational attainment among the children of immigrants". Statistics Canada, Catalogue no. 11F0019M, no. 332. http://www.statcan.gc.ca/pub/11f0019m/11f0019m2011332-eng.pdf.

Portes, Alejandro, and Ruben Rumbaut (2001). *Legacies: The story of the immigrant second generation*. Berkeley, CA: University of California Press.

Purkayastha, Bandana (2005). *Negotiating ethnicity: Second-generation South Asian Americans traverse a transnational world*. New Brunswick, NJ: Rutgers University Press.

Purkayastha, Bandana (2010). "Interrogating intersectionality: Contemporary globalisation and racialised gendering in the lives of highly educated South Asian Americans and their children". *Journal of Intercultural Studies* 31(1):29–47.

Rahman, Zaynah, and Matthew A. Witenstein (2014). "A quantitative study of cultural conflict and gender differences in South Asian American college students". *Ethnic and Racial Studies* 37(6): 1121–1137.

Reitz, Jeffrey G. (2012). "The distinctiveness of Canadian immigration experience". *Patterns of Prejudice* 46(5): 518–538.

Reitz, Jeffrey G., and Raymond Breton (1994). *The illusion of difference: Realities of ethnicity in Canada and the United States*. Toronto: C.D. Howe Institute.

Reitz, Jeffrey G., and Rupa Banerjee (2007). "Racial inequality and social cohesion in Canada: Findings from the ethnic diversity survey". In Keith Banting, Thomas J. Courchene, and F. Leslie Seidle (eds.), *Belonging? Diversity, recognition and shared citizenship in Canada* (pp. 489–545). Montreal: Institute for Research on Public Policy, 2007

Reitz, Jeffrey G., Heather Zhang, and Nako Hawkins (2011). "Comparisons of the success of racial minority immigrant offspring in the United States, Canada and Australia". *Social Science Research* 40: 1051–1066.

Reynolds, Tracey, and Elisabetta Zontini (2014). "Bringing transnational families from the margins to the centre of family studies in Britain". *Families, Relationships and Societies*, 3(2): 251–268.

Reynolds, Tracey, and Elisabetta Zontini (2016). "Transnational and diasporic youth identities: Exploring conceptual themes and future research agendas". *Identities* 23(4): 379–391.

Rumbaut, Rubén G. (2002). "Severed or sustained attachments? Language, identity, and imagined communities in the post-immigrant generation". In P. Levitt and M. Waters (eds.), *The changing face of home: The transnational lives of the second generation* (pp. 43–95). New York, NY: Russell Sage Foundation.

Rumbaut, Rubén G. (2008). "Reaping what you sow: Immigration, youth, and reactive ethnicity". *Applied Developmental Science* 12(2): 108–111.

Samuel, Lina (2010). "Mating, dating and marriage: Intergenerational cultural retention and the construction of diasporic identities among South Asian immigrants in Canada". *Journal of Intercultural Studies* 31(1): 95–110.

Sano, Yujira, Lisa Kaida, and Eric Y. Tenkorang (2015). "Racial variations in ethnic identity among the children of immigrants in Canada". *Canadian Ethnic Studies* 47(3): 49–68.

Saran, Rupam (2009). "In between Indianness and Americanness: Second-generation Asian Indian youths in New York". In Anand Singh (ed.), *Indian diaspora: 21st century challenges: Globalisation, ethnicity, and identity* (pp. 51–64). Delhi: Kamla Raj Enterprises.

Shankar, Shalini (2008). *Desi land: Teen culture, class and success in Silicon Valley*. London: Duke University Press.

Somerville, Kara (2008). "Transnational belonging among second-generation youth: Identity in a globalized world". In Anand Singh (ed.), *Youth and migration* (pp. 23–33). Delhi: Kamla-Raj Enterprises.

Somerville, Kara (2009). "Marriage and childbirth as transnational triggers: Homeland attachments of second-generation Indo-Canadians". In Anand Singh (ed.), *Indian Diaspora: 21st century challenges: Globalisation, ethnicity, and identity* (pp. 41–50). Delhi: Kamla Raj Enterprises.

Somerville, Kara (2013). "Transnational care-giving practices among Indo-Canadian women migrants: Creating and maintaining families through cooking and healthcare". *Transnational Social Review* 3(2): 211–227.

Somerville, Kara, and Oral Robinson (2016). "Keeping up appearances within the ethnic community: A disconnect between first and second generation South Asians' educational aspirations". *Canadian Ethnic Studies* 48(2): 99–117.

Srinivasan, Sharada (2018). "Transnationally relocated? Sex selection among Punjabis in Canada". *Canadian Journal of Development Studies* 39(3): 408–425.

Sriskandarajah, Anuppiriya (2008). "Demonstrating identities: Multiculturalism, citizenship, and Tamil Canadian identities". *Diaspora: A Journal of Transnational Studies* 17(2): 172–195.

Statistics Canada (2011). "Generation status: Canadian-born children of immigrants". National Household Survey, Catalogue no. 99-010-X2011003.

Statistics Canada (2016). "Children with an immigrant background: Bridging cultures". Census of Population, Catalogue no. 98-200-X2016015.

Statistics Canada (2017). "Immigration and ethnocultural diversity: Key results from the 2016 Census". *The Daily*, Wednesday, October 25.

Vertovec, Steven (2001). *Transnational challenges to the "new" multiculturalism*. Working Paper WPTC-01-06. Oxford: Transnational Communities Programme.

Walton-Roberts, Margaret (2001). "Returning, remitting, reshaping: Non-resident Indians and the transformation of society and space in Punjab, India". Working Paper Series No. 01-15. Vancouver: Vancouver Centre of Excellence.

Walton-Roberts, Margaret (2003) "Transnational geographies: Indian immigration to Canada". *The Canadian Geographer* 47(3): 235–250.

Walton-Roberts, Margaret (2011). "Multiculturalism already unbound". In May Chazan, Lisa Helps, Anna Stanley, and Sonali Thakkar (eds.), *Home and native land: Unsettling multiculturalism in Canada* (pp. 102–122). Toronto: Between the Lines.

Wong, Lloyd, and Vic Satzewich (2006). "Introduction: The meaning and significance of transnationalism". In Vic Satzewich and Lloyd Wong (eds.), *Transnational identities and practices in Canada* (pp. 1–17). Vancouver: University of British Columbia Press.

Wu, Zheng, Christoph Schimmele, and Feng Hou (2012). "Self-perceived integration of immigrants and their children". *Canadian Journal of Sociology* 37(4): 381–408.

Zaidi, Arshu U., Amanda Couture-Carron, Elenor Maticka-Tyndale, and Mehek Arif (2014). "Ethnic identity, religion and gender: An exploration of intersecting identities creating diverse perceptions and experiences with intimate cross-gender relationships amongst South Asian youth in Canada". *Canadian Ethnic Studies* 46(2): 27–54.

9
NEGOTIATING TRANSNATIONAL IDENTITY AMONG SECOND-GENERATION INDIAN RESIDENTS IN OMAN

Sandhya Rao Mehta

Introduction

The Arabian Gulf is one of the most fertile areas for the exploration of transnational homes, given the absence of permanence by citizenship but with the possibility of long-term settlement for some workers. Historically, the Indian Ocean has long been the center of transnational flows, as trade flourished right from the Bronze Age onward between the Indian coasts and the Arabian peninsula, over toward Iraq and Turkey in the spice route (Gilbert, 2002; Keshodkar, 2014; De Bel Air, 2018). In the late twentieth and early twenty-first centuries, following the oil boom and resulting national developmental programs undertaken by the 6 Gulf Cooperation Council (GCC) countries of Saudi Arabia, Qatar, United Arab Emirates, Kuwait, Oman and Bahrain, the migratory flow increased substantially, giving rise to a large population whose presence is temporary and directly dependent on their work status, primarily owing to the kafala system which ensures that all residents are directly linked to an individual or institutional sponsor. While the narrative of exploitation and migrant worker rights have been extensively discussed in the context of the Gulf (Gamburd, 2009; Gardner, 2013), a considerable vacuum exists in the exploration of guest workers who eventually lived for a long period of time[1] in any of the countries of the Gulf and whose children grow up and reside for the first 18 years of their life in a country where they cannot legally continue their lives (unless supported by their own permits sanctioned by work, education or marriage to a resident). Torn from the geographical spaces which they call home, these individuals must either return to their home countries or go to a third country to continue to study and work. Having been rejected by the only space they call "home," these second- (at times third-) generation children of residents in the Gulf adopt a variety of transnational practices in order to negotiate their identity and place in a global world.

This paper focuses on second-generation Indian residents in Oman, most of whom were either born there or came as very young children but are not entitled to any benefits by the State once they turn 18 and are considered adults as opposed to their earlier status of being dependents of the worker. This has implications on the way these individuals perceive meanings of home, languages adopted and choices made about their future. Transnational identity is here not a choice but the resultant reality of their social situation. Based on interviews and questionnaires with more than 30 individuals born and raised in Oman, this research explores the creation of homes in a transnational context where identity is determined by institutional forces outside the control of individuals. Using Appadurai's (1990) notion of transnational belonging and Avtar Brah's (1996) work on diasporic space, this paper reflects on the creation of a Gulf-based Indian community whose home becomes more potent in the imagination as its physical presence erodes. This research suggests that transnational identities among residents in the Gulf are problematized by their inability to reside in the country of their birth while being disconnected to their country of origin, but that such non-belonging, in turn, creates opportunities for reconceptualization of home within this particular diaspora which could be termed as creative transnationalism.

The Indian community in the Gulf is almost always thought of as consisting of temporary migrant workers who spend a few years at varying levels of the manufacturing, infrastructural or services sector and return to their home states with enough means to support themselves for life. Ever since the first large group of workers in the early 1970s, the continuing cyclical pattern of migration has been unrelenting. Not only do these migrants represent the largest foreign work force but also their combined remittances are larger than all other remittances received in India. While much research has focused on these temporary migrant workers, the relative permanence of families who have lived and worked in the region over a larger period of time, in some cases more than 30 years or more, has largely gone unnoticed. For these families, migration is not just a temporary sojourn to fulfill a three-year contract but one that spans their entire careers. For the children of these migrants, often born in the Gulf and growing up there, migration has an entirely different meaning. Labelled by the state as a foreigner in the country of their birth and the place of their formative years, the second generation finds itself forced to redefine the framework within which it sees itself as Indian/foreigner. While children of diasporic communities in various contexts across the world have often been seen to merge more successfully with the land their parents have settled in (Bhattacharya, 2008; Hussain, 2005), in the context of the Gulf countries, no such assurance is possible. In fact, if anything, the children of migrants in the Gulf embody a larger sense of displacement and non-belonging owing to the peculiar circumstances determined by two factors which they cannot control: the state; and the decisions of their family. Coupled with global opportunities of the new millennium, the transnational possibilities of these residents create spaces in which their identities are re-formed and re-articulated in ways that reflect an emotional non-belonging to their country of citizenship and the enforced disconnect to the country of their youth. Such a disconnect in turn allows for a creative transnational identity that looks back as much as it looks forward to forging past and future lives.

Framing the transnational

UNESCO uses Vertovec's (2001) notions of interlinking communities through economic, cultural and political ties as reflecting transnationalism in the age of globalization. Given that communities are increasingly interlinked through technology, increased mobility and economic interdependence, migration is often re-framed in the context of transnationalism. Such tendencies affect a vital relationship between sending and receiving countries where a migrant's cord with the homeland is not completely cut. This has social, economic and even political implications, as migrants continue to impact and determine the political climate and outcomes of their home countries. For example, religious transnationalism as determined by global Hindu movements which are seen to account for the rise of the Hindu right in India spurred by Western donors and pressure groups are an important example of transnational identity. As Appadurai noted as early as 1990 that:

the overseas movement of Indians has been exploited by a variety of interests both within and outside India to create a complicated network of finances and religious identifications, in which the problems of cultural reproduction for Hindus abroad has become tied to the politics of Hindu fundamentalism at home.

(Appadurai, 1990: 296)

So, while the connections between nations are increasingly interlinked, the borders themselves are being redefined through this process of interconnectedness. An essential component of postmodern geographies and migration studies, it is commonly connected to the major migratory corridors in the world, including the Mexican–American border, the African–European one and various forms of the Indian diaspora as well (Sahoo, Baas and Faist, 2012; Safran, Sahoo and Lal 2009; Bhattacharya, 2008). While these migrations and diasporic experiences from the Global South to the North have been substantially documented, the South–South migrations, of which the South Asian to the Arabian Gulf is the most prominent, has been less explored. Not only is this a significant group of people but also their study works into Vertovec's call to study specific cases of transnationalism without bringing all experiences of diasporas under one umbrella: "Research needs to detail the current extent, structural and technical capacities, and migrants' own desires, strategies and practices of remaining connected around the world, and exactly how these are continuous with, or distinct from, earlier patterns of linkage" (2001: 577).

Homemaking and transnationalism

In the context of millennial families, homemaking strategies stand in contrast, if not in opposition, to diasporic representations of home which are centered around nostalgia, memory and the (im)possibility of return. Technology, travel and real-time connectivity with the homeland ensures that the home-and-away binary of diaspora is translated into a more complex network of interconnectedness whereby home is re-imagined and re-created through images available in the imagined and virtual world (Henry and Mohan, 2003; Parreñas, 2005). Avtar Brah (2005: 4) explains home as:

> the place where feelings of rootedness ensue from the mundane and the unexpected of daily practice. Home here connotes our networks of family, kin, friends, colleagues and various other "significant others." It signifies the social and psychic geography of space that is experienced in terms of a neighbourhood or a home town. That is, a community "imagined" in most part through daily encounter. This "home" is a place with which we remain intimate even in moments of intense alienation from it. It is a sense of "feeling at home."

This sense of home and memory is further complicated in situations where the real home cannot be easily accessed, for legal (as opposed to political or economic) reasons. In the context of transnational workers in the Middle East, this is particularly relevant to the lived experiences of a large community of individuals who grow up in a land (which is not the country of their citizenship) which they have to leave upon turning 18. Having left behind the land of their memories and childhood friendships, these young adults have to negotiate an entirely different life, finding creative ways to connect to the countries which they cannot easily access any more. This is a fairly typical situation with children of workers in the GCC countries who are compelled to leave their parents to pursue higher education and subsequently work.

The multiple ways in which these individuals stay connected, interact and remember the land of their childhood is an apt example of creative transnationalism.

The case of Oman

As has been pointed out frequently in Indian Ocean studies, transnationalism in the Arabian Gulf predates the oil encounter by centuries (Onley 2014; Oonk, 2016; Hofmeyer, 2007). With trade between Indian shores and along the spice route facilitating movement of traders and, with them, cultures and religion, increased interactions between South Asia, East Africa and the Gulf corridor has been extensively documented. The pastoral nature of life in the Gulf ensured the irrelevance of latter-day borders. Even under British rule of South Asia, the Middle East was controlled by agents who were often Indian, working in the ports of the Gulf and representing the British. Such early examples of transnational contact continued through the discovery of oil, for specifically economic considerations as more labor was required to develop the infrastructure of newly emerging nation states. While the early participants in the economic development of these countries were Arab (Kapiszewski, 2006; Birks, Seccombe and Sinclair, 1986), the impulse to distance workers from participation in contemporary political realities created a switch to the demand for labor from non-Arabic-speaking Asian nations. These workers included every spectrum of the labor market, from domestic work, farming and construction to while collar work including doctors, engineers, teachers and employers at every level of public and private administration. This led to a very particular demographic in which foreign workers found themselves living and working for long periods of time, at times their entire career, in a land they knew they would have to eventually leave (Kanna, 2010; Ong, 1999).

Irrespective of the nature of work, all expatriates in the Gulf, including Oman, work under the commonly known kafala system. This entails the sponsorship of each individual worker by a citizen or a recognized organization. Such sponsorship suggests that each employer can stay in the country only as long as their sponsorship by a certain entity is valid and renewed every two years. Once the employee is relieved of a specific job, they automatically lose the right to live in the country, unless they have another job in hand. This system of sponsorship applies not only to an employee but also to their immediate family, only some of whom are entitled to accompany them. This is entirely dependent on the policies of the country. At present, those earning a minimum of OMR 300 are entitled to bring their family to Oman. This amount was decreased from OMR 600 in 2010.[2]

Ethnographic studies of the Indian middle class in Oman are rare. Deffner and Pfaffenbach (2011), Mehta and Onley (2015) and Mehta (2017) have documented the daily lives of the Indian community in Muscat city, exploring the various strategies of diaspora and belonging used to create homes in spaces where they are seen to be foreigners and temporary, even if they have lived more than three decades in the country. The structure of the rentier system based on the kafala implies that an individual could live for decades in the country, working for the same organization, but not be eligible for permanent residency or citizenship. In the case those who may have lived and been employed for a large part of their lives in Oman, they would retire around the age of 65[3] at which point they would have to return to India or look elsewhere for other opportunities for which they may have planned (such as joining their children in other countries or returning to countries where they may have taken citizenship, usually Canada, Australia or New Zealand and, in some cases, the United States or South Africa[4]).

Within the Arab Gulf, transnationalism remains relatively unexplored, given the perceived temporary nature of its migrant population and, at times, the relatively lower levels of education and consequent absence of strategies of transnationalism through extensive use of technology or frequent travel. As used by Gardner (2008), Vora (2008) and Ali (2011), it remains essentially a middle- (including trading) class, white-collar phenomenon whereby the realities of non-citizenship and temporary residence are addressed in strategic and creative ways which impact individuals and families in ways diametrically different to cases in more permanent migration contexts.

Migration studies have almost uniformly focused on the temporary nature of migrancy, determined by state forces to restrict cultural intermingling:

> Since the 1990s, the Gulf monarchies have tried to have a tighter grip on migration. They have been openly endorsing "anti-integration" policies aimed at preventing the settlement and incorporation of migrant workers in host societies.... They have cultivated a model of migration management anchored in the paradigm of "temporary labor import," promoting short-term contracts and the turnover of migrants, preventing family reunification and naturalisation, limiting socio-economic rights and implementing deportation programmes for irregular migrants. This set of policies and practices in transnational migration management may be called the "Gulf model."
>
> *(Thiollet, 2016: 4)*

Yet, as increasing ethnographic research in the region suggests, such temporary migratory patterns, while not permanent, are long lasting, often covering entire career spans. While this is relevant to workers on all levels of the social spectrum (with workers often being renewed contracts multiple times and those on free visas and business visas using the official system to stay),[5] its impact on the second generation applied primarily to white-collar workers, who are more likely to be eligible to bring their families and stay for a longer period of time, working out successive series of three-year contracts.

It is the children of these resident white-collar workers who face the uncertain future which is symptomatic of the working lives in Oman. A previously demarcated 600 OMR was reduced to 300 OMR in 2017 to be eligible to bring families, adding to the population of dependents for whom a variety of facilities such as schools would be necessary. By May 2018, more than 50 000 children are documented as studying in the 19 Indian schools across Oman and the more expensive private schools in Muscat and Sohar.[6] Anecdotal evidence suggests that more than half of these students who begin school here are likely to finish here, except for unforeseen circumstances as the loss of their parent(s)' job or other emergencies. Thus most of them know of no other home than Oman as they are forced to choose another destination for their higher education at age 19. As they navigate between their physical and emotional homes in Oman and the new places they opt to continue to study, the choices of home and its ever-increasing complexities become more apparent. The transnational strategies adopted suggest that, while Oman remains an essential component of their formative life, the exigencies of state policy separates this geographical space from continuing to be part of their life. As such, they rationalize their experiences in Oman as a separate and disconnected aspect of their life.

This study is based on 26 Indian residents between 20 and 26 years old who spent a substantial part of their lives in Oman and have then moved to other places after having turned 18. Of the 26, 88.5 percent of them said that they had lived in Oman for more than 12 years and 57.7 percent said that their parents had been in Oman for more than 20 years. Almost all of them (92.5%) said that they went to Oman at least once a year. Half of them (56.5%) are presently studying in India, while the other half are spread in United States, Singapore and Canada. All of them are undergraduate students who left Oman in the last two to three years.

Asked about whether they would have liked to continue to study in Oman, most of them said that they preferred to go away, bearing in mind that the universities offer very few options and no career opportunities.[7] Yet, when asked about whether they would come back, the answers were more ambivalent:

- Not really. Again there are many restrictions and there isn't a guarantee of staying there for a particular number of years so uncertainty everywhere.
- No, due to lack of personal growth.
- Definitely, it is a better environment.
- I wouldn't as job opportunities for expat. women are limited.
- Not in the immediate future, but definitely in the later stages of my career.
- I would consider working here because it is home.
- Yes because one can offer a better lifestyle.
- Yes, home environment and friendly locals.
- I think I would. Life is very comfortable.
- Definitely. It was the perfect place to grow up and I'd like my kids to have at least the same (if not better) quality of life in the future.
- Yes I would consider working in Oman but only when I was older and more experienced as the companies there do not provide as many opportunities for development to new recruits.

Thus, not all participants have rejected the possibility of returning to work in Oman as their parents had come earlier, but this would be contingent on their getting a job and subsequent work permits. For all purposes, Oman is not their place of residence anymore.

Yet, when asked about what Oman meant to them, the answers were uniformly nostalgic and celebratory:

- Yes always! I lived in Oman since I was some months old so that's the only place that makes me feel like home.
- Yes definitely.
- Everyway. It's an emotion.
- Yes, I associate Oman with my childhood.
- Home is and will always be home to me. It is the place I go back to every now and then and feel the most "at home." It has a familiar sense of warmth that is absent in any other place.
- Yes, it gives me a different feeling being in Oman.
- Yes, my parents are there as are my friends. I also have the earliest and most treasured memories there.
- I don't consider it "Home" but I've been here a long time and it does have sentimental value to me as I've grown up here.
- Yes. I was born in Oman and I've had my whole childhood here. India is my home country yes but Oman is a country I have a different type of connection to.
- Yeah, since I've grown up there a part of my heart will always belong to Oman.
- Yes, been there for 20 years.
- Yes as I have lived most of my life there.
- Yes, because this is the place where I have hundreds of memories.
- Yes, having spent 22 years in Oman, more time than anywhere else, Oman is more home than any other place will ever be.
- Oman is home. I've spent my whole life there and there's no other place I would go.
- If my family stays I will but it's on my job also.

- Yes. I've always believed that home is where the heart is. And to this day, there hasn't been a doubt about where that is. If not now, Oman would always be another home away from home. Any day.
- Grew up there from the age of 2 and completed my entire education there. Thus I have an obvious attachment to the places in Muscat and its friendly people, not to mention most of my friends I grew up with, I'd say are my best friends.
- Was born and brought up there.
- Yes I lived there all my life.
- Yes, I mostly definitely think it is home. After spending 18 years of my life in Oman I can't call any other place home.
- Yes Oman is home. I grew up there and almost all my memories bot from there. Most of my friends are from there and we still talk about Oman as going back home. When I get homesick I think of Oman.
- I was born and brought up there for 18 years. It's definitely a home to me!
- Yes, I mostly think it is home. After spending 18 years of my life in Oman I can't call any other place home.

When asked about their favorite memories, "Friday mornings, beaches, friends, shawarma, wadis, the corniche, the beautiful roads" were the most popular responses.

While 95 percent of those questioned said that they came back annually, most of them will now require another form of official entry as they are not entitled to be residents after turning 18. The process to acquire a tourist or visit visa is fairly complex, requiring a sponsor (the parent's organization) and the issuance of an insurance policy. This entitles them to a three-month visit visa. When asked about the new rules they would have to follow, most of them said that they felt "bad" and uncomfortable to have to request a visa to visit the country of their childhood. Typically, one respondent said, "I mean, I have lived here all my life and now I need so many papers to be photocopied and submitted . . . and then I have to stand in a long line to get my passport stamped!" The previously owned resident card which allowed them to enter the country without passport stamping is now denied to them, and they can only be temporary visitors in the country of their birth.

Syed Ali suggests that, on the face of it, second-generation migrants would show lesser tendencies toward transnationalism as they would be more closely connected to their adopted countries. Clearly, this is not the case in the Arabian Gulf, where citizenship or even official permanent residency is not an available option, even if desired. Given such a disconnect between aspiration and reality, the strategies employed by those who have remaining roots in Oman through family and friends is no longer determined by physical ties but by the various forms of transnational connections such as social media and other online participation as school alumni and other social groups on facebook and twitter. For example, many of the respondents remain connected to teachers and tutors from high school as well as the teachers of other activities such as dance and music. They continue to participate virtually in productions of their old schools and institutions, often commenting on them, making suggestions and just "liking" such events on facebook. Their interactions with events in Oman are thus an extension of their lives here, participating in the only way that it would be possible for them. This is particularly interesting in individuals who are now based in a country other than India, commenting on Indian festivals and Indian cultural events in Oman. Such seamless interactions point to creative ways in which transnational identities are constructed among young Indians from Oman, inhabiting an imaginary space that links the country of their birth (Oman), the country of their parents (India) and the country in which they currently live.

Two case studies will better point the negotiations made by these second-generation Indian residents in Oman:

Ronald's[8] parents came to Oman in 1991. They are both doctors from Kerala. Ronald's father is an anesthetist, and his mother is a pediatrician. They both responded to advertisements in an Indian newspaper placed by the Ministry of Health of Oman to join the rising number of hospitals and clinics in various parts of Oman. Ronald's father was appointed in a large publicly funded hospital in Muscat, while his mother joined a clinic in another part of the city. A few years later, Ronald's mother Mamata also joined the same hospital as her husband. As doctors, they were considered to be representing the diasporic elite, earning much more than many of their compatriots in Oman who were either living in single-income families with the man earning.[9] Roland was born in 1993 in Oman, as his mother was already working here in the hospital and she had access to medical facilities.[10] Ronald first went home, back to Kochi, when he was one year old and, subsequently, after every two years. Having spent his early childhood with a neighbor who informally babysat him, he went to the Indian school closest to his house at the age of three. Like many expatriate children, he went on to learn karate, music and swimming, which his parents would coordinate with other parents to pick and drop. His entire social life consisted of participating in social events of his school and observing the various religious events of his community in Oman. He spent some of his holidays on a package tour of Europe and one in Singapore, but the rest of his holidays were spent with his grandparents and extended families in Kochi. Ronald finished grade 12 in 2011 and, in his words,

> only then did I realize that I could not live in Oman anymore. I had to find a future somewhere else. My friends were going to India but I also had the option of going somewhere else. I was not sure what to do or where to go but the idea of being forced to go away from Oman hit me very hard. . . . I always knew I had to go away but when the time came, it was very upsetting.

As many respondents earlier had mentioned, the education standard in Oman is not considered very competitive, and there are very few choices in terms of programs and specializations. The professional field is also very uncertain, and students do not know what opportunities, if any, would be available to them upon completion of a degree which may not be valuable in any other part of the world. Ronald went on to a university in the United States to pursue finance. In his early years he would come back and work as an unpaid intern for the two-month summer break at a private company. These companies are multinational but with an Omani sponsor. Ronald, an Indian citizen, brought his international (American) expertise to an Omani company. When asked about his reaction to this transnational moment, he reminisced that he liked to work here in the early years as it brought him closer home: "I like being at home but also being able to visit my grandparents in India from here . . . it was closer and cheaper." Asked if he wanted to continue working here, he was more ambivalent:

> I don't know . . . I feel I like Oman because of what it gave me growing up but I don't feel I have a connection now. It's not the same, most of my friends have gone away and my parents live in another locality which I don't know very well. Sometimes I come when my friends and I meet up but otherwise, I meet my parents when they come to me (in US) or in India. Getting a visa is very complicated and we can't leave the country and visit Dubai or anywhere, so what it the point of coming here?

Like many others of his cohort, Ronald is hoping to find work in the United States and eventually get a green card, which would finally grant him permanent residency denied to him in the country of his birth. But as long as he remains a student there, he finds himself in a state of permanent impermanence, a foreign student in the United States with temporary access to Oman and a citizen of a country where he has not spent any meaningful length of time. Ronald introduced an important limitation in the lives of residents' children which is determined by their nationality. When they come back to visit Oman on a three-month, single-entry-visit visa, they cannot leave the country to visit India or anywhere else and come back. So all holidays are planned in ways that include a single visit to Oman followed by a trip to other countries, including neighboring Dubai or even India. This limits their interaction with their former host country as they negotiate ways in which to socialize with their childhood friends or revisit places important to them.

Women have even more complex ways of negotiating transnational identities in Oman, as the patrilinear form of residency legitimizes their stay there only as daughters or wives. Unless recruited as teachers, doctors or nurses, most women are on dependent visas, which officially prohibit them from working. Single women under 30 are not given independent visas, and so girls who have gone to college outside Oman cannot come back to visit the country unless their parents are still working in Oman.[11] Yet, the attraction of Oman as a safe place to live and work makes it an aspirational destination: girls who may have grown up here and were made to leave upon completion of school, desire to marry and return to Oman, this time as dependent wives.

Lata grew up in Oman and attended an Indian school here. She left Oman after grade 12 to attend college in Chennai. She completed an undergraduate degree, visiting her parents every year for more than two months at a time, as she missed her family and community. Having earned an MBA from Chennai, she worked for a year in a firm in Chennai, all the while knowing that this would be temporary, as her parents were very keen to get her married to someone "in the Gulf," preferably Oman. Using online platforms and their community network, they introduced her to her future husband who was working in a private company in Oman. Lata was very happy to have an opportunity to return to Oman, where she got a job in her husband's firm. Within two years and one child later, however, her husband was transferred to Sharjah, and Lata found herself working in Oman until she decides to join her husband in Sharjah or live out a long-distance relationship. She also has another plan, which is to apply for Canadian or Australian residency, which would allow her family to finally be together. Meanwhile, her father had retired (at 60) and returned to their home in Bangalore, a city that Lata had never been to. Of this predicament Lata says,

> I love Oman and would love to stay here. I wish I could stay here all my working life and send my children to school here as I did . . . it was very nice, but I don't think I can stay her long. The pressure to nationalize the jobs is very high and I will have to have other plans. But I tell my husband that we can stay here as long as they let us. After that, we will see . . . all my friends in the church as in my neighborhood feel the same way. We don't want to go but I know we cannot stay here forever.

Lata now spends her time between Sharjah, Bangalore and Muscat, keeping an eye on an eventual Australian residency.

In her iconic work on home in the diaspora, Avtar Brah articulates the inherent struggles of negotiating homes:

What is home? On the one hand, "home" is a mythic place of desire in the diasporic imagination. In this sense it is a place of return, even if it is possible to visit the geographical territory that is seen as the place of "origin." On the other hand, home is also a lived experience of a locality.

(Brah, 2005: 192)

Such a perspective helps to view the formation of multiple homes within communities for whom home is not a binary space of here-and-there but a fleeting combination of different homes. The strategies adopted to negotiate within these physical and virtual spaces are necessitated by a variety of circumstances which range from the political to the personal. Such transnational behavior as cited above is necessitated by the knowledge of the permanent state of impermanence in the Gulf that is largely determined by the state. But it is also a creative coping strategy to live between borders as a way of reconciling the various push and pull factors in a postmodern context. While the Arabian Gulf countries determine temporary residency for its guest workers, many white-collar workers have spent their entire working lives here, bringing up families and establishing a rich community and successful life. Being denied permanent residency has implications, not only on their lives but on their children, those second-generation Indians who were born and spent over 18 years of their lives in a country which turns them into visitors upon completion of school. For these people, Oman is the only home they know, and the ways they adopt to such foreignness is an indication of the multiple ways in which transnationalism creates a space within which their multiple identities are rehearsed and enacted.

Acknowledgment

This research has been made possible by the Humanities Research Centre, Sultan Qaboos University, Oman (DVC/PSR/RD/2016/1180).

Notes

1 Although workers in different industries, including domestic workers, have been documented to spend their entire working lives in the Gulf, they are most often not entitled to family visas. Second- and third-generation transnationalism thus primarily relates to children of white-collar professionals as well as traders, some of whom have stayed for generations in these countries. See Parween (2013) and Vora (2013) for a detailed discussion of these workers.
2 This limit was lowered as an incentive to the local market economy, which would be activated with a larger dependent population spending their earnings within the country instead of sending it all back home.
3 While the official age of retirement is 65 for expatriates, this can and has been very loosely followed, and some professionals are kept on as consultants beyond this retirement limit.
4 For a more detailed study of the white-collar workers and their everyday lives in Oman, see Deffner and Pfaffenbach (2011) and Mehta and Onley (2015).
5 Such examples of extended stays have often been recognized and addressed by the Gulf governments, the suggestion of implementing a fixed maximum number of years per worker (six years) being commonly extended. For a number of external and internal considerations, such moves have not been successfully implemented in any country so far.
6 The country's most popular newspaper, *The Times of Oman*, states that two more schools are scheduled to open by 2019 to accommodate the large cohort of students who are forced to attend an evening shift of some classes as the increasing numbers cannot be accommodated in the existing system.
7 The process of Omanization ensures that, while experienced foreign workers continue to be recruited at various levels of the private sector, entry-level jobs for expatriates are almost non-existent, as nationals are given priority at this level.

8 Names are fictitious, but the respondents have given consent for their life narratives to be discussed in an academic paper.
9 Many professionally qualified women marry, join their husbands in Oman and then find themselves without a career opportunity. The consequences of this is subject to an entirely new study on the women of the Gulf diaspora.
10 Most women go back to India for maternal care, as the hospital fee in Oman is high and residents are no longer eligible for public hospital care. Women also go back home to be cared for by their families.
11 This rule was only changed in 2017 when certain single women (with valid visit visas from the United States or Europe) are being allowed on a tourist visa.

References

Ali, S. (2011). Going and Coming and Going Again: Second-Generation Migrants in Dubai. *Mobilities* 6(4), 553–568.
Appadurai, A. (1990). Disjuncture and Difference in the Global Cultural Economy. *Theory, Culture & Society* 7(2–3), 295–310.
Bhattacharya, G. (2008). The Indian Diaspora in Transnational Context: Social Relations and Cultural Identities of Immigrants to New York City. *Journal of Intercultural Studies* 29(1), 65–80, DOI: 10.1080/07256860701759949.
Birks, J., Seccombe, I. and Sinclair, C. (1986). Migrant Workers in the Arab Gulf: The Impact of Declining Oil Revenues. *The International Migration Review* 20(4), 799–814, DOI:10.2307/2545737.
Brah, A. (2005). *Cartographies of Diaspora: Contesting Identities*. London: Taylor & Francis. (Original work published 1996.)
De Bel Air, F. (2018). Asian Migration to the Gulf States in the Twenty-First Century. In M. Chowdhury and I. Rajan (eds.). *South Asian Migration in the Gulf*. Cham: Palgrave Macmillan. 7–34.
Deffner, V. and Pfaffenbach, C. (2011). Zones of Contact and Spaces of Negotiation: The Indian Diaspora in Muscat (Sultanate of Oman). Retrieved from http://www.rc21.org/conferences/amsterdam2011/edocs/Session%2028/28-DP-Deffner.pdf.
Gamburd, M. R. (2009). Advocating for Sri Lankan Migrant Workers: Obstacles and Challenges. *Critical Asian Studies* 41(1), 61–88.
Gardner, A. (2008). Strategic Transnationalism: The Indian Diasporic Elite in Contemporary Bahrain. *City and Society* 20(1), 54–78.
Gardner, A. (2013). A Portrait of Low-Income Migrants in Contemporary Qatar. *Journal of Arabian Studies* 3(1), 1–17.
Gilbert, E. (2002). Coastal East Africa and the Western Indian Ocean: Long-Distance Trade, Empire, Migration, and Regional Unity, 1750–1970. *The History Teacher* 36(1), 7–34.
Henry, L. and Mohan, G. (2003). Making Homes: The Ghanaian Diaspora, Institutions and Development. *Journal of International Development: The Journal of the Development Studies Association* 15(5), 611–622.
Hussain, Y. (2005). *Writing Diaspora*. London: Routledge.
Hofmeyr, I. (2007). The Black Atlantic Meets the Indian Ocean: Forging New Paradigms of Transnationalism for the Global South – Literary and Cultural Perspectives. *Social Dynamics* 33(2), 3–32, DOI: 10.1080/02533950708628759.
Kanna, A. (2010). Flexible Citizenship in Dubai: Neoliberal Subjectivity in the Emerging "City-Corporation." *Cultural Anthropology*, 25(1), 100–129.
Kapiszewski, A. (2006). Arab versus Asian Migrant Workers in the GCC Countries. Retrieved from https://pdfs.semanticscholar.org/6512/6c08bb15b1dfbd7c0951fc09e6f0bb8a50a3.pdf.
Keshodkar, A. (2014). Who Needs China When You Have Dubai? The Role of Networks and the Engagement of Zanzibaris in Transnational Indian Ocean Trade. *Urban Anthropology and Studies of Cultural Systems and World Economic Development* 43(1–3), 105–141.
Mehta, S. R. (2017). Contesting Victim Narratives: Indian Women Domestic Workers in Oman. *Migration and Development* 6(3), 395–411, DOI: 10.1080/21632324.2017.1303065.
Mehta, S. R. and Onley, J. (2015). The Hindu Community in Muscat: Creating Homes in the Diaspora. *Journal of Arabian Studies* 5(2), 156–183, DOI: 10.1080/21534764.2015.1122979.
Ong, A. (1999). *Flexible Citizenship: The Cultural Logics of Transnationality*. Durham, NC: Duke University Press.

Onley, J. (2014). Indian Communities in the Persian Gulf, c. 1500–1947. In L. G. Potter (ed.). *The Persian Gulf in Modern Times*. New York, NY: Palgrave Macmillan.

Oonk, G. (2016). Diaspora and Nation in the Indian Ocean: Transnational Histories of Race and Urban Space in Tanzania. *Journal of World History* 27(3): 587–589.

Parreñas, R. S. (2005). *Children of Global Migration: Transnational Families and Gendered Woes*. Stanford, CA: Stanford University Press.

Parween, A. (2013). "Invisible" Indian White Collar Workers in the Gulf. *Middle East Institute*. Retrieved from https://www.mei.edu/publications/invisible-white-collar-indians-gulf.

Safran, W., Sahoo, A., and Lal, B. (eds.). (2009). *Transnational Migrations: The Indian Diaspora*. New Delhi: Routledge.

Sahoo, A., Baas, M. and Faist, T. (eds.). (2012). *Indian Diaspora and Transnationalism*. New Delhi: Rawat Publications.

Thiollet, Hélène (2016). Managing Migrant Labour in the Gulf: Transnational Dynamics of Migration Politics Since the 1930s. Retrieved from https://spire.sciencespo.fr/hdl:/2441/j960aji478olr2anb4oo4i0ca/resources/wp131-managing-migrant-labour-in-the-gulf-thiollet.pdf.

Vertovec, S. (2001). Transnationalism and Identity. *Journal of Ethnic and Migration Studies* 27(4), 573–582.

Vora, N. (2008). Producing Diasporas and Globalizations: Indian Middle-Class Migrants in Dubai. *Anthropological Quarterly* 81(2), 377–407.

Vora, N. (2013). *Impossible Citizens: Dubai's Indian Diaspora*. London: Duke University Press.

PART III

Political engagement in transnational spaces

10
TRANSNATIONALISM AND INDIAN/AMERICAN FOREIGN POLICY

Pierre Gottschlich

Introduction: the Indian diaspora in the United States

According to official figures, there were close to four million Non-Resident Indians (NRIs) and People of Indian Origin (PIOs) living in the United States by 2015, making Indian Americans one of the fastest growing minorities in the country. Since 1980 their number has almost doubled every decade. By 2016 Indians had become the second-largest group of foreign-born immigrants in the United States after Mexicans (Zong/Batalova 2017). This development is astonishing considering that a visible immigration from India began only after the comprehensive reform of U.S. immigration laws in 1965. While there had been some immigration from South Asia before that watershed date and even some noticeable political activism, the overall number of NRIs and PIOs remained negligible. Discriminatory immigration regulations and quota laws made it virtually impossible for people from India to enter the United States legally. The liberalization of U.S. immigration laws in 1965 coincided with a surplus of highly skilled workers in India. In contrast to many other immigrant groups, these Indians did initially not compete with Americans in the employment market but instead filled vacancies. While earlier migrants from South Asia had to face numerous hardships, the post-1965 immigrants from India were widely seen as "quality migrants". For the most part it was and continues to be an elite migration, which particularly in the first decades consisted almost exclusively of highly skilled workers, academics, and their closest relatives. Hence the Indian American community has to be seen as the deliberate result of U.S. immigration policy and as a "diaspora by design". Indian migrants do not come to the United States without presuppositions. All collective characteristics of the Indian American community have to be interpreted in the light of these specific circumstances.

The Indian diaspora in the United States is widely regarded as one of the most successful immigrant groups in the country. The socioeconomic data are indeed noteworthy. In 2015 the median household income of Indian immigrants was 107,000USD, almost doubling the respective number for the native-born population (Zong/Batalova 2017). At the same time, the rate of Indian Americans living in poverty is remarkably low. At 7.5 percent, it was not even half the number for the general population in 2015. An important reason for this economic success is a comparatively high degree of English proficiency coupled with remarkable educational attainments of NRIs and PIOs. Almost three-quarters of all Indian Americans aged 25 and older have obtained at least a Bachelor's degree (Lopez/Cilluffo 2017). Language skills and a good education are crucial for socioeconomic achievements. They have paved the way for the Indian American community to become a well-established ethnic minority in the United States. Their success has also laid the foundation for a more active political involvement and continued attempts to influence U.S. foreign policy.

Early political activism and the Cold War years

In the first half of the 20th century, transnational political activities of Indians in the United States focused on gathering support for Indian independence from British colonial rule. From 1913 on, San Francisco became the center of the anti-colonial Ghadar Party led by Lala Har Dayal and Ram Chandra. Their efforts, however, were as unsuccessful as earlier attempts by Taraknath Das and others to bring the United States to side with the independence movement in India (Gould 2006: 148–230). As a matter of fact, with the American entrance into the First World War, the Ghadar Party and their anti-British stand was increasingly seen as harmful to the geostrategic interests of the United States, which eventually led to the ban and dissolution of the party. Although short-lived, the Ghadar Party gained importance beyond the United States and had an ideological and political impact throughout the worldwide Indian diaspora (Shukla 2013: 169). The New York-based India League of America (ILA), founded by Lajpat Rai in 1917, continued the political lobby work for India's independence, as did several secular Indian American Muslim organizations created in the 1920s (Agarwala 2016: 929). None were able to create much resonance among decision makers in Washington. When the introduction of more restrictive immigration and naturalization measures closed the door for migrants from South Asia and led to some return migration, the limited political influence of NRIs in the United States was even further reduced. In 1940 there were not even 3,000 Indians left in the country. The Indian American community was virtually invisible. The NRI population and diplomatic relations to their homeland India were insignificant to both the general public and the political sphere (Rubinoff 2005: 172).

While all efforts to help India gain its independence were fruitless, attempts to initiate a reform of the strict immigration laws in the 1940s were more successful. For this the ILA joined hands with the National Committee for India's Freedom (NCIF) and the India Chamber of Commerce (ICC). Although the Indian American community was still very small, their concentration in relatively compact demographic pockets, particularly along the West Coast and in major cities such as New York City or Philadelphia, aided their lobbying efforts (Calder 2014: 204–205). In a very efficient campaign, they helped to push through the Luce-Celler Act of 1946 that lifted some restrictions on immigration from India and for the first time in decades allowed legal entrance to the United States for a limited number of Indians.

This success was only made possible by the commitment and leadership of individual NRIs. The most prominent of these early community leaders was Jagjit ("J.J.") Singh, who on personal advice from Jawaharlal Nehru established the ICC in 1938. In 1940 J.J. Singh became the president of the ILA and revitalized the organization, which at that point had a mere thirteen members. The "one man lobby" J.J. Singh was exactly what the Indian American community needed – "an indefatigable, socially prominent, media-savvy figure who was exotic enough to be exciting to other Americans but assimilated enough in economic position, dress, and language to be nonthreatening on a personal level" (Shaffer 2012: 94). Arguably, nothing demonstrates the significance and influence of J.J. Singh more than the fact that the ILA disbanded after he went back to India in 1959. The high importance of personal leadership during this period is further illustrated by the example of the NCIF, which was also discontinued after three of its four main leaders decided to return to newly independent India in 1947. During the first years of independence, J.J. Singh and the ILA had a crucial role as de facto ambassadors of India in the United States while the diplomatic corps of the nascent nation was only slowly developing towards a working level. Although there are signs that "Indian leaders were not always happy with such extra governmental diplomacy" (Shaffer 2012: 91), it cannot be denied that it was important to India during that stage to have such a transnational "bridge" that could function as an interpreter and thereby correct inaccurate depictions of India in the United States (Shaffer 2012: 77–78).

Ten years after the passage of the Luce-Celler legislation, the Indian American community earned a second remarkable success when Dalip Singh Saund was elected to the U.S. Congress in 1956. Saund, a Punjabi Sikh who came to the United States in 1920, had been the first president of the Indian Association of America (IAA). Just like J.J. Singh and the ILA, Saund and the IAA had campaigned for immigration and naturalization reform in the 1940s. While J.J. Singh and other early community leaders always remained Indian citizens and eventually returned to India, Saund opted for U.S. citizenship as soon as he could (Shaffer 2012: 91). Upon assuming office in 1957, Saund became the first U.S. Congressman of Asian descent. He was re-elected twice, in 1958 and 1960, and was particularly committed to improving the relationship between the United States and India. The Luce-Celler Act and Saund's six-year congressional career were "the high water marks of India in Washington for nearly four decades" (Calder 2014: 205). When Saund suffered a stroke in 1962 and did not win re-election, the Indian American community lost its most prominent voice. In addition, an important and influential transnational political supporter of better relations between both countries was gone.

Tensions between India and the U.S. had already been growing in the very first phase of the Cold War. After India had gained independence, the ILA and other Indian American anti-colonial voices embarked on a broader transnational political project by lobbying in the United States for the independence of other Asian nations such as Indonesia or Vietnam. In fact, the ILA had some influence in changing Washington's Indonesia policy in 1949. However, more often than not, these "pan-Asian solidarity efforts" brought the ILA into conflict with U.S. foreign policy and did not help to alleviate the difficult bilateral relationship between the United States and India (Shaffer 2012: 79–81). At the onset of the Cold War, India refused to enter the Western alliance and followed a non-alignment policy. When the United States reached out to Pakistan and incorporated India's regional rival into its collective security treaty organizations in 1954 and 1955, relations between New Delhi and Washington further deteriorated. With their political leverage declining, transnational actors in the United States were unable to overcome the Cold War logic in U.S. foreign policy towards India, which led to several low points in the relationship. Washington not only entered an alliance with Pakistan but also took anti-India positions on the Goa question in 1961 and during the Bangladesh crisis of 1971. Additionally, there were severe political conflicts over aid, trade, and currency issues (Rubinoff 2005: 171–176).

During much of the 1960s and 1970s, there was virtually no voice for India in U.S. foreign policy. The negative view of India among decision-makers such as President Lyndon B. Johnson, President Richard Nixon, or Congressman Lee Hamilton largely prevailed without correcting influences from the Indian American community. For much of the American foreign-policy leadership, India was "associated with problems rather than opportunities". After the Indo-Soviet treaty of friendship in 1971, mutual perceptions became openly hostile. Now the political establishment in Washington viewed India as irrevocably "on the wrong side" of the Cold War. Republican "India bashers" in the U.S. Congress such as Dan Burton and Robert Dornan found fertile ground for their opinions without a powerful pro-India lobby being able to offer an alternative voice. The negative image of India also found its way into the general public, for instance through school books where India was depicted as a "backward society". Textbooks in the 1970s regularly presented India as the most negative of all Asian countries (Rubinoff 2005: 173–176).

Things slowly started to change during the 1980s, primarily because the number of Indians in the United States was steadily growing after the reform of U.S. immigration laws in 1965. New Indian American organizations were formed, particularly along religious lines. Several newly founded Hindu associations in the United States mirrored the organizational structure of the Sangh Parivar in India, thereby linking transnationalism and nationalism (Jaffrelot/ Therwath 2012: 343). By far the most influential among these groups is the Vishwa Hindu Parishad of America (VHPA), founded 1970 in New York. Other organizations within this so-called "Yankee Hindutva" cycle include the Hindu Swayamsevak Sangh (HSS), founded 1977 in New Jersey, and the India Development and Relief Fund (IDRF), founded 1989 in Maryland, whose connections to Hindu nationalist ideology have drawn much criticism from secular Indian American groups. While Hindutva groups initially mostly stayed away from attempts to influence U.S. foreign policy, other associations were more active. In the mid-1980s, Sikh organizations tried to bring attention to the Khalistan issue and anti-Sikh riots in India and to raise awareness of their culture (Agarwala 2018: 113). Similarly, Indian American Muslim associations such as the Indian Muslim Relief Committee (IMRC) sought to expose anti-Muslim violence in India and lobbied for American and international action (Agarwala 2016: 936). These transnational efforts, however, had only very limited success in altering U.S. foreign policy.

The formation of an Indian American lobby

It was only in the early 1990s that NRIs and PIOs engaged in serious concerted efforts to gain more political influence in the United States. The initial focus was to counter the at-that-time very powerful pro-Pakistani lobby in Washington. Here the Indian American Forum for Political Education (IAFPE), which had been founded in 1982, became a key player. IAFPE is one of the oldest and most important lobby groups for the Indian American community. The "Forum" is not only active in educating the American public about India but also works directly with politicians and decision-makers. In a landmark success, an IAFPE initiative led to the establishment of the Congressional Caucus on India and Indian Americans in the U.S. House of Representatives in 1993. The Caucus has developed into one of the crucial links between the Indian American community and lawmakers in Congress. At its high point, it had roughly 200 members. It continues to be the largest country-specific parliamentary group, a fact that has not gone unnoticed and is a source of pride within the community. The Congressional Caucus on India and Indian Americans was the first institutional base for India on Capitol Hill and had an important role in the 1990s in defeating the annual Burton Amendment to cut aid towards India. The Caucus also helped limit the influence of the Pakistan lobby. Critics, however, argue that the strength and accomplishments of the Caucus are exaggerated and that its main activity so far has been the drafting of "feel-good resolutions" with little or no political impact (Rubinoff 2005: 182). While its actual political clout may indeed be hard to measure, the institutionalized dialogue that the Caucus represents is in itself a valuable achievement for the Indian American population and has raised the visibility of the community (Gottschlich 2008: 160–161). Both the Caucus and its counterpart in the U.S. Senate, which was founded in 2004, have certainly helped creating a more favorable climate for India on Capitol Hill.

The 1990s also saw a substantial shift in India's diaspora policy. Since the mid-1980s, governments in New Delhi had increasingly looked to the global NRI and PIO population as a supporting factor for the development of India. The economic crisis of 1991 and the subsequent reforms in India accelerated this process. After decades of benign neglect, there was a new interest in the economic power and financial capabilities of the diaspora, which now re-entered the public and political discourse in India as an important actor (Varadarajan 2015: 293). The Indian American community, which had created the Global Organization for People of Indian Origin (GOPIO) in 1989, became a driving force in this shift. While economic development remained the main focus of the rapprochement, New Delhi also saw potential for transnational political assistance in improving the bilateral relationship between India and the United States (Agarwala 2018: 110–111).

Despite the successful establishment of the Caucus, Indian American lobby work initially remained inefficient. Many times, political positions were not articulated through a single unified voice, not least because of the remarkable heterogeneity of a growing Indian American population. Additionally, there was a noticeable uneasiness in using political resources, particularly campaign finance, and an unfamiliarity with the unwritten rules of Washington lobbying. Ambitious community leaders started looking for support from outside and a role model that Indian Americans could emulate. When the India Abroad Center for Political Action (IACPA) was established in the early 1990s, its founder Gopal Raju was advised by Ralph Nurnberger, an experienced and influential politician and lobbyist who had worked for the American Israel Public Affairs Committee (AIPAC). Nurnberger wrote a handbook for the Indian American community in which he detailed the successful political work of Jewish lobby groups and laid out a path to follow for NRIs and PIOs (Nurnberger 2000). He also participated in the founding of the United States India Political Action Committee (USINPAC) that went on to become one of the main lobby organizations for the Indian American population. The usually highly effective and efficient work of the Israel lobby functioned as an exemplary role model, particularly with regard to forging a strong relationship between the United States and India. The American Jewish Committee (AJC) even organized training sessions for Indian Americans in grassroots lobbying (Calder 2014: 210). Despite its apparent success, the collaboration with the Israel lobby and the (self) presentation of Indians and particularly Hindus in the United States as "the new Jews" has also sparked criticism within the community, not least because of its anti-Muslim undertone (Prashad 2012: 61–99).

The learning process in replicating the successful tactics of Jewish lobby groups was tested early. The nuclear question had been a highly controversial issue between Washington and New Delhi for decades. When the newly elected government of the Bharatiya Janata Party (BJP) in India conducted a series of nuclear tests in 1998, the United States responded with swift and harsh economic sanctions. Politically active Indian American lobby groups became de facto spokespersons for the BJP government and helped to mitigate the effects of the sanctions, working towards their eventual lifting (Varadarajan 2015: 293). During the time of the sanctions, there was noticeable resistance to improving bilateral ties among Members of Congress, as Sanjay Puri, founder and chairman of USINPAC, recalls: "When we started working on Capitol Hill about U.S. India relations there was a lack of awareness and lack of interest. [. . .] We spent a lot of time explaining to Members of Congress as to how India shared common values with the U.S." (Puri interview).

From 2005 on, the full potential of the transnational political weight of the Indian American community was displayed for the first time in their coordinated and extensively unified work for the passage of the nuclear deal between India and the United States. GOPIO joined hands with USINPAC and other political associations as well as with professional interest groups like the American Association of Physicians of Indian Origin (AAPI) or the Asian-American Hotel

Owners Association (AAHOA) and with economic lobby organizations such as the U.S.-India Business Council (USIBC) and the Confederation of Indian Industry (CII). The community used grassroots activities and other traditional means of influence such as briefings and information events. An important part of the overall strategy was the targeting of influential individual politicians such as Senator Hillary Clinton, at that time co-chairperson of the Senate Caucus "Friends of India" (Sharma 2017: 154–157). USINPAC specifically worked with parliamentarians who were heads of key committees such as the Foreign Relations Committee or the Energy and Commerce Committee (Puri interview). According to former Indian Ambassador to the United States Nirupama Menon Rao, "the diaspora was very effective in working with Members [of Congress] to push the pros of the deal" (Rao interview).

The Indian American community and the government in New Delhi also used the help of professional lobbyists. Here foreign policy analyst and political adviser Ashley Tellis played a crucial role. Tellis, an Indian American, had worked for Robert Blackwill, the former U.S. Ambassador to India. In 2006 the Indian government hired Blackwill and his lobby firm and used his old connections on Capitol Hill. Additionally, tactics of indirect lobbying were used. The Indian American Security Leadership Council (IASLC) mobilized U.S. veteran associations to speak out for a closer security cooperation between Washington and New Delhi (Kamdar 2007: 33–38). With the help of a pro-active Indian embassy, a broad transnational interest coalition was forged, reaching far beyond the Indian American community itself. The message and the basic premise were that the nuclear pact would bring the United States and India closer together, to the benefit of both (Puri interview).

Although direct causal connections between lobby activities and political outcomes are virtually impossible to quantify, there can be little doubt that the efforts of the Indian American community had a substantial impact on the passage of the nuclear pact. The legal framework cleared both houses of the U.S. Congress with vast majorities in 2006, which is particularly noteworthy since this success was achieved against the work of the powerful non-proliferation lobby. In order to obtain the necessary approval of the Nuclear Suppliers Group (NSG), the USINPAC engaged in a unique form of transnational lobby work by urging NRIs and PIOs in NSG countries such as France or Germany to support an exemption for India with the governments of their countries of residence (Calder 2014: 216–217). In 2008, all hurdles were cleared, and the nuclear deal was finalized. While this success was truly remarkable, political strategists warned that geostrategic frame conditions had helped enormously and that such a friendly global environment would not be reproducible at will (Gupta 2009: 319).

Current issues and the road forward

The nuclear deal between India and the United States has been widely regarded as the beginning of a new era in bilateral relations. It has also been seen as the coming of age of the Indian American community as a powerful transnational political lobby. Much had already been accomplished before, particularly regarding the perception of India in the United States. With the decisive help of the diaspora, the image of India was "transformed from a malnourished skeleton in a filthy dhoti to a highly educated prosperous professional in a designer business suit" (Rubinoff 2005: 169). Critics argue, however, that this shift still does not represent an accurate picture of India or the NRI and PIO population in the United States. They point to the elite and "model minority" status of the Indian American community and its diaspora organizations. In their view, the lobby work for the nuclear deal was just another epitomization of transnational elite-to-elite collaboration that left out substantial parts of both the Indian and the Indian American population (Mishra 2012).

While the question of representation and agenda setting is certainly debatable, it is beyond doubt that the elite status of Indian Americans has not only helped them gain political leverage in the United States but also gives them legitimacy and influence in India. Their assistance in foreign policy is increasingly seen as a transnational two-way street with certain returns expected (Agarwala 2018: 108–114). Government schemes such as the Overseas Citizenship of India (OCI) not only show that the contributions of the diaspora are appreciated in New Delhi but also help to forge a closer attachment to the homeland. Additionally, the availability of OCI or other measures that come close to dual citizenship encourages higher naturalization rates in the country of residence, especially among newer migrant cohorts. This "naturalization effect" oftentimes leads to a more vocal political involvement in the United States, opening up opportunities for transnational advocacy on behalf of India (Naujoks 2017: 208–210).

Since its return to power in 2014, India's BJP government has sought to tap the potential of the diaspora as a transnational economic and political facilitator even more. Prime Minister Narendra Modi's efforts to "turn every Indian abroad into an ambassador of India" clearly show that New Delhi no longer views the diaspora as a liability but sees it as an asset for the homeland (Suryanarayan 2017: 99–100). The Indian American community has been a prime target of Modi's unprecedented and at times unconventional outreach to the diaspora. In a remarkable appearance in New York City's world-famous Madison Square Garden in September 2014, Modi addressed the capacity crowd in the manner of a "rock star" (Pant 2016: 31). In his speech, Modi clearly attempted to evoke nationalist sentiments among the Indian Americans present. The New York City mega-event and other outings show that Modi "reinvents the nation in extra-territorial terms", emphasizing the close bond between India and the diaspora (Hedge 2018: 270). While enduring loyalty to India is expected, a total return to the homeland is not intended, with the topic being carefully avoided in the discourse. Instead, NRIs and PIOs in the United States are urged to engage as transnational ambassadors for India. Modi's message to the diaspora is that "you do not have to be in India in order to be connected and work for the betterment of the motherland" (Hedge 2018: 279).

As far as foreign policy is concerned, supporting the homeland from abroad means working for a strong alliance between India and the United States. This has been the lobby focus for Indian American Hindu and particularly Hindutva groups for years. They want to raise India's global status in order to protect and empower Hindus and Hinduism. The pathway for this is a reliable bilateral relationship to the world's only superpower. More than other organizations of the "Yankee Hindutva", the Overseas Friends of the BJP (OFBJP) have engaged in political advocacy on behalf of closer Indo-U.S. relations. They have been active in the United States as well as in India, where the OFBJP are committed to a foreign policy friendly towards Washington (Agarwala 2016: 934–935). Modi's election in 2014 has reinforced the transnational connection between the BJP and the OFBJP. At the first U.S. convention of the OFBJP in December 2014, a BJP representative emphasized the "overall Indian interests" and called on the Indian population in the United States to support Modi's governance program in India (Rohit 2014).

The new activism towards the NRI and PIO population raises the question of how far New Delhi should go in encouraging the diaspora to lobby on India's behalf. The notion of being used as a mere instrument to reach foreign-policy goals might spark criticism among parts of the diaspora. Additionally, there may be situations where differing priorities or even conflicts of interest between Indian Americans and the government in New Delhi arise. While Prasad Thotakura, president of the Indian American Friendship Council (IAFC) and long-time community leader, emphasizes the strong ties between India and its diaspora and sees "only cordial relations" between the Indian government and NRIs and PIOs in the United States

(Thotakura interview), other voices are more skeptical. According to Sanjay Puri of USINPAC, "New Delhi should do its own advocacy and leave the Indian Americans as U.S. citizens to figure out the issues they care about" which many times may be different at least in nuances (Puri interview). The mobilizing and unifying effect the work on the passage of the nuclear deal in the mid-2000s had within the Indian American community may have been a rare occurrence and not easy to replicate. As former Ambassador Nirupama Menon Rao stated, "this cannot happen for all issues that concern the relationship" (Rao interview). In addition, Indian foreign policy and the bilateral relationship between India and the United States might not always be the focus of Indian American activity. New Delhi will have to accept that politics and international relations "are not the only issues Indian Americans care about", as Sonali Lappin, president of the IAFPE Massachusetts, pointed out. Other topics such as community service, education, culture, and art are also important and oftentimes much closer to the everyday-life of NRIs and PIOs in the United States (Lappin interview).

Even without a galvanizing political issue such as the nuclear question, there are certain areas in which the Indian American community can be a valuable transnational asset for New Delhi. In the words of Nirupama Menon Rao, "the diaspora is an important go-to that multiplies access and outreach for the Indian government in the United States" (Rao interview). Indian Americans can also help to enhance India's soft power in international diplomacy by spreading its spiritual and philosophical wealth, its popular culture, and its democratic values. Furthermore, the diaspora could and should continue to alleviate the trust deficit on both sides, which has not yet been completely overcome and has hindered further progress in bilateral relations. According to some observers, segments of the strategic establishment in New Delhi still view the United States with deep suspicion, particularly regarding defense cooperation and military supply (Karnad 2015: 187–195). Even ten years after the completion of the landmark nuclear pact, there are anxieties in India about the reliability of the United States and the durability of the bilateral partnership, which was also bemoaned by U.S. Ambassador to India Kenneth Juster in his inaugural policy address in early 2018 (Juster 2018). Here the Indian American community may work as a transnational bridge by bringing policy makers from India to the United States and work for mutual understanding and confidence in each other's sincerity and reliability.

This strategy has worked vice versa in the past: Visits of U.S. politicians to India have had a remarkably positive effect on their willingness to engage with issues relevant to India and work for a better bilateral relationship. According to Prasad Thotakura, almost all U.S. Congressmen and Senators who travel to India come back "with a lot of excitement and enthusiasm to build better relations between the two great countries" (Thotakura interview). In this respect, another group of transnational actors is gaining significance. Since the 2000s, Indian returnees from the United States have developed into an important lobby for a better relationship with Washington in India. Representing another effect of transnationalism, U.S.-educated politicians and government officials in India can also have an impact. Their knowledge and understanding of American politics, culture, and values builds yet another bridge for improved U.S.-India relations (Rubinoff 2005: 177–178).

Conclusion

The Indian American community has established itself as an important transnational actor in Indian and American foreign policy. It has developed from a rather small advocacy group driven by the work of extraordinary individuals to a powerful lobby with real political influence. According to many analysts, the bilateral relationship between India and the United States has evolved to a stage where it no longer matters which parties or politicians are in power in New Delhi and Washington. Similarly, the Indian American lobby is no longer dependent on paramount personalities such as J.J. Singh, Dalip Singh Saund, or Gopal Raju. It has established strong and durable organizational and institutional structures and has learned to use its vast resources efficiently. At its core, however, the India lobby in the United States continues to be elitist in nature. With Prime Minister Narendra Modi reaching out only to the elite segments of the diaspora, this characteristic might become even stronger in the future (Hedge 2018: 279).

Critical observers claim that the importance of the diaspora in the field of foreign policy might be overestimated. The Indian American lobby, they argue, does play a role, but rather facilitative and not necessarily causal. Indian Americans "have helped push through certain agendas [but] have not shaped the agenda itself" (Varadarajan 2015: 296). It is certainly true that U.S. foreign policy is primarily interest-oriented. Nevertheless, being able to frame and amplify existing interests is no small accomplishment for the Indian American community. While hard to quantify, the effect of transnational lobby work is far from negligible.

References

Agarwala, Rina (2016). Divine Development: Transnational Indian Religious Organizations in the United States and India, in: *International Migration Review*, Vol. 50 No. 4 (Winter 2016), pp. 910–950.

Agarwala, Rina (2018). Transnational Diaspora Organizations and India's Development, in: Hedge, Radha Sarma/Sahoo, Ajaya Kumar (eds.). *Routledge Handbook of the Indian Diaspora*. London: Routledge, pp. 104–116.

Calder, Kent E. (2014). *Asia in Washington: Exploring the Penumbra of Transnational Power*. Washington, D.C.: Brookings Institution Press.

Gottschlich, Pierre (2008). The Indian Diaspora in the United States of America: An Emerging Political Force?, in: Raghuram, Parvati/Sahoo, Ajaya Kumar/Maharaj, Brij/Sangha, Dave (eds.). *Tracing an Indian Diaspora: Context, Memories, Representations*. New Delhi: Sage, pp. 156–170.

Gould, Harold A. (2006). *Sikhs, Swamis, Students, and Spies: The India Lobby in the United States, 1900–1946*. New Delhi: Sage Publications.

Gupta, Amit (2009). The Indian Diaspora as "Strategic Asset", in: Ray, Jayanta Kumar/Mishra, Binoda Kumar (eds.). *Interpreting the Indian Diaspora: Lessons from History and Contemporary Politics*. New Delhi: Centre for Studies in Civilizations, pp. 315–330.

Hedge, Radha S. (2018). Renewing Diasporic Bonds and the Global Branding of India, in: Hedge, Radha Sarma/Sahoo, Ajaya Kumar (eds.). *Routledge Handbook of the Indian Diaspora*. London: Routledge, pp. 269–281.

Jaffrelot, Christophe/Therwath, Ingrid (2012). The Global Sangh Parivar: A Study of Contemporary International Hinduism, in: Green, Abigail/Viaene, Vincent (eds.). *Religious Internationals in the Modern World: Globalization and Faith Communities since 1750*. Basingstoke: Palgrave Macmillan, pp. 343–364.

Juster, Kenneth I. (2018). U.S.–India Relations: Building a Durable Partnership for the 21st Century (Ambassador Kenneth I. Juster's Inaugural Policy Address, January 11, 2018). Retrieved from: https://in.usembassy.gov/full-transcript-ambassador-kenneth-justers-inaugural-policy-address/ (20.03.2018).

Kamdar, Mira (2007). *Planet India: The Turbulent Rise of the Largest Democracy and the Future of Our World*. New York: Scribner.

Karnad, Bharat (2015). *Why India Is Not a Great Power (Yet)*. New Delhi: Oxford University Press.

Lappin, Sonali (interview): President of the Indian American Forum for Political Education Massachusetts (IAFPE-MA), interviewed by author on March 28, 2018.

Lopez, Gustavo/Cilluffo, Anthony (2017). Indians in the U.S. Fact Sheet. Washington, D.C.: Pew Research Center. Retrieved from: http://www.pewsocialtrends.org/fact-sheet/asian-americans-indians-in-the-u-s/ (16.01.2018).

Mishra, Sangay (2012). The Limits of Transnational Mobilization: Indian American Lobby Groups and the India-US Civil Nuclear Deal, in: Sahoo, Ajaya Kumar/Baas, Michiel/Faist, Thomas (eds.). *Indian Diaspora and Transnationalism*. Jaipur: Rawat Publications, pp. 414–431.

Naujoks, Daniel (2017). The Transnational Political Effects of Diasporic Citizenship in Countries of Destination: Overseas Citizenship of India and Political Participation in the United States, in: Carment, David/Sadjed, Ariane (eds.). *Diaspora as Cultures of Cooperation: Global and Local Perspectives*. Cham: Palgrave Macmillan, pp. 199–221.

Nurnberger, Ralph (2000). *Lobbying in America: A Primer for Citizen Participation*. Washington, D.C.: India Abroad Center for Political Awareness.

Pant, Harsh V. (2016). *Indian Foreign Policy: An Overview*. Manchester: Manchester University Press.

Prashad, Vijay (2012). *Uncle Swami: South Asians in America Today*. New York: The New Press.

Puri, Sanjay (interview): Founder and Chairman of the United States India Political Action Committee (USINPAC), interviewed by author on February 18, 2018.

Rao, Nirupama Menon (interview): Indian Ambassador to the United States 2011–2013, interviewed by author on March 13, 2018.

Rohit, Parimal M. (2014). Overseas Friends of BJP Urges Diaspora to Build Stronger India, in: *India West* (December 19, 2014). Retrieved from: http://www.indiawest.com/news/global_indian/overseas-friends-of-bjp-urges-diaspora-to-build-stronger-india/article_5461a2ec-86e9-11e4-b0ce-0f0132a610be.html (16.01.2018).

Rubinoff, Arthur G. (2005). The Diaspora as a Factor in U.S.-India Relations, in: *Asian Affairs*, Vol. 32 No. 3, pp. 169–188.

Shaffer, Robert (2012). J.J. Singh and the India League of America, 1945–1959: Pressing at the Margins of the Cold War Consensus, in: *Journal of American Ethnic History*, Vol. 31 No. 2 (Winter), pp. 68–103.

Sharma, Ashok (2017). *Indian Lobbying and Its Influence in US Decision Making: Post-Cold War*. New Delhi: Sage.

Shukla, Sandhya (2013). South Asian Migration to the United States: Diasporic and National Formations, in: Chatterji, Joya/Washbrook, David (eds.), *Routledge Handbook of the South Asian Diaspora*. New York: Routledge, pp. 166–179.

Suryanarayan, V. (2017). India's Policy towards Indian Communities Living Abroad, in: Vinodan, C. (ed.). *India's Foreign Policy and Diplomacy: Emerging Scenario and Challenges*. New Delhi: New Century Publications, pp. 86–102.

Thotakura, Prasad (interview): President of the Indian American Friendship Council (IAFC), interviewed by author on February 12, 2018.

Varadarajan, Latha (2015). Mother India and Her Children Abroad: The Role of the Diaspora in India's Foreign Policy, in: Malone, David M./Mohan, C. Raja/Raghavan, Srinath (eds.). *The Oxford Handbook of Indian Foreign Policy*. Oxford: Oxford University Press, pp. 285–297.

Zong, Jie/Batalova, Jeanne (2017). Indian Immigrants in the United States. Washington, D.C.: Migration Policy Institute. Retrieved from: https://www.migrationpolicy.org/article/indian-immigrants-united-states (09.01.2018).

11
CONSTRUCTING HINDU IDENTITIES IN FRANCE AND THE UNITED STATES

A comparative analysis

Lise-Hélène Smith and Anjana Narayan

Introduction

This chapter focuses on the articulation and construction of Hinduism in the United States and France. Most studies on the South Asian diaspora provide a comparative analysis of the United States vis-à-vis Canada or the United Kingdom, where Hindu communities have grown significantly in the last several decades. These countries follow a similar model of multiculturalism unlike France, which stands out because of its policy on *laïcité* or secularism that continues to influence the experiences of ethnic groups in its context. In addition, while a growing body of work addresses the Hindu diaspora in the United States, little scholarly attention has been paid to the Hindu presence in France. Accordingly, we trace the representation and transformation of Hindu communities across the United States and France, two countries with distinct migration histories, conceptions of nationhood, and understandings of religion. Drawing on existing scholarship available in the English and French languages as well as on primary data from web-based sources including social media sites and religious organizations, we analyze whether the experiences of Hindus in France and the United States transcend the specificities of their national and local contexts. We conclude our study by reflecting on the applicability of transnational frameworks when analyzing ethno religious minority groups across national contexts.

Conceptions of nationhood and religion in France and the United States

As French historian Gérard Noiriel (1992) has argued, the French have never regarded their country as a country of immigration, a view that has shaped their conception of race and ethnicity over the years. The historiography of France has traditionally emphasized its uniformity, universality, and homogeneity rather than focus on visible cultural difference. The French Revolution established the nation specifically as a voluntary association between free individuals in the Rousseauist tradition (Silverman 1992, 19). Repudiating its mythical origins ("our ancestors the Gauls"), the French nation relocated itself in "the people" to ensure equality of conditions and the common good, based on the universal right of Mankind. According to Noiriel (1992), however, this contract should be read as a way of discrediting aristocratic privilege rather than as a concrete social reality (9). This new conception of the nation creates but another myth, that of its unitary constitution for the common good. Such an ideal has become increasingly difficult for the French to reconcile with the heterogeneity, pluralism, and decentralization of its society resulting from regular influxes of immigrants, often originating from former French colonies. Unable to face its complex colonial legacy, the French nation-state continues to rely on centralizing and assimilationist tendencies that depend on a distinction between French nationals and foreigners – rather than between racialized minorities and a white majority, as has been the case in the United States (Silverman 1992, 13). The steady rate at which immigrants have been securing French citizenship has eroded such a distinction, thereby posing a threat to the French conception of the nation. What is more, since the separation of church and state in the early 20th century, the French Republic has insisted on its secularism to enforce the absence of all signs of religious affiliation, belief, or practice in the public arena. Immigrants, regardless of race, culture, or faith, are expected to adhere to all French laws and customs, in an effort to encourage integration and conformity (Trouillet 2013).

Unlike the French Republic, the pluralistic American nation relies on the equally powerful myth of the United States as a melting pot and safe haven for all (Noiriel 1995, 368). Despite being conceived as a "federation of self-governing communities of individuals," the nation has allowed racialized minorities to be recognized institutionally over time, because it acknowledges the reality of racial and cultural amalgamation (Greenfeld 2011, 181). With its longstanding history of mass immigration and the size of its territory, the American democracy has relied on the principles of federalism and republicanism and the self-proclaimed values of liberty and equality despite marked economic disparities between minority groups and a (decreasing) white majority. Liah Greenfeld (2011) actually proposes that in the United States, "ethnic diversity is both glorified and deprived of cultural significance" because of the high tolerance for the "individualistic American nationalism" that protects the identity of hyphenated Americans, which, she argues, negates the socio-political power of ethnicity (188). Yet the prevalence of minority groups within its national community has prompted debates about religious expression in light of the United States' culture of religiosity (Ali 2012). Secularity in the United States is commonly understood as protecting freedom of expression while supporting religious autonomy, rather than enforcing assimilationist policies (Ajrouch 2007, 322). While France uses secularism to relegate religious expression to the private sphere and ban religion from politics, Americans allow private matters to become public concerns and use religion to unite themselves, believing the United States to be a predominantly Christian nation (Ali 2012). Despite its defense of individual liberties against religious persecution, the United States remains a religiously charged nation that, like France, can rob minority groups of a sense of national belonging because of its understanding of the relation between church and state (Ali 2012).

Hindus in France and the United States: migration histories and population growth

Interestingly, as late as the mid-nineteenth century, the word "immigrant" hardly appears in French documents; access to citizenship was relatively easy, and the concept of the foreigner extremely vague (Silverman 1992, 28). While five hundred thousand foreigners were living in France in 1860, their number had increased to one million by 1880. In addition, the notion of France as a country not grounded in immigration is an erroneous one, since 11 percent of the French population was of foreign origin in 1942 (Noiriel 1992, 53). By the 1960s, France was a leading industrialized nation based on its size of it immigration population (Noiriel 1996, 5). An estimate by the French national institute of statistics (INSEE) indicates that 5.3 million foreign-born immigrants and 6.5 million direct descendants of immigrants were living in France in 2008, for a total of 11.8 million or 19 percent of the 62.1 million total population in metropolitan France (*INSEE* 2011). About 20 percent of the population has a grandparent of immigrant origin, which increases to one-third of the population if one takes great grandparents into account (Noiriel 1995, 368). Of the 20 percent who claim immigrant origins, between 400,000 and 500,000 were of South Asian descent in 2008 according to Sylvie Dauvillier (2008). Within the Indian diaspora in France, 170,000 individuals self-identified as Hindu in 2012 (Lesegretain 2012). The first Hindus to arrive in France came to port cities as sailors and merchants in the 18th century, followed by artists such as dancers and musicians during the colonial era in the 19th century (Trouillet 2013). Hindu businessmen, mostly jewelers, settled in Paris in the early 20th century while the Independence of India led to the relocation of Pondicherrians and Tamil families who had acquired French citizenship during the colonial period. Finally, the arrival of 60,000 Indo-Mauritians on French soil and of more than 100,000 Sri Lankan Tamils fleeing the civil war in the 1970s accounts for the presence of most Hindus in France today (Trouillet 2013, Goreau-Ponceaud 2014).

By contrast, mass migration has informed the history of the United States, initially allowing population growth rather than meeting work-related demands, as was the case in most of Europe post-WWI and II. Because of the early influx of White Anglo-Saxon Protestants and because of restrictive, discriminatory laws intended to protect their economic power and social class, the first immigrants from India came to the United States predominantly as farm laborers in the early 19th century (Zong and Batalova 2017). Bauman and Saunders (2009) report the presence of 13,600 immigrants specifically from India between 1820 and 1960. This number had increased substantially by 1980, at which time the U.S. Census registered 387,223 individuals who self-identified as Americans of Indian descent (Bauman and Saunders 2009). This demographic increase is explained by significant legislative changes that took place between 1965 and 1990: the removal of national-origin quotas, the introduction of temporary skilled-worker programs, and the creation of permanent employment-based visas, all of which encouraged the migration of highly skilled young Indian professionals (Zong and Batalova 2017). By 2007 the number of Americans of South Asian descent had increased to 1.7 million and to 2.4 million by 2015 (Bauman and Saunders 2009), making the foreign-born from India the second largest immigrant group in the United States – accounting for close to 6 percent of the 43.3 million foreign-born population (Zong and Batalova 2017). Today, most immigrants of South Asian descent arrive through the family reunification program that continues to regulate immigration laws (Bauman and Saunders 2009). In 2015, 2.23 million of the 2.4 million self-declared Americans of Indian descent identified as Hindu, making Hinduism the fourth largest faith in the United States (Louis 2015). According to the Pew Research Center's "Religious Landscape Study" published in May 2015, the number of Hindus in the United States increased by 1.03 million between 2007 and 2014, which corresponds to an 85.8 percent increase over a short seven-year period (Louis 2015). Another 2015 Pew report projects that Hindus could number 4.78 million by 2050, constituting 1.2 percent of the total American population (Louis 2015).

Construction of Hinduism in the United States

In the United States, the religious practices and institutions of post-1965 immigrants from Asia, Africa, and Latin America have attracted much scholarly attention. Although the literature on the Hindu diaspora in the United States is relatively new, the number of studies published on the topic has grown rapidly in recent decades. Some of the early studies focused on providing a general overview of the migration and settlement of Hindu immigrant communities in the United States while chronicling the experiences of specific Hindu groups and organizations (Dempsey 2005, Leonard 1997, Shattuck 1996, Williams 1988). In addition, scholars focused on making available the texts and traditions of Hinduism by providing both interpretations and translations (Beane 1977, Coburn 1991, Eck 1993, Kupperman 2001, Miller 1986). Although these studies succeeded in making the traditions and symbols of Hinduism accessible to predominantly Christian audiences, they did not focus on the larger social, historical, and political context of Hinduism.

Instead, scholars have tended to trace the specific transformation of Hinduism in the United States to demonstrate how religious practices change post-migration in receiving host societies, as individuals encounter new barriers and opportunities for practicing their religions. First, scholars claim that, unlike in South Asia where worship is more personal and often confined to the family and private sphere, in the United States, temples have emerged as an important community institution. Temples provide Hindu Americans a platform both to come together as a community as well as to gain visibility and public recognition (Rayaprol 1997, Narayanan 1992, Kurien 1998, 2002, Eck 2000, Jacob and Thakur 2000, Mazumdar and Mazumdar 2006). Second, studies show that, in order to conform to Christianity, the dominant religion in the United States, the more diverse and historically grounded forms of religion that make up the Hindu world are being slowly replaced by a more homogenized and simplified articulation of Hinduism on American soil (Kurien 2004, Narayan and Purkayastha 2011). Finally, scholars explain the transformation of Hinduism into a well-defined and congregational religion in the United States based on the pressures to conform to a bureaucratic structure of religion like that of Christianity (Vertovec 2000, Kurien 2004, Joshi 2006). Studies cite the emergence of Hindu Sunday schools, of Hindu summer camps, of sermons and speeches, and of large communal gatherings on weekends in temples as examples of new congregational patterns of Hindu religious practices that are not the norm in India.

A small but growing body of literature has also focused on the religions of "new immigrants" to determine whether new immigrants are assimilating into the American mainstream (Carnes and Yang 2004, Ebaugh and Chafetz 2000). These studies argue that religious institutions such as temples provide the social and cultural ties that can aid ethnic groups in the assimilation process. Moreover, scholars have observed a shift towards more modern and gender-neutral ideas as well as practices among immigrant religious institutions and their members in the American context (Yang and Ebaugh 2001a). These findings, however, have recently been challenged in the context of the Hindu diaspora. A number of scholars now argue that the homogenization of Hindu religio-cultural norms and practices have actually created new gender hierarchies in the United States. Scholars such as Kurien (1999) and Narayan and Purkayastha (2011) demonstrate that the processes of bureaucratization—homogenization, the centralization of power, and the establishment of sharp boundaries—creates distinctively demarcated roles for males and females while facilitating the emergence of more conservative sections of the Hindu American community. Furthermore, they argue, the new structural circumstances give rise to groups that are more patriarchal, subjecting women to more scrutiny and control.

Paradoxically, the same studies also demonstrate that Hindu organizations in the American context very often deploy the image of the "strong woman" in their discourse (Narayan and Purkayastha 2009, 2011). These groups profess the distinctiveness of Hindu women to present Hinduism as a religion that grants high status to Hindu women, unlike other religions such as Islam. Scholars contend that such assertions need to be understood as a way for Hindu groups to demonstrate the superiority of their culture and religion, which is often dismissed as traditional and non-modern by mainstream Americans. However, studies reveal that the idealization of Hindu women's superiority is conducted within culturally prescribed gender roles, where women become responsible for upholding the community honor; their behaviors are strictly controlled to maintain the coherence and specificity of their ethnic groups (Das Gupta and Das Gupta 1996, Das Gupta 1997).

By contrast, the rise of Hindu Nationalism in the American diaspora has been studied much more extensively, as studies document the dramatic growth and visibility of Hindu nationalist organizations in the last few decades in the United States (Kurien 2004 and 2007, Lal 1999, Mathew and Prashad 2000, Bhatt and Mukta 2000, Therwath 2012). Scholars attribute this phenomenon to both the multicultural context of American society as well as to the rise of cyberspace as a crucial platform for representing religious identities. Scholars show that Hindu Nationalist groups utilize the internet strategically to promote select dimensions of Hinduism by emphasizing histories, values, and traditions that are likely to appeal to new believers. Unlike the pluralistic and diverse forms of Hinduism, these organizations promote a simplified and homogenized version of the religion that not only emphasizes the superiority of Hindus but also distances itself from other religions, particularly from Islam.

Scholars have also documented the dynamics of racialization and religion and observed the growth of fundamentalism in the U.S. diaspora (Kurien 2005, Rajagopal 2000, Purkayastha 2005, Joshi 2006, 2012, 2013). They argue that experiences of racism and marginalization on American soil have encouraged Indian immigrants to turn to religion and religious institutions: privileging their religious over their cultural identity is one way that minorities have avoided racial categorizing (Kurien 2005, Rajagopal 1997). Studies document mostly the experiences of post-immigrant generations who face the further worry of being associated with a religion like Hinduism that is misunderstood and stereotyped by mainstream societies (Joshi 2006, Purkayastha 2005, Narayan et al. 2011). One important ramification of this phenomenon is the adoption of radical strands of religion by young post-immigrant generations. The racism and marginalization they have experienced make the rhetoric of Hindu nationalist organizations attractive as these organizations emphasize cultural nationalism and Hindu superiority. This is most evident in the emergence of transnational Hindu nationalist organizations, specifically student organizations in the South Asian diaspora in the United States and the United Kingdom. In the United States, Hindu student organizations numbered in the hundreds are currently asserting a specific Hindu identity while simultaneously codifying Indian ethnicity. These groups take it upon themselves to communicate to second-generation immigrants what Indian culture and Indian religion entail, despite the particularity of their stance on South Asian diasporic identities.

Finally, recent studies have also explored the transnational links between Hindus in the U.S. diaspora and their connections to the homeland. One of the first scholars to examine transnational Hindu migrants, Peggy Levitt (1998, 1999, 2007), demonstrated how Hindu immigrants in Massachusetts not only sent remittances to India but also influenced the religious and political life in their home country. Similarly, research by Yang and Ebaugh (2001b) shows how immigrant communities in the United States are contributing to more congregational forms of religion in their countries of origin. In addition to the transnational connections at the individual and community level, studies have also focused on the role of religious organizations in the diaspora in shaping the society and politics of India. These studies analyze in particular the rise of Hindu nationalist organizations in the United States, which, thanks to their overseas remittances and technological resources, have been able to create platforms to engage with the homeland (Mathew and Parshad 2000, Rajagopal 2000, Kurien 2006). In addition to the connectivity of the Hindu diaspora to the homeland, studies have also highlighted networks that groups maintain with Hindu immigrants in other receiving countries such as the United States, the United Kingdom, Australia, or Canada (Jaffrelot and Therwath 2007, Narayan et al. 2011, Zavos 2013). These studies demonstrate how common experiences of marginalization and racism in multicultural host societies facilitate the creation of transnational ethnic networks. This set of scholarship above all underscores the importance of virtual spaces to understand fully the transnational activities of Hindu organizations in the diaspora.

Construction of Hinduism in France

By contrast, very few studies have been conducted on the representations and manifestations of Hinduism in the French context (Altglas 2005, Weibel 2007, Trouillet 2013, Goreau-Ponceaud 2009 and 2014). Most studies focused on immigrant communities have privileged the North African diaspora, including the growing influence of Islam in France, and the Southeast Asian diaspora. In other words, studies have tended to focus on ethnic groups whose presence in France is directly linked to the country's complex, and often violent, colonial history. Because France did not enter into direct armed conflict with India, the South Asian migration to its territory is often overlooked. Our findings suggest that Hindus in France have used their historical invisibility to their advantage by presenting themselves as assimilated into mainstream French society in an attempt to remain inconspicuous at a time of rising racial and religious tensions.

Since the Law of December 9, 1905, that separated Churches and the State in France, the Republic no longer recognizes any religion in an official capacity (Loi de 9 décembre 1905). To engage in the exercise of religion, groups can register as religious organizations (*associations cultuelles*) or as cultural organizations (*association culturelles*). Registering as a religious organization allows for tax exemptions but restricts all activities to the purposes of worship, according to Title IV of the 1905 Law. In parallel, Act 1 of the July 1901 Law defines the purpose of such an organization as exclusively religious and therefore limited to the celebration of religious ceremonies, the maintenance of buildings used for worship, and the training of the persons necessary for the exercise of religion. All social, cultural, humanitarian or educational activities, efforts, and publications are excluded (Leclerc 2005). By contrast, a cultural organization can promote social and educational activities but is not tax exempt and may not engage in religious activities of any sort. It is therefore common for religious groups to attempt to register under both categories, although funding sources and state or municipal authorization can prove quite restrictive. Indeed, since the enactment of the 1905 Law, associations of worship are no longer eligible for state funding or prefectural support. Ironically, Catholic churches, chapels, and cathedrals in existence prior to the 1905 Separation of the Churches and the State continue to be maintained at public expense, suggesting the favoring of traditional religion.

This means that without private or international funding, it is difficult to establish clearly marked sites of religious worship, such as the prominent Hindu temples restricted mostly to the Parisian area, which likely benefit from transnational monetary support. Unlike in the United States, where Hindu temples function as cultural hubs that become sites of celebration, commemoration, and of community building, well-established Hindu temples in France, such as the Ganesh Temple and the Sri Sri Radha Parisisvara Temple in Paris or the Sri Ashtalakshmi Thevasthanam Temple in Choisy-le-Roi, focus strictly on worship and religious ceremonies, as their websites make clear. Many of the Hindu temples in France, numbered at about twenty in 2013, are commonly established inside shops, private apartments, and converted basements (Trouillet 2013, Goreau-Ponceaud 2014). As a result of funding restrictions, they operate away from the scrutinizing eye of the French authorities. Hindus in France typically worship in small groups, behind closed doors, in the privacy of a member's residence to avoid stigmatization (Weibel 2007, 179). Because of the close monitoring of religious and cultural gatherings, public displays of Hindu identities are also limited to two annual events: the celebration of *rathayātrā* or chariot processing in the month of July and of *vināyakacaturtti/gaṇeśacaturthī*, also known as the Ganesa Festival, in the month of September. In spite of their scarceness, such celebrations are extremely popular, gathering Hindus nation-wide regardless of sect or language (Trouillet 2013).

While Trouillet's claims that these processions "testif[y] to the settling of Hindu traditions in France and to its increasing visibility in the French landscape" (2013), Goreau-Ponceaud (2014) suggests that the "public spatialization of religion" also "challenges French attachment to secular tradition," as this type of religious festival "puts into question the loyalty of French society beyond ethnic and religious affiliation" (213). Likewise, we propose that these selective public appearances speak to the construction of Hinduism in France as an increasingly spiritual movement, which serves to diffuse the fear of being categorized as a sect (Weibel 2007, 179; Trouillet 2013). Indeed, the French have a long-documented interest in alternative spiritualities, Eastern philosophies, ayurvedic medicine, and yoga practices, which renders Hinduism particularly appealing to the laymen (Weibel 2007). Specifically, Hinduism seems to be adapting to the peculiar secularity of the French public arena by emphasizing its spiritual dimension through the promotion of yoga, of meditation, and of breathing techniques inspired by Hindu tradition (Trouillet 2013). French individuals who join Indian groups seem more interested in their own personal development than in embracing the principles of Hinduism per se. Bourrier (2006) reports that while some seek spiritual appeasement, others appreciate the values of the four Veda texts; yet all claim to be attracted to the open-mindedness and freedom that Hinduism promotes. Hinduism attracts those whose spiritual quest is not satisfied by structure or strict dogma and who are eager to adopt only the values that suit them (Bourrier 2006, Lesegretain 2012). Members of forums such hindouisme.forumactif or forum.indeparis attest to the warm welcome reserved to all who attend Hindu temples in Paris, regardless of origin. What is more, Weibel (2007) cites the emergence of neo-hinduist groups that organize around the spiritual figure of a guru (living or deceased) to unite body and soul, in search of truth and transcendence (179–80). These groups of "spiritual exploration" engage an India of the mind that is more clearly aligned with a Western construction of India as envisioned by Orientalists and French Romantics than to the nation of India today (180).

Thus, rather than celebrating a cultural heritage and religious traditions separate from those of the French, Hindus are careful to present themselves as an integral part of contemporary secular French culture. According to Weibel (2007), Indian cultural associations go to great lengths in France to promote cultural discovery, interaction, and exchange rather than emphasize community-building, for fear of religious discrimination (177). To adhere visibly to a religion in France is typically seen as suspect and as possibly at odds with one's citizenry (Weibel 2007, 178) in a country where *laïcité* as a specific type of secularism is "the civil religion of the French Republic" (Martín-i-Pardo 2011, 498). According to Meritxell Martín-i-Pardo (2011), the dichotomy between the private sphere and the "legal requirements of French public policy" has resulted in what he terms a "French civil Hinduism" (504–505). French individuals who identify as Indian have learned to define "Indian culture in a manner that echo[es] the government's expectations. That is, they represented Indian culture as having the ability to exist independently of Hinduism" (505). In short, the dichotomy between public and private spheres that emerges when considering how Hindus worship and their relationship to their faith is essential to understanding the construction of Hinduism in France as increasingly (and falsely) secular. On the one hand, Hinduism is attracting the French through its promotion of its spiritual dimension, seemingly separate from religious precepts. On the other hand, Hindus worship in the privacy of their own homes while continuing to engage in clearly religious ceremonies within legally regulated places of worship. Rather than demonstrating a lack of coherence or uniformity within the Hindu religion in France, this duality remains closer to the iteration of Hinduism found in India, where plurality and heterogeneity prevail, than to that found in the United States, where Hinduism is increasingly modeled after the principles of Christianity.

The emergence of a civil Hinduism in France, to use Martín-i-Pardo's term, does not imply that Hindus are better accepted by French mainstream society. Having repressed their colonial legacy, the French continue to envision their nation as predominantly white and Christian. Heirs to the Enlightenment, the French also continue to associate civilization with modernity, with literacy and print capitalism, with technological advancements and scientific progress. Our analysis of internet and news sources suggest Hindu groups have been forced to challenge the view that relegates Hinduism to the realm of superstition and social backwardness. Specifically, we understand concerted efforts to advocate for the rights of Hindus in France and to document hate-based incidents against the Hindu community as protestations against the delegitimization and marginalization of Hinduism. This is reflected in the coverage of particular local events, such as the possibility of serving vegetarian food in public school cafeterias, a social issue that is perceived as problematic enough to become a focal point for the media (*The Hans India* 2015b). In this particular instance, reporting of Hindus in France centered on a French governmental order mandating public schools to serve fish and meat for lunch. Articles document efforts by Hindu groups to launch a campaign supporting vegetarian school meals while denouncing the government for not taking into consideration the diversity of the French population in deciding menus for school-aged children. The same is true of the discriminatory portrayal of Hindu symbols and deities in movies and apparel, the object of an article entitled "French Comedy film offends Hindus" (BBC News 2006). The article criticizes the French Film *Les Bronzés* for depicting the Hindu Goddess Durga as carrying alcohol and quotes a spokesperson from the Hindu Forum of Britain: "To mock the worship of the Hindu religion, as this French film does, does little to increase understanding our different cultures. . . . To depict a Hindu Goddess holding bottles of alcohol is extremely offensive." Similarly, a French footwear company was criticized by Hindu organizations for selling shoes that commodify the image of Lord Rama (Hassan 2005). The article titled "French Shoes with Lord Rama's Image Annoys UK Hindus" comments,

> Because Lord Rama is one of the most revered gods in Hinduism and is known as an ideal man: his image is adored by believers, his status respected and he encapsulates the peace and humanity of Hindus. After all, religion, any religion, is not fashion, and Hinduism is the oldest religion of them all.

Interestingly, the lack of reverence towards and misappropriation of Hindu religious symbols seems to infuriate British Hindus more than their French counterparts, despite denunciations by Hindu organizations of the unfair treatment of Hindus in France.

Hindu organizations have used the controversial status of Roma refugees, also known as gypsies, to call attention to their perceived discrimination of Hindus on French soil. While the violence and racism against the Roma has received worldwide media attention, Hindu organizations in particular have been very critical of the French authorities cracking down on the Roma, who are now recognized by historians as being of Indian or Hindu origin (Nelson 2012, Khati 2016). Coverage in the media features articles that are critical of French politician Jean-Marie Le Pen for implying that the Roma are thieves (Rothwell 2013); other articles by Hindu groups call for a public apology from President François Hollande for denying a deceased Roma infant a burial space (*The Hans India* 2015a). Media reports also focus on Hindu lobbying to pressure the European Commission into providing reparations to the Roma community for being evicted from France (*Romea.cz* 2010). Another article focuses on attempts by Hindu groups to raise awareness of what they describe as a "Roma apartheid." An article titled "Hindus Express Shock at the Demolition of Roma Settlement in France" quotes Hindu leader Rajan Zed, who states, "Instead of unleashing repression, France and Europe needed to work on social inclusion and rehabilitation of Roma communities. Europe's most persecuted and discriminated community, Roma were reportedly facing apartheid conditions in Europe" (*Daily News and Analysis* 2010). By drawing attention to such socio-political incidents, Hindu groups are attempting to promote the integration of Hindus in France and to hold the French government accountable for the delegitimizing of Hinduism in France.

Yet such denunciations are voiced in the media by Hindus implanted in the United Kingdom and in the United States rather than by Hindus residing in France, who seem to remain silent in the face of prejudice. In fact, there is a noticeable absence of narratives documenting what it means to be a Hindu in France. Several factors can explain the challenges French Hindus confront in trying to present a strong and unified response to the discrimination they experience. First, the absence of Hindu nationalist organizations in France, due in part to the constant monitoring of organized religious and political organizations by the French authorities, can account for the minimal web presence of French Hindus. French media have been particularly critical of the rise of Hindu nationalism in India, denouncing the role played by Prime Minister Narendra Modi in the Muslim genocide in the state of Gujarat (*France 24* 2015). The comic book by French journalist William de Tamaris similarly educates French readers of the dangers of right-wing Hindu nationalism by using the example of the recent ban on beef in parts of India (Tiwari 2018, Senghar 2017). Such media coverage and negative attention could make it more difficult for nationalist organizations to seek implantation on French soil. Second, French assimilationist policies that affect Hindus, such as the serving of non-vegetarian meals in schools, do not necessarily target Hindus alone. These policies are couched in neutral terms that deprive Hindus of the tools frequently used as the backbone of political counternarratives by disfavored groups. Third, the underdeveloped use of the internet in France, as compared to the United States, severely restricts efforts of self-representation, dissemination, and community-building. According to Joel Dreyfuss (2017) with CNBC, technology companies are underrepresented in France, posing a risk to its market economy that remains "alarmingly underexposed to technology." Nick Colas, co-founder of market analysis firm DataTrek Research, goes as far as to claim that "the internet essentially never happened" in France (Dreyfuss 2017). Early French institutional practices based on centralization, the absence of a service-based culture, the limited web-based services offered by French companies that rely very commonly on pay-per-call phone assistance, and weak institutional infrastructure continue to limit the role of the internet in France today. Rather than pointing to a lack of public articulation, the discreet online presence of the French Hindu community confirms its roots on French national soil where the web is underutilized. Finally, the lack of a Hindu public response to perceived acts of discrimination can be explained by the extreme diversity of the Hindu community, which poses a challenge to the establishment of a unified group identity. Although Hindus in France share a common status as a markedly new religious minority, they are also an extremely diverse group with differing national origins, migration histories, and class backgrounds (Weibel 2007, Trouillet 2013, Goreau-Ponceaud 2009, 2014). In the United States, Hindus tend to be well-paid professionals with privileged access to technology and education and therefore the means to control the discourse (Bauman and Saunders 2009).

By contrast, in France, most Hindus are small business and restaurant owners who are part of the working class and who may not favor access to technology to make their community more visible (Weibel 2007, Goreau-Ponceaud 2009, 2014).

By insisting on the victimization of French Hindus, British- and American-based organizations have portrayed themselves as the only voices willing and able to stand up for the French Hindu community. These organizations have consistently denounced the grievances of Hindus in the diaspora and are presenting themselves as the guardians of Hindus around the globe. Financial resources have allowed these organizations to use technology to increase their access to Hindus residing in the West. They design sophisticated and popular websites that offer discussion forums, news items, and commentaries. They seem united around clear pan-Hindu themes, show a strong sense of collective identity, and feel strongly about promoting the expansion of Hindu nationalist groups in France specifically and in Europe generally. Recent articles document the desire to start a branch of the RSS in France (Uttam 2014), while signature campaigns have circulated to establish a statue of RSS founder, Veer Sarvarkar, in Marseille (*Hindu Janajagruti Samiti* 2014). The official launching in October 2015 of the Veda Federation of France, a foundation that brings together eight associations of Hindu tradition, similarly suggests a desire to be known and acknowledged in France (Gaulmyn 2017). Its founding speaks specifically to a desire to conform to a vision of India and Hinduism that aligns with that of the nationalist party currently in power in India and of its Prime Minister Narendra Modi (Gaulmyn 2017). These recent efforts could indicate the possibility of stronger transnational ties in the future between the Hindu communities in France, the United Kingdom, the United States, and India.

Conclusion: rethinking transnationalism

Theories of transnationalism offer a useful conceptual and empirical framework through which to investigate the experiences of Hindus in the United States and France. The transnational paradigm is commonly based on the critique of the nation-state as a unit of analysis and is founded on the notion that lives of contemporary migrants involve social, symbolic, and material ties that are decentered from national-boundaries (Glick-Schiller et al., 1995; Portes 1997; Vertovec 2001). Literature on transnationalism transcends the limitations of earlier models of assimilation into single nation-states and focuses on how lives of immigrants transcend national borders (Portes 1997, 812; Kasinitz et al. 2009). Consequently, research has studied networks and relationships that tie migrants to their homeland. In keeping with such objectives, the primary goal of this study was to examine whether emerging similarities could be observed between the experiences of Hindus in the United States and in France. Particularly, this study was interested in assessing whether the articulation of Hinduism transcends specific contexts, given that Hinduism as a religion does not ascribe to a uniform set of practices. Instead, its religious texts, customs, rituals, and beliefs vary from family to family and remain culturally and regionally defined. Its plurality therefore provides a strong basis for investigating if Hindu groups in France and the United States are constructing identities that are transnational. We chose to focus our study on the United States and France because both are home to a growing Hindu population, yet the two nations offer differing political models, frameworks, and philosophies.

Despite pronounced national variations, our analysis shows some similar patterns across the two contexts. First, Hindus in both countries face the difficulty of overcoming overt and covert forms of discrimination and delegitimization of their religion. Our study shows that Hindus both in the United States and in France experience racialization and otherness. Second, Hindus in both countries show attempts to make their religion more consistent with American and French mainstream societies, whether it be congregational forms of worship in the United States or the privatization of religion and the promotion of more spiritual dimensions of Hinduism in France. Our analysis also reveals profound differences in the experiences of Hindus in France and the US – differences that have led to divergent articulations of Hinduism, unique to each national context. For example, Hindus in France have been far less politically effective in bargaining with the state. As compared to Hindu groups in the United States, Hindus in France have been relatively less successful in creating national organizations that can advocate for and represent them. Furthermore, while temples emerge as important spaces for gathering and networking in France, they are locally controlled and relegated to the private sphere, thereby limiting Hindus' ability to express a coherent national presence in France. In fact, our study shows that American- and British-based Hindu organizations have emerged as transnational representatives for Hindus across the world, including France, thanks to their technological resources and outreach efforts. These groups evoke common religious roots and utilize simplistic messages or symbols to organize Hindu audiences who are experiencing new forms of racism and anxieties in their respective host societies. Hindus in the diaspora are attracted to such organizations because of their need to come together and gain a collective voice in the face of discrimination.

Based on this study, we make two interrelated arguments about the theoretical framework of transnationalism. First, we argue that beyond the recognition of the trans-territorial connections, transnationalism as a framework needs to take into account the social realities of nation-states that influence immigrants' lives and experiences. This study questions the national/transnational binary and underscores the impact of structural realities on the lived experiences of individuals, which becomes central to the emergence of transnational ties. We simply cannot dismiss the variables of the nation-states that both impose constraints on minority groups and continue to define the nation, nationalism, citizenship, and citizenry. Second, while much of the literature on transnationalism has focused on immigrants' activities that influence the homeland, our study indicates the emergence of transnational organizations that are trying to transform the politics and structure of other host societies. It is evident that American and British Hindu organizations are engaged in transnational activities not only to influence politics in India but also to exercise pressure on other host societies with a significant Hindu presence, such as France. We simply cannot ignore the marginalization, intolerance, racism, and prejudice that minorities face in countries like France and the United States and the ways in which local, national, and transnational infrastructure shape their responses to such experiences of oppression, shaping the construction of Hinduism in nation-states in the process. Unlike in the United States, where minority groups are encouraged to overtly assert their ethnicity, in France the tension between the political mobilization of transnational Hindu groups and the structural constraints placed on minorities make it difficult for Hindus to assert a public presence. Interestingly, in the United States, multiculturalism is actually encouraging the emergence of a certain right-wing discourse that proposes to unite people in the diaspora against discrimination, whereas in France, structural constraints have actually discouraged the dissemination of such ideologies in the Hindu context, at least up until now. It will be interesting to see how differences in the articulation of Hinduism continue to play out in the United States and in France, especially for post-immigration generations raised exclusively on French soil. It would worth adopting a more intersectional approach in the future to examine problematics of class, gender, or sexuality and to track how successful transnational Hindu organizations are in making their presence felt in France.

References

Ajrouch, Kristine J. "Global Contexts and the Veil: Muslim Integration in the United States and France." *Sociology of Religion* 68.3 (Fall 2007): 321–325.

Ali, Huma. "Religion, Discrimination and Assimilation: A Comparison of Contemporary France and The United States." Thesis, Carnegie Mellon University, April 2012. ProQuest.

Altglas, Véronique. *Le nouvel hindouisme occidental*. Paris: Broché, 2005.

Bauman, Chad M. and Jennifer Saunders. "Out of India: Immigrant Hindus and South Asian Hinduism in the United States." *ReligionCompass* (2009): 116–135. http://digitalcommons.butler.edu/facsch_papers/79.

BBC News. 2006. "French Comedy Film Offends Hindus." February 21, 2006. http://news.bbc.co.uk/go/pr/fr/-/2/hi/entertainment/4735198.stm.

Beane, Wendell. *Myth, Cult and Symbols in Sakta Hinduism: A Study of the Indian Mother Goddess*. New Delhi: MunshirmManoharlal Publications, 1977.

Bhatt, Chetan and Parita Mukta. "Hindutva in the West: Mapping the Antinomies of Diaspora Nationalism." *Ethnic and Racial Studies* 23.3 (2000): 407–441.

Bourrier, Ani. "L'hindouisme se répanden France." *Radio France Internationale (Rfi)*, January 26, 2006. http://www1.rfi.fr/actufr/articles/073/article_41400.asp.

Carnes, Tony and Fenggang Yang, eds. *Asian American Religions: The Making or Remaking of Borders and Boundaries*. New York, NY: New York University Press, 2004.

Coburn, Thomas. *Encountering the Goddess: A Translation of the Devi Mahatmya and a Study of its Interpretation*. Albany, NY: SUNY Press, 1991.

Daily News and Analysis. "Hindus Express Shock at Demolition of Roman Settlement in France." August 10, 2010. http://www.dnaindia.com/world/report-hindus-express-shock-at-demolition-of-roma-settlement-in-france-1420592.

Das Gupta, Monisha. "What is Indian About You? A Gendered Transnational Approach to Ethnicity." *Gender & Society* 11 (1997): 572–596.

Dasgupta, Sayantani and Shamita Das Dasgupta. "Women in Exile: Gender Relations in the Asian Indian Community in the U.S." In *Contours of the Heart South Asians Map North America*, edited by Sunaina Maira and Rajni Srikanth, 381–400. New York, NY: Asian American Writers' Workshop, 1996.

Dauvillier, Sylvie. "Diasporas Indiennesen France." *Banques des Savoirs*, March 3, 2008. http://www.savoirs.essonne.fr/thematiques/les-hommes/ethnologie/diasporas-indiennes-en-france/.

Dempsey, Corinne. *The Goddess Lives in Upstate New York: Breaking Convention and Making Home at a North American Hindu Temple*. Oxford: Oxford University Press, 2005.

Dreyfuss, Joel. "French President Emmanuel Macron Wants France to Become Start-up Nation." *CNBC*, November 27, 2017. .https://www.cnbc.com/2017/11/27/french-president-emmanuel-macron-wants-a-nation-of-internet-start-ups.html

Ebaugh, Helen Rose and Janet Saltzman Chafetz. *Religion and The New Immigrants: Continuities and Adaptations in Immigrant Congregations*. Walnut Creek, CA: Altamira Press, 2000.

Eck, Diana. *Encountering God: A Spiritual Journey from Bozeman to Banaras*. Boston: Beacon Press, 1993.

Eck, Diana. "Negotiating Hindu Identities in America." In *The South Asian Religious Diaspora in Britain, Canada and the United States*, edited by Harold Coward, John R. Hinnells, and Raymond Brady Williams, 219–237. Albany, NY: SUNY Press, 2000.

France 24. 2015. "Who really is Narendra Modi?" April 10, 2015. http://www.france24.com/en/search/?Search%5Bterm%5D=who+really+is+Narendra+Modi&Search%5Bpage%5D=1.

Gaulmyn, Isabelle. "Hindouisme: offensive de charmeen France à travers la tradition védique." *Franceinter*, March 11, 2017. https://www.franceinter.fr/emissions/faut-il-y-croire/faut-il-y-croire-11-mars-2017.

Glick-Schiller, Nina, Linda Basch, and Cristina Blanc Szanton. "From Immigrant to Transmigrant: Theorizing Transnational Migration." *Anthropology Quarterly* 68 (1995): 48–63.

Goreau-Ponceaud, Anthony. "La diaspora tamouleen France: entre visibilité et politisation." *EchoGéo*, 2009. http://echogeo.revues.org/11157.

Goreau-Ponceaud, Anthony. "Ganesha Chaturthi and the Sri Lankan Tamil Diaspora in Paris: Inventing Strategies of Visibility and Legitimacy in a Plural 'Mono-Cultural' Society." In *Migration and Religion in Europe: Comparative Perspectives on South Asian Experiences*, edited by Ester Gallo. Burlington, VT: Ashgate, 2014.

Greenfeld, Liah. "The Reality of American Multiculturalism: American Nationalism at Work." In *Contemporary Majority Nationalism*, edited by Alain-G. Gagon, André Lecours, and Geneviève Nootens, 181–196. Montreal: McGill-Queens University Press, 2011.
The Hans India. 2015a. "Hindus Want Apology from French President Hollande on Burial Denial to Roma Baby." January 5, 2015. http://www.thehansindia.com/posts/index/NRI/1970-01-01/Hindus-want-apology-from-French-President-Hollande-on-burial-denial-to-Roma-baby/124481.
The Hans India. 2015b. "Hindus Back Vegetarian School Meals in France." August 22, 2015. http://www.thehansindia.com/posts/index/2015-08-22/Hindus-back-vegetarian-school-meals-in-France-171888.
Hassan, Steven. "French Shoes with Lord Rama's Image Annoys UK Hindus." *Religion News Blog*, July 12, 2005. http://www.religionnewsblog.com/11651/french-shoes-with-lord-ramas-image-annoys-uk-hindus.
Hindu Janajagruti Samiti. 2014. "Approve the Veer Sarvarkar Memorial in France." https://www.hindujagruti.org/national-issue/veer-savarkar-memorial-in-france.
INSEE (Institut National de la Statistique et de Etudes Economique). 2011. "Répartition des immigrés par pays de naissance 2008." https://www.insee.fr/fr/statistiques.
Jacob, Simon and Pallavi Thakur. "Jyothi Hindu Temple: One Religion, Many Practices." In *Religion and the New Immigrants: Continuities and Adaptations in Immigrant Congregations*, edited by Helen Rose Ebaugh and Janet Saltzman Chafetz, 151–162. New York, NY: AltaMira Press, 2000.
Jaffrelot, Christophe and Ingrid Therwath. "The Sangh Parivar and the Hindu Diaspora in the West: What Kind of Long Distance Nationalism?" *International Political Sociology* 1 (2007): 278–295.
Joshi, Khyati. *New Roots in America's Sacred Ground*. New Brunswick, NJ: Rutgers University Press, 2006.
Joshi, Khyati. "Religion in the Lives of Second Generation Indian American Hindus." In *Sustaining Faith Traditions: Race, Ethnicity, and Religion among the Latino and Asian American Second Generation*, edited by Carolyn Chen and Russell Jeung. New York, NY: New York University Press, 2012.
Joshi, Khyati. "Standing Up and Speaking Out: Hindu Americans and Christian Normativity in Metro Atlanta." In *Asian Americans in Dixie: Race and Migration in the South*, edited by Khyati Joshi and Jigna Desai, 190–215. Urbana, IL: University of Illinois Press, 2013.
Kasinitz, Philip, John Mollenkopf, Mary Waters, and Jennifer Holdaway. *Inheriting the City: The Children of Immigrants Come of Age*. Cambridge, MA: Harvard University Press, 2009.
Khati, Pooja. "Meet the Roma: 2,000 Years Ago, the First 'Indians' to Go to Europe." *The Indian Express*, February 23, 2016. http://indianexpress.com/article/explained/meet-the-roma-2000-years-ago-the-first-indians-to-go-to-europe/.
Kupperman, Joel. *Classic Asian Philosophy: A Guide to The Essential Texts*. New York, NY: Oxford University Press, 2001.
Kurien, Prema. "Becoming American by Becoming Hindu: Indian Americans Take Their Place at the Multicultural Table." In *Gatherings in Diaspora: Religious Communities and the New Immigration*, edited by Stephen Warner and Judith Wittner, 37–70. Philadelphia, PA: Temple University Press, 1998.
Kurien, Prema. "Gendered Ethnicity: Creating a Hindu Indian Identity in the U.S." *American Behavioral Scientist* 42.4 (1999): 648–670.
Kurien, Prema. "'We Are Better Hindus Here': Religion and Ethnicity Among Indian Americans." In *Religions in Asian America: Building Faith Communities*, edited by Pyong Gap Min and Jung Ha Kim, 99–120. New York, NY: AltaMira Press, 2002.
Kurien, Prema. "Multiculturalism, Immigrant Religion, and Diasporic Nationalism: The Development of an American Hinduism." *Social Problems* 51.3 (2004): 262–285.
Kurien, Prema. 2005. "Being Young, Brown, and Hindu: The Identity Struggles of Second-Generation Indian Americans." *Journal of Contemporary Ethnography* 34.4 (2005): 434–469.
Kurien, Prema. "Multiculturalism and 'American' Religion: The Case of Hindu Indian Americans." *Social Forces* 85 (2006): 723–741.
Kurien, Prema. *A Place at the Multicultural Table: The Development of an American Hinduism*. New Brunswick, NJ: Rutgers University Press, 2007.
Lal, Vinay. "The Politics of History on the Internet: Cyber-Diasporic Hinduism and the North American Hindu Diaspora." *Diaspora: A Journal of Transnational Studies* 8.2 (1999): 137–172.
Leclerc, Caroline. "Le statut d'association cultuelle et les sectes." *RFDA*, 2005. https://actu.dalloz-etudiant.fr/fileadmin/actualites/pdfs/OCTOBRE_2013/RFDA2005-565.pdf.

Leonard, Kareen Isaksen. *The South Asian Americans*. Westport, CT: Greenwood Press, 1997.
Lesegretain, Claire. "Les Hinduistes de France enquête de visibilité." *La Croix*, August 30, 2012. https://www.la-croix.com/Religion/Actualite/Les-hindouistes-de-France-en-quete-de-visibilite-_EP_-2012-08-30-847942.
Levitt, Peggy. "Local-Level Global Religion: The Case of US-Dominican Migration." *Journal for the Scientific Study of Religion* 37 (1998): 74–89.
Levitt, Peggy. "Social Remittances: A Local-Level, Migration-Driven Form of Cultural Diffusion." *International Migration Review* 32 (1999): 926–49.
Levitt, Peggy. *God Needs No Passport: Immigrants and the Changing American Religious Landscape*. New York, NY: New Press, 2007.
Loi du 9 décembre 1905 concernant la séparation des Eglises et de l'Etat. *Legifrance: le service public de diffusion du droit*. https://www.legifrance.gouv.fr/affichTexte.do?cidTexte=JORFTEXT000000508749
Louis, Arul. "Muslims Third-Largest Group; Hindus, Buddhists Fourth in United States." *Ummid*, May 13, 2015. http://www.ummid.com/news/2015/May/13.05.2015/hindu-muslim-population-in-us.html.
Martín-i-Pardo, Meritxell. "The Articulation of a French Civil Hinduism." *Journal of the American Academy of Religion* 79.2 (June 2011): 497–519.
Mathew, Biju and Vijay Prashad. "The Protean Forms of Yankee Hindutva." *Ethnic and Racial Studies* 23 (2000): 516–34.
Mazumdar, Shampa and Sanjoy Mazumdar. "Hindu Temple Building in California: A Study of Immigrant Religion." *Journal of Ritual Studies* 20.2 (2006): 43–57.
Miller, Barbara, trans. *Bhagavad-Gita*. New York, NY: Bantam, 1986.
Narayan, Anjana and Bandana Purkayastha, eds., *Living Our Religions: Hindu and Muslim South Asian Women Narrate Their Experiences*. Springfield, VA: Kumarian, 2009.
Narayan, Anjana and Bandana Purkayastha. "Talking Gender Superiority in Virtual Spaces." *Journal of South Asian Diaspora* 3.1 (2011): 53–69.
Narayan, Anjana, Bandana Purkayastha, and Sudipto Banerjee. "Constructing Transnational and Virtual Identities: A Study of the Discourse and Networks of Ethnic Student Organizations in the US and UK." *Journal of Intercultural Studies* 32 (2011): 495–517.
Narayanan, Vasudha. "Creating the South Indian 'Hindu' Experience in the United States." In *A Sacred Thread: Modern Transmission of Hindu Traditions in India and Abroad*, edited by Raymond Brady Williams, 147–176. USA: ANIMA Publications, 1992.
Nelson, Dean. "European Roma Descended from Indian 'Intouchables,' Genetic Study Shows." *The Telegraph*, December 3, 2012. https://www.telegraph.co.uk/news/worldnews/europe/9719058/European-Roma-descended-from-Indian-untouchables-genetic-study-shows.html.
Noiriel, Gérard. *Population, immigration, et identité nationale en France/ XIXe–XXe siècle*. Paris: Hachette, 1992.
Noiriel, Gerard. "Immigration: Amnesia and Memory." *French Historical Studies* 19.2 (Fall 1995): 367–380.
Noiriel, Gérard. *The French Melting Pot: Immigration, Citizenship and National Identity*. Minneapolis, MN: University of Minnesota Press, 1996.
Portes, Alejandro. "Globalization From Below: The Rise of Transnational Communities." Paper presented at Princeton University, 1997. http://maxweber.hunter.cuny.edu/pub/eres/SOC217_PIMENTEL/portes.pdf.
Purkayastha, Bandana. *Negotiating Ethnicity: Second-Generation South Asian Americans Traverse a Transnational World*. New Brunswick, NJ: Rutgers University Press, 2005.
Rajagopal, Arvind. "Transnational Networks and Hindu Nationalism." *Bulletin of Concerned Asian Scholars* 29.3 (1997): 49–50.
Rajagopal, Arvind. "Hindu Nationalism in the United States: Changing Configurations of Political Practice." *Ethnic and Racial Studies* 23 (2000): 467–96.
Rayaprol, Aparna. *Negotiating Identities: Women in the Indian Diaspora*. Delhi: Oxford University Press, 1997.
Romea.cz. "Hindus Ask for Compensation for Maltreated Roma in France and Italy." November 9, 2010. http://www.romea.cz/en/news/world/hindus-ask-for-compensation-for-maltreated-roma-in-france-and-italy.

Rothwell, James. "French Far-Right Politician Jean Marie Le Pen Fined for Racist Roma Remarks." *The Independent*, December 19, 2013. https://www.independent.co.uk/news/people/news/french-far-right-politician-jean-marie-le-pen-fined-for-racist-roma-remarks-9016617.html.

Senghar, Shweta. "French Author Comic Whacks Cow Vigilantism and Hindu Nationalism Through Art and Relevant Questions." *India Times*, July 28, 2017. https://www.indiatimes.com/news/india/french-author-s-comic-whacks-cow-vigilantism-hindu-nationalism-through-art-relevant-questions-326549.html.

Shattuck, Cybelle. *Dharma in the Golden State: South Asian Religious Traditions in California*. Santa Barbara, CA: Fithian Press, 1996.

Silverman, Maxim. *Deconstructing the Nation: Immigration, Racism, and Citizenship in Modern France*. London: Routledge, 1992.

Therwath, Ingrid. "Cyber-Hindutva: Hindu Nationalism, The Diaspora and The Web." *Social Science Information* 51.4 (2012): 551–577.

Tiwari, Noopur. "A French Comic Book Uses India's War on Beef to Illustrate the Dangers of Hindutva." *Scroll.in*, March 22, 2018. https://scroll.in/magazine/844269/a-french-comic-book-uses-indias-war-on-beef-to-illustrate-the-dangers-of-hindutva.

Trouillet, Pierre-Yves. "Hinduism in France." In *Brill's Encyclopedia of Hinduism*, volume 5, edited by Knut Jacobsen, Helene Basu, Angelika Malinar, and Vasudha Narayan, 235–239. 2013. https://brill.com/view/db/enhi.

Uttam, Kumar. "RSS Plan to Join Hindu Groups, Expand in the West." *Hindustan Times*, August 8, 2014. https://www.hindustantimes.com/india/rss-plans-to-join-hindu-groups-expand-in-the-west/story-MjgW5tnSeTEtYnCtIROajL.html.

Vertovec, Steven. *The Hindu Diaspora: Comparative Patterns*. London: Routledge, 2000.

Vertovec, Steven. "Transnational Challenges to the 'New' Multiculturalism." Paper presented at The ASA Conference, University of Sussex. 30 March 2001. http://www.transcomm.ox.ac.uk/working%20papers/WPTC-2K-06%20Vertovec.Pdf.

Weibel, Nadine. "Spiritualités indiennesen Alsace." *Hommes et migrations 1268–1269* (2007): 174–182.

Williams, Raymond Brady. *Religions of Immigrants from India and Pakistan: New Threads in the American Tapestry*. Cambridge and New York: Cambridge University Press, 1988.

Yang, Fenggang and Helen Rose Ebaugh. "Religion and Ethnicity: The Impact of Majority/Minority Status in the Home and Host Countries." *Journal for the Scientific Study of Religion* 40 (2001a): 367–378.

Yang, Fenggang and Helen Rose Ebaugh. "Transformation of New Immigrant Religions and Their Global Implications." *American Sociological Review* 66 (2001b): 269–288.

Zavos, John. "Hinduism in the Diaspora." In *Routledge Handbook of the South Asian Diaspora*, edited by Joya Chatterji and David Washbrook, 306–317. London: Routledge, 2013.

Zong, Jieand and Jeanne Batalova. "Indian Immigrants in the United States." *Migrationpolicy.org.*, August 31, 2017. https://www.migrationpolicy.org/article/indian-immigrants-united-states.

12
FACING STRONG HEAD WINDS
Dalit transnational activism today

Peter J. Smith

Introduction

In recent decades there has been a growing resurgence of previously marginalized peoples occurring on a transnational scale. These forms of collective resistance have been highlighted by the blossoming of new identity-based social movements (Castells 2010). Common among these social movements is a profound sense of being excluded, coupled with an assertion of their dignity and human rights. The focus of this chapter is Dalit transnational movements from India. Desai defines transnationalism as "both organizing across national borders as well as framing local, national, regional, and global activism in 'transnational discourses'" (2005: 319). In this chapter I shall argue that transnational activism and the appropriation of a discourse of human rights have played a significant role in shaping the activism and the organizational formation of transnational Dalit (formerly untouchables) movements. The objectives of these movements include international recognition, a more responsive Indian state, and ultimately the abolition of caste and untouchability.

Dalit transnational activists are making connections with peoples around the world who have been marginalized in a variety of ways including African Americans, landless workers in Brazil, indigenous peoples, and other groups bearing the stigma of caste wherever they are located: Japan, Africa, and South Asia. Here they use the universalist discourse of human rights to articulate their issues and assert their demands. Their notion of rights, however, is broad and includes economic, social, cultural, and women's rights. This broad concept of rights tied to notions of justice has assisted the Dalits in becoming part of a larger global justice movement (GJM) participating in a variety of venues beyond the UN, including the World Social Forum (WSF). In addition to these venues, the Dalits have worked with like-minded groups and solidarity movements in South Asia and Europe, including lobbying the European and UK parliaments as well as the United States Congress.

This chapter discusses the involvement of Dalit movements in transnational activism in terms of their struggle for social justice, recognition, and human rights as well their struggle against casteism and the debilitating effects of neoliberal globalization. In so doing it recognizes, as Desai noted previously, that this is a struggle that takes place on a variety of scales and within a framework of transnational discourses. The framing of these discourses is contested, as the chapter indicates. For example, should caste be "recast" as an international phenomenon;

or is it a particularly Indian phenomenon, as Indian governments insist? The movements examined in this chapter include a distinct Dalit women's movement led by the National Federation of Dalit Women and the National Campaign on Dalit Human Rights. As the chapter indicates, Dalit transnational activism is very much contested, with considerable opposition coming from Indian governments as well conservative elements of the Indian diaspora. This struggle taking place today is acknowledged to be taking place in a chilly human rights climate.

The chapter begins by providing context in terms of who the Dalits are, what their status is within India—legally and politically as well as in terms of the Indian social structure. Following this section, the chapter discusses the impact of neoliberal globalization on India, both in terms of its ideological hegemony within India's governing parties and with regard to its negative impact on hundreds of millions of India's poor, in particular the Dalits. Next the chapter provides considerable attention to the transnationalism of Dalit movements. Here it employs Karl Polanyi's (2001) concepts of the "double-movement" and "countermovement," which are used to discuss the dynamic connections between the global and the local as well the emphasis of Dalit movements on social protection not only in an economic, material sense but also in terms of social recognition and human dignity. It then concludes by asking, what has Dalit transnationalism accomplished?

Context: who are the Dalits?

Answering this question necessitates that one begin with caste, "one of the most controversial fields of Indian studies" (Jaffrelot 2013: 107). However controversial, it is a phenomenon that "continues to pervade India's society, economy and politics" (Kapadia 2017: 4). In its basic form the caste system divides Indian society into a rigid hierarchy based upon the fourfold varna system of the ancient Hindu scriptures. According to these ancient scriptures the Brahmins, the priestly caste, were created from God's head; the warrior caste, the Kshatriyas, were created from his arms; the merchants and artisans, Vaishyas, from his thighs; and agricultural workers and servants, Shudras, from his feet. Outside, beyond, and below the caste system—and, therefore polluted—were the untouchables, today, the Dalits.

The term "Dalit" can be traced to the root "dal" in Sanskrit, which means "oppressed," "broken," "crushed," or "cracked" and was popularized by the great Dalit leaders Mahatma Jotirao Phule in the nineteenth century and Dr. B.R. Ambedkar in the twentieth. Today, as Kapadia notes, the term "Dalit" "is the self-referential term of choice for activists and intellectuals from this social group" (2017: 2). The castes associated with Dalits are known otherwise as the "scheduled castes" (SC) according to the Indian constitution, which confirms their rights to "reservations," public sector jobs, and places in higher education. According to the 2011 Indian census, the Dalit population was 201.3 million or about 16.6 percent of India's population (Teltumbde 2017: 53).

Officially, untouchability is banned by the Indian constitution, and a host of laws have been passed since Independence in 1947 to ameliorate the condition of the Dalits, for example, laws against manual scavenging (the practice of cleaning dry toilets by hand). Yet the practice of untouchability in many ways survives, particularly in rural areas. According to a survey conducted in 2011–2012 in more than 42,000 households across India by the National Council of Applied Research and the University of Maryland, 27 percent of respondents agreed that they practiced untouchability in some form. When asked "Will you let an SC enter your kitchen, use your utensils?" 54 percent of Brahmins said no as did 35 percent of those adhering to the Hindu religion. (Chishti 2014) Since the Indian state as often as not has been dominated by Brahmins (Teltumbde 2017), there has been little inclination historically to challenge the deep rootedness of this social structure.

In virtually every social category—poverty, health care, education, welfare provision—Dalits are at the bottom. Caste thus pervades all aspects of Indian society. As Tharamangalam puts it: "The abysmal socio-economic condition of the lower castes is not a random occurrence but is embedded in historically inherited structures that have resisted radical change" (2012) Even today, despite its high growth rate, India, in particular the Dalits, has fallen behind even Pakistan in terms of international rankings of social indicators (Tharamangalam 2012). For Dalit women the situation is even worse, exploited as they are by the intersection of caste, class, and patriarchy and therefore subjected to multiple, interconnected oppressions (Kapadia 2017) which intensify their exclusion and marginality. To this must be added the fact of continuing acts of violence, atrocities, upon Dalit women including rape, a situation in which "more than four Dalit women are raped in India, everyday," acts designed to intimidate and keep Dalit women in their place (NCDHR 2015, Irudayam et al. 2006, Kapadia 2017).

At a formal level the Indian state has passed numerous pieces of legislation to protect and enhance the daily lives of Dalits. However, historically, there has been a gap between promise and performance, between formal, political democracy and substantive democracy. As Gorringe puts it "significant symbolic victories co-exist with continuing casteism and deprivation" (2013: 124), a situation that very much concerned the great Dalit leader B.R. Ambedkar, a leading architect of the Indian Constitution. Speaking on the eve of enacting the Indian Constitution, Ambedkar (1949) spoke of his fear of a disjuncture between the legal, political status of the Dalits and the deep-seated social reality of India.

> On 26th of January 1950, we are going to enter into a life of contradictions. In politics we have equality and in social and economic life we have inequalities. In politics we will be recognizing the principles of one man one vote and one vote one value. In our social and economic life, we shall, by reason of our social and economic structure, continue to deny the principle of one man, one vote. How long shall we continue to live this life of contradiction?

Too long, it would appear, as this "contradiction" is, today, very much a part of the lives of India's Dalits, one exacerbated by the implementation of neoliberal policies beginning in the early 1990s.

The impact of neoliberal globalization on India

When neoliberal globalization arrived in India in 1991, it represented a *volte face* in terms of the role of the Indian state in the economy and society. Gone was Nehru's vision of a democratic socialist republic ushering in development and secular modernity through state planning, import substitution industrialization, and a commitment to political and social justice—which, in fact, had improved the lives of Dalits somewhat (Corbridge and Harris 2003). In its place was "an enthusiastic pro-capitalist state with a neoliberal ideology" (Kohli and Singh 2013: 9) which has become hegemonic in India today.[1] The result is a state-capital alliance emphasizing economic growth. Indeed, economic growth figures are impressive, often exceeding 7 percent per year. (Statista 2018) Yet not everyone has benefited from this growth. According to Kohli and Singh, the Indian state has thrown "its weight behind the winners of the new economy without compensating those left behind" (2013: 9). Indeed, inequality is widening between the better off and the common people of India (Kapadia 2017: 11).

According to Himanshu and Sen, poverty is particularly bad among the Dalits and Adivasis (tribal peoples, Scheduled Tribes), the result being that "poverty incidence in these two groups ... has not lessened significantly over time, in spite of the phase of rapid growth in the past three decades" (2014: 68).

Privatization and retrenchment by the state is having a negative effect on the limited Dalit advancement that has occurred, particularly privatization in the public sector with its reservations (affirmative action) of 15 percent of the public sector workforce for Dalits. Today the emphasis on the market as the allocator of resources is viewed as a threat by many Dalits. Put differently, the Dalits have had representation in the state but not in the market. Of particular concern is the loss of jobs in government. According Jaffrelot (2013: 24, 25), "There were 19.5 million jobs in the public sector in 1992–93, when the Indian population was 839 million. Though Indians now total 1.3 billion, the number of jobs in the public sector has shrunk to 17.6 million." The pervasiveness of casteism makes it hard for Dalits to find good jobs in the private sector, particularly in the burgeoning IT sector. According to Kapadia "the best jobs in the much-sought-after IT sector are entirely monopolized by the well-educated upper caste middle classes who get the high salaries and foreign postings it offers" (2017: 11). In effect, age-old occupational segregation attached to casteism continues to hamstring the progress of the Dalits in India's private-sector labor markets, women in particular. The already low participation rate of women in the work force has declined in recent years (Ghosh 2016).

Neoliberal policies have also had a negative on public provision of services, with cutbacks in already meager public health and public education budgets. Budget allocations targeted especially for special protection and provisions for Scheduled Castes and Tribes have only occasionally met their required targets, often being diverted into unrelated activities with the actual spending far less that what was budgeted (Teltumbde 2016: 11). Under the Bharatiya Janata Party (BJP) of Prime Minister Modi, the situation seems to be getting worse. According to Teltumbde, "the two years of Modi have been grossly devastating to Dalits in the short term and utterly ruinous in the long term" (2016: 11). Overall then, neoliberalization has not been good for the Dalits (Kapadia 2017, Teltumbde 2017).

There are some exceptions to this, with social conditions for Dalits improving in Uttar Pradesh but with very little progress in economic terms. Two states, Kerala and West Bengal, where poverty has gone down have long experience with leftist governments (Kohli and Singh 2013). There have also been efforts to balance neoliberalism with humane social and economic policies. In 2005, for example, the Congress-led coalition government (2004–2014) passed the Mahatma Gandhi National Rural Employment Guarantee Act (MGNREGA), which provided at least 100 days of guaranteed wage employment in a financial year to every rural household whose adult members volunteer to do casual unskilled work, a program which proved to be popular and supported by the voters (Jaffrelot 2013). Yet, here once again, a gap arose between promise and performance. The program which delivered concrete benefits and reduced gender wage differences, has eroded since 2010. According to Ghosh (2015):

> Essentially central government has been slowly trying to kill this programme by starving it of essential funds. The cynical process was started by the very Congress-led government that put the law into force, but it has intensified under the government of Narendra Modi.

Indeed, the Modi-led BJP government have been unabashed champions of neoliberalism, with economic growth being the answer to and equated with development encapsulated in the slogan, "participation of all, development for all" (Mitra and Schöttli 2016).

Internationalizing the Dalit movement

Frustrated by the slow pace of change, the paternalism of the Indian government, and fearing the negative impact of neoliberal globalization upon their community, the Dalits in the 1990s shifted scales and began engaging in transnational activism. In taking their struggle for social, economic, and cultural recognition and protection to the transnational level, the Dalits drew their inspiration from Ambedkar. For Dalits, Ambedkar is a source of immense pride and respect, not for only his remarkable educational achievements—two doctorates, one from the London School of Economics, the other from Columbia University—but also for his leadership in the struggle against untouchability and Hinduism and his role as a founder of the modern Indian state. Today Ambedkar serves not only as an inspiration for Dalit movements but also as a source of legitimacy for actions, including the fight against casteism, not only nationally but globally.

Today the struggle, domestically and transnationally, of the Dalits, particularly in reaction to the effects of neoliberal globalization, can best be understood from a Polanyian perspective, as a countermovement for social protection. In sum, the Dalits are acting as the other half of Polanyi's double movement, that is, as a protective countermovement. For Karl Polanyi (1886–1964) the double movement was key to understanding how history advances. The nineteenth century's "great transformation" led to the expansion of the free market as part of an attempt to disembed the market from society. At the same time, however, a counter-movement occurred, one that reflected an impulse for social protection and which ultimately led to the creation of the welfare state. In both instances the role of the state was critical. First, the state acted to "disembed" the economy from existing social relationships and to facilitate and protect the expansion of the market. Then the state itself came under great pressure to make the "process of economic improvement" "socially bearable" (Polanyi 2001: 40). Polanyi argues, "Indeed, human society would have been annihilated but for protective countermoves which blunted the action of this self-destructive mechanism" (2001: 79). This impulse towards social protection, however, was not merely economic. According to Polanyi (2001: 48):

> The outstanding discovery of recent historical and anthropological research is that man's economy, as a rule, is submerged in his social relationships. He does not act so as to safeguard his individual interest in the possession of material goods; he acts so as to safeguard his social standing, his social claims, his social assets.

This is particularly true of the Dalits, who, as much as they are fighting for material goods, are fighting for social recognition, human rights, and dignity. Today Polanyi's analysis in terms of the national level can be scaled upwards to the global level (Munck 2007).

In moving the scales beyond India, Dalit movements were challenging the tentative hold the state has upon politics, justice, and concepts of citizenship. As Fraser tells us, "globalization is changing the way we argue about justice," away from a concept of justice focused solely on the state to other venues beyond the state (2005: 1). Likewise, Dalit movements exemplify the contested and changing notions of citizenship in society today. According to Seyla Benhabib (2005: 674), "The crises of the nation-state along with globalization and the rise of multi-cultural movements have shifted the lines between citizens and residents, nationals and foreigners. Citizenship rights today must be situated in a transnational context." Ambedkar himself set the precedent of Dalit internationalism through his intervention before the British Round Table Conference in London in 1930–1931. According to two activists in the transnational Dalit movement (Divakar and Ajai 2004: 18:

Ambedkar showed that boundaries for solutions to the problem of caste discrimination are not to be drawn around the village, district, state or nation. What is an internal solution or an external solution should not be determined by geographic borders or national borders.

In moving their struggle for economic justice and cultural recognition beyond India, Dalit activists were able to access a wide range of new political opportunity structures, including the UN and the UN-sponsored World Conference Against Racism, Racial Discrimination, Xenophobia and Related Intolerance in 2001 (WCAR). Most of the activities at these venues focused on issues of human rights broadly understood—political, economic, and social. However, the World Social Forum is where the Dalits have delivered their strongest indictment of the effects of global capitalism on the Dalit people.

Until the 1990s the internationalization of the Dalit issue was not done so much by Dalits in India but by a transnationally linked Dalit diaspora. During the 1950s and 1960s, Dalits began to emigrate: to the United Kingdom, the United States, Canada, and other countries.

Fewer in numbers than the dominant castes, they were often scattered. They kept in touch where they could, and during the 1990s the connections among themselves and the Dalit movement in India became more extensive and complex, "not least due to their communication via the Internet" (Hardtmann 2003: 150). The Dalit diaspora was instrumental in first raising Dalit issues outside India; for example, making representations on behalf of India's Dalits at the United Nations in the early 1990s, a practice they continue today, particularly in the United Kingdom. In fact, it was the Dalit diaspora that was first engaged in transnational activism at the UN.

By 1998, thanks to the emergence of a Dalit middle class, improved organizational capacity (Bob 2007), and communicative structures, more extensive Dalit movements had taken shape, composed of a variety of networks within India and abroad. While there is no central hub to the movement, key nodes have emerged. Discussed in the next section is the early transnational leadership of the Dalit diaspora, followed by discussion of the formation of the National Federation of Dalit Women (NFDW) in 1995, followed by the creation of the National Campaign for Dalit Human Rights (NCDHR) in 1998.

The Dalit diaspora and the United Nations

Lead by Ambedkar, Dalit activists have been long-time advocates for universal human rights including the Dalit diaspora. Among them was Yogesh Verhade from Canada, who in 1991 became an accredited participant at the UN and advocate for human rights. One major problem the Dalit diaspora faced at the United Nations was that the dominant discourse of international human rights was silent on the issue of caste discrimination until 1996. The Universal Declaration of Human Rights, for example, makes no reference to caste. The necessity of finding room within existing UN discourse for Dalit concerns on including casteism was of no small consequence.

With pressure coming from many non-Dalit non-governmental organizations, including Human Rights Watch, to address the issue of caste discrimination in 1996 the UN Committee on Elimination of Racial Discrimination (CERD) invited Verhade to come and testify before their committee. The crucial question before the committee was whether or not the binding International Convention to Eliminate All Forms of Racial Discrimination to which India was a signatory "should be interpreted as also barring caste discrimination" (Cabrera 2017, 287). In a formative decision CERD stated: "The term 'descent' mentioned in article 1 of the Convention does not solely refer to race. The Committee affirms that the situation of the scheduled castes and scheduled tribes falls within the scope of the Convention" (CERD/C/304/Add.13).

This was an historic ruling, one strongly opposed by the Indian government, which had argued that caste was uniquely an Indian phenomenon beyond the purview of the UN's mandate. In effect, CERD had re-framed, "recast," the meaning of caste to include similar instances of discrimination based on work and descent in other countries in Asia and Africa. This opened the door for later investigations and reports by the UN Rapporteurs on the phenomenon of caste discrimination and to later Dalit transnational organizing networking with others discriminated against in a variety of countries, a process that continues to this day.

The transnationalization of the Dalit women's movement

At about the same time of advocacy by the Dalit diaspora at the UN in the mid-1990s, Dalit women in India were preparing to take their cause to the UN, but this time at another venue, the UN Fourth Women's World Conference in Beijing in 1995. Prior to 1995 Dalit women had been virtually invisible politically; their particular issues involving the intersectionality of caste, class, and gender had been ignored. According to Vimal Thorat, "both the Dalit movement and women's movement have consciously ignored the Dalit women's issue" (2001: 1). By 1995 this occlusion was in the process of being rectified where, at a conference of Dalit women preparing to attend the Beijing Conference, Dalit feminists decided to establish the National Federation of Dalit Women (NFDW). Dalit women wanted to create a new category of identity and becoming that would offer new critical dimensions to the Indian Women's Movement and the Dalit movement as well.

At the Beijing Conference the eighty-member Dalit delegation led by longtime activist Ruth Manorama and now president of the NFDW addressed from their perspective the crucial issue of Women's Rights as Human Rights. In doing so they advocated for a broad conceptualization of human rights, one that included not only civil and political rights but economic and social rights as well. In the week prior to the Conference, activists Raghuram and Manorama in September 1995 delivered a strong critique of neoliberal globalization condemning: "First, the ascendance of market ideology which have promoted inequities and second, the unsustainable economic growth in industrialized regions which have jeopardized the quality of women's lives" (Raghuran and Manorama 1995: 263). Clearly, in their estimation, women's rights as human rights and globalization were closely linked with economic globalization being a threat to any gains received from the Indian state. In going to Beijing Manorama stated that "Dalit women in India look towards international women for solidarity and support" (Quoted in Mehta 2013: 199).

However, while Manorama made it clear the Dalit women's movement had to differentiate itself from the Indian women's movement and the Dalit movement, it had to do so in a way that did not strongly alienate either. As Ruth Manorama, a founder and first president of the NFDW, expressed it at the establishment of the NFDW (Manorama 2006):

> Conscious that the call for a separate platform could be interpreted as divisive move by both Dalit men and non-Dalit women, the proponents of such a special forum emphasize that their initiative must not be mistaken for a separatist movement. Rather, they assert that there is need for strong alliances between the Dalit movement, the women's movement and the Dalit women's movement....

Acting on this belief in the necessity of strong alliances, the NFDW made common cause with the National Campaign for Dalit Human Rights at the WCAR Conference in 2001. For the Dalit and Dalit Women's movements, the WCAR promised to provide the largest international event to date in which to have caste recognized as a form of discrimination based on work and descent, which would serve to both legitimize and internationalize the Dalit struggle.

WCAR and the national campaign on Dalit human rights

Underlying the formation of the NCDHR in 1998 is the desire to publicize the plight of the Dalits at both the national and international levels, the latter with the intent of internationalizing the Dalit issue. Accordingly, the NCDHR (2003) has two overarching aims closely linked to its primary concerns of publicity:

1   that India and the international community recognize that Dalit rights are human rights and decide to effectively abolish untouchability
2   to cast out caste so as to build a new, just social order.

For the NCDHR, internationalizing Dalit human rights meant working with other organizations such as Human Rights Watch to bring their messages to global audiences (Cabrera 2017). This also included assisting in the creation of the International Dalit Solidarity Network (IDSN) in 2000 as a coordinating platform for other national advocacy organization in caste-affected countries as well as national Dalit solidarity networks in Europe. Together the IDSN, advocacy organizations, and solidarity networks assisted the NCDHR (and NFDW) in lobbying at the UN and bodies in the European Union.

WCAR proved to be the biggest overseas venture for the NCDHR, NFDW, and IDSN, with more than 200 Dalit activists attending. According to Cabrera, NCDHR leaders "cited the Durban [WCAR] conference as a watershed for raising international awareness of caste discrimination in India, and as a momentum builder" (2017: 288). Both the Dalit Movement and Dalit Women's movement hoped that the WCAR would place a clause on the conference agenda prohibiting discrimination on the basis of work and descent, which, in turn, would bring huge international and global pressure on a recalcitrant Indian government. The NFDW, which worked closely with the NCDHR, reiterated the language of CERD in their "NGO Declaration on Gender and Racism" at the WCAR on the matter but then added (2001: 363):

> All these forms of racism and racial discrimination are gendered and have specifically troubling consequences for women of dalit, indigenous, and religious and ethnic minority communities in the fields of employment, right to life, livelihood and dignity, housing, education, political participation, to name a few.

With the support of the United States, the Indian government delegation succeeded in deleting the clause linking caste to discrimination based on work and descent from the WCAR agenda. Nonetheless, the Dalits reaped a publicity bonanza, internationally as well as in India.

Converging at the World Social Forum

With its slogan "Another World is Possible", the WSF was particularly attractive to the Dalits who were searching for another transnational venue that would complement their activity at the UN on human rights. According to Manoharan (2004):

> So when I went to [the] WSF I thought it was the right platform by which we have got two legs. Earlier it was one, casteism. Now it is capitalism also. Casteism reflected in the form of untouchability, capitalism in the form of globalization.

Combined, then, venues at the UN and the WSF provided opportunities for the Dalits to fight against what Ambedkar identified as their main two sources of oppression—caste and class. While the Dalits had attended earlier meetings of the WSF, the 2004 meeting of the WSF in Mumbai proved to be a golden opportunity, with up to 130,000 participants attending each day, most from India but thousands from the rest of the world as well.

The Dalits, an estimated 30,000-strong, made skillful use of the WSF as a public space. The Dalits, the NCDHR, the IDSN, and the NFDW among them, organized events where they focused on key issues, in particular the impact of neoliberalization on the Dalits, including its intensification of casteism. There was an awareness that the market posed an obstacle to Dalit advancement. As one Dalit participant asked, "How can people denied basic rights compete in the market?" Finally, the WSF was used to highlight the importance of internationalizing the caste issue, including other international communities discriminated against on the basis of work and descent. The intent was to put pressure on India and other governments with caste-like systems to apply international and national norms.

Together, the NCDHR and the NFDW have attended all World Social Forums, but given that they have been held in other countries, the Dalit presence has been reduced. Ever since WCAR and WSF Mumbai, the issue of Dalit human rights and the issue of discrimination based on descent have been on the international agenda. Space does not permit a full articulation of all that has occurred in an ongoing campaign to gain visibility, publicity, and positive results for the Dalit cause. In this effort they have encountered the intransigence of Indian governments, most recently from the BJP (2014–?) who have "characterized the Dalit activists not as pathbreaking cosmopolitan citizens, but primarily as poor or disloyal domestic citizens who had no business bringing India's internal challenges to a global audience, much less a would-be global judge" (Cabrera 2016: 293).

Indeed, one could argue that the BJP government's relationship with civil-society organizations, in particular, human rights organizations, in India have become very chilly. At the heart of a growing controversy is the Foreign Contribution Regulation Act (FCRA) of 2010, intended to regulate the flow of foreign funds to individuals or organizations in India, particularly NGOs (Chauhan 2017). The Modi government is perceived to have taken advantage of this act to silence dissenters, in particular human rights organizations, by cutting off their sources of foreign funding and thereby forcing them to cease their activities. According to Human Rights Watch (2017: 5), "The impact of the FCRA on Indian civil society has been severe." How effective the efforts of the government to silence its critics in receipt of foreign funding is yet unknown, but many of its decisions have been rejected in the courts (Human Rights Watch 2016).

In recent years the transnational Dalit movements have continued to expand their network connections with, for example, the creation of the Asia Dalit Rights Forum, a platform for civil-society organizations in South Asian countries as well Japan. In 2013 the South Asia Parliamentarians Forum for Social Justice was formed. In Europe, the United States, and the United Kingdom anti-caste groups have been formed, some affiliated with the IDSN, others not, for example, the UK Anti Caste Discrimination Alliance (ACDA), an association of groups and organizations working for the elimination of caste discrimination among the Indian diaspora in the UK. In sum, the international network of Dalit and Dalit solidarity organizations appears to be thickening, a sign of the vitality of transnational Dalit activism.

Along with their friends and allies, the Dalit transnational movements have succeeded in maintaining a high profile internationally. For example, in 2009 the UN Commissioner for Human Rights, Navi Pillay, issued a scathing indictment of caste-based discrimination, calling it "an abhorrent form of marginalization and exclusion" whose barriers must be torn down (quoted in IDSN 2009). UN Special Rapporteurs have reported extensively on various facets of caste-based discrimination and in 2014 committed to prioritize caste discrimination and extend it across the mandates each pursues (IDSN 2014a).

Efforts have been made to profile the treatment of Dalit women, including tours of activists to the United States and Europe as well as conferences such as the 2006 Hague International Conference on the Human Rights of Dalit Women organized in part by the IDSN, the NFDW, the NCDHR, and other international organizations. At the UN, representations have been made to the Committee on the Elimination of Discrimination Against Women on the treatment of Dalit women and girls, including the 2014 committee meeting when Ruth Manorama and other Dalit women attended. When the Indian government delegation listed all the legislation in place to deal with these issues, the committee made it clear that these laws were not being implemented and urged India to do so (IDSN 2014b).

Currently the NCDHR and the Asia Dalit Rights Forum have concentrated efforts on the UN post-2015 development goals to ensure that the concerns of Dalits and other excluded communities are included in the new global development agenda. These include an emphasis on gender justice and affirmative action in the private sector to compensate, in part, for jobs lost in the public sector as a result of neoliberal globalization.

Elsewhere the NCDHR and the IDSN have been successful in raising the profile of the Dalits within the EU. Their lobbying efforts led the European Parliament to pass critical resolutions on the poor treatment of the Dalits in 2007, 2012, and 2013. At a national level there has been considerable activism and contention within the Dalit and broader Indian diasporas in the UK and the US. For example, in the UK, the ACDA and the UK Dalit Solidarity Network, which has been chaired by Jeremy Corbyn of the Labour Party, have been lobbying the UK Parliament to amend the Equality Act so as to outlaw caste-based discrimination after a government study in 2010 confirmed the existence of the phenomenon. Previously, as the chair of the UK Dalit Solidarity Network, Corbyn (2006) spoke to the influence and impact of forums such as the WSF stating:

> I first became truly aware of the extent of caste discrimination in India, and of the resistance to it, when I attended the World Social Forum in Mumbai in January 2004. . . . I was . . . horrified to realise that caste discrimination has actually been exported to the UK through the Indian Diaspora.

Hindu diaspora leaders in the UK deny the problem, saying that the caste system "is not something that is part and parcel of our beliefs and ideologies" (Samani and Ahmad 2017), a claim that Ambedkar and the Dalits have adamantly rejected. In 2017 the UK government conducted an extensive public consultation on amending the Equality Act, keeping the issue in the public eye.

Conclusion: what has been accomplished?

What emerges from the activities of the NCDHR, the NFDW and the Dalit movement generally at the UN, the WSF, and elsewhere is a strategy that recognizes in a globalizing world with a growing dispersal of power and influence that all structures—local, national, international, global, within civil society or the market—affecting casteism and their welfare must be contested. At the heart of this contestation is a "mobilization of shame" directed at creating a global awareness of casteism in an effort to bring about domestic changes within India; to have the Indian government live up to national and international norms of human rights, and to place greater emphasis on social justice.

The question is, has this strategy been working? Have the Dalits been successful, first, in internationalizing and globalizing awareness of casteism and, second, in bringing about changes within India and the Indian state? In terms of the first, there are clear indications of success; in terms of the second, success has been modest at best.

Using existing international norms on human rights, Dalits have clearly been successful at making themselves visible to an international audience, to international NGOs, international organizations, and governments. The UN WCAR was a publicity bonanza for the Dalits. Ever since its landmark decision on discrimination based on work and descent, UN agencies and Special Rapporteurs have proven supportive of Dalit human rights. Elsewhere, as previously noted, the European Parliament has passed resolutions supporting Dalit human rights as well. Debates and resolutions have also been passed in parliaments of some European countries. Caste discrimination has become a significant issue politically in the United Kingdom, an issue with friends in high places such as Jeremy Corbyn, elected leader of the Labour Party in 2015.

In the United States and Europe, conferences on Dalit issues and country visits by Dalit activists occur on a regular basis. Newspaper stories and online documentaries about the Dalits are becoming more common. In 2006 Ruth Manorama was awarded the Right Livelihood Award—otherwise known as the Alternative Nobel Prize—by the Swedish parliament. All the above indicates that Dalit rights issues are becoming mainstream and legitimate internationally.

At the same time, India's essential position at the UN has not changed. It does everything it can to stymie the efforts of Dalit activism, not only at WCAR but also at the UN itself. For example, its reaction to the UN Universal Periodic Review of its human rights record in 2012 and 2016 was decidedly negative. In 2016, for the eighteenth time in a row, it refused, as member states of the UN have the right to do, to recognize the IDSN, which means that the organization does have consultative status as the UN.

Within India itself the efforts of the NCDHR to have public-sector reservations extended to the private sector have not found traction. Initiatives such as the rural employment act (MGNREGA) have not lived up to expectations. In brief, there are two trends in India today: 1) gains to the Dalits in terms of legal rights which are often not implemented; and 2) increasing inequality. Moreover, the social structure of caste remains deeply entrenched. Coupled with a government chill towards human rights groups, Dalit movements are facing stronger headwinds.

That said, the Dalits are highly visible in the public sphere (Gorringe 2013) and vote, as do the poor and disadvantaged in general, in higher numbers than the rich and upper castes, meaning they cannot be ignored altogether. As neoliberalism comes increasingly into question, the possibility exists of a government and a state more willing to listen to those most excluded in society.

Note

1 For more background on the transition to neoliberalism in India, see Corbridge and Harriss 2003.

References

Ambedkar, B.R., "Speech to Constituent Assembly Constituent Assembly of India Proceedings, Volume XI. Available at https://thewire.in/featured/ambedkar-constitution-assembly-democracy 1949.
Benhabib, Seyla, "Borders, Boundaries, and Citizenship," *PS: Political Science and Politics*, 38(4), Oct. 2005, 673–677.

Bob, Clifford, "'Dalit Rights Are Human Rights': Caste Discrimination, International Activism, and the Construction of a New Human Rights Issue," *Human Rights Quarterly*, 29(1), 2007, 167–193.

Cabrera, Luis, "Dalit Cosmopolitans: Institutionally Developmental Global Citizenship in Struggles against Caste Discrimination," *Review of International Studies*, 43(2), 2017, 280–301.

Castells, Manuel, *The Power of Identity*, 2nd edition, Malden MA: Wiley Blackwell, 2010.

CERD (Committee on Elimination of Racial Discrimination), United Nations Document, CERD/C/304/Add.13 1996. http://www.unhchr.ch/tbs/doc.nsf/0/30d3c5041b55e561c12563e000500d33?Opendocument.

Chauhan, Neerja, "Drastic Reduction in Foreign Funding to NGOs: Govt to RS," *Times of India*, December 20, 2017. https://timesofindia.indiatimes.com/india/drastic-reduction-in-foreign-funding-to-ngos-govt-to-rs/articleshow/62181970.cms. Accessed May 9, 2019.

Chishti, Seema, "Biggest Caste Survey: One in Four Indians Admit to Practising Untouchability," November 29, 2014, *Indian Express*. http://indianexpress.com/article/india/india-others/one-in-four-indians-admit-to-practising-untouchability-biggest-caste-survey/. Accessed February 2, 2018.

Corbridge, Stuart and Harriss, John, *Reinventing India: Liberalization, Hindu Nationalism and Popular Democracy*, 2nd edition, Oxford: Oxford University Press, 2003.

Corbyn, Jeremy, "No Escape – Caste Discrimination within the UK," Dalit Solidarity Network UK. http://dsnuk.org/caste-discrimination/caste-discrimination-in-the-uk/ 2006. Accessed March 10, 2018.

Desai, Manisha, "Transnationalism: The Face of Feminist Politics Post-Beijing," *International Social Science Journal*, 57(184), 2005, 319–330.

Divakar, N. Paul and Ajai, M., "UN Bodies and the Dalits: A Historical Review of Interventions," in Sukhadeo Thorat Umakant (ed.), *Caste, Race and Discrimination: Discourses in International Context*, New Delhi: Rawat, 2004, 3–31.

Fraser, N., "Reframing Justice in a Globalizing World," *New Left Review*, 36 (2005), 69–88.

Ghosh, Jayati, "India's Rural Employment Programme is Dying a Death of Funding Cuts," *The Guardian*, February 5, 2015. https://www.theguardian.com/global-development/2015/feb/05/india-rural-employment-funding-cuts-mgnrega. Accessed March 7, 2018.

Ghosh, Jayati, "What Works for Women at Work," *The Indian Express*, January 14, 2016. http://indianexpress.com/article/opinion/columns/what-worksfor-women-at-work-maternity-protection-ministry-of-women-and-childdevelopment/. Accessed on February 25, 2018.

Gorringe, Hugo, "Dalit Politics: Untouchability, Identity, and Assertion," in Atul Kohli and Prerna Singh, eds., *Routledge Handbook of Indian Politics*, New York: Routledge Press, 2013, 119–128.

Hardtmann, Eva-Maria, *Our Fury is Burning*, Stockholm: Stockholm Studies in Social Anthropology, 54, 2003.

Himanshu and Sen, Kunal, "Measurement, Patterns and Determinants of Poverty', in Nandini Gooptu and Jonathan Parry (eds.), *Persistence of Poverty in India*, New Delhi: Social Science Press, 2014, 67–88.

Human Rights Watch, "India: Foreign Funding Law Used to Harass 25 Groups," November 8, 2016. https://www.hrw.org/news/2016/11/08/india-foreign-funding-law-used-harass-25-groups. Accessed March 3, 2018.

Human Rights Watch, "India: Key UN Rights Recommendations Ignored," September 7, 2017. https://www.hrw.org/news/2017/09/21/india-key-un-rights-recommendations-ignored. Accessed March 4, 2018.

IDSN, "UN High Commissioner: Tear Down the Barriers of Caste," October 8, 2009. https://idsn.org/un-high-commissioner-tear-down-the-barriers-of-caste/. Accessed September 19, 2018.

IDSN, 2014a. Annual Report. http://idsn.org/portfolio-items/idsn-annual-report-2014/. Accessed February 25, 2018.

IDSN, 2014b, "UN CEDAW Committee Raises Serious Concern for Dalit Women and the Lack of Implementation of Laws." http://idsn.org/un-cedaw-committee-raises-serious-concern-for-dalit-women-and-the-lack-of-implementation-of-laws/. Accessed February 27, 2018.

Irudayam, Aloysius S.J., Mangubhai, Jayshree, and Lee, Joel (eds.), "Dalit Women Speak Out – Violence against Dalit Women in India: Overview Report," New Delhi: National Campaign on Dalit Human Rights, March 2006.

Jaffrelot, Christophe, "Caste and Political Parties in India: Do Indians Vote Their Caste – While Casting their Vote?" in Atul Kohli and Prerna Singh, eds., *Routledge Handbook of Indian Politics*, New York: Routledge Press, 2013, 1–11.

Kapadia, Karin, "Introduction: We Ask You to Rethink: Different Dalit Women and Their Subaltern Politics," in S. Anandhi and Karin Kapadia, eds., *Dalit Women: Vanguard of an Alternative Politics in India*, New York: Routledge Press, 2017, 1–50.

Kohli, Atul and Singh, Prerna, "Introduction: Politics in India – An Overview," in Atul Kohli and Prerna Singh (eds.), *Routledge Handbook of Indian Politics*, New York: Routledge Press, 2013, 1–17.

Manohoran, Vincent, Interview with author, New Delhi, 8 November 2004.

Manorama, Ruth "Background Information on Dalit Women in India." http://www.rightlivelihood.org/manorama_publications.htm 2006. Accessed March 7, 2007.

Mehta, Purvi, "Recasting Caste: Histories of Dalit Transnationalism and the Internationalization of Caste Discrimination," PhD dissertation, University of Michigan, 2013. Interview of Ruth Manorama, by Purvi Mehta, September 2009, Bangalore, India.

Mitra, Subrata K. and Schöttli, Jivanta, "India's 2014 General Election, A Critical Realignment in Indian Politics?" *Asian Survey*, 56(4), 2016, 605–628.

Munck, Ronaldo, *Globalization and Contestation*, London: Routledge, 2007.

NCDHR (National Campaign on Dalit Human Rights), "Voicing Dalit Concerns at Asian Social Forum," 2003. http://www.dalits.org/asfreport.htm.

NCDHR, "Reclaiming Equity and Justice," New Delhi, 2015. http://www.ncdhr.org.in/resources/publications/NCDHR_TriManual_28Feb.pdf. Accessed January 25, 2018.

NFDW (National Federation of Dalit Women), "NGO Declaration on Gender and Racism," reprinted in Anupama Rao (ed.), *Gender and Caste*, London: Zed Books Ltd., 2001, 363–367.

Polanyi, Karl. *The Great Transformation: The Political and Economic Origins of Our Time*, Boston, MA: Beacon, 2001.

Raghuran, Shobba and Manorama, Ruth, September 1995 "Fourth World Conference on Women: "Gendering' Development: Issues and Politics," *Economic and Political Weekly*, September 1995, 2162–2164.

Samani, Vishva and Ahmad, Athar, "Why are UK Hindus Against a Caste Law?" BBC Asian Network. January 18, 2017. http://www.bbc.com/news/uk-england-38663143. Accessed March 8, 2018.

Statista, "India: Real Gross Domestic Product (GDP) Growth Rate from 2012 to 2022 (compared to the previous year)," 2018. https://www.statista.com/statistics/263617/gross-domestic-product-gdp-growth-rate-in-india/. Accessed March 1, 2018.

Teltumbde, Anand, "Foreword: Dalits, Dalit Women and the Indian State," in S. Anandhi and Karin Kapadia (eds.), *Dalit Women: Vanguard of an Alternative Politics in India*, New York: Routledge Press, 2017, 53–74.

Teltumbde, Anand, "Two Years of an Ambedkar Bhakt and the Plight of Dalits," *Economic and Political Weekly*, June 4, 2016, 10, 11.

Tharamangalam, Joseph, "Caste in Politics is Linked to Lived Realities," *The Hindu*, March 7, 2012. www.thehindu.com/opinion/op-ed/caste-in-politics-islinked-to-lived-realities/article2967566.ece. Accessed on February 8, 2018.

Thorat, Vimal, "Dalit Women Have Been Left Behind by the Dalit Movement and the Women's Movement," *Communalism Combat*, May 2001 Year 8 (6)9. Archived at https://sabrangindia.in/article/%E2%80%98dalit-women-have-been-left-behind-dalit-movement-and-women%E2%80%99s-movement%E2%80%99.

PART IV
Gender and Indian transnationalism

13
EXPERIENCES OF EMPOWERMENT AND CONSTRAINT

Narratives of transnational Indian women entrepreneurs

Manashi Ray

Introduction

Despite enormous advances made in immigrant entrepreneurship literature beginning with Bonacich (1973), Light and Bonacich (1988), and others (Light and Bachu 1993; Zhou and Logan 1989; Aldrich and Waldinger 1990; Light and Gold 2000, etc.), including ethnic group-specific research (Gold 1998, 1994; Gold and Kibria, 1993; Zhou 1992; Hosler 1998; Min 1988; Min and Bozorgmehr 2000; Basu and Goswami 1999; Ram 1994; among others), gender has been under-investigated in immigrant economies. Women have often been described as 'silent contributors' (Dhaliwal 1998) to male-run businesses, facilitating the success of immigrant economies by providing unpaid labour as an extension of their domestic, maternal, and socially reproductive household activities (Zhou and Logan 1989). This has been denounced as 'exploitation' or explained as women's 'traditional' place in immigrant cultures (Zhou 1992, 152–84). Since the early 2000s this changed, with steadily growing research addressing women and immigrant women in particular as entrepreneurs, innovators, and businesswomen who use their class, ethnic, culture, and gender resources for starting and sustaining businesses in ethnic and mainstream economies (Knight 2016; Valdez 2011; Javadian and Singh 2012; Collins and Low 2010; Tan 2008; Lee et al. 2009; Rutashobya, Allan, and Nilsson 2009; Brettell 2007; and others).

However, no research addresses how women realise entrepreneurial aspirations across national borders or how gender relations affect transnational entrepreneurship and vice versa. Similarly, little research studies highly skilled migrant women entrepreneurs' use of human and cultural capital for entrepreneurship, as most research focuses on the 'push' elements driving their engagement in entrepreneurship, such as discrimination and marginalisation in the labour market, unemployment, poverty, the need to provide for family, dissatisfaction with past/present employers, and cultural norms (Azmat 2013; Poggesi, Mari, and De Vita 2016, 751–52). But women may also be 'pulled' into entrepreneurial enterprise to pursue opportunities to develop ideas, earn a higher income or for self-fulfilment, be their own boss, or leverage cross-border resources (Tan 2008). These aspects have received scant attention in empirical research. This chapter, therefore, makes a vital contribution by studying the specific experiences of migrant and returnee[1] Asian Indian women who are owners or co-owners/partners of transnational businesses located in the US and India. It explores several aspects of these women's entrepreneurial experiences that impact their entry into transnational business, including education, professional career, English-language proficiency, class background, migratory process, membership in multiple networks, and family. I investigate how they draw extensively on these forms of human, cultural, class, social, and ethnic capital that define their experiences and empowerment as women transnational entrepreneurs (TEs) at different stages of entrepreneurship and during their life course.

I first show how US immigration policy changes, dramatic shifts in Indian state policies since the 1980s, and selective migration from India created an enabling economic and political environment that resonated with Indian women migrants' aspirations to initiate transnational entrepreneurship and influenced the location of their businesses. I then present several typical cases illustrating the resources women entrepreneurs bring to their enterprises that redefine gender expectations and thus entrepreneurial experiences. Finally, I consider the heterogeneity and complexity of their experiences and examine changing nuances of gender relations.

Methods

The experiences of women transnational entrepreneurs discussed in this chapter were collected during fieldwork in the US and India over a ten-year period (2007–2017/18) by conducting narrative interviews in multiple urban centres in both countries. For longitudinal analysis, a few women were interviewed again eight to ten years after the initial interview, to capture if and how they dealt with family responsibilities at different life stages and how this affected their business growth. As Indian migrants are a widely dispersed population in the US (Portes and Rumbaut 2014), I sought multiple data sources to obtain a representative sample of migrant and returnee women entrepreneurs from wide-ranging business sectors (info-tech, professional services, manufacturing, and retail/wholesale). First, the interviewees were selected via snowballing with the help of personal networks of family and friends to gather information about women transnational entrepreneurs residing in both countries. Second, I used public data sources on the web and the mailing lists of Indian trade and business associations to build a roster of potential respondents' names, office addresses, and type/sector of transnational business in the US and India. In India, I visited the office of NASSCOM (The National Association of Software & Service Companies) in New Delhi, where I interviewed the secretary and officials of this premier trade institution of the Information Technology-Business Process Outsourcing (IT-BPO) industries. Respondents' business offices were contacted directly by email and phone for interviews. To supplement the primary data, I used secondary data from the Department of Homeland Security's Office of Immigration Statistics (OIS) for 2016, Pew Research Center and Migration Policy Institute publications, and online articles to analyse transnational business trends among Indians.

The interviews lasted one to two hours. Topical questions were prepared beforehand covering educational background, the societal or institutional structures that contributed to respondents' cultural and social capital, occupational history, migratory moves (including their decision for returning to India), and the respondents' utilisation of diverse networks. But the interviewees were encouraged to elaborate on aspects of their lives they considered important and to provide in-depth interpretation of any episodes. The interviews were conducted in English and Hindi and were recorded and transcribed verbatim. Pseudonyms are used to protect identity.

The respondents were born in India, range from forty-three to sixty-two years old, and have been owners and founders or partners of transnational businesses between ten and thirty years. All the respondents were married, excluding three, and all had children except for two.

Framing the case: immigration from India to the US

Contemporary migration from India to the US, according to Chakravorty, Kapur, and Singh (2016), can be divided into three major phases: 1) the 'Early Movers' (1965–1979); 2) the 'Families' (1980–1994); and 3) the 'IT Generation', which represent the profiles of an estimated 3.98 million Asian Indians living in the US (Pew Research Center 2017). The revision of the Immigration and Naturalization Act of 1965, a momentous shift in US immigration policy, allowed the admittance of a large number of skilled professionals and students from India for the first time. Many highly trained Indian migrants took advantage of the visa allocation preference given to 'priority workers; professionals with advanced degrees, or aliens of exceptional ability', contributing to the 'brain drain' from India at that time.

While this movement corresponded to a significant gain for the US in highly trained and skilled personnel (Portes and Rumbaut 2014), there was also a corresponding 'push' factor in India: the transformation of the social basis of political power as a consequence of universal franchise. Over time this policy permitted the ascendancy of marginalised groups while gradually eroding the social and political power of elites and upper castes, leading them to migrate abroad for better prospects. Furthermore, Chakravorty, Kapur, and Singh (2016, 27–31) note the existence of a well-ingrained selection process for the best and brightest Indians who voluntarily chose to leave for the US. The social system favoured individuals from urban, educated, and higher/dominant classes and castes to receive higher education, and an examination system selected individuals from this socially privileged group to be trained in technical fields. These factors complement the US immigration system's selection process, which prefers individuals with specific technical skills, particularly in IT since the 1990s.

In the mid-1970s the immigration flow from India shifted towards family reunification (phase 2) as the early settlers sponsored family members, relatives, and kin. This became the predominant mode of Indians entering the US until the late 1980s. Although these immigrants were educationally accomplished by American and Indian standards, they were less so in comparison to the 'Early Movers'. Twenty-five years later, another revision of immigration law—the Immigration Act of 1990—substantially increased the number of technical and specialty temporary workers arriving in the US under the temporary H-1B visa program, which has become the primary channel for the arrival of huge numbers of skilled professional Indian migrants (phase 3, the 'IT generation'). Additionally, throughout the three phases mentioned above, Indians have entered the US as students pursuing higher education.

During this period India's domestic policies underwent drastic changes that powerfully influenced migration from India to northern countries. After the Cold War and particularly from the mid-1980s, India replaced socialistic-leaning policies with 'pro-business' development strategies, like many emerging economies. The government became highly interventionist[2] by giving precedence to economic growth as a national goal (Kohli 2007). Domestic policies shifted due to global changes and domestic compulsions, thus impacting policies towards the Indian diaspora. Changes in foreign policy particularly targeted influential Non-Resident Indians (NRI), wherever they settled, to engage in the Indian economy, services, academics, politics, health sector, and entrepreneurship. To that end, the government started the innovative Overseas Citizenship of India (OCI) scheme, which granted overseas Indians Indian citizenship and other benefits, though they could not participate in elections or hold constitutional posts. The OCI scheme's main intention was to facilitate economic investment from NRIs without giving them political rights and to bring capital and investment into India (Tiwari 2013, 223). The government provided special savings, investment schemes, and instruments for NRIs, such as foreign currency accounts, bonds with attractive interest rates, and tax benefits to encourage saving and investment (Tiwari 2013, 212–30). Further, starting in 1991, import quotas were lifted (albeit not fully until 2001), tariffs declined steadily, currency was devalued, the foreign investment regime was liberalised, and restrictions on external financial transactions were eased. These policy changes signalled that the state had entered into a new social contract with Indian businesses, supporting them with the understanding that they had to become more competitive in the international arena. As a result of these dramatic shifts in political, economic, and social policies, between the 1980s and 2005, India's economy grew from the world's fiftieth largest, in nominal US dollars, to the tenth largest (Ahmed and Varshney 2012). And India has remained the top international remittance-receiving nation in the world, with $62.7 billion in 2016 (World Bank 2017), despite the recent decline of remittances by 8.9 percent for two successive years.

The biggest beneficiary of these policy revisions has been the IT sector. Indian expatriates in the US have played a crucial role in India's global integration through the transfer of technology, social and financial remittance, start-up capital, and mobilising capital from well-established entrepreneurs (Saxenian 2006; Gold 2018). The Indian state wishes to maximise 'brain gain/circulation/return' and use foreign-trained Indian immigrants and nationals as a magnet for foreign and diasporic investments in knowledge-based industries (Kapur and Ramamurti 2001). This opening of the Indian economy to the global market presented an unprecedented opportunity to the overseas Indian migrant community, and particularly to Asian Indians in the US, to invest and establish business with India. Given their own professional success and resources, members of this community in the US felt compelled to participate in India's economic growth and development. By 2002 the combination of a recession in Silicon Valley, enormous difficulties with complicated and outdated immigration laws (Wadhwa and Salkever 2012), and growing professional and entrepreneurial opportunities in India prompted an ongoing and sustained interest among US-educated Indians, particularly in STEM fields, to initiate transnational business ventures with India (Saxenian 2006). India thus reversed the 'brain drain' of earlier decades by establishing 'brain gain/circulation' opportunities for Indian migrants in the US (Ray 2013).

Consequently, this makes the 'context of exit' for contemporary Indian migrants a selective process inspired by a complex range of motives, and one that affects their career paths and assimilation/acculturation in American society. Indian migrants' major modes of entry to the US (either as international students or H-1B workers[3] filling jobs requiring a university degree) create a positive image for this ethnic group, which comprised 2.4 million immigrant residents in 2015 with a median age of thirty-nine years. With 68 percent employed in the civilian labour force in 2015, the group's occupational profile demonstrates a close association between high levels of education (77% ages twenty-five and over with a bachelor's degree or higher) and their socio-economic location in American society, with their median household income at $107,000 (Zong and Batalova 2017). These figures strongly reflect the specific channels Indian use to enter the US.

Theory

For all entrepreneurs, irrespective of gender, mobilising resources is key to their success. Cross-border networks are especially critical for the growth and survival of transnational entrepreneurship, just as networks are imperative for entrepreneurs from immigrant and dominant groups. While TEs hold considerable class and ethnic resources, transnational networks provide access to information, markets, capital, technology, mentoring, and emotional support (Davidsson and Honig 2003; Light and Gold 2000). These networks enable them to combine connections, resources, and identities from multiple locations to maximise their independence from restrictions associated with societal hierarchies, gender ideologies, patriotism, and citizenship (Gold 2002, 13).

Cross-border networks connect the demand side and the supply side, structures and resources, and opportunities and individuals at different levels (Chen and Tan 2009). As a meso-level analytical framework,[4] cross-border networks help to focus on the *relationships* entrepreneurs have that offer resources for transnational business endeavours (Granovetter 1992; Greve and Salaff 2003). As Light and Gold (2000) mention, 'the contribution of social networks to entrepreneurship is the most important research discovery in the last generation' (94). It is therefore no surprise that scholars have extensively used social networks for examining transnational migration, entrepreneurship, settlement patterns, and other engagements (Poros 2011; Landolt 2001; Levitt 2001; among others).

But, membership and use of transnational networks and economic practices are decidedly affected by migrants' and non-migrants' diverse motivations and forms of resource mobilisation. The use of these networks also depends on migrants' social locations in their home and host countries, their 'context of exit', and other ascribed characteristics, notwithstanding their shared ethnic membership or nationality. Only recently has the importance of non-economic resources—family, identity, community, philanthropic and nationalistic aspirations—been emphasised as vital to the success of cross-border businesses. These resources add value and complement global business strategies and innovation (Gold 2018; Salaff, Wong, and Greve 2010; Ray 2013). Members consider network relationships to be priceless for providing 'social capital'—a sense of commitment or mutual obligation that motivates people to extend favours, expect preferential treatment, and look out for each other. Social capital defines the depth and durability of networks and interlocks actors in long-term relationships, and its consumption usually increases rather than depletes its availability in a given context (Rutashobya, Allan, and Nilsson 2009; Gold 2005).

However, differential social capital accumulation within networks can affect productive capacity and thereby create unequal outcomes for members. Hence dissimilarities in entrepreneurial performance among various groups in migrant populations can be explained by differential access to social capital within a network or by differential possession of other forms of capital (human, cultural, and financial). Specifically, in the context of transnational migration and subsequent cross-border business, Bourdieu's notion of capital provides a deeper description of how different forms of capital interact, resulting in iniquitous outcomes for TEs.

Bourdieu and Wacquant (1992) emphasise the overall composition of an individual's capital, made up of economic (income, wealth, financial inheritances, and assets), social (resources based on connections, group membership generated in social networks), and cultural capital. Cultural capital can take three forms: embodied (long-lasting disposition of mind and body, e.g., bi-cultural literacy, English language proficiency), objectified (cultural goods), and institutionalised (educational degrees). As these forms of capital are recognised as legitimate, they become symbolic capital. Bourdieu contends that these different forms of capital are interlinked and convertible.

Closely associated with 'capital' is Bourdieu's 'theory of practice' (1990), which is related to an individual's 'habitus'. Bourdieu defines habitus as a product of history that produces individual and collective practices ... it ensures the active presence of past experiences, which, deposited in each organism in the form of schemes of perception, thought and action, tend to guarantee the 'correctness' of practices and their constancy over time, more reliably than all formal rules and explicit norms.

(cited in Drori, Honig, and Ginsberg 2010, 7)

Habitus informs practices or strategies that might not be planned or explicit but that 'guide the individual entrepreneur in managing change and uncertainty' (Drori, Honig, and Ginsberg 2010, 8). The TE's habitus is a product of material and social conditioning echoing one's experiences because of one's social location, and collectively constitutes a 'class habitus', learned in immediate and extended family, school, and neighbourhood (Light and Gold 2000, 92–94).

For the habitus to be produced and activated, the notion of 'field' becomes important. A network of relations can be defined as a 'field'[5] wherein different kinds of capital (social, economic, cultural, and symbolic) are embedded and individuals strategize to gain degrees of control (Drori, Honig, and Ginsberg 2010; adapting from Bourdieu and Wacquant 1992). Put differently, 'at the individual level, the *habitus* interacts with the collective through common relationship of the field', and thus the relationship of the habitus and the accompanying 'field' explain the predisposition of entrepreneurs towards action at the intersection of the collective and the individual (Drori, Honig, and Ginsberg 2010, 9).

Bourdieu is often critiqued for theorising 'class formation' within a nation-state framework, but his model can include sources of capital produced and utilised in more than one country. Several scholars have adopted Bourdieu's framework, like Nowicka's (2013) research on Polish entrepreneurs in Germany highlighting how the use of economic, social, and cultural capital acquired in different countries helps position entrepreneurial strategies for success. Similarly, Erel (2010) uses Bourdieu's concepts to illustrate the transformative aspects of migration-specific capital and how skilled Turkish and Kurdish women in Britain are able to valorise their cultural resources as capital in their country of residence. Additionally, Kelly and Lusis (2006) use Bourdieu's habitus to explain that economic, social, and cultural capital do not simply transfer to new settings but that a process of valuation and exchange continues between home and host countries well after settlement. Thus the role of transnational networks and the intersection of different forms of capital in the process of migration—over time and between geographical sites—is crucial for analysing ways existing capital or resources brought from the home country are appreciated and transformed or acquired in the host country within transnational fields.

Women transnational entrepreneurs

In this section I trace the trajectories of women TEs who have engaged in cross-border entrepreneurship, primarily between the US and India. These case studies show the wider complexities of migration and strategies and constraints for transnational entrepreneurship. For some women, immense personal effort and determination, combined with social networks, was required to migrate for better opportunities, while for others it was the pursuit of higher education and global recognition. Family trajectories mattered as well, particularly the partner's migratory history and professional growth and progression, as many decisions to migrate and pursue an entrepreneurial career were taken within the immediate and extended family. Not everyone had a choice. These case studies illustrate that a confluence of factors—motives, choices, opportunities, available resources, and support systems—and a combination of successive migratory and professional movements led these women to entrepreneurship across multiple national borders.

The power couples: Kavita, Rekha, Vani, Tara, Gowri, Rukmini, and Durga

Kavita, Rekha, Vani, Tara, and Gowri migrated to the US in the mid- to late 1990s as graduate students in STEM fields, except for Vani, who received her terminal degree in law. Among the seven respondents whom I call 'power couples', only Rukmini and Durga entered the US as spouses when their husbands were either transferred by their companies or decided to relocate to the US from the UK. Kavita's inspiration for migrating to the US as a single woman was pursuing a PhD:

> I had a senior college friend who had come to the University of X. He convinced one [of] his professors, who had a lot of projects, having preference for Indian students. This prof. made funds available for me to go to the US. I was a gold medallist from my university, which helped getting a quarter-time assistantship for the first semester. After that I supported myself.

Tara also migrated to pursue an advanced degree:

> This urge to go to the US was always behind me so I decided to leave home . . . my father was very supportive of me coming to the US to study. I'm sure they were very worried about sending a girl alone to the US, I was one of the top rankers in my class so he felt this was my opportunity to fulfil my potentials . . . my mother was sad but gave in. I had got admission in a few universities; I chose to be at R as my aunt lived in a town close to the university.

Vani and Gowri stated similar reasons for their migration. Gowri said:

> When I was growing up that was the American dream. One was to get into A [premier Indian institution] and the second was to go to the US. [The] American dream existed in our campus . . . it was the normal course of things then . . . a kind of herd mentality. For me going to the US was an independent decision, although if I had not met my partner I might have done something else. So it was both influenced by my fiancé and my brother who had gone to the US ahead of me.

Being female and 'single' might have been concerning in the Indian context, where conventional gender roles place reproductive and household duties before the pursuit of higher education, but the women's individual human and class capital, context of exit, and having family members and friends in the US outweighed these concerns. Another respondent, Rukmini, was established in her advertising career in India but chose to be a full-time 'homemaker' during her stay in the US. The other four women met their partners, who were graduate students in similar disciplines, in the US, and entered the US labour force together as couples.

What is striking in these narratives is the women's agency, even though their migratory decisions were supported by family members and influenced by their peers and the macro environments in the premier institutions they attended. These women left their home countries in their twenties for self-actualisation and to fortify their human capital. But their independent streak and the values that shaped their personalities reflect the embodied cultural capital of urban, Western-educated, professional upper-middle-class or rich backgrounds in India, which helped them adapt to multicultural American society and validated their cultural capital brought from home. The cultural capital within the Indian families in which they were raised—irrespective of region and caste—set in place the mechanisms that redrew boundaries and expectations for them, so that defiance of normative gender roles was tolerated and encouraged.

When questioned on this issue, Vani, Rekha, Rukmini, and others fiercely rejected the notion of being undervalued compared to male siblings, stressing the privileges of being girls/women in their families as impartial and gratifying, with a strong emphasis on education, as evident in these recollections:

> The way we grew up maybe was slightly different from others in India. It was different because we were encouraged to make our own decisions from a very early age and all three of us read a lot. Looking back I feel I had a lot of freedom from my childhood. . . . We also had many discussions at the kitchen table, my parents encouraged plenty of debates on various issues, we were asked to speak and voice our thoughts.
>
> *(Rekha)*

> . . . my dad adored his three daughters, made us feel like we were the most important people on this earth and provided for us the very best that could be offered in India—best school, the best opportunities in nurturing my passion for performing arts, sports, social life, etc. That gave me confidence and courage to take on the world.
>
> *(Rukmini)*

These women's cosmopolitan upbringing, English-language proficiency, and bi-cultural literacy were assets and markers of distinction that they could easily convert into economic capital upon joining the US labour force as professional workers. All the respondents in this category except two were employed in middle and upper management in engineering or technological multinational corporations or in scientific research laboratories for five to ten years in the US before transitioning to entrepreneurship. Rukmini honed her skills in 'communication and advertising' by volunteering in Indian and American organisations, whereas Durga, a delayed entrepreneur,[6] waited until her children went to college to start her cross-border business in event management and real estate.

There was no clear-cut separation of push and pull factors for these interviewees; rather, it was a combination of both, and life course events—like raising children, care-giving responsibilities for aging parents, a partner's relocation—that motivated them to entrepreneurship in partnership or with unequivocal support and mentoring from their spouses, who were also TEs. Nor did these women TEs perceive potential difficulties in integrating family and professional life, defying the notion that entrepreneurship is detrimental to balancing family and work life (Poggesi, Mari, and De Vita 2016, 744). Rather, they asserted it was a deep desire for self-expression, achievement, and empowerment along with an enabling ecosystem that propelled them to entrepreneurship—an important reflection of how their understanding of gender expectations, their career stages, and family status influenced their high-growth entrepreneurship.

Further, obtaining greater autonomy was important for these women, along with the joy, success, and satisfaction of building relationships with customers and employees and accomplishing something they considered worthwhile. Kavita explained:

> I worked for five years in the industry and as an independent consultant a couple of years in the Silicon Valley . . . it was when [the] web was booming, people were starting out companies here, . . . it was contagious, I wanted to do something exciting next. In the end, my husband who is an electrical engineer and I decided to float

a company that would look into the software needs of the pharmaceutical industry. My husband had been [an] entrepreneur for a long time. Raising a family comes with the territory.

Similarly, Gowri said:

> I am one of those persons who [has] a big appetite of taking risks ... perhaps the risk-taking ability has been my strength and an enduring trait that has served me well, so transitioning to entrepreneurship was predictable and easy. My husband had [a] finance background, I had more IT kind of background besides being a 'people' person. ... So, [the] decision about being the CEO has to do with [an] individual's forte. My husband had no issues about me being the face of the company. In the end I think it has worked out well for us both professionally and at home. We share parenting equally and other familial responsibilities. It's [a] team!

Rekha also expressed similar sentiments, describing her and her partner's success and satisfaction with their business in the technology sector after seventeen years:

> It was the best decision we made together. As we were among the first few to return to India in 2000, nothing was laid out, there were no procedures then, I discovered as I went along ... which is my strength and gives me a huge sense of satisfaction.

As successful first-generation TEs from elite backgrounds, their enterprises were aided by the spreading of new technology, the diversity of organisations, and the global economy, which has erased many older stereotypes and substantially reduced structural barriers for women since the mid- to late 1990s.

Above all, the power couples took advantage of a strong and enabling entrepreneurial ecosystem found on both the East and West coasts of the US and the prevailing 'culture of co-operation', a 'work culture where openness, complementary skill sets and collaboration is rewarded' (Gold 2018, 137). But, their success was driven by their access to social capital, embedded in multiple networks (peer, co-ethnic, educational institutions' alumni networks, professional, trade, and familial networks), where they received guidance, funding, referrals, advice, and support that augmented their business connections. Wadhwa and Salkever (2012) recall the monumental contribution of the first generation of successful Indian entrepreneurs in Silicon Valley, who built organisations like the Indus Entrepreneurs[7] to help those who followed in their path. These pioneer Indian entrepreneurs, who overcame stereotypes and cultural challenges, shared their experience and knowledge to ease the entry of other Indian TEs, including women (Chakravorty, Kapur, and Singh 2016).

Notably, these women also attributed their entrepreneurial success to previous work experience in the industry, to supportive husbands who in all seven cases were equally connected to extensive networks, and to their synergy with their spouses. The couples' financial and emotional security allowed the women TEs to withstand failures and setbacks in their enterprises and to take more risks for their businesses' long-term growth, a finding that resonates with Tan's (2008) study of Chinese women entrepreneurs in the electronics industry. So, for these women TEs, one's entrepreneurial career was as much environmental as personal and the product of a combination of cultural and social capital and migratory exposure that encouraged creativity focused on transnational entrepreneurship.

The inheritors: Maya, Sonia, and Deepa

For Maya, Sonia, and Deepa, entrepreneurship was a natural progression as their lives unfolded. All three were born into well-established, multi-generational business families in India belonging to a prosperous merchant community and caste. Sonia explained,

> I knew as a girl this to be my life's aspiration, though I was given complete freedom to make choices . . . for my career, go abroad to study . . . entrepreneurship is in my blood. The women in our family have always been discreetly involved in business as trust or board members, partners, shareholders, etc. . . . I wanted to be on [the] forefront, create opportunities and help my dad!

All three respondents travelled overseas—to the US, France, and the UK—for graduate education in business, food and beverage management, and supply-chain management. As part of their families' business expansion into global markets in the mid-2000s, Sonia and Deepa resettled in the US with their families, making substantial investments in assets/property in the US and the American market. Maya, however, chose to work alongside her father in India. She said:

> He definitely needed me . . . we mutually learnt from each other. I work in his industry and in our family business. He taught me the nuts and bolts of how to operate the business and the tremendous amount of attention to detail that is needed to hold everything together . . . so that we sustain our growth. I am professionally successful because of my dad, although not totally. I would say 90 percent because of my father and 10 percent would be me. Yes, we joke I used to be known as his daughter but now he is known as my father. I have had my share of mishaps and failures, but plenty of advantages and doors opened for me because of my father. I am jointly in charge of our overseas clients and started our operations with American businesses and corporations.

This was a sentiment Deepa and Sonia shared, despite belonging to different industries on different continents. They called attention to their familiarity, on-the-job learning, and lived experiences in India before and after the economic reforms since the mid-1990s, and incorporated the dimensions of transforming structural power relations, both globally and in India, in their understanding of transnational business practices.

Akin to the 'power couples', these women prudently used their bourgeois class capital, which provided them with Western-oriented embodied cultural capital. In Deepa's case, her knowledge of Western cultural tastes was important for marketing her products—like different flavours of tea—to mainstream Americans. Above all, their key to success lay in embracing the 'culture of entrepreneurship' as inheritors of their families' legacies. Light and Gold (2000) describe the culture of entrepreneurship as class resources including 'supportive values, attitudes, knowledge and skills transmitted in the course of socialization from one generation to another . . . [and] contain[ing] all the skills they need to practice their occupation [in the market economy]' (84). This cultural endowment distinguishes bourgeois entrepreneurs from non-bourgeois co-ethnic entrepreneurs while connecting them to similar non-ethnic bourgeois elsewhere. In other words, the respondents cultivated a multi-cultural habitus with economic value. This habitus is especially evident in Deepa's recollection of her use of trade networks, an important channel for advancing business growth and overseas operations:

Trade networks... invite members from different countries to interact... every year we meet at a particular location and spend three days networking with each other... it is quite intense with back-to-back meetings and you pick and choose the members that you want to do business with... there is the fun side too in the evenings... where you socialise, if you are a regular part of the network then you develop enduring relationships, become friends, all that goes to increase our business. Besides, these networks provide financial protection for working with members in the same network, say if there is default in payment... [the] network reimburses your financial costs. And, long-standing business connections, and network of people we have been working with for many years—they are vendors or clients—they bring us lots of business in the US.

When these participants were asked about the constraints they contended with in their entrepreneurship, they cited gender discrimination. Deepa described it as 'in the air, both men and women breathe, some see and feel it and others don't'. Despite being members of reputable family businesses with financial and emotional security, they mentioned a robust presence of 'men's/good ol' boys' networks' and being judged at the beginning of their careers by conventional masculine traits of being aggressive, arrogant, dominant, and using foul language, stemming from cultural assumptions that free enterprise is a hyper-masculine activity and women do not possess the traits or skills necessary for success. Juggling these constraints has been tough for these respondents, particularly in managing employees inclined to ignore their management style and inner-core strength. Deepa explained,

> ... you never really know whether my peers and employees [men] are patronising or they actually respect my work. The challenge is that when you work in a man's world in India, you have to keep your pride, you cannot have them see you weak, or angry or sympathetic. You can't let them see your tears; you can't let them see you fumble. I cannot always be strong and heartless... but I am one of the alpha women when it comes to making decisions and its execution.

Interestingly, these women did not mention a collective support group or network of women entrepreneurs, but thrived on their families' encouragement and confronted discriminatory experiences. Their determination spurred them to further action, leading to their empowerment as leaders of their industries (Gill and Ganesh 2007). These women TEs did not accept the limited opportunities offered to them because of their gender, but overcame these barriers to re-narrate their own biographies.

The lone crusaders: Radha, Simi, and Eda

The women TEs in this category did not overtly choose entrepreneurial careers but discussed the overwhelming joy, self-fulfilment, and personal growth their careers brought them. They were either 'displaced' due to personal circumstances—like separating and later divorcing while caring for an infant—or experienced 'restrictive growth opportunities' in their previous employment. Their prime motive was finding a solution to their existing situations, rather than a genuine wish to become entrepreneurs. Two interviewees came from professional families, whereas one hailed from a modest background. Two of the women had graduate degrees in management from Indian universities; one had a college degree in finance. Radha and Simi joined their spouses who were employed in the US, while Eda was sponsored by her church family and lived in the US for a few years before returning to India. These respondents worked in upper-management positions in the hospitality and fashion industries and in the service sector before starting their own enterprises. Radha and Simi were driven by their beliefs in social entrepreneurship—business with a social good component. Simi explained:

> A passion for social justice and thinking about opportunities that would get the best market price/value for handcrafted furniture, artefacts, and textiles for the vulnerable and poor craftspeople . . . when there was nothing available was central to me. I could bring my management skills, corporate experience, contacts and resources to this population. . . . the main concern is for better livelihoods for this population, so that people can stay in their natural work environment.

Similarly, Radha shared,

> I returned to be with my parents, but I knew my forte. I started really small by organising exhibitions for my artist friends, which were highly successful. . . . I soon realised I could organise such events professionally. So, that is how I grew into an entrepreneur. I have a symbiotic relationship with craftspeople of all type[s] . . . they are my creditors/lenders, workers, and trust me with their goods, to which I add value and sell worldwide. My work is bringing together people who have some kind of synergy . . . and to get the best value for their merchandise.

These women TEs perceived their entrepreneurship as part of a social commitment, as a way of fulfilling nationalistic aspirations, and as an opportunity for expanding their careers and building enduring relationships with local communities. Moore (2005, 43) calls this trend among women entrepreneurs a 'protean' style of career development, where boundaries no longer have the same meaning. For the 'Lone Crusaders', career advancement was no longer seen as limited within one's particular organisation, job, or firm but evolved together with personal interests, passion, faith, and competence in a global economy. Simi echoed this sentiment:

> I got fed up very quickly at my job [as a senior executive in the hospitality industry] and so I went on to join an organisation that deals with high fashion, craft-based women's clothing who exported their creations. I was managing their retail stores at [City A]. Then I moved to [City B] where I coordinated their design studio. I was managing their production and sales. That was [a] good break for me because it exposed me to [a] lot of handmade textiles, crafts, etc. . . . by sheer good luck, I found a meaning in my work . . .

Strategic opportunities, or blocked advancement to the top of the organisation, as in Eda's case, led these women to leave their jobs to start on their own. While Eda benefited enormously from businesses/clients she formerly worked for in her employment and maintained a close relationship with her former employers, the opportunity allowed her to develop a fresh, creative approach to balancing her professional growth, financial security, and community service. She explained,

> my faith community has always supported me, and taught me leadership qualities, given me confidence . . . I believe I have a life of purpose and put my effort in lifting the community. . . . I'm happy with what I'm doing and I have grown with it.

For these women it was not just employment crossover but also multiple relationships that benefitted their immediate communities.

Notwithstanding being owners and leaders of cross-border businesses, these women's business operations were self-funded. They were averse to taking high risks, which meant their enterprises incurred fewer loses, grew at a modest pace, and had lower growth expectations, unlike their counterparts in the previous categories.

To deepen their global connections, these respondents stressed building network diversity to reach different customers in the US and other advanced nations. The heterogeneity of networks served to avoid redundancy in instrumental information exchanged among members, lobby for international support and legitimacy for their merchandise, and further their business opportunities worldwide (Granovetter 1973). Radha explained the virtues of networking at public international events, where buyers and sellers with common interests converge—a novel method of entering the American market in this millennium:

> Networking was how I could get into transnational business. I became a member of [the] World Craft Council, Surface Design Association of United States Museums Store Association, U.S.A., and Craft Council of India. At the conference of Surface Design Association at Kansas City in early 2000, I did a trunk show of our stuff... I managed to sell almost 95 percent of my stuff at this venue. I realised that the people in the US appreciate handcrafted things. The US has a very upper-end market, while there is a regular market. In the US I started supplying garments at small exclusive boutiques who had attended the conference. Many museum stores are my regular customers now.

Simi referenced similar mechanisms and international networking opportunities. Through strategic use of their social skills, multi-cultural sensitivities, and interpersonal competencies, these women TEs gave meaning and added economic value to their merchandise in overseas markets, mostly within particular social and spatial contexts in keeping with Bourdieu's concept of habitus.

The survivalists: Asha and Hema

Asha entered the US with her son on a visitor's visa to visit family in New York. She overstayed her visa and filed for asylum to escape violent domestic physical and emotional abuse from her partner. After years of uncertainty, turbulence, financial hardship, and perseverance, she attained asylee status in the US. Lacking English language skills and a high school diploma from India, and with no resources except ties with her immediate family and the local Indian ethnic community, she had no chance of employment in the formal economy. She laboured for poor wages at a beauty salon owned by a co-ethnic businessman for several years before becoming an assistant and occasionally substituting for an Indian lady who threaded eyebrows. As Asha steadily grew in experience and confidence, with her sister's support she rented a chair at the salon for a few hours to do eyebrows for customers. She emotionally recalled,

> ... that was the start to my business... I was extremely frugal, I had a son to take care [of]. My sister was kind but I had to be responsible... While working at the salon I learnt everything to do with Indian bridal make-up from 'head to toe'... gradually my skills and mehndi (henna) artwork and application got well known [in the community] and I got very very busy. My son got neglected... it was good income. There

are lots of lavish Indian weddings. I left the salon to work full time as a make-up artist at Indian weddings . . . I started bringing wedding stuff and accessories, bridal make-up and genuine herbal products from India, on my trips and with help from family. I have travelled with [my] patron's family for weddings to India and to other American cities. My son helps now, he is thinking of going to college.

[Translated from Hindi]

Asha's route to self-employment involved making the most of ethnic resources, transnational linkages, personal skills, and social capital. Hema too had a similar narrative, having entered the US on the family reunification immigration system in the early 1980s with her husband and child. Her husband had a comfortable income from his government salary in India; she was a homemaker. On moving to the US, the family experienced financial adversities, as her husband, despite his education in accountancy, could not find suitable employment in New York (for more, see Khandelwal 2002, 91–116). He settled to work as a sales clerk in an ethnic-owned business. To make ends meet and from fear of economic instability, Hema worked for an hourly wage on the shop floor of an Indian-owned garment business, where her skills as a tailor and seamstress were highly valued, mainly by the Indian community:

I had to commute [a] very long distance to work in all sorts of weather . . . my employer was ruthless and exploitative. I found it problematic to continue with my job with a growing family . . . in the beginning I started by taking orders for stitching 'saree blouse' and Indian dresses. I did this from my house and no help. I had to be quiet about it. . . . I did this for many years, till I quit my job. Many of my patrons have remained with me . . . now I supervise and service large orders. As my loyal client base grew, business owners from India contacted me for retailing their garments and accessories. . . . Trust, old and new contacts, and goodwill matters a lot.

[Translated from Hindi]

Both respondents were 'pushed' into entrepreneurship for survival in harsh economic and social environments but benefitted from growing Indian ethnic niches in New York City's changing economy in the 1970s–1990s (Khandelwal 2002). Their journey to entrepreneurship was a daily struggle to achieve financial stability and security and was closely linked with their 'context of exit' from India and the limited skills and opportunities they brought with them as migrants.

Both respondents also remembered being humiliated in work situations and business transactions by co-ethnic employers and customers. Asha, for example, recalled how rich Indian clients bitterly bargained with her about rates: 'They have not abandoned their despicable habits when making millions . . . they don't see the struggling Indians desperately trying to survive. . . .' This example resonates with the findings of Dhaliwal (1998), Azmat (2013), Poggesi, Mari, and De Vita (2016), and others describing the 'double/triple disadvantage' confronted by South Asian women entrepreneurs in the UK and immigrant self-employed women from developing countries. Low-status wage work, low levels of formal education, lack of prior employment and managerial skills, poverty, and vulnerability caused by fewer options available to enter the labour market because gender, ethnicity, and migrant status create special challenges for women entrepreneurs. Despite these challenges, Asha and Hema experienced empowerment and constraints simultaneously. By employing creative practices in everyday interactions they subverted the hegemonic representations of class privileges for economic mobility.

In contrast to the previous categories, these women depended entirely on patronage and support from the Indian ethnic community and its social capital and networks. They were able to sustain and gradually grow their humble businesses at a transnational level because they functioned in an Indian ethnic enclave economy in the US (Light and Gold 2000),[8] maintained close ties with co-ethnics in India on whom they frequently depended for purchasing merchandise or financial help, and remained active both socially and communally at places of worship such as the Hindu temple. However, being exclusively embedded in ethnic business environments, their networks were restricted and consisted predominantly of co-workers, friends, and families of Indian origin. This led to 'homophily', or the degree to which network actors are similar in identity, thus reducing their access to vital information and business connections from a wide range of groups in American society. Hence their transnational businesses grew modestly and remained isolated from both countries' mainstream economies.

So, transnational entrepreneurship is not limited to ethnic elites' means to self-empowerment but also allows 'semi-proletariats' to meet basic needs for survival in the home and host country (Lin and Tao 2012). This is also illustrated by Landolt's (2001) study of Salvadorian immigrants in the US and in studies of low-skilled Vietnamese and Chinese migrant entrepreneurs who maintain close ties with their home countries to enhance their businesses (Wong and Ng 2002; Bagwell 2006).

Conclusion

The above case studies demonstrate that the distinctive socio-cultural and economic contexts in which the women TEs were grounded exacerbated or minimised difficulties and liabilities and created or limited transnational business opportunities (Poggesi, Mari, and De Vita 2016). Each unique case showcases the interplay of various forms of capital used by women TEs to access worldwide networks and confront the challenges of functioning at a global level. These cases reveal how the class positions of women entrepreneurs' partners and extended family are equally crucial for their trajectory, success, empowerment, and agency. The findings also shed light on how human, cultural, and class capital function as markers of different types of transnational networking—multidimensional, diasporic, and ethnic—that create paths of upward mobility for some while reinforcing inequalities for others in host and home countries.

These women were not only 'pushed' into entrepreneurship primarily with co-ethnics by necessity and discriminatory factors but also some were highly educated and skilled migrant and returnee entrepreneurs motivated by 'pull' factors. Analysing the heterogeneity of these women's experiences moves the debate beyond collective 'ethnic' explanations of business development by introducing personal factors into the analysis and by avoiding the narrow individualistic premises of neo-classical theory (Struder 2003; Poggesi, Mari, and De Vita 2016; Lin and Tao 2012). By acknowledging these complexities and the importance of agency and practice when unpacking the process of seeking and exploring cross-border business opportunities in multiple settings, this chapter looks beyond simplistic explanations of Indian women TEs' motives—in contrast to the existing literature's depiction of women mainly mirroring male TEs' experiences and ventures—to see how their biographies, socialisation, migratory experiences, gender relations, and place constitute cross-border entrepreneurial experiences. Future research should explore the cultural influences—traditions, religious affiliations, sex-based social norms, and nationalistic aspirations—on women's transnational entrepreneurship, as this would differ by religious and/or ethnic background. Such research would also explain how women TEs structure their cross-border business environments—for example, by introducing measures allowing employees to balance their business and family or religious life locally and globally. It is important to recognise the particularities of ethnic and national groups to avoid reifying the experiences of dominant TE groups.

Notes

1 Migrant entrepreneurs are defined as Indians who live and have their business headquarters in the US, whereas returnees are migrant entrepreneurs who have chosen to reside and operate from India. All of them spent a minimum of five years in the US before relocating to India. Most of the returnees are US citizens.
2 Kohli (2007) defines an 'interventionist state' as one that prioritises economic growth as a state goal and therefore ruthlessly supports capitalists, represses labour, mobilises economic nationalism to act as a social glue, and channels firm activities to produce for protected domestic markets and exports (89; cited in Ray 2013).
3 In 2016, Indians were the top recipients of high-skilled H-1B temporary visas and were the second-largest group of international students in the US (Zong and Batalova 2017).
4 It is considered a meso-level analytical framework because it takes into account features of macro structure—like the pre-migration context in the home country (Portes 2003), state policies affecting institutional infrastructure, immigration, return, visa and citizenship policies, and market conditions in the home and host countries—and features of micro-level individual and collective resources and conditions that facilitate or constrain transnational entrepreneurship (Chen and Tan 2009).
5 Faist (2000) has called the field a transnational space. Transnational spaces are relatively stable, lasting, dense ties reaching across the borders of sovereign states and consisting of combinations of ties and their contents, positions in networks and organisations, and networks or organisations cutting across at least two nation-states' borders.
6 Moore (2005, 45) defines 'delayed entrepreneurs' as women who start their businesses after a first career of raising a family.
7 See https://tie.org/.
8 'Ethnic enclave' refers to small enterprises owned by (self-employed) members of an ethnic community and confined to a geographic location. Usually the labour force is drawn extensively from co-ethnics: family, friends, social contacts, and ties. Networks are an integral part of such enclaves, providing the essential information for setting up businesses, financial support, labour requirements, etc.

References

Ahmed, Sadiq, and Ashutosh Varshney. 2012. "Battles Half Won: Political Economy of India's Growth and Economic Policy Since Independence." In *The Oxford Handbook of the Indian Economy*, edited by Chetan Ghate, 56–104. New York, NY: Oxford University Press.

Aldrich, Howard, and Roger Waldinger. 1990. "Ethnicity and Entrepreneurship." *American Review of Sociology* 16 (1): 111–35.

Azmat, Fara. 2013. "Opportunities or Obstacles? Understanding the Challenges Faced by Migrant Women Entrepreneurs." *International Journal of Gender and Entrepreneurship* 5 (2): 198–215.

Bagwell, Susan. 2006. "UK Vietnamese Businesses: Cultural Influences and Intracultural Differences." *Environment and Planning C: Politics and Space* 24 (1): 51–69.

Basu, Anuradha, and Arati Goswami. 1999. "South Asian Entrepreneurship in Great Britain: Factors Influencing Growth." *International Journal of Entrepreneurial Behavior and Research* 5 (5): 1–16.

Bonacich, Edna. 1973. "A Theory of Middleman Minorities." *American Sociological Review* 38 (5): 583–94.

Bourdieu, Pierre. 1990. *The Logic of Practice*. Stanford, CA: Stanford University Press.

Bourdieu, Pierre, and Loïc Wacquant. 1992. *An Invitation to Reflexive Sociology*. Chicago, IL: University of Chicago Press.

Brettell, Caroline B. 2007. "Immigrant Women in Small Businesses: Biographies of Becoming Entrepreneurs." In *Handbook of Research on Ethnic Minority Entrepreneurship: A Co-Evolutionary View on Resource Management*, edited by D. Leo Paul, 83–98. Cheltenham, UK: Edward Elgar.

Chakravorty, Sanjoy, Devesh Kapur, and Nirvikar Singh. 2016. *The Other One Percent: Indians in America*. New York, NY: Oxford University Press.

Chen, Wenhong, and Justin Tan. 2009. "Understanding Transnational Entrepreneurship Through a Network Lens: Theoretical and Methodological Considerations." *Entrepreneurship Theory and Practice* 33 (5): 1079–91.

Collins, Jock, and Angeline Low. 2010. "Asian Female Immigrant Entrepreneurs in Small and Medium-Sized Businesses in Australia." *Entrepreneurship and Regional Development* 22 (1): 97–111.

Davidsson, Per, and Benson Honig. 2003. "The Role of Social and Human Capital Among Nascent Entrepreneurs." *Journal of Business Venturing* 18 (3): 301–31.

Dhaliwal, Spinder. 1998. "Silent Contributors: Asian Female Entrepreneurs and Women in Business." *Women Studies International Forum* 21 (5): 463–74.

Drori, Israel, Benson Honig, and Ari Ginsberg. 2010. "Researching Transnational Entrepreneurship: An Approach Based on Theory of Practice." In *Transnational and Immigrant Entrepreneurship in a Globalized World*, edited by Benson Honig, Israel Drori, and Barbara Carmichael, 3–30. Toronto: University of Toronto Press.

Erel, Umut. 2010. "Migrating Cultural Capital: Bourdieu in Migration Studies." *Sociology* 44 (4): 642–60.

Faist, Thomas. 2000. *The Volume and Dynamics of International Migration and Transnational Social Spaces*. Oxford: Oxford University Press.

Gill, Rebecca, and Shiv Ganesh. 2007. "Empowerment, Constraint, and the Entrepreneurial Self: A Study of White Women Entrepreneurs." *Journal of Applied Communication Research* 35 (3): 268–93.

Gold, Steve J. 2018. "Israeli Infotech Migrants in Silicon Valley." *RSF: The Russell Sage Foundation Journal of the Social Sciences* 4 (1): 130–48.

Gold, Steve J. 2005. "Migrant Networks: A Summary and Critique of Relational Approaches to International Migration." In *The Blackwell Companion to Social Inequalities*, edited by Mary Romero and Eric Margolis, 257–85. Hoboken, NJ: Blackwell.

Gold, Steve J. 2002. *The Israeli Diaspora*. Seattle, WA: University of Washington Press.

Gold, Steve J. 1998. "Refugees and Small Business: The Case of Soviet Jews and Vietnamese." *Ethnic and Racial Studies* 11 (4): 411–38.

Gold, Steve J. 1994. "Patterns of Economic Co-Operation Among Israeli Immigrants in Los Angeles." *International Migration Review* 28 (1): 114–35.

Gold, Steve, and Nazli Kibria. 1993. "Vietnamese Refugees and Blocked Mobility." *Asia and Pacific Migration Journal* 2 (1): 27–56.

Granovetter, Mark. 1992. "Problems of Explanation in Economic Sociology." In *Networks and Organizations: Structure, Form, and Actions*, edited by Nitin Nohria and Robert G. Eccles, 25–56. Boston, MA: Harvard Business School Review.

Granovetter, Mark. 1973. "The Strength of Weak Ties." *American Journal of Sociology* 78 (6): 1360–80.

Greve, Arent, and Janet Salaff. 2003. "Social Networks and Entrepreneurship." *Entrepreneurship Theory and Practice* 28 (1): 1–22.

Hosler, Akiko S. 1998. *Japanese Immigrant Entrepreneurs in New York City: A New Wave of Ethnic Business*. New York, NY: Garland Publishing.

Javadian, Golshan, and Robert Singh. 2012. "Examining Successful Iranian Women Entrepreneurs: An Exploratory Study." *Gender and Management: An International Journal* 27 (3): 148–64.

Kapur, Deepak, and Ravi Ramamurti. 2001. "India's Emerging Competitive Advantage in Services." *Academy of Management Executives* 15 (2): 20–31.

Kelly, Philip, and Torn Lusis. 2006. "Migration and the Transnational Habitus: Evidence from Canada and Philippines." *Environment & Planning* 38 (5): 831–47.

Khandelwal, Madhulika. 2002. *Becoming American, Being Indian: An Immigrant Community in New York City*. Ithaca, NY: Cornell University Press.

Knight, Melanie. 2016. "Race-ing, Classing and Gendering Racialized Women's Participation in Entrepreneurship." *Gender, Work and Organization* 23 (3): 310–27.

Kohli, Atul. 2007. "State, Business, and Economic Growth in India." *Studies in Comparative International Development* 42(1–2) (July): 87–114.

Landolt, Patricia. 2001. "Salvadoran Economic Transnationalism: Embedded Strategies for Household Maintenance, Immigrant Incorporation and Entrepreneurial Expansion." *Global Networks* 1 (3): 217–41.

Lee, Sang, Timothy Stream, Jerome Osteryoung, and Harriet Stephenson. 2009. "A Comparison of the Critical Success Factors in Women-Owned Business Between the United States and Korea." *International Entrepreneurship and Management Journal* 5 (3): 259–70.

Levitt, Peggy. 2001. *The Transnational Villagers*. Berkeley, CA: University of California Press.

Light, Ivan, and Parminder Bachu. 1993. *Immigration and Entrepreneurship: Culture, Capital and Ethnic Networks*. New Brunswick, NJ: Transaction Publishing.

Light, Ivan, and Edna Bonacich. 1988. *Immigrant Entrepreneurs*. Berkeley, CA: University of California Press.

Light, Ivan, and Steve Gold. 2000. *Ethnic Economies*. Bingley, UK: Emerald Group Publishing Limited.

Lin, Xiaohua, and Shaw Tao. 2012. "Transnational Entrepreneurs: Characteristics, Drivers, and Success Factors." *Journal of International Entrepreneurship* 10 (1): 50–69.

Min, Pyong Gap. 1988. *Ethnic Business Enterprise: Korean Small Business in Atlanta*. Staten Island, NY: Center for Migration Studies.

Min, Pyong Gap, and Mehdi Bozorgmehr. 2000. "Immigrant Entrepreneurship and Business Patterns: A Comparison of Koreans and Iranian in Los Angeles." *International Migration Review* 34 (3): 707–38.

Moore, Dorothy Perrin. 2005. "Career Paths of Women Business Owners." In *International Handbook of Women and Small Business Entrepreneurship*, edited by Sandra Fielden and Marilyn Davidson, 42–51. Cheltenham: Edward Elgar Publishing.

Nowicka, Magdalena. 2013. "Positioning Strategies of Polish Entrepreneurs in Germany: Transnationalizing Bourdieu's Notion of Capital." *International Sociology* 28 (1): 29–47.

Pew Research Center. 2017. "Indian Population in the U.S., 2000–2015." Accessed July 9, 2018. http://www.pewsocialtrends.org/chart/indian-population-in-the-u-s/.

Poggesi, Sara, Michela Mari, and Luisa De Vita. 2016. "What's New in Female Entrepreneurship Research? Answers from the Literature." *International Entrepreneurship Management Journal* 12 (3): 735–64.

Poros, Maritsa. 2011. *Modern Migrations: Gujarati Indian Networks in New York and London*. Stanford, CA: Stanford University Press.

Portes, Alejandro. 2003. "Conclusions: Theoretical Convergencies and Empirical Evidence in the Study of Immigrant Transnationalism." *International Migration Review* 37 (3): 874–92.

Portes, Alejandro, and Rubén Rumbaut. 2014. *Immigrant America – A Portrait*. 4th ed. Berkeley, CA: University of California Press.

Ram, Monder. 1994. "Unravelling the Social Network in Ethnic Minority Firms." *International Social Business Journal* 12 (3): 42–53.

Ray, Manashi. 2013. "The Global Circulation of Skill and Capital: Pathways of Return Migration of Indian Entrepreneurs from the United States to India." In *Diaspora Engagement and Development in South Asia*, edited by Tan Tai Yong and Md Mizanur Rahman, 75–102. Houndmills: Palgrave Macmillan.

Rutashobya, Lettice, Issack Allan, and Kerstin Nilsson. 2009. "Gender, Social Networks, and Entrepreneurial Outcomes in Tanzania." *Journal of African Business* 10 (1): 67–83.

Saxenian, Annalee. 2006. *The New Argonauts: Regional Advantage in a Global Economy*. Cambridge, MA: Harvard University Press.

Salaff, Janet, Siu-lun Wong, and Arent Greve. 2010. *Hong Kong Movers and Stayers: Narratives of Family Migration*. Chicago, IL: University of Illinois Press.

Struder, Inge. 2003. "Self-Employed Turkish-Speaking Women in London." *The International Journal of Entrepreneurship and Innovation* 4 (3): 185–95.

Tan, Justin. 2008. "Breaking the 'Bamboo Curtain' and the 'Glass Ceiling': Experiences of Women Entrepreneurs in High-Tech Industries in an Emerging Market." *Journal of Business Ethics* 80 (3): 547–64.

Tiwari, Smita. 2013. "Diaspora Engagement Policy in South Asia." In *Diaspora Engagement and Development in South Asia*, edited by Tan Tai Yong and Md Mizanur Rahman, 212–30. Houndmills: Palgrave Macmillan.

Valdez, Zulema. 2011. *The New Entrepreneurs: How Race, Class, and Gender Shape American Experience*. Stanford, CA: Stanford University Press.

Wadhwa, Vivek, and Alex Salkever. 2012. *The Immigration Exodus: Why America Is Losing the Global Race to Capture Entrepreneurial Talent*. Philadelphia, PA: Wharton Digital Press.

Wong, Lloyd L., and Michele Ng. 2002. "The Emergence of Small Transnational Enterprise in Vancouver: The Case of Chinese Entrepreneur Immigrants." *International Journal of Urban and Regional Research* 26 (3): 508–30.

World Bank 2017. "Migration and Remittances: Recent Developments and Outlook; Global Compact on Migration." Washington, DC.

Zhou, Min. 1992. *Chinatown: The Socioeconomic Potential of an Urban Enclave*. Philadelphia, PA: Temple University Press.

Zhou, Min, and John R. Logan. 1989. "Return on Human Capital in Ethnic Enclaves: New York City's Chinatown." *American Sociological Review* 38 (3): 1040–74.

Zong, Jie, and Jeanne Batalova. 2017. "Indian Immigrants in the United States." Washington, DC: Migration Policy Institute. Accessed June 1, 2018. https://www.migrationpolicy.org/article/indian-immigrants-united-states.

14
INDIAN ORIGIN WOMEN
Organising against apartheid

Quraisha Dawood and Mariam Seedat-Khan

Introduction

This chapter briefly discusses the history of Indians in South Africa, specifically highlighting women who created a legacy for the success of future generations. We subsequently discuss the hybrid identity of South African Indian women in terms of their diasporic, gendered and professional identity. We argue that while some South African Indian women have maintained cultural and religious links to India, some have worked hard to promote equality and go to battle for social justice and equality. Ultimately, this chapter looks at the role played by Professor Fatima Meer, while making reference to Dr. Goonam, and Mrs. Amina Cachalia in their fight against the apartheid regime. They paved the way for equality and provided a voice for South African Indian woman; this chapter broadly traces their legacies and how this relates to the challenges South African Indian women face today.

The inimitable Indian community in South Africa exemplifies the largest non-immigrant Indian population outside of India. With the first indentured, passenger and merchant Indians arriving in South Africa 158 years ago; their South African-born descendants have become an integral part of the country's past and current rainbow nation. The political participation of South African Indian women such as Professor Fatima Meer, Frene Ginwala, Amina Cachalia, Dr. Goonam, Ela Gandhi and Phyllis Naidoo intensified in the 1950s with the struggle against the apartheid regime. However, in a patriarchal racially divided society, scholars mostly acknowledged the likes of Yusuf Dadoo, Dr. Naicker and Mahatma Gandhi for their political activism and Gandhi's passive resistance ideology.

We argue that the equally important struggle that was fought by South African Indian women was often discounted in favour of the role played by Indian men – a practice not uncommon within a patriarchal system. Women provided the foundation for the fight against apartheid in establishing support structures for their families, maintaining cultural anchors and preserving Indian heritage. This facilitated the breeding ground for writers, teachers and political activists. Indian women were the backbone of the liberation struggle that facilitated Indian men and women's entry into the political arena. The South African Indian women paved the way for future generations, who continue to confront gender- and race-related challenges demanding equality and social justice for all.

Indians in South Africa: a historical perspective

Literature on South Africa's history of colonialism and apartheid is extensive. However, authors have failed to highlight the struggle of Indian women in particular living under the harshness of the apartheid regime. Fewer studies focus on the unique plight and gendered inequalities faced by Indian women. Govinden (2000: 69) asserts that 'much of the research on Indian history (in South Africa) assumes that the term is inclusive of male and female. Indian women's histories have been insufficiently documented.' Nevertheless, it is evident from the writings of activist Phyllis Naidoo during the 1980s (1990), Farida Karodia (1986) and academics such as Fatima Meer (1969), Mariam Seedat-Khan (2012), Nasima Carrim (2012), Goolam Vahed, Vishnu Padayachee and Ashwin Desai (2006) that South African Indian women bore the brunt of 'double discrimination,'[1] under an oppressive regime. Under British rule, all indentured Indians were promised a rent-free home, in addition to an abundance of water and vegetables in return for working on the sugar cane plantations in Natal; yet women were only allotted half the wages and half the rations compared to their male counterparts. Seedat-Khan (2012: 36) relates, 'The advertisement read like a tropical holiday.'[2] In reality, Indian women arrived in Natal only to be discriminated against for their skin colour and gender. Govinden's (2000) study on the histories of Indian women in South Africa confirms that indentured women of all ages were treated poorly on the ships, and unmarried women were labeled as 'promiscuous.' They were particularly vulnerable and took a husband on board the ship as a form of protection from male sexual predators. This was a form of survival adopted by the indentured women. Indian women were paid poorly and worked under harsh conditions even while sick or pregnant (Beall, 1990). Many of them were forced into child marriages, as a means of survival. Oppressive and patriarchal conditions were reproduced, thereby further subjugating women, forcing them into an unequal system which made them increasingly dependent on men.

After the end of the indentured period, a sizeable number of Indians made the choice not to return to India. They had established a community outside of India and began making a success of their lives in their new home. With the legalization of apartheid, they quickly learnt that they could not own land or vote and that they were forced to live in racially demarcated areas such as Phoenix, Chatsworth, Isipingo and Overport in Natal. They were forcibly removed from income-generating communities and areas that they had long established.

Wealthier merchant Indians who elected to migrate to South Africa in search of improved economic prospects were affected by South African apartheid pass laws, which determined where they could live, work and establish businesses (South African History Online, 2018). The immediate success of wealthy Indian traders posed a threat to existing white and Afrikaner traders in different parts of South Africa. Indian traders were, as a result, relegated to poor underdeveloped rural communities in which white and Afrikaner traders were not interested. South African Indian traders' current presence in small rural communities all over South Africa is evident today. Indians faced compounded discrimination from the Boers, who believed anyone with darker skin was inferior (Carrim, 2012: 33). In an effort to preserve Afrikaner values and promote division among the race groups, Indians were subjected to curfews, segregated amenities and housed in 'Coolie Compounds.'

In an effort to preserve Indian culture, and maintain a sense of community and familiarity to India, South African Indians established 'little Indias' wherever they settled in South Africa (Govinden, 2000: 87). These replicas of Indian communities comprised mosques, temples, saris, spice, vegetable, prayer and food shops. These served as a reminder of their ancestral homes and cemented the 'cultural transplant' from India to South Africa which is still visible today. Limited space in designated Indian areas, far removed from the three identifiable race groups[3] in South Africa, reinforced a caste system[4] among Indians living in South Africa. The Group Areas Act saw Indians, Blacks and Coloureds shunted into racially segregated homelands, where they were forced to live in close proximity to each other, regardless of class differences and ethnicities. Despite this, Indians from different castes, language and religious groups seemed to symbolize one homogenous group.

The harsh conditions under apartheid experienced by Indians in South Africa resulted in the arrival of British-educated Indian lawyer Mahatma Gandhi, in Natal. He was a beacon of hope for Indians, who facilitated the rise of the South African Indian Congress[5] and the Natal Indian Congress.[6] These organisations advocated for the rights of Indians in South Africa. Gandhi's philosophy of passive resistance was adopted to resist the pass law, which was a mechanism used to control the movement of black[7] people, control urbanisation and manage migrant labour. Gandhi was a catalyst for the mobilization of the struggle for equal rights for Indians living under racist colonial rule in South Africa.

After South Africa gained independence from British rule in 1948, black South Africans endured oppressive and inhuman treatment under apartheid.[8] In order to maintain and secure white domination and subjugate black people, discrimination was legitimized through various laws and social constructs (Carrim, 2012: 38–43). These included the Group Areas Act[9] and the Separate Amenities Act[10] among hundreds of others that sought to promote white privilege. The hierarchy of race was legalized via the Population Registration Act of 1950, which decreed that Whites were legitimately superior, at the top of the hierarchy, while Blacks occupied the lowest rungs. Coloureds and Indians were 'sandwiched' in between (Maharaj, 2012: 79). Families were torn apart based on the colour of their skin, and many were subjected to the 'pencil test,' a degrading test where a pencil was placed in some persons' hair: if the pencil fell out, the person was classified as White; if it did not, the classification was Coloured. This resulted in family members being classified into different race groups, with catastrophic results that impacted on the structure of the family. The apartheid regime fractured personal lives, preventing people from marrying across race lines, and this was legalized via the Mixed Marriages Act of 1949. The Indian Education Act legalized Indians receiving an inferior education, with males being taught subjects in trade and females being taught needlework. This further entrenched a patriarchal system, which was already imported and reinforced from India. This was realized when Indian families began placing added emphasis on the education of male children compared to their female children (Carrim, 2012: 40). Securing a university education in South Africa was a challenge for all black people. In order to further their studies, Indians had to obtain a permit from the Minister of Education allowing them to attend university. A privileged few women such as Dr. Goonam had the opportunity to travel abroad to obtain a medical degree.

Working life was particularly harsh, and Indians had difficulty securing formal employment ahead of Whites and Coloureds under apartheid. In a post-apartheid South Africa, they have difficulty securing jobs ahead of African women and men. The architects of apartheid ensured that the Job Reservations Act would secure the best senior positions for Whites, while Blacks were relegated to menial, semi-skilled work, which groomed them for a life of servitude. Carrim (2012: 40) aptly notes that these measures ensured that Blacks would 'internalise and maintain the inferiority of their race.' These discriminatory practices however, were not received without resistance.

Enter women

Govinden (2000: 51) reminds us that 'a scattering of people inevitably leads to their gathering.' In this spirit, women banded together to create stokvels,[11] which would ultimately benefit their families and empower them financially. They also came together to form prayer groups in a call for solidarity under the harsh conditions that women experienced as a collective (South African History Online, 2018). The Zenzele club, funded by Josie Palmer and Madie-Hall Xuma, ensured that women earned a living from their knitting skills. Many African women were forced into domestic work as a means of survival. The exodus of men to mining towns and communities left women behind to take care of their families. Despite the danger and risk of arrest that pass laws presented, women risked everything to sustain their families and supplement their household incomes.

Between the 1940s and 1950s, a sisterhood against resistance developed, when the SAIC (South African Indian Congress), African National Congress and Communist Party South Africa resolved to rise against the oppressive regime, along with the ANC Women's League. Many South African Indian women were arrested in 1946, including Fatima Meer, Dr. Goonam and N.P. Desai for speaking out against apartheid and encouraging all other women to do the same. P.K. Naidoo, Mrs. Veeramah Pather, Khatija Mayet, Zohra Meer, Ms. Suriakala Patel and Amina Cachalia became the faces of the resistance movement by South African Indian women. While there were previous instances of women gathering to oppose discrimination, in 1913 and 1930, the momentum gained momentum and culminated in the historical Women's March of 1956. It is on this occasion that approximately 20,000 South African women of all races marched on the union buildings on the 9th of August to voice their political will in the fight against discrimination practices. Lillian Ngoyi, Amina Cachalia, Helen Joseph and Bertha Mkhize were among the women who stood at the forefront of a historic moment that South African women continue to celebrate and emulate. The outcry of women on this scale signified that apartheid had infiltrated every element of personal life, threatening the very core of the family and its survival:

> When it was women who resisted, it was because the crisis reached into the inner sanctum of home and family life. Each of the three [episodes of resistance] . . . reflects a time when women themselves were directly and negatively affected by shifts in the application of the pass laws.
>
> *(Wells 1993: 9)*

The 'claiming of their voice' through active political activism and through their writing provided personal and communal value to the experience of South African Indian women. In the 1960s Phyllis Naidoo and Amina Cachalia became prominent figures of the resistance of South African Indian women.

Prof. Fatima Meer's, political activism can be traced back to 1944. She was 16 years old when she took the initiative to raise funds for famine victims in Bengal (SAPA, 2010). It was her idea to bring the shared experiences between Indian and African women in her fight for equality and justice. Her ideas saw a coming together of all women, and this was the catalyst for a sisterhood that resulted in the Women's March in 1956.

Freedom dawned on South Africa in 1994, with the hope of equality for all. Women rose in the ranks of government and business. Yet the effect of apartheid has left a legacy of inequality, racism, unemployment and poverty which is difficult to overcome. Indians still find themselves 'sandwiched' between Whites, Coloureds and Blacks and are often invisible.

Negotiating a hybrid identity

Indian indentured labourers were brought into South Africa by the British when they found local labour unreliable. The British experience of securing cheap labour in India was met with fewer challenges and less resistance than they had faced in South Africa. The malicious and divisive nature and history of indenture which pitted Africans against Indians for British economic gain 'systematically othered' Indians. South Africans continued to view Indians as 'foreigners,' despite their 158-year presence and their substantial political and economic contributions. In a post-apartheid South Africa in 2002, ANC MP Mbongeni Ngema's song about Indians fuelled an anti-Indian sentiment, creating political conflict. The growing bond between Indians and Africans in the Warwick Avenue triangle threatened the strategy of the apartheid government. The apartheid state was responsible for the 1949 Durban riots, which created conflict between Africans and Indians while police stood on the side-lines watching and to some degree encouraging the violent conflict that resulted in the separation of the two races.

Diasporic/hybrid identity

Family life of South African Indian families is socially constructed, shaped by their lived experiences since their arrival on the east coast of South Africa. Their lived experiences have resulted in the social construction of a unique South African Indian family which is determined by a series of key factors. Religion, education, family history, political affiliations, socio-economic position and social networks determine the particular position of the South African Indian family in contemporary South Africa. Notwithstanding this, education is believed to be the foundation upon which any form of success can be attained within this unique community. It was under the harshest conditions on the sugarcane plantations, with meagre wages, that women came together to contribute limited and scarce funds on a monthly basis to ensure that their children received an education in makeshift schools on the sugarcane plantations (Desai and Vahed, 2010). Votti Veeramah Somayya, indenture number 42129, was a strong, single, beautiful woman with a determination for justice and equality, a fearless woman who was not afraid to speak her mind. 'Votti's story draws our attention to ways in which some women confronted the multiple layers of oppression' (Desai and Vahed, 2012: 6). Like Votti, women like Amina Cachalia and Fatima Meer also fought and resisted all forms of patriarchy and exploitation. Their resistance came at a price, family was sacrificed, their children were sent away and many women like them became mothers to a nation while leaving their own children in the care of surrogates for protracted periods of time. Their struggle was no different or any more difficult than the woman who was forced to leave her child behind to seek domestic employment in a location far from her rural home for protracted periods of time.

One cannot understand or define the hybrid identity of the South African Indian woman without addressing the impact of indenture, apartheid and racially divisive practices that have not been expunged from society as a whole. The dawn of democracy did not automatically reset our minds to view people of different races in new ways. The apartheid system was strategically designed to present a racial divide and a hierarchy of people based on race. Evidence of racism and a strong anti-Indian sentiment is an actual challenge for people who are South Africans and identify with an Indian culture. South African Indians grapple with the notion of a transnational or a diasporic identity. On the one hand, the term 'Indian' is a persistent reminder of one's link to another country, religion, language, culture and way of life. On the other hand, being South

African (being an active citizen, working and living in a country that once enslaved you) is deeply embedded in the identity as well. When dissecting the South African Indian identity, it is imperative to take into account the complex dynamics of identifying with two 'homes.' The notion of this duality of 'homes' does not contribute equally to the identity of the South African Indian woman. Vally (2012) asserts, 'with each new generation, India gradually retreated as the quintessential home or space of origin.' Thus the link to India weakens over time. Despite this, it cannot be disregarded that the South African Indian identity is heavily influenced by spatial relationships. South African Indians faced geographic discrimination during the apartheid era, which had resulted in areas that remain predominantly Indian. Due to the Group Areas Act, Indians – who were accustomed to cultural parameters such as a caste system, different languages, religions, styles of cooking, dressing and music among other influences – were forced to live together. This 'collapsing of space' produced a 'pan-Indian culture' or a forced homogenous identity (Govinden, 2000: 37–39). The manifestation of such coercive identities is still apparent in 'Indian' areas such as Chatsworth, Lenasia, Laudium. Overport, Phoenix and other areas in South Africa. Such tangible symbols of identity such as space, words such as 'coolie' and BEE (ticking 'Indian' as race) is an amalgamation of a fractured Indian and South African identity.

Gendered identity

The gender identity of the South African Indian women, much like women of colour in the country, have lived under colonialism, indenture, apartheid and patriarchy. Women still largely continue to maintain, execute and fulfil household tasks despite their entry into the formal sector, experiencing a double burden. The household and familial domain continue to remain the responsibility of the women in a patriarchal South African society, irrespective of race. Men of all races continue to earn more than women and occupy higher paying positions within an unequal economic system. They continue to outnumber women in positions of leadership, power and influence. This South African Indian identity is fluid. Political, economic and social evolution has resulted in transformations over protracted periods of time. While sometimes viewed as outsiders, Indian women have made substantial contributions to the South African rainbow nation and remain as South African as Africans, Whites and Coloureds, all of whom form the rainbow nation.

Identity work

It is important to establish that this group of people identify themselves as South Africans first and foremost; only thereafter do they attach labels that represent aspects of gender, religion, culture, ancestry and other classifications. Escaping stratified, racially divisive labels is particularly difficult for South Africans, considering the complex history of slavery, colonialism, indenture and apartheid. In a society that sought to execute separate development premised on race, clear divisions in wealth, language, education, politics, religion and recreation are among the key areas that indicated race and rank in society. Fatima Meer played an important role as a sociologist. She aimed to study human behaviour objectively, seeking to provide scientific explanations for social problems that existed in her community, society and country at large. She delved into areas of labour, suicide, politics, gender, religion, justice and later on began documenting the history of political activist such as Andrew Zondo, Nelson Mandela (1990), Mahatma Gandhi (1970) and Dr. Goonam. The inclusivity of people across all race groups and religion was indicative of her inclusive approach to understanding the fractures caused by historical oppressions.

Against the milieu of the complex gendered hybrid identity of the South African Indian as well as historical oppression, Fatima Meer emerged as an icon of resistance. Her education and ability to take a political stand and challenge patriarchy in both the traditional South African Indian household as well as government was because she was politically conscious from an early age: hosting literacy classes in her father's garage in the 1940s, to becoming a student leader at the age of 17. Meer was determined to contribute to the education of women and raise funds to advance the passive resistance campaign. While challenging the status quo, she continued to embrace elements of her Indian heritage. Her Indian heritage did not prevent her from identifying with other women of different race and religious groups or from finding ways to empower them through her clinical practice as a sociologist. Meer emerged as the epitome of how the South African Indian woman could negotiate and redefine her identity in new ways, free from patriarchal influence. Her close friendship with Winnie Mandela did much for women of both race groups, working together to advance the cause for women in an apartheid society. Mandela believed that 'At a time when most Indian girls were helping their mothers in the kitchen making samosas, this young woman was leading protest marches and challenging the most oppressive system in the world' (Wajid, 2010). While this takes nothing away from Indian women who supported their husbands and sons in the struggle against discrimination and fought an emotional struggle of their own, it is important to note that Meer was an anomaly in the context of traditional Indian female identity, which was tied to the husband, children and home. Meer had numerous roles: she balanced the role of wife to political activist and lawyer Ismail Meer; she was mother to Shehnaaz, Shamin and Rashid; and was a sister, sociologist, activist, community leader and writer. Her greatest strength was her ability to identify with women across all racial, religious, cultural and political lines. In doing so, she held immeasurable power, despite her diminutive appearance. Wajid (2010) writes, 'describing her characteristic intervention during an incident of student unrest, one of her students said: 'It was an unbelievable sight to see this petite little woman, wrapped in a sari, march in front of a Hippo [an armoured police vehicle] and order it to stop them.' Forging the first common membership between Africans and Indians, Fatima Meer founded the Durban and District Women's' League in the early 1950s, where she held the post of secretary, along with Bertha Mkhize, then president of the ANC Women's League. During this time Fatima married her cousin Ismail Meer. She frequently contravened discriminatory laws and challenged the government with her writing and demonstrations. Her activism resulted in a political banning; she was prevented from publishing her work and confined to the magisterial district of Durban. In spite of this, her political activism and fundraising continued to have an impact on discriminatory laws that governed all people. While Fatima Meer never officially joined a political party, she was regarded as a child of the ANC, based on her political affiliation with the Mandela, Kathrada, Sisulu, Naidoo and Zondo families. She believed in promoting justice and equality for all South African people irrespective of race and religion. She was one of the first black women to be employed as an academic at the University of Natal in Durban.

South African Indians: Hurdles in contemporary South Africa

In the almost 140 years of our presence in South Africa, there has been no such regular publication dedicated to Indian lifestyles as well as being significantly owned by us. Although our buying power is some R4 billion annually, our custom is taken for granted, our heritage is devalued, our contributions to society (especially our fledgling democracy) tend to be overlooked.

(Cooper 1998: 5)

Racism, anti-Indianism, corruption and rising unemployment continues to plague South Africa post-democracy. Measures aimed to reduce historical inequalities, including Black Economic Empowerment and Employment Equity, have not successfully achieved their objectives. South African Indian women face a further sense of isolation and exclusion in the current economic climate. Adverts similar to the one that offered women half rations and half payment for their labour excludes white, Indian and coloured South Africans from applying for employment. Adverts openly call for black African applicants, thus excluding all other black people that faced discrimination under apartheid. While some South African Indians and Africans have found wealth and success in post-apartheid South Africa; large numbers still find themselves underprivileged, living in neglected conditions with no access to basic amenities and limited employment opportunities. BEE has in fact created an elite few, while the poor, unemployed masses have remained poor, the gap between the rich and the poor has widened and the opportunities promised by a democratic government have failed the poorest of the poor, At the bottom of this hierarchy black women remain the most marginalized and subjugated in a society that has always failed to prioritise them. The discrimination agonised over by South African Indians who contributed to the economy has fundamentally been overlooked in order to prioritise black Africans exclusively.

> While those in the business and professional sectors thrived in the post-apartheid era and jostled with the political elites for power, privilege, patronage and position, working-class Indians increasingly feel disillusioned, marginalized and excluded from the rainbow nation.
> *(Maharaj, 2012: 79)*

Indian women in particular are underrepresented in skilled professions such as engineering, medicine, academia and science. Their identities are still tied to traditional Indian values of the home. With only a limited number of women rising to challenge the status quo, it remains largely unchanged. While many older South African Indian women do retain cultural elements (cooking, dressing, religion and language) that are linked to their Indian heritage, it is visibly clear that generations that have followed do not seem as tied to India as their grandmothers. India, through these generational stages, has retreated as the homeland and remains a distant memory to South African Indians who no longer identify it as home (Govinden, 2000).

South African Indian women in particular share stronger ties with other South African women who have experienced apartheid, motherhood and the gender bias nature of the workplace. Their shared lived experiences in the liberation movement created a spirit of sisterhood that bound a generation of women like Winnie Mandela and Fatima Meer as sisters. The unity of black women is encapsulated in the words of Winnie Mandela in her tribute to Prof. Fatima Meer at her funeral in 2010 when she referred to her as:

> my sister, my friend and a mother to my children, during the difficult times of apartheid; I could depend on her to take care of my children when I was away, arrested or in hiding. She understood me and we shared a similar goal.
> *(Seedat-Khan, 2012: 45)*

It is against this backdrop that South African Indian women should be acknowledged and celebrated for their perseverance in pursuit of democracy and social justice and for their efforts to help build a rainbow nation. Winnie Mandela, speaking about Meer, notes the she indubitably, has a place in the rainbow nation of South Africa and should be recognised for her contribution. The battle to discover and assert her space in a multiracial, multicultural society is ongoing, and in the spirit of justice and equality South African Indian woman will rise to the challenge as she has in the past. She will draw on the strength and endurance displayed by women before her (like Votti, Meer, Dr. Goonam, Chachalia, Naidoo) to effect change in a society that presents a series of multifaceted problems.

Notes

1 Women were subjugated based on both race and gender.
2 Enticing poor Indians to sign a contract of Indenture.
3 Whites, Coloureds, Indians and Africans.
4 A caste system is a form of social stratification.
5 SAIC was a political organization of Indian men who fought against the injustice of apartheid.
6 NIC a branch of the SAIC in Natal.
7 Black includes Africans, Indians and Coloureds.
8 Separate development of Whites, Coloureds, Indians and Africans.
9 Separate developments of Whites, Coloureds, Indians and Africans legitimised by the government of South Africa. The acts assigned racial groups to different residential and business sections in urban areas in a system of urban apartheid.
10 The Act legalized the racial segregation of public premises, vehicles and services. Only public roads and streets were excluded from the Act.
11 An informal group that contributes money into a pool every month, so that each member benefits from a larger sum of money.

References

Beall, J. (1990) Women Under Indentured Labour in Colonial Natal 1860–1911. In C. Walker, ed. *Women and Gender in Southern Africa to 1945*. Cape Town: David Philip, 147–167.
Carrim, N. (2012) "Who am I?" – South African Indian Women Managers' Struggle for Identity: Escaping the Ubiquitous Cage, Unpublished Doctoral Thesis, School of Industrial Psychology, University of Pretoria, South Africa.
Cooper, S. (1998) http://scnc.ukzn.ac.za/doc/B/Cs/Biography_Cs/COs/Cooper_Family_Politics_SASO/Cooper,Saths_and_Others.pdf (accessed on 11 November 2017).
Desai, A. and Vahed G. (2010) *Inside Indian Indenture: A South African Story 1860–1914*. Cape Town: HSRC Press.
Desai, A. and Vahed G. (2012) Indenture and Indianness in South Africa, 1860–1913. In S. Patel and T. Uys (eds.) *Legacies, Identities and Dilemmas: Understanding Contemporary India and South Africa*. India: Routledge.
Govinden, D. (2000) "Sister Outsiders" – The Representation of Identity and Difference in Selected Writings by South African Indian Women, Unpublished Doctoral Thesis, School of English, University of Natal, Durban, South Africa.
Karodia, F. (1986) *Daughters of the Twilight*. Ann Arbor, MI: Women's Press, University of Michigan.
Maharaj, B. (2012) Commemoration, Celebration or Commiseration? 150th Anniversary of Indentured Labourers in South Africa. In S. Patel and T. Uys (eds.) *Legacies, Identities and Dilemmas: Understanding Contemporary India and South Africa*. India: Routledge.
Meer, F. (1969). *Portrait of Indian South Africans*. Durban: Avon House.
Naidoo, P. (1990) *Waiting to Die in Pretoria*, Harare: P. Naidoo.
SAPA (2010) *Tributes Pour in for Fatima Meer*. Available at: https://www.timeslive.co.za/news/south-africa/2010-03-13-tributes-pour-in-for-fatima-meer/ (accessed 20 February 2018).
Seedat-Khan, M. (2012) Tracing the Journey of South African Indian Women from 1860. In S. Patel and T. Uys (eds.) *Legacies, Identities and Dilemmas: Understanding Contemporary India and South Africa*. India: Routledge.

South African History Online (2018) Fatima Meer Timeline. Available at: https://www.sahistory.org.za/topic/fatima-meer-timeline-1928-2010 (accessed 15 February 2018).

Vahed, G. H., Padayachee, V., & Desai, A. (2006) Beyond Apartheid: Race, Transformation and Governance in KwaZulu-Natal Cricket. *Transformation: Critical Perspectives on Southern Africa*, 61(1), 63–88.

Vally, R. (2012) 'Made in India, Proudly South African': Commemorating 150 Years of Indian Presence in South Africa. In S. Patel and T. Uys (eds.) *Legacies, Identities and Dilemmas: Understanding Contemporary India and South Africa*. India: Routledge.

Wajid, A. (2010) Fatima Meer: Academic and Activist. Available at: http://www.thehindu.com/opinion/op-ed/Fatima-Meer-academic-andactivist/article16634562.ece (accessed: 20 February, 2018).

Wells, J. (1993) *We Now Demand! The History of Women's Resistance to Pass Laws in South Africa*. Johannesburg: Witwatersrand University Press.

15
WORKERS, FAMILIES, AND HOUSEHOLDS

Towards a gendered, raced, and classed understanding of Indian transnationalism in Canada

Amrita Hari

Introduction

The Indo-Canadian diaspora consists of persons who can trace their histories to the territorial boundaries of a post-independence (1947) India, second- and third-generation Indians, as well as twice- or thrice-migrated persons of Indian origin (Singh and Singh 2008). India has been one of the top five source countries for Canada since at least 1980. After a long, complex, and arduous immigration application process, numerous health and criminal checks in India, a twenty-four-hour journey, biometric checks, and countless signatures in one of Canada's ports of entry, Indian newcomers are greeted with the "Welcome to Canada" sign. The sign, however, is deceptively simple.

The very formation of diaspora is largely dependent on resistance and/or barriers to assimilation, which become catalysts for political action (Singh and Singh 2008: 155). The Indo-Canadian diaspora has contributed to Canada's economic, social, cultural, and political fabrics; however, Indian immigrants to Canada have long struggled with Canada's racist past. In this chapter I discuss the more contemporary iterations of racist discrimination experienced by a particular group of Indian newcomers to Canada. Despite the prominence of Indians as transnational actors in Canada and the increasing politicization of the Indo-Canadian diaspora (Singh and Singh 2008; Singh 2006), newcomers are still subject to new iterations of Canada's racist past. To demonstrate this, I will discuss the gendered, raced, and classed negotiations that occur within Indian newcomer households, and among heterosexual partners, when managing the transition to the Canadian labour market and arranging childcare in a post-migratory context.

The particular group of Canadian newcomers under study arrived within the last decade, primarily through labour migration streams, as highly skilled professionals, aspiring to enter Canada's growing Information and Communications Technology (ICT) sector. The study included the narratives of forty-two heterosexual partnered immigrants of Indian origin. This group arrived in intact nuclear family units, with their spouses/partners and young or pre-school-aged children. A few participating families had a child soon after arrival. Participants were invited to describe in detail their dual transition into the labour market and parenthood.

Participants explained that their decision to migrate rested on the assumption that both partners would rebuild their professional lives in the new host country, Canada. On the contrary, they faced of a set of ongoing material conditions that resulted in greater gender inequality in the division of domestic labour after migrating. Analysis of semi-structured interviews with this group revealed experiences of racial discrimination in the Canadian labour market, which offset newcomers' career trajectories. Moreover, participants realized that their buying power is lower in Canada, which led to them take gender-typical paths to negotiate post-migratory gender roles and expectations of contributions to social reproduction.

Methodologically, in-depth semi-structured interviews fit well with the stated purpose of the study: to reveal the microcosm of household negotiations. In order to control for some degree of social desirability bias, all couples were interviewed separately but using the same interview guide. All participants were recruited from Canada's Technology Triangle (Waterloo Region, Ontario, Canada) using snowball sampling. The region attracts Indian immigrants looking to enter the growing and diverse technology sector. All participants were between 30 and 45 years of age; 24 had a Bachelor of Science or Bachelor of Engineering degree; and 18 had a Master of Science or Master of Business Administration degree. Twenty participants were working as computer/information technology engineers; 12 were computer/software programmers, eight were computer/software analysts; and two worked as systems testers. At the time of the interviews, ten couples had one pre-school age child, six couples had two pre-school age children, one couple had one pre-school age child and two school-age children, and four couples had no children.

All interviews, lasting between 60–90 minutes, were recorded and transcribed. The interview guide included both closed- and open-ended questions on demographic information, labour market experiences, resourcing childcare for pre-school-aged children, and the division of household work. Interviews were conducted at separate times in the participants' homes. The transcripts captured verbatim responses and were coded manually, using a grounded theory approach (Glaser and Strauss 1967). The codes reflected major topics covered in the interview schedule (to a point of data saturation). Pseudonyms were used to maintain anonymity and confidentiality.

The chapter proceeds in three sections towards its conclusion. In the next section I will discuss Canada's history of a systematic exclusion of Indian migration outside of restrictive labour streams. This is followed by a brief discussion of the shift of the dominant stream of Indian migration to Canada from predominantly family class[1] to a growing group of hi-tech professional migrants who arrive in intact family units. In the penultimate section I discuss the gendered, raced, and classed negotiations that occur among heterosexual partnered couples of Indian origin after arriving in Canada. The concluding section provides an overview of the existing and ongoing research on the Indo-Canadian diaspora and provides some directions for future research.

A racist history of Indian labour migration to Canada

The complex colonial relationships between Britain, India, and Canada contributed to a long history of Indian labourers migrating to Canada to fill critical labour shortages. Indian migrants, primarily from the Punjab region, arrived in the late nineteenth century to contribute to Canada's resource economy (logging, agriculture, and railroads). They traveled with the British Army or worked their way through Chinese and Japanese ports as merchant sailors (Buchignani 1977). Their arrival was met with largely unfounded fears expressed by the local white community over competition for the supposedly limited number of jobs in factories, mills, and lumberyards (Singh and Singh 2008).

The growing anti-immigrant sentiment resulted in a number of discriminatory government policies, including the Continuous Journey Regulation in 1908, which forced passenger ships to make a single continuous trip from port of departure to the port of arrival. Given geographical constraints, this regulation categorically stopped immigration between India and Canada. The arrival of the Komagata Maru in 1914, a chartered Japanese passenger ship carrying 376 Indian immigrants that was denied entry, was a critical moment in Canada's racist past and simultaneously a pivotal event for political organization within the Indian diaspora in Canada (Singh and Singh 2008).

In general, Canadian immigration laws from 1885 until 1962 were explicitly racist in both wording and intent. Immigration and citizenship policies were specifically designed to prohibit non-white and non-European migration to build a preferred Canadian identity as a white British settler colony in demographic, cultural, and institutional terms (Abu-Laban 1998; Kelley and Trebilock 1998). In addition to the single-continuous-journey requirement mentioned above, the 1885 Chinese Immigration Act (placing a head tax exclusively on Chinese immigrants) and the 1906 Immigration Act permitted the government to effectively prohibit the landing of any immigrant group construed as not belonging to the white European settler nation-state. As a result, this early group of Indian migrants was categorically denied permanent settlement and resided primarily in "bachelor communities."

Until the early 1990s, Indians arrived primarily through the family class category in compliance with the Canadian government's family reunification measures. A small number of Indian women and children were admitted to Canada between the 1920s and 1930s to compensate for historically racist immigration policies, which restricted the entry of accompanying family in fear of threats to the White-European identity. Family class includes a variety of sub-categories; however, the most significant components are spouses and parents. The limited allowances made for family reunification were exclusive to those with existing familial and kinship links. Additionally, the majority of the then-newcomer women were restricted to working in the home. The family sponsorship process was integral to the formation of the Indo-Canadian diaspora and provided a mechanism to reconstitute extended family (Walton-Roberts 2003). As a result of these policies, there were no opportunities for non-family class migration from India. Overall, entries were further restricted by the quota system implemented in 1951, placing limits on all arrivals to Canada.

Declining fertility rates and growing labour shortages in the post-World War II period in Canada led to three significant immigration policy changes, which made it possible for independent-class Indian migration to Canada, including refugee claimants and professional immigrants. In addition, India's independence from British colonial rule in 1947 led to a re-enfranchisement of Indians in Canada (Singh and Singh 2008). First, the long-standing system of European preference was revoked in 1962. Second, the 1966 White Paper on Immigration, under the Liberal Pearson government, proposed the development of a more universally applicable framework to determine admissibility to Canadian territory and nationhood. The Points System, implemented in 1967, led to a more objective assessment of the admissibility of applicants for permanent residency regardless of their place of origin or their ethnocultural similarities to the dominant construction of a White-European Canada. Third, in 1978 the Liberal Trudeau government allowed for refugee class admissions.

These policy changes in effect replaced the historical Indian "bachelor communities" with primarily economic immigrants arriving from India as intact nuclear family units – with spouses, common-law/conjugal partners, and children not requiring separate family sponsorship – to settle permanently in Canada. By the 1960s and 1970s, there was a significant rise in the number of skilled Indian immigrants to Canada. Several scholars have tracked the evolution of Indian settlement in Canada (Buchignani, Indira and Srivastiva 1985; Sharma 1997). The percentage of economic migrants from India as compared to the total number of Indian immigrants has grown from 18.1 percent in 1981 to 55.4 percent in 2009 and the percentage of Indian immigrants arriving through the family class has dropped from 81.5 percent in 1981 to 41.7 percent in 2009. Indian immigrant women, however, continue to be admitted primarily as dependents: spouses, parents/grandparents, or elderly dependents of skilled Indian immigrant men (Walton-Roberts 2004). Despite the broad strokes that statistics can provide, scholars have discussed the connectivity and complexity that permeates all Indian immigration classes in Canada (Walton-Roberts 2003). These connections complicate the simple imaginaries of separateness to show that the Indo-Canadian diaspora is constitutive of various migratory trajectories, which are intimately linked.

A new class of Indian hi-tech migrants

Canada–India bilateral relations were revived as India, in the early 1990s, implemented a series of privatization and deregulation measures. Simultaneously, India developed itself as the preferred destination to outsource a large share of global trade in software services. In particular, the deregulation of telecommunications in 2000 led to a rise in Indian software vendors offering competitive low prices to global and transnational businesses (Arora et al. 2001; Khadria 2001; Dossani and Kenney 2009). The highly successful ICT-Business Process Outsourcing (BPO) sector allowed India to capture a growing share of the global exchanges of software services. India soon became the first offshoring stop for global, transnational, and multinational businesses. Indian workers could provide these services at a low-cost advantage, and the Indian environment became a financially attractive location for foreign direct investments.

Although India's share of global software market revenues of more than US$ 300–500 billion in 1999–2002 is still a tiny fraction (US$ 5.7 billion), India attracts a disproportionate share of interest as a source of software (Arora et al. 2001). At the same time, India invested in a national vocational framework to train a new class of technology professionals (Saxenian 2002). The supply of low-cost software professionals is believed to be the key to India's success and dominance within its borders and in providing software services globally. Scholars of Indian mobility and modernity have shown that the pre-migration context (India) is dynamic; it is rapidly changing with increasingly neoliberal and global trends (Oza 2006; Radhakrishnan 2011).

The ICT downturn in 2001 and the United States' growing restrictive settlement and naturalization polices contributed to Indian IT workers looking for newer destinations (Xiang 2007). In recognition of India's growing reputation as a global player in software and ICT services, Canada conducted three separate missions to capture India's attention: Finance Minister Roy MacClarenin 1992, Secretary of State for Asia Raymond Chan in 1994, and the Team Canada delegation in 1996. The final mission, led by Prime Minister Jean Chretien, included several business stakeholders, provincial premiers, and trade officials intent on growing the Indo-Canadian business and professional communities (Singh and Singh 2008). As a result, more immigrants work in ICT and related occupations than any other sector in Canada (Habtu 2003). Overall, two countries contribute a disproportionate number of foreign-born and trained technology professionals: India and China (ICTC 2011).

Gendered, classed, and raced negotiations in a post-migratory context

Gender exerts a powerful influence on migration processes (Willis and Yeoh 2000), yet research that employs a transnational framework often inadequately considers the structuring effects of gender (Mahler and Pessar 2006). Several scholars in areas of migration and diaspora studies have noted the racist and sexist tendencies of migration policy (Hari 2014; Knowles 1997; Laquian, Laquian, and McGee 1997; Ralston 1994); there is little work on specific transnational migratory networks from an explicitly gender perspective, however (Walton-Roberts 2004). Transnational social spaces, consisting of "a combination of ties and their contents, positions in networks and organizations, and networks of organizations" can only form when there is long-distance communication and travel (Ghosh 2007: 220). These spaces facilitate an exchange of social and symbolic capital and ties: "a continuing series of interpersonal transactions to which participants attach shared interests, obligations, expectations, and norms" (Faist 2000: 101). Migrant Indian families maintain their transnational nature through new communication technologies and more affordable travel that helps to keep the immediacy of family relationships alive across borders (Ghosh 2007).

Indian women's increased mobility and engagement with paid labour outside the home has the potential to complicate narratives of modernity and in turn challenge gender hierarchies (Walton-Roberts 2015). Migration does not necessarily erase traditional gender norms and relations; it does have the potential to transform and reshape gender roles and expectations in a post-migratory context. Patterns of support and care are expressed through different arrangements across time (Singh 2006). The transnational Indian family and the emergence of a special kind of transnational money has meant that Indian women do not have to choose between paid work and childcare even when they continue to bear the additional burden of social reproduction. While in India, there are various childcare arrangements that aid the continuation of paid work, including servants, relatives or a mix of relatives and a part-time servant (Singh 2006: 383). This study sought to explore how gender roles and expectations are transformed and reshaped in the Canadian context, where participants are losing specific household and childcare arrangements, which were more readily available and affordable in India.

Scaling-back and restructuring career commitments

Compared to the attainments of Canadian-born and educated workers with similar qualifications and experience, foreign-trained professionals tend to have lower incomes and higher levels of unemployment and underemployment (Bauder 2006; Hum and Simpson 1999). Academics perplexed by this paradox have attributed skilled immigrants' higher levels of unemployment and underemployment (both in terms of skills utilization and involuntary part-time) to the complex interactions of several related factors. These factors include the non-recognition of foreign qualifications and experience, perceived linguistic abilities or a foreign accent, cultural stereotypes and discrimination based on different social characteristics, in particular, race, ethnicity, skin colour, gender, and age. These factors are evaluated and associated with penalties in the labour market (Bauder 2006; McDowell 2009; Wills et al. 2009). Despite having relevant skills and work experience, many skilled immigrants suffer from deskilling, occupational downgrading, and loss of previous labour-market position and social status (Man 2004). The discriminatory effects are more acute for immigrants entering regulated occupations such as medicine, healthcare, engineering, and law. The onus is placed on immigrants to integrate, conform, and assimilate to the economy and wider society.

Participant narratives confirmed the persistence of labour-market struggles for skilled newcomers. However, India's reputation, success, and dominance in the global ICT sector resulted in participants who were trained in the technology fields to circumvent the permanent effects of marginalization and exclusion suggested in previous Canadian studies (Hari 2013). Despite this positive trend, a significant gendered pattern of labour-market participation emerged: couples negotiated and placed limits on female partners' career progression. Scholars have discussed scaling-back strategies employed by couples to manage career progression over the life course, often involving investing in two careers at different life stages (Becker and Moen 1999; Moen and Yu 2000). These strategies predominantly align with conventional gender roles whereby men retain a career focus and women focus on social reproduction. This staged progression affects women's occupational outcomes to a greater extent and promotes a vicious cycle whereby women continue to disproportionately scale back to balance work, family, and the household budget.

Such decisions are not without emotional and economic costs. Participants in my study described this gender-typical path: upon arrival in Canada, both men and women sought to enter the labour market but came up against two significant barriers. First, as discussed above, participants faced barriers to labour-market entry; second, there was a lack of available, accessible, and affordable childcare. In cases where both partners secured any type of employment, women were often paid less or not enough to cover the costs associated with non-parental childcare; therefore, they were also more likely to opt out of the labour market and assume full-time responsibility for the household and childcare. The long periods spent outside the labour market also made them less competitive when looking for opportunities at a later stage. Most newcomer families initially adopted a male breadwinner–female caregiver model or, in some cases, a one-career–one-job strategy, with women engaged in paid (often minimum wage survival jobs) or volunteer work on a part-time basis. These negotiations were dynamic, and the majority of families aspired to a two-career marriage.

Gendered negotiations of childcare within transnational families

Just as gender is a powerful influence on migration and post-migratory labour practices, feminist scholars established gender as the dominant system of social relations, shaping the organization of reproductive work (Graham, 1991). Resourcing care through mainly informal means and through marriage and kinship relationships reproduced women's disadvantaged position within marriage, the labour market, and the social security system. This informal organization of care reinforced a gendered division of labour, (re)producing and maintaining women's disproportionate responsibility for the day-to-day work of keeping families going (Graham, 1993; Hawkins et al. 1993, 1994; Tuominen, 1994).

A legacy of these contributions is that the household remains a critical realm for the study of the persistence of gender inequality by using the gendered division of household labour (childcare and domestic work) as a proxy measure. The household is broadly defined as a unit of co-residence, characterized by members who are usually but not exclusively related by blood or a conjugal relationship, and designated by certain functions toward the wellbeing of its members. The definition of a household has become less stable with the increase in global migrations and persons living transnationally. Processes of migration and transnationalism have complicated household arrangements and the resourcing of care. As a result, earlier theorizations of women's disadvantaged position within marriage, the labour market, and the social welfare system came into question with the feminization of migration.

The earliest studies of the intersection of gender, migration, and caring/motherhood emerged in the 1980s, through to the 1990s, focusing primarily on the experiences of Jewish, Italian (Foner 1998), Latin American (Hondagneu-Sotelo 1992), Caribbean (Grasmuck and Pessar 1991; Pessar 1984, 1995), and Asian (Kibria 1993; Lim 1997; Min 1992, 1998) immigrant working mothers in the United States. A common observation in all these studies on immigrant families in North America is that men's declining contributions to the family economy after migrating to a new host country (primarily as a result of a decline in manufacturing and a shift towards service economies) constructed a need for wives, who did not engage in labour markets in their home countries, to participate in waged work out of economic necessity. Migration changes women's status in complex and contradictory ways – for better and for worse (Foner 1998).

Women's incorporation into the workforce enhances their sense of economic independence with their regular access to wages (Pessar 1984, 1995), improving their position in the household and broadening their social horizons. Childcare constraints, however, often limit women to low-paid jobs with flexible schedules, preserving and in some ways intensifying gendered divisions of childcare and housework (Foner 1998; Grahame 2003; Greenlees and Saenz 1999; Min 1992; Moon 2003). Studies on Asian middle-class professional migrant women in the U.S. found that wives continue to cope with the double burden of combining waged and reproductive work, doing a greater share of both childcare and housework (Min 1992, 1998; Moon 2003). A significant difference between migrant women in the earlier studies in the American context and the Indian women in my study is that my participants were engaged in productive work prior to their migration to Canada. Whilst in India, both partners had worked full time, sharing their caring duties with extended family members and paid domestic help, who generally lived in the same household or within small distances.

In Canada, participants' childcare arrangements were influenced by employment status, combined incomes, working hours, access to information about childcare options, previous experiences with childcare centers in the region, the availability of childcare spaces, the age of children, and the ability and willingness of extended families living in India to provide support. All families were faced with a care deficit in Canada and chose different combinations of four main strategies (Hari 2015). The first strategy was working opposite shifts at work and home, ensuring an even division between productive and reproductive work for each adult. This arrangement was only used for one year or less; all families transitioned to a different arrangement as soon as possible. Second, a small number of families used government-sponsored, not-for-profit or for-profit centre-based childcare spaces. Although this was the preferred option, most families had to contend with three main challenges: accessibility due to long wait lists; affordability, as most of the families were not eligible for needs-based subsidies; and, finally, difficulties in negotiating the centres' hours of operation with the work schedules of both parents. The third and most common strategy was the use of unregulated home-based day cares. These spaces were more easily available than the previous option, less expensive, and with more flexible hours of operation; however, these spaces were often unregistered and unregulated. Most families relied on social networks to identify reliable and trustworthy home-based childcare options.

Only a few families employed the fourth strategy: intergenerational transnational care arrangements. These families sent children to live with their grandparents in India or brought their elderly parents to care for their grandchildren in Canada on a visitor or tourist visa. There is scholarship and policy that recognizes such forms of transnational care (Baldassar 2007; Phua and Kaufman 2008; Treas 2008; Treas and Mazumdar 2004). In 2011 Canada introduced the Parent and Grandparent Super Visa, meeting its national objective of family reunification while also providing up to ten years of multiple-entry (CIC 2012; Hari 2015). In general, there is a rise in the numbers of transnational, globalized, and flexible families who both maintain a sense of family connections across national borders and also provide transnational intergenerational support. Canada is not an exception to this growing trend.

When it came to negotiating non-parental and non-familial childcare arrangements, all participants emphasized the limited options available to them; however, women were also more likely to express feelings of guilt and disappointment. In all households except one, women continue to undertake the role of organizer and manager, bearing the "triple burden" of worker, manager of the multiple demands of all members of the family, and primary care provider (Skinner 2005). Secondly, immigrant families' childcare arrangements are flexible and open to negotiation and re-evaluation over time. Arrangements changed in relation to different combinations of internal and external constraints. These constraints included the levels of actual and potential family income, gender ideologies of both adults in the family, the lack of coordinated support from partners, stated preferences to "be there" for their children (generally expressed by women), intergenerational transnational relationships, and the age of the children, especially as the cost and hours of non-parental care needed is indirectly proportional to the age of the child. All families relied on a web of social networks and multiple forms of care to complement inadequate market-based provision (as a result of challenges of affordability, accessibility, and conflicts between work hours and hours of operations of centres). These constraints contributed to the construction of a complex "childcare jigsaw" (a term borrowed from Skinner 2005).

In summary, the restrictive and limited public support for childcare and other forms of reproductive work under the Canadian liberal welfare state means that the majority of childcare spaces are based on market delivery and also shaped by the social and economic circumstances of the family. Moreover, Indian newcomers are contending with restricted entry to Canadian labour markets, thereby adopting gender-typical paths by scaling back women's career progression. The cumulative effect of both factors is that immigrant women are disproportionately affected, perpetuating a gendered division of productive and reproductive work. This is not because Indian newcomers are becoming less modern, more conservative, or more traditional than when they were in India; rather, all adults in the household are working harder, earning more, and contributing more to the household than when they were in India (Hari 2018).

Concluding remarks and future directions

In this chapter I have discussed both historical and contemporary contributors to Indian transnationalism in Canada and briefly discussed the patterns of migration, immigration, and settlement that contributed to the formation of the Indian diaspora in Canada. This Indo-Canadian diaspora has grown considerably in size from the early "bachelor communities" to the expansive communities across the country (Ghosh 2007). There are town such as Brampton, Ontario, and Surrey, British Columbia, which reflect the strong culture and influence of the Indo-Canadian diaspora. In addition, the diaspora has continued a long traditional of political organizing, beginning with protests against the denial of entry of the Komagata Maru (Singh and Singh 2008) to current Indo-Canadian activists addressing gender- and sexual-based violence (Kang 2006) and the election of Jagmeet Singh as the current leader of the National Democratic Party.

Current research on the Indo-Canadian diaspora includes a variety of lines of inquiry. Activists and scholars have discussed the ways in which Indian immigrant women face a double threat on the basis of gender/sex as well as national origin and insecure migration status.

A few scholars have also studied gendered labour migration streams (e.g., Indian nurses) (George 2006) and also streams associated with familial, kinship, and marital ties (Walton-Roberts 2003, 2004). In the study informing this chapter, the relative success of Indian ICT immigrants in circumventing persistent labour market disadvantages and management of a childcare jigsaw does not minimize the concerns with contemporary iterations of Canada's racist past. Instead, it is demonstrative of the agency, creativity, and resilience of the growing Indo-Canadian diaspora. The dedicated scholarship and activism have come to demonstrate the heterogeneity of the growing and active Indo-Canadian diaspora.

There is still more to be known about Indian transnationalism and transnational connections that spans over time and in diverse locations. South Asians or Indo-Canadians in Canada, however, suffer from a problem of overgeneralization, and there is a need for future studies to challenge the validity of the homogenous identities and associated experiences ascribed to this group. Examinations of migration and settlement patterns, labour-market trajectories, strengths and types of transnational ties, and transnational spaces should distinguish by region, religion, caste, languages spoken, and stream of admission to Canada.

Note

1 "Family class" can include spouses, common-law or conjugal partners, dependent children, parents, grandparents, or sibling, nephew, niece, or grandchild under 18 years who is unmarried and whose parents are deceased. In this research, intact family units imply the nuclear family (spouse, common-law or conjugal partner, and dependent children only).

References

Abu-Laban, Yasmeen. 1998. "Welcome/Stay Out: The Contradiction of Canadian Integration and Immigration Policies at the Millennium." *Canadian Ethnic Studies Journal* 30(3):190–211.

Arora, Ashish, V.S. Arunachalam, Jai Asundi, and Ronald Fernandes. 2001. "The Indian Software Services Industry." *Research Policy* 30(8):1267–1287.

Baldassar, Loretta. 2007. "Transnational Families and the Provision of Moral and Emotional Support: The Relationship between Truth and Distance." *Identities* 14(4):385–409.

Bauder, Harald. 2006. *Labor Movement: How Migration Regulates Labor Markets*. New York, NY: Oxford University Press.

Becker, Penny Edgell, and Phyllis Moen. 1999. "Scaling Back: Dual-Earner Couples' Work-Family Strategies." *Journal of Marriage and Family* 61(4):995–1007.

Buchignani, Norman. 1977. "A Review of Historical and Sociological Literature on East Indians in Canada." *Canadian Ethnic Studies* 9(1):86–108.

Buchignani, Norman, Doreen Indira, and Ram Srivastiva. 1985. *Continuous Journey: A Social History of South Asians in Canada*. Toronto, ON: McClelland & Stewart.

Citizenship and Immigration Canada (CIC). 2012. "News Release: Parent and Grandparent Super Visa a Great Success." Accessed May 23. http://www.cic.gc.ca/english/department/media/releases/2012/2012-05-18.asp.

Dossani, Rafiq, and Martin Kenney. 2009. "Service Provision for the Global Economy: The Evolving Indian Experience." *Review of Policy Research* 26(1–2):77–104.

Faist, Thomas. 2000. *The Volume and Dynamics of International Migration and Transnational Social Spaces*. Oxford, UK: Clarendon Press.

Foner, Nancy. 1998. "Benefits and Burdens: Immigrant Women and Work in New York City." *Gender Issues* 16(4):5–24.

George, Sheba Mariam. 2006. *When Women Come First: Gender and Class in Transnational Migration*. Berkeley, CA: University of California Press.

Ghosh, Sutama. 2007. "Transnational Ties and Intra-Immigrant Group Settlement Experiences: A Case Study of Indian Bengalis and Bangladeshis in Toronto." *GeoJournal* 68(2–3):223–242.

Glaser, Barney G., and Anselm L. Strauss. 1967. *The Discovery of Grounded Theory: Strategies for Qualitative Research*. Chicago, IL: Aldine.

Graham, Hilary. 1991. "The Concept of Caring in Feminist Research: The Case of Domestic Service." *Sociology* 25(1):61–78.

———. 1993. "Social Divisions in Caring." *Women's Studies International Forum* 16(5):461–470.

Grahame, Kamini Maraj. 2003. "'For the Family': Asian Immigrant Women's Triple Day." *Journal of Sociology and Social Welfare* 30(1):65–90.

Grasmuck, Sherri, and Patricia R. Pessar. 1991. *Between Two Islands: Dominican International Migration*. Berkeley, CA: University of California Press.

Greenlees, Clyde S., and Rogelio Saenz. 1999. "Determinants of Employment of Recently Arrived Mexican Immigrant Wives." *International Migration Review* 33(2):354–377.

Habtu, Roman. 2003. "Information Technology Workers." *Perspectives* July (Catalogue No. 75–001 XIE):5–11.

Hari, Amrita. 2013. "Foot in the Door or Double-Edged Sword: The Construction of Indian Hi-Tech Immigrants in Canada's Technology Triangle." *Journal of South Asian Diaspora* 5(2):197–210.

———. 2014. "Temporariness, Rights and Citizenship: The Latest Chapter in Canada's Exclusionary Migration and Refugee Policy." *Refuge: Canada's Journal on Refugees* 30(2):35–44.

———. 2015. "Intergenerational and Transnational Familyhood in Canada's Technology Triangle". In *Engendering Transnational Voices: Studies in Family, Work, and Identity*, edited by Dr. Guida C. Man and Dr. Rina Cohen. Waterloo: Wilfrid Laurier University Press. (pp. 53–74.)

———. 2018. "'Someone Kept Sacrificing': Disentangling Gender Ideology in Immigrant Narratives of Social Reproduction." *Signs: Journal of Women in Culture and Society* 43(3):1–24.

Hawkins, Alan J., Shawn L. Christiansen, Kathryn Pond Sargent, and E. Jeffrey Hill. 1993. "Rethinking Fathers' Involvement in Child Care: A Developmental Perspective." *Journal of Family Issues* 14(4):531–549.

Hawkins, Alan J., Tomi-Ann Roberts, Christina M. Marshall, and Shawn L. Christiansen. 1994. "An Evaluation of a Program to Help Dual-Earner Couples Share the Second Shift." *Family Relations* 43(2):213–220.

Hondagneu-Sotelo, Pierette. 1992. "Overcoming Patriarchal Constraints: The Reconstruction of Gender Relations among Mexican Immigrant Women and Men." *Gender & Society* 6(3):393–415.

Hum, Derek, and Wayne Simpson. 1999. "Wage Opportunities for Visible Minorities in Canada." *Canadian Public Policy* 25(3):379–394.

Information and Communications Technology Council (ICTC). 2011. Outlook for Human Resources in the ICT Labour Market, 2011–2016 [online]. Ottawa: ICTC. Available from http://www.ictc-ctic.ca/Outlook_2011/index_en.html [Accessed October 5 2011].

Kang, Neelu. 2006. "Women Activists in Indian Diaspora: Making Interventions and Challenging Impediments." *South Asia Research* 26(2):145–164.

Kelley, Ninette, and Michael Trebilock. 1998. *The Making of the Mosaic: A History of Canadian Immigration Policy*. Toronto, ON: University of Toronto Press.

Khadria, Binod. 2001. "Shifting Paradigms of Globalisation: The Twenty-First Century Transition towards Generics in Skilled Migration from India." *International Migration* 39(5):45–69.

Kibria, Nazli. 1993. *Family Tightrope: The Changing Lives of Vietnamese Americans*. Princeton, NJ: Princeton University Press.

Knowles, Valerie. 1997. *Stranger at our Gates: Canadian Citizenship and Immigration Policy 1540–1997*. Toronto, ON: Dundurn Press.

Laquian, Eleanor R., Aprodicio Laquian, and Terry McGee (eds.). 1997. *The Silent Debate: Asian Immigration and Racism in Canada*. Vancouver, BC: Institute of Asian Research, University of British Columbia.

Lim, In-Sook. 1997. "Korean Immigrant Women's Challenge to Gender Inequality at Home: The Interplay of Economic Resources, Gender, and Family." *Gender & Society* 11(1):31–51.

Mahler, Sarah J., and Patricia R. Pessar. 2006. "Gender Matters: Ethnographers Bring Gender from the Periphery toward the Core of Migration Studies." *International Migration Review* 49(1):27–63.

Man, Guida. 2004. "Gender, Work and Migration: Deskilling Chinese Immigrant Women in Canada." *Women's Studies International Forum* 27(2):135–148.

McDowell, Linda. 2009. *Working Bodies: Interactive Service Employment and Workplace Identities*. Chichester: Wiley-Blackwell.

Min, Pyong Gap. 1992. "Korean Immigrant Wives' Overwork." *Korea Journal of Population and Development* 21(1):23–36.

———. 1998. *Changes and Conflicts: Korean Immigrant Families in New York*. Boston, MA: Allyn & Bacon.

Moen, Phyllis, and Yan Yu. 2000. "Effective Work/Life Strategies: Working Couples, Work Conditions, Gender and Life Quality." *Social Problems* 47(3):291–326.

Moon, Seungsook. 2003. "Immigration and Mothering: Case Studies from Two Generations of Korean Immigrant Women." *Gender & Society* 17(6):840–860.

Oza, Rupal. 2006. *The Making of Neoliberal India: Nationalism, Gender, and the Paradoxes of Globalization*. Abingdon, Oxon: Routledge.

Pessar, Patricia R. 1984. "The Linkage between the Household and Workplace of Dominican Women in the United States." *International Migration Review* 18(4):1188–1211.

———. 1995. "On the Home Front and in the Workplace: Integrating Immigrant Women into Feminist Discourse." *Anthropological Quarterly* 68(1):37–47.

Phua, Voon Chin, and Gayle Kaufman. 2008. "Grandparenting Responsibility among Elderly Asian Americans." *Journal of Intergenerational Relationships* 6(1):41–59.

Radhakrishnan, Smitha. 2011. *Appropriately Indian: Gender and Culture in a New Transnational Class*. Durham, NC: Duke University Press.

Ralston, Helen. 1994. "Immigration Policies and Practices: Their Impact on South Asian Women in Canada and Australia." *Australian-Canadian Studies* 12(1):1–47.

Saxenian, Annalee. 2002. "Transnational Communities and the Evolution of Global Production Networks: The Cases of Taiwan, China and India." *Industry and Innovation* 9(3):183–202.

Sharma, Kavita A. 1997. *The Ongoing Journey: Indian Migration to Canada*. New Delhi: Creative Books.

Singh, Milan, and Anita Singh. 2008. "Diaspora, Political Action, and Identity: A Case Study of Canada's Indian Diaspora." *Diaspora: A Journal of Transnational Studies* 17(2):149–171.

Singh, Supriya. 2006. "Towards a Sociology of Money and Family in the Indian Diaspora." *Contributions to Indian Sociology* 40(3):375–398.

Skinner, Christine. (2005). "Coordination Points: A Hidden Factor in Reconciling Work and Family Life." *Journal of Social Policy* 34(1):99–119.

Treas, Judith. 2008. "Transnational Older Adults and Their Families." *Family Relations* 57(4):468–478.

Treas, Judith, and Shampa Mazumdar. 2004. "Kinkeeping and Caregiving: Contributions of Older People to America's Immigrant Families." *Journal of Comparative Family Studies* 35(1):105–122.

Tuominen, Mary. 1994. "The Hidden Organization of Labor: Gender, Race/Ethnicity and Child-Care Work in the Formal and Informal Economy." *Sociological Perspectives* 37(2):229–245.

Walton-Roberts, Margaret. 2003. "Transnational Geographies: Indian Immigration to Canada." *The Canadian Geographer* 47(3):235–250.

———. 2004. "Transnational Migration Theory in Population Geography: Gendered Networks of Practices Linking Canada and India." *Population, Space and Place* 10:361–373.

———. 2015. "Femininity, Mobility and Family Fears: Indian International Student Migration and Transnational Parental Control." *Journal of Cultural Geography* 32(1):68–82.

Wills, Jane, Kavita Datta, Yara Evans, Joanna Herbert, John June, and Cathy McIlwane. 2009. *Global Cities at Work: New Migrant Divisions of Labour*. London: Pluto Press.

Willis, Katie, and Brenda Yeoh (eds.). 2000. *Gender and Migration. The International Library of Studies on Migration Series*. Cheltenham: Edward Elgar Publishing.

Xiang, Biao. 2007. *Global "Body Shopping": An Indian Labour System in the Information Technology Industry*. Princeton, NJ: Princeton University Press.

16
IS MIGRATION A TICKET TO FREEDOM?

Exploring sense of freedom among Indian women in Toronto

Sutama Ghosh

Since the mid-1980s, several Indian women novelists have enriched mainstream English literature with stories of educated middle-class Indian women migrating to and settling in North America – a predominantly white patriarchal landscape (Razack 2002). Like the authors themselves, the protagonists had permanently migrated to the U.S. or Canada as dependants of a male family member[1] in the latter half of the twentieth century. In the process of making North America home – the Kaminis, Taras, and Ashimas – challenged various aspects of "race" – and gender-related subjugations and, ultimately, "gladly renounce[d] security within the confines of four walls to walk the path of freedom" (Das Dasgupta 1998). For them, migration is integrally tied to achieving "freedom" – *freedom from* the gender and sexual norms of home and the homeland.

In her recent feature film titled *English Vinglish* (2012; see Balki 2013), Gauri Shinde adds another dimension to this story: transnationalism. In the movie, Shashi (based on Shinde's mother's experiences) is an educated middle-class heterosexual Indian mother living in India. Often ridiculed by her family for not being able to speak in English, she lacks self-confidence. Life, however, presents her with an opportunity to travel alone to New York to help her sister prepare for her niece's wedding. Upon her arrival in the U.S., Shashi enrols herself into an ESL crash course, but keeps it a secret from her husband and children (with whom she is in frequent contact by phone) as well as her sister in New York. Within a few weeks, Shashi learns to converse in English, earns respect from the teacher and her fellow classmates, and develops affections for a French chef who also happens to be her classmate.[2] In the meantime, her husband and children also arrive in New York. This is when her familial obligations create unsurmountable barriers for Shashi to continue with her ESL course, and she is unable to appear for the final exam. The film ends on a "feel good" note, however, as, despite all her troubles, Shashi proves herself by delivering a speech in English at the wedding. By correlating with the novels mentioned earlier, *English Vinglish* adds an important dimension to the existing narrative by demonstrating that even a temporary sojourn (e.g., as a visitor) can provide an educated middle-class married Indian woman with an opportunity to experience 'freedom' and self-worth.

It has been widely recognised that stories penned by immigrants themselves are an extremely powerful tool in developing a wholistic and nuanced understanding of their settlement experiences. This is primarily because being able to tell their own stories enables "the objectified others to turn into subjects of [their own] history and experience" (Bhabha 1994). While this may be true for the novels and the film mentioned above, the immediate association between "freedom" and migration perhaps needs a thorough examination.

The academic literature does not seem to question whether migration necessarily leads to freedom for women in general, and Indian women more particularly. Concerning the general population, the migration literature recognises that forced migration (e.g., of refugees) is not always a good thing, as it may often cause family fractures; however, the effects of migration by choice (e.g., of economic migrants) remains unquestioned. While research on the migration and settlement experiences of Indian women is more abundant in the U.S., it is particularly scarce in the Canadian context.[3] In Canada, although there is some research on feminization of migration of professionals (e.g., Walton-Roberts and Hennebry 2012), most policy makers and academics seem to be preoccupied with their settlement processes.[4] Canadian studies on immigrant women from South Asia more generally have demonstrated that women not only leave but also enter gendered societies, gender-segregated labour markets, and gendered immigration policies (e.g., Silvey 2004; Sheel 2005; Dyck and Dossa 2007; Bastia, Piper, and Prieto Carrón 2011; Das Gupta et al. 2014; Maitra 2018). While the security of the domestic space is variously destabilised by violence, the path outside often presents itself as an intricate and complex labyrinth that presents agents and institutions of malevolence for many women navigating it (Hari 2018; Walton-Roberts and Pratt 2005).

Beyond this overwhelming narrative, there is also an emergent trend. First, recent studies have found that many Indian women are now arriving alone as independent professionals (e.g., Walton-Roberts and Hennebry 2012; Sangha and Gonsalves 2013). Also, even if they arrive as spousal dependants, the Canadian immigration policy now guarantees[5] that those who have come to Canada since the mid-1990s embody a specific human capital – they are of working age, with university degrees and related work experiences, and fluency in English.[6] Therefore it is not surprising that not only the structure but also the individuals themselves expect to fully participate in the Canadian economy and integrate socially. Some studies have further highlighted that, unlike some of the characters in the novels who were shaky about their imminent immigrant life and felt unmoored, the more recent arrivals have strong pre- and post-migration transnational connections (Ghosh 2007, 2014).[7] As a result, at the time of starting a new life in Canada, they are empowered with detailed knowledge about Canadian life and, after arrival, are able to retain their familial and social connections. Finally, research has further demonstrated that, despite the barriers they face in Canada, many women are able to challenge the "social constructions of work and family as separate spheres" (Collins 1994: 47) and are often the most crucial fulcrum in the lives of their spouses and children (Maitra 2018). In light of these findings, it is quite possible that, in comparison to the protagonists in the novels, the more recently arrived Indian women may have specific personal and familial aspirations associated with migration that can influence their understanding of "freedom" differently.

Questioning whether international migration necessarily leads to "freedom" for this cohort of Indian women, it was also evident that perhaps their histories and experiences of subjugation and emancipation are not necessarily in binary opposition, and that there may be a space for multiplicity (Butler 2004). From that perspective, this paper seeks to understand two interrelated issues: (1) How do young educated working middle-class Indian women living in Toronto conceptualise "freedom" – what does "freedom" mean to them?; and (2) Have they achieved "freedom" by migrating to Canada/Toronto, and if so, what is the geography of their freedom – where (space) and when (time) do they feel free – at home, work, or places of socialization? In the next section of the paper, I first explore the meaning of "freedom," following the French philosopher Henri Bergson. Following that I argue that, because the act of being free is geographically contextual, to understand the experiences of this specific cohort of Indian women, it is important to visit the concept of the transnational habitus. Finally, I attempt to unwrap the geography freedom by focussing on the literature concerning "home/inside" and "out of home/outside".

Freedom and the transnational habitus

In conceptualising freedom, Bergson (1889, 1896) argues that freedom cannot be defined easily. Bergson (1889) conceptualised freedom as a *freedom to act*. Finding the deterministic and libertarian conceptualization of "act" problematic,[8] Bergson (1889: 172) stated that the psychology of the subject changes while performing acts. This change, however, may not be quantifiable but, rather, should be understood qualitatively. Secondly, even when a subject is forced to perform a certain way (e.g., when another person's will is imposed upon her), she functions through "fusion and interpretation". Meaning that her acts are not just in response to the current cause but, rather, are born out of her previous experiences. Thirdly, acts are both spatial and temporal in nature. Acts are not only performed in current space and time but also are affected by previous experiences in space and time. In Bergson's view, "we are free when our acts spring from our whole personality . . . which one *sometimes* [emphasis added] finds between the artist and his work" (Grosz 2010: 146) – i.e., freedom is an exception rather than the rule, because the extent to which a subject has the freedom to act depends on the autonomy the subject possesses in specific contexts.

Elizabeth Grosz (2010) argues that, even though concepts of autonomy, agency, and freedom are often evoked in feminist theory to understand subjectivity, these terminologies have not been adequately defined, explained, or analysed. Instead, the concept has functioned "as a kind of mantra of liberation, a given ideal, not only for a politics directed purely to feminist questions but to any politics directed to class, race or national and ethnic struggle" (Grosz 2010: 139). Building on Bergson's ideas of freedom to act, Grosz questions whether feminist theory is best served by focussing on *freedom from* (e.g., patriarchy, racism, colonialism and heteronormativity) and underscores the value in exploring *freedom to* [act] – i.e., "what the female or feminist subject is capable of making and doing" (2010: 141).

Following Grosz's lead, if it is important to understand the true meaning of freedom, one must explore *freedom from* and *freedom to* in tandem. In the case of migrant women, their capability to make and do depends on the contexts of home and the migrant societies. This is because *what they can do here* is not just influenced by the material, socio-psychological, and political geographies of the migrant country but is also variously modulated by their *past* and *ongoing* norms of their home country, i.e., the context matters. I argue that this understanding of the context is closely connected to Pierre Bourdieu's concept of the habitus.

For Bourdieu (1986), the habitus is an inclination to behave in a certain way in society, as an individual and as a part of the larger collective. Habitus is also where economic, social, and cultural capital is exchanged, evaluated, and transformed. Building on Bourdieu's ideas, the literature on migration and settlement experiences has established that immigrants' habitus does not only include "here" (i.e., the migrant country) and "there" (i.e., the home country) but, rather, it is both here and there simultaneously. It may be argued that the social practices of immigrants are constructed not only by the contexts from where they have emigrated but also by an evaluation of their current circumstances (e.g., the social and structural conditions of the society where they have settled), thereby providing a duality of being both here and there, as well as acquiring a dual lens for evaluating one's life in reference to both here and there. In other words, the habitus is transnational in nature. First coined by Guarnizo (1997: 7), transnational habitus is defined as:

> A particular set of dispositions that inclines migrants to act and react to specific situations, in a manner that can be, but is not always, calculated, and that is not simply a question of conscious acceptance of specific behavioural or socio-cultural rules.... The transnational habitus incorporates the social position of the migrant and the context in which transmigration occurs.

In the transnational habitus[9] (Guarnizo 1997), while certain pre-migration social practices remain unaltered (i.e., the habitus is transposed), others fade, and new practices are adopted based on the norms of the migrant society, and the immigrant's socio-economic and political circumstances – i.e., the current habitus (Ghosh 2014). As a concept, transnational habitus has been used to understand the everyday social practices of immigrants in the city.

Freedom: inside and/or outside?

It was mentioned earlier that in the novels and the feature film *English Vinglish*, the "inside" and "outside" are in fact described as geographical spaces/places intricately connected to the concept of "freedom". Most of the protagonists in those stories are immigrant women who were subjugated "at home" and found freedom "outside of home", and in that regard, the connotations of home were expansive, including the country/city/dwelling.

Several feminist scholars have enriched research on "home" both theoretically and empirically (see Valentine 2007).[10] Problematizing "home" as a space and a place,[11] they have shown that as a physical place, "home" may constitute the dwelling, the neighbourhood, the city, as well as the nation (Mallett 2004; Young 2005), and as an abstract space, the "home" is economic, social, cultural, and political. As Blunt and Dowling (2006) describe, "feelings of home can be stretched across the world, connected to a nation or attached to a house; the spaces and imaginaries of home are central to the construction of people's identities".[12]

Processes of homemaking are often gendered – i.e., the domain of the women, created through an intricate tapestry of everyday material and social relations. Just as it is argued in the context of the production of place, homes are produced as "complex and sometimes fragmented time-space" (Power 2009: 1025) and "the multiple times, rhythms and temporalities that flow through the home co-exist, interact, entwine, coincide and conflict" (ibid).

With respect to making a home in the diaspora, the meanings that spaces acquire within the "home" are not necessarily similar for all users (Blunt and Dowling 2006). Even though gender relations (and roles) may be transformed by migration and may lead to some "gender gains," immigrant women (and children) are seldom immune to "patriarchal relations [which may] return in different guises in different times and places" (Pratt and Yeoh 2003: 161; also Ahmed 1999; Ahmed et al. 2003; and Bastia, Piper, and Prieto Carrón 2011). In that sense, while in some spheres of everyday life equity may be achieved in certain domains of the domestic space, in other spaces and times women may remain subjugated, negotiating the boundaries of patriarchy – the "permitted and prohibited" (Collins 1994; Brah 1996). Thus, as Rose (1993: 57) reminds us, "home" is both constructed and experienced relationally: "[homes] are constructed in particular ways, by discourses, institutions, desires. All of them mediate the others in specific ways in specific circumstances, to produce particular sorts of relations and spaces".

Both men and women may become home dependent when it suits their need(s) or desire(s). Attachment to one's home is grounded in the everyday, localized spatial interaction with a physical space, which may change over time (e.g., one's dwelling or one's neighbourhood). Just as in the case of place attachments (Livingston, Bailey, and Kearns 2010), attachment to home may be functional or emotional or both. The extent to which such attachments may develop depends on both sensory cues and/or social encounters. Whether functional or emotional, attachments with one's home may often lead to a strong desire to preserve and maintain the characteristics of the associated physical space. Despite such a long tradition of research, there is much more to explore in the context of home. For instance, Long (2013) notes that "greater attention [needs] to be paid to the expansive and integrative capacities of domestic space".

One component of the "outside" is the labour market – place of work[13] – where an immigrant woman spends much of her every day. In the era of flexible production and precarious labour-market conditions, immigrant women are no longer just secondary or temporary workers; in fact, they often assume the role of the main earner. Whether they are working from home or at an office space, they are subjected to "formal organizational structures and informal workplace practices . . . saturated with gendered meanings and practices that construct both gendered subjectivities at work and different categories of work as congruent with particular gender identities" (McDowell 1999: 135). Specifically, in the context of migrant working women in Canada, the literature demonstrates that women's class identities (e.g., from being professionals to working class)[14] and responsibilities (e.g., as workers both outside and at home, and as wives and mothers)[15] change as a result of migration.

Spaces, whether they are public or private, are often contested (Lehrer and Keil 2006). In the context of public space, scholars argue that spatial use creates "defensible space" – that is, a space which is controlled to maintain monitoring and management of use (Chaskin and Joseph 2013). While defensible spaces allow for a greater sense of safety and security, such spaces often transform previously "open" space into private/semi-private space, available only to a limited constituency. Seldom is the dwelling (arguably a private space) or place of work (arguably a public space) discussed in a similar vein, but the same dynamics may occur within these spaces as well. In this regard, *time spent at home*/at work may be considered as another important element in the development of a sense of being.

Keeping in mind the work of innumerable scholars who have contributed to the literature on "house as home" and "work/workplaces," it is therefore important to explore the experiences of Indian women – do they feel that they are free in these spaces or are they the subjugated "others" both at home and/or at workplaces? How do they evaluate their situation? Do they use a dual lens: how she is now in comparison with how she was prior to migration?

Research design

In order to explore the intersectionality of migration and freedom, two focus groups (with ten participants in each) were conducted with South Asian women (nine of whom were Indian) in Toronto. Based on a thematic analysis of transcripts, salient issues that had emerged in the focus-group discussions formed the basis of a topical protocol which was then used to conduct individual, semi-structured, in-depth interviews with another twelve participants. All participants in this study came to Canada as spousal dependants between 1990 and 2003. Entering Canada under the revised "point system," most of these women were young and highly-educated; almost all of them were working full-time outside the home prior to coming to Canada, and they were fluent in English. The demographic questions further revealed that at the time of interview, all participants were working at gendered workplaces[16] as accountants, engineers, medical technicians, doctors, and real estate agents. They were in a heterosexual married relationship, were mothers, and owned homes in Toronto.

Research findings

In order to explore the whether/how freedom is linked to the act of migration, the following interrelated research questions were explored in the focus groups, as well as in the in-depth interviews: What does freedom mean to these women, as a concept? Where and when are they free – i.e., what is the geography of freedom – is it at home and/or at the workplace? Do they perform specific acts at home and/or at their workplace that frees them from the gender norms of their home societies?

What is freedom?

All participants were asked to describe what freedom means to them. Without prompting, they began reminiscing about their lives in India, specifically highlighting the extent of freedom they enjoyed at two specific time periods: pre- and post- marriage. Nostalgic about their pre-marital days, they fondly recollected the times when they were living with their parents and siblings in their parental home, and following that when they were living alone as a university student/as a working-woman.

> We were brought up in the same way – my brother and me. There were some restrictions, but no difference in terms of going out with friends or wearing whatever I want to. I had huge freedom in India . . . even when I was working alone, I did everything – I stayed alone in a city. . . . I did not have to come to Canada to get those things.
>
> *(#Rashi)*

> Freedom oh my God I did everything, we ate slept drank worked everything with my friends. My parents are very open, even when I was seeing Soumyo [her husband] they knew everything. . . . I even stayed at his place for days no one said anything. After marriage . . . well I hardly stayed with [in laws]. We continued our life as I was before.
>
> *(#Surabhi)*

Recalling freedom after marriage, the participants recalled the days with their husbands and in-laws in India (not all women, however, lived with their in-laws post-marriage). Even then, most of them claimed that there was never any feeling of subjugation or lack of freedom. As #Koli said: "I could wear anything even after marriage . . . no one forced me to do anything". Similarly, #Aditi stated: "After marriage, well, I hardly stayed with my in-laws, but even then, we continued our life as before. Nothing had changed".

During the focus-group discussions, among all respondents, only #Mohua had stated that she had felt a lack of freedom post-marriage when she was living with her in-laws. Following up on that topic during the in-depth interview, #Mohua – a school teacher from Kolkata – revealed that, as the daughter-in law, she was expected to complete household chores before leaving for work, as well as contribute her entire salary toward the running of the joint-family household. Her anguish was particularly compounded when her sisters-in law or her husband were not bound by similar familial expectations. Living in that situation, #Mohua felt that despite being educated and financially independent, she had little economic and social freedom. As #Mohua explains: "We [husband] could not even go shopping together, and after coming back, we had to show everything to the mother-in-law . . . had to share everything with everyone. There was no privacy".

As the above quotations reveal, for all respondents, the word "freedom" meant the ability to do (or not) certain things (Grosz 2010). It is important to note here that the very fact that these women were able to choose what to wear, whether to earn a living, where and with whom to socialize with, whether to live away from home, and most importantly, to be able to live "the same way" both pre- and post-marriage, posits them in a specific social rung which is far above that of the others, who remain victims of gender-based subjugations both in their familial situations and in the society at large. It also seems that, since for most respondents the ability to choose was a "normal thing" and not a privilege earned, some even enquired about my intention behind asking this question. As #Koli asked, "what do you want to know, freedom from what?"

The geography of freedom – where and when are you free?

To explore the geography of freedom further, I tried to understand the extent to which the ides of "home" and "freedom" were interconnected. Following Blunt and Dowling (2006), it was contended that the connotations of "home" is expansive and can include multiple countries, cities, neighbourhoods, and dwellings. Toward that goal, the following interrelated topical questions were asked: what does "home" mean to you? Where is "home"? Are you free at home? There was unanimous agreement on the first question: associating home with family, the respondents stated: "home is where I live with my family" (#Roma). Answering "where is home", most participants answered, "both India and Canada", thereby reflecting their self-awareness of being transnational.

When asked whether, after several years of migration, the participants still consider India as their home, most explained: "of course, that is who we are" (#Roshni), a part of their primordial identity. Having said that, many women also lamented about the rapid societal changes in India in recent years and their inability to identify with India as their home anymore. For instance, #Mohua recalls the case of Nirbhaya, a student who was gang raped by several men as a juvenile in a running bus in New Delhi in December 2012. Nirbhaya was left on the street, brutally mutilated, and ultimately died at a Singapore hospital. Almost all Indian television channels (e.g., NDTV; Zee TV, ABP), which are now readily available in Canada, and the international media (e.g., BBC, CBC) reported on the Nirbhaya case for several months. As a result, besides second-guessing one's own safety back home, some women had to struggle to defend their own country as a safe place to be to their non-Indian friends and especially their co-workers.

> When I read the news stories about girls being gang raped in India, I seriously feel ashamed. . . . this is not where we grew up, what is happening to my country . . . after the Nirbhaya case, my colleagues keep asking me, and I don't know how to answer.
> (#Mohua)

As was expected, most respondents were in constant touch with their friends and family in India through social media, telephone conversations, Skype, WhatsApp, and FaceTime. They also seem to visit India at least every couple of years, mainly to see their aging parents. Sometimes travelling alone and at other times with their family, many respondents expressed that they are no longer seen or treated as the same person, or even as an Indian. As #Anita says: "they see me as foreigner, and therefore [with] lots of money". Stating how she is expected to spend lavishly, #Roshni also expressed that she feels that the people back home do not understand or value the sacrifices she makes every day for her family: "they see us with money, lots of money . . . if I say oh today was hard day today, they 'LOL' me".

Additionally, pointing out that their family and friends treat them differently if they speak critically about any issues concerning India (e.g., environmental or social), many respondents questioned whether they can even refer to India as their home anymore.

> . . . When you first arrive . . . wow finally I touched the soil of my country, now I will see everyone, shop, eat, and have fun. I will rejuvenate and go back. Then you realise, it is not what it was anymore, even if you came to visit just a couple of years ago, people have changed, the roads have changed, even my parents have become different. I sometimes feel that they treat me more as a foreign visitor than their daughter.
>
> (#Sulagna)

> Even my brother says, NRIs only see faults in India. If I say anything about India – they deny it. Even pollution or rape. They say yes now you will say everything is bad about India because you are a NRI. Then come here and make it all good.
>
> (#Mohua)

When thinking about whether Canada was home and whether they feel free in Canada, many respondents provided ambiguous answers – "yes and no" – often contingent upon their pre- and post-migration experiences. For instance, during the focus-group meetings, #Mohua was the only participant who explicitly stated that migrating to Canada gave her freedom. In #Mohua's words: "When I left India, the main thing was that I wanted to be free". Although others disagreed and pointed out that this was not their experience at all, still, their specific reasons and processes of migration seemed to have influenced whether migrating to Canada was necessarily a positive experience.

> We came to Canada of our own free will. No one forced us. From the very first day I landed in Canada I felt very welcomed. I have a lot of respect for Canada. I will tell you a story – I was standing in line with my little baby in my arms for immigration. The immigration officer gave me a place to sit. That little thing touched my heart.
>
> (#Koli)

> Canada is not yet my home . . . umm maybe because I went to the U.S. first?
>
> (#Aditi)

The quotations reveal that while for #Koli and her husband, their decision to immigrate to Canada was out of their "own free will", for #Aditi, in contrast, Canada was not her first choice of destination. Leaving India just ten days after her wedding, #Aditi had migrated to the U.S. as a new bride, with her heart filled with the dreams of "making home in New Jersey". However, after only a short stay, the couple was "forced" to uproot and resettle in Canada.[17] Thus it seems that not only their specific reasons for moving to Canada but also their imaginations of that place where they would want to make a home played an important part in limiting the development of their sense of belonging to Canada. For #Koli, however, the random acts of kindness she had received from individual strangers upon her arrival made her develop special affections for Canada as a nation.

For most participants, their post-migration experiences evoked strong emotional responses and influenced place attachments. Often evaluating their situations here and there, the respondents revealed ambivalent feelings about Canada in general, and Toronto more particularly. While satisfaction with "where they lived" created spatial bonds, their struggles of (re)finding their social positions (e.g., a sense of recognition) often isolated them from the country/city.

At the time of the interviews, several respondents had lived in the Indian enclaves in the Greater Toronto Area, particularly in Mississauga and Brampton. As #Chandni said: "I don't know about Toronto, but Brampton feels like home, because it is like home. Shops, people, you just have to think you are living among the Punjabis, that you have to do if you were living in Chandigarh". Interestingly, like the Bangladeshis in Toronto (Ghosh 2014), several Indian women also referred to Toronto as "a White area" (#Rashi). This may be because as #Anita explained: "I can only see it [Toronto] from far. Its white, all affluent people". Even though for most respondents "neighbours [did not] matter much here in Canada" (#Anita), they spoke fondly about their specific neighbourhoods and described their localities as being "just like home" (#Koli).

All respondents were asked to describe whether the act of owning a home in Canada made them feel free. Almost all respondents agreed that to them, owning a home meant "freedom to do what I want in my own home" (#Sulagna) and also gave them "a sense of pride and achievement as an immigrant" (#Rashi). However, #Surabhi stated that her sense of freedom was not necessarily associated with just buying a house but a house where she has more autonomy. Comparing her life in an ownership condominium and her current freehold residence she described: "when we lived in a condo . . . it did not feel like home. There were many restrictions . . . on curtains, common spaces . . . this house is ours, it feels much better".

In contrast, for #Sonia, owning a detached home could not provide her with a sense of stability, nor freedom. #Sonia is a computer engineer from a reputed Indian university and had first migrated with her husband to the U.S. on an H1B visa. After living there for five years (like #Aditi), when they did not receive "the G card" they had immigrated to Canada. In Canada the couple faced various forms of barriers in the labour market, including the "glass gate, the glass door and the glass ceiling" (Guo 2013). Frustrated, her husband took up a job in Oman, while she continues to live with her now adolescent children in Mississauga.

> Yes, I am married but I live alone with my kids . . . my husband shuttles between Toronto and the Middle East, he is hardly here – what to do this is the job he got. . . . I also feel I am not permanent here. Our [aged] parents are in India . . . so I have to go [to India] often. I go to husband too . . . but when I go there I feel it is his place not mine. I am not free anywhere.
>
> *(#Sonia)*

Even though her ability to shuttle between three countries (Canada/Oman/India) may seem like a privilege, for #Sonia, a working mother, it is both physically and psychologically exhausting. Long separations from her husband and sometimes even from her children has complicated her family dynamics, which is further compounded by her social/familial obligations "back home".

To explore Indian professional women's feelings of being free at home in the outside world, it was important to understand their experiences at their workplace. With respect to workplace, the literature informs that high levels of satisfaction in employment often positively correlates with a decreased sense of alienation. Toward that goal, several objective and subjective markers of satisfaction with employment were considered. The objective markers included their pre- and post- migration academic achievements, earnings, position within an organization, and associated professional aspirations. The subjective markers included gender and ethnicity of co-workers, and social relationships with co-workers (e.g., the frequency of their interactions and levels of comfort).

With respect to the objective markers: all respondents had completed at least a bachelor's degree in India and many of them had a master's degree or a professional equivalent or held a doctorate. This is not surprising, as most of them had entered Canada under the new points system. It is important to note here that most women stated that they were "good students" and had aspired to become a professional.[18] At the time of their wedding (pre-migration), most women were working. After their arrival in Toronto, while only a few respondents had entered the labour market directly, a majority retrained (e.g., early childhood education, human resources, ultrasound technology, real-estate management, accountancy, and public administration) and entered the labour market following the completion of their diploma/degree.

The respondents adopted a dual lens (what they were in India/ where they are now) to evaluate their current employment situations – i.e., current positions within an organisation and future professional goals. During the in-depth interviews, most respondents said that if had they not migrated, they would have progressed in their field of expertise and would not be forced to follow a different career path. As #Rashi explained: "I would have been at least two to three levels higher than where I am now". Despite retraining, several women experienced de-professionalization and alienation at their workplaces, and as a result, for some "it is daily struggle to get to work" (#Rakhi).[19]

While they seem frustrated by unmet career aspirations, there is also a practical understanding that "both partners to earn in Canada" (#Soma). Therefore, many women compromised their careers – settling in jobs that would suit their familial needs rather than their personal goals. As #Aditi said: "I started this business because mortgage needs to be paid", and #Rashi explains: "I took this job because it was good for the family – this job gave me flexible hours . . . flexible time, work from home opportunities. I cannot take a job that cannot give me these things . . . so I often don't even look at those ads". In contrast, #Mita – who holds a PhD in Sociology and is a mother of a toddler – revealed that, although she was devalued both by the Canadian society and her husband in particular (who reminds her that her degree does not have any value in Canada), she "feel[s] like a prisoner here and every time I visit home, I don't want to come back. But I have to, because of my parents". Besides battling deskilling and isolation, many women find their sense of freedom also curtailed by the fact that as an immigrant family they were expected to send regular remittances. #Roshni explains:

> It seems we are here on our own, so we are free, but you know, we are not really free . . . we have to be careful on what we spend here . . . you have to continue supporting back home . . . we have aged parents. In our community, it is our duty to look after them, they have done so much for us, they are now old and our responsibility . . . we are here but always going back and forth – anything happens we run home . . . I would say I am less free now

As revealed in some of the quotations, social, familial, and economic obligations and reciprocities and loyalties to both places meant that these women had to make several personal and professional sacrifices at both geographical places – here and there (Hari 2018).

In responding to the subjective questions, most women revealed that they were comfortable working with men and members of different ethnic groups at the workplace. Women who worked in gendered workplaces (e.g., as an ultrasound technician, statistician, office administrator) said that they often spent time with their co-workers, primarily at office parties. Comparing with their lives in India, several women said that this situation was not new for them but, rather, was a continuation of their life back home. As #Anita says:

> I grew up in Muscat, and then I lived in Delhi. When I got married at 27, by then, I had worked and stayed alone as a working woman in India. I have worked with different people – Indians and foreigners. I go to office parties, drive myself back home at 1am in the morning.

Similarly, #Aditi mentions: "When I got married, by then, I was already working. I also worked in the U.S. for several years. So, working with men or people of other ethnicities was not a big deal".

While discussing office parties, although several issues were brought up by the respondents during the focus-group discussions, a debate ensued on what constitutes pleasure/entertainment after work. Although from the same country of birth, the participants expressed unique views from their individual cultural and social locations and associated ideas of social permissibility. It was also observed that their transnational connections played a vital role in determining "what they can or cannot do" as working women in Toronto. The respondents also seemed concerned about the proverbial Western gaze. For #Anita, "freedom has nothing to do with being able to go out and party. Maybe it is for others but not for me . . . my husband still goes out, I don't". For #Soma, a Canadian woman's sense of entertainment after work was somewhat in opposition to her own sensibilities, mainly now that she is a mother. #Soma expressed that, even though drinking is not a problem for her, "bar hopping [with office colleagues] is a thing of the past. Been there done that in India . . . now I am a mother I have to take care of my daughter first".

Discussion and conclusions

Novels and films on young educated middle-class heterosexual married immigrant Indian women in North America assert that their freedom is inextricably linked to migration. These semi-autobiographical stories also depict that "freedom" is a relational concept – *freedom from (what* and *where)*. The protagonists of these stories seem to have found freedom *from* the gender norms of their home society (what) in North America (where). Arguing that by focussing too much on "*freedom from*", feminist scholars have often disregarded another important dimension of freedom, which revolves around the *act of freedom* (Grosz 2010). In that light the supposition is that it is the *act of migration* that made them free. In this paper questioning that causal relation between migration and freedom, I attempted to explore the following interrelated research questions: *What* does freedom mean to this cohort of Indian women as a concept? What is the geography of freedom – i.e., *where* (e.g., in India/Canada/Toronto/at home and/or at their workplace) and *when* (pre-migration, post-migration, or when visiting back home) do they feel free? Which specific acts do they perform spatially and temporally, that give them a sense of freedom?

This research establishes that in explaining what freedom means, most respondents related the act of being free to a specific geographical space (where) and time (when). In this regard, the participants understood, felt, and articulated "'home" both contextually and relationally, and in complex ways. "Home" to them seems to be connected to a sense of place, related to the feelings of being at home at various geographical spaces and scales in Canada and India, including, the dwellings, the neighbourhood, the city, and the country. Therefore, when thinking of being free, they referred to their lives at their parents' home, at their in-laws' home in India. Similarly, in the context of Toronto, they related the idea of freedom with that of feeling "at home" in their dwellings. Freedom "outside" was understood and articulated not only with respect to the permissibility of the Western society with regards to dressing a certain way outside of home but also with the act of being able to secure (or not) a desired employment and/or socialize outside the home (e.g., at office parties, going to pubs).

Secondly, it seems that although they were physically separated from their country of origin, their feelings of freedom were associated with the circumstances "both here and there" simultaneously – the transnational habitus. Comparing their current situations in Toronto with their pre-migration experiences, the respondents pointed out two main elements: first, that they were leading the same lifestyle as before (pre-migration). In this regard, they specifically mentioned dressing, working, and socializing outside of home. Second, they expressed that they were perhaps freer in India than they are currently in Canada. In explaining why they feel that way, many respondents described their complex everyday life situations in Toronto – especially at home and at the workplace.

It is important to note that, in each of the geographical sites, this specific cohort of Indian women seem to understand and experience freedom differentially. For them the senses of freedom and imprisonment, stability and instability, power and powerlessness exist simultaneously, thereby positioning them both at the centre and at the margins. In the transnational habitus, for most respondents, their dwellings and their neighbourhoods provided a sense of being at home in the migrant city. These geographical places were filled with symbols, smells, colours, and meanings, thus providing these immigrant women with a unique normality – a new way of being "at home". At the same time, however, unfair labour market conditions (e.g., non-recognition of foreign credentials, loss of employment) added financial pressures on some women and put them in precarious family situations. As a result, many women were forced to compromise their own career aspirations and felt unmoored when families were dislocated. Additionally, many women (and men) were expected to send remittances, as well as visit and care for their relatives left behind in India. All these circumstances sometimes made them feel that they were "stuck". In these ways, based on their changing power positions, the respondents were placed simultaneously at the centre and at the margins in their own homes, at work, and at the places of socialization. Therefore, it is not surprising that most participants described Toronto/Canada as a space of both alienation and marginalisation, imprisonment and liberation. In other words, the respondents are in liminality – the characteristic of "threshold people" where they are necessarily in an ambiguous zone – "neither here nor there they are betwixt and between the positions assigned and arrayed by law, custom, convention, and ceremonial" (Turner 1969).

Notes

1 For instance, Kamini in *Tamarind Mem* (Badami 1996), Tara in *Desirable Daughters* (Mukherjee 2002), Ashima in *The Namesake* (Lahiri 2004), Kiran, Preeti, and Rani in *The Hindi-Bindi Club* (Pradhan 2007), and Nina in *The Immigrant* (Kapur 2008). Even though in *The Namesake* Gogol is the protagonist, Ashima, Gogols's mother, is an important character.
2 The relationship does not blossom, however, as Shashi must remain a loyal mother from India.
3 See, e.g., the work of Purakayastha and her colleagues 2004, 2010.

4 This is understandable, since successful integration of immigrants in the housing and labour markets has been the main goal of the Canadian government, particularly since the mid-1990s.
5 This was not a requirement for those who had arrived in the 1970s and 1980s under the family reunification program.
6 The application process is extremely stringent. Even if they are not the main applicant, in order to secure the minimum cut off points, they must be of working age, with university degrees and related work experiences, and must be able to speak fluently in English (cic.gc.ca)
7 Previous studies have shown that compared to those who came to Canada prior to the 1990s, newer immigrants come with specific knowledge of the housing and labour-market conditions in their intended place of settlement, as well as the societal and cultural norms of that space.
8 Determinists argue that an act is the effect of a cause and libertarians say that acts are unpredictable and that different acts can occur with or without the same cause. Bergson demonstrates that both groups assume that the subject does not change during and after performing the acts – in other words the subject remains the same.
9 Pierre Bourdieu's concept of the habitus may help to sort out this particular complexity in social practices. For Bourdieu, habitus is an inclination to behave in a certain way in society, as an individual and as a part of the larger collective. Habitus is also where economic, social, and cultural capital is exchanged, evaluated, and transformed.
10 The flow of inquiry with respect to house as home has followed two interlinked threads. First, the *Material Geographies of Home*, including studies on Residential Segregation, Residential Mobility and Location, Gentrification, and Household Demographic Change. The other stream has concentrated on the lived experiences in the domestic space (i.e., dwelling/house). In this regard, immigrant and refugee experiences, social relations and emotional significances of domestic life, home as a place of safety and security as well as danger, fear and violence, and transnational geographies of home are some of the main areas of focus.
11 In the geographical literature, "space" and "place" are often discussed as separate yet intertwined concepts (see Knox and McCarthy 2011).
12 Arguing that it is at "home" where materialism intersects with "race", gender, sexuality, age, and ability, Blunt and Dowling (2006) suggest that various members of the household, particularly women, are posited in specific rungs of power and identity.
13 Although home is also a place of work for women and men, the general understanding is that the place of work is not home (see McDowell, 1999: 123).
14 See Walton-Roberts and Pratt 2005.
15 See Devasahayam and Yeoh 2007; Giles and Preston 1996.
16 Gendered workplaces include banks, real-estate, and the IT sector (see McDowell 1999).
17 Similar stories of Indians first migrating to the USA on H1B visa and then having to either return back to India or re-migrate to another country have been captured by various researchers (Maitra 2018; Purakayastha 2010; Ghosh 2013).
18 As was mentioned in the previous section, for some of the participants these aspirations were never fulfilled because they came to Canada.
19 #Rakhi is a trained software engineer who, prior to coming to Canada, worked for a reputed multinational company and now works for a bank in a "nominal position". Similarly for #Roshni: "When I go to work I feel very depressed . . . what has happened to me I feel like they don't even know how much training I had behind me, data entry was not my job, data analysis is what I did – I feel humiliated – I am stuck".

References

Ahmed, S. 1999. "Home and Away: Narratives of Migration and Estrangement." *International Journal of Cultural Studies* 2 (3): 329–347.
Ahmed, S., C. Castaneda, A. M. Fortier, and M. B. Sheller, eds. 2003. *Uprootings/Regroundings Questions of Home and Migration*. Oxford: Berg.
Badami, A. R. 1996. *Tamarind Mem*. New York, NY: Penguin Books.
Balki, R. 2013. *English Vinglish*. London: Eros International.
Bastia, T., N. Piper, and M. Prieto Carrón. 2011. "Geographies of Migration, Geographies of Justice? Feminism, Intersectionality, and Rights." *Environment and Planning A* 43 (7): 1492–1498.

Bergson, H. 1889. *Time and Free Will: An Essay on the Immediate Data of Consciousness* (*Essai sur les données immédiates de la conscience*. Doctoral Dissertation.
Bergson, H. 1896. (*Matière et mémoire*, 1896). Mineola, NY: Dover Publications.
Bhabha, H. 1994. *The Location of Culture*. New York, NY: Psychology Press.
Blunt, A., and R. Dowling. 2006. *Home*. London: Routledge.
Bourdieu, P. 1986. "The Forms of Capital." In *Handbook of Theory and Research for the Sociology of Education*, edited by J. G. Richardson, 241–258. New York, NY: Greenwood Press.
Brah, A. 1996. *Cartographies of Diaspora: Contesting Identities*. London: Routledge.
Butler, J. 2004. *Undoing Gender*. New York, NY: Routledge.
Chaskin, R. J., and M. L. Joseph. 2013. "'Positive' Gentrification, Social Control and the 'Right to the City' in Mixed-Income Communities: Uses and Expectations of Space and Place." *IJURR* 37 (2): 480–502.
Collins, R. 1994. *Four Sociological Traditions*. New York, NY: Oxford University Press.
Das Dasgupta, S. 1998. *A Patchwork Shawl: Chronicles of South Asian Women in America*. New Brunswick, NJ: Rutgers University Press.
Das Gupta, T., G. Man, K. Mirchandani, and R. Ng. 2014. "Class Borders: Chinese and South Asian Canadian Professional Women Navigating the Labor Market." *Asian And Pacific Migration Journal* 23 (1): 55–83.
Devasahayam, T., and B. S. A. Yeoh (eds.). 2007. *Working and Mothering in Asia: Images, Ideologies and Identities*. Singapore and Copenhagen: NUS Press and NIAS Press.
Dyck I., and P. Dossa. 2007. "Place, Health and Home: Gender and Migration in the Constitution of Healthy Space." *Health & Place* 13 (3): 691–701.
Ghosh, S. 2007. "Transnational Ties and Intra-Immigrant Group Settlement Experiences: A Case Study of Indian Bengalis and Bangladeshis in Toronto." *Geojournal* 68 (2–3): 223–242.
Ghosh, S. 2014. "Vertical Neighbourhoods as Spaces of Hope and Despair: Exploring Bangladeshi Residential Spaces in Toronto." *International Journal of Urban and Regional Research* 38 (6): 2008–2024.
Giles, W., and V. Preston. 1996. "The Domestication of Women's Work: A Comparison of Chinese and Portuguese Immigrant Women Homeworkers." *Studies in Political Economy* 51 (Fall): 147–181.
Grosz., E. 2010. "Feminism, Materialism and Freedom." In D. Coole and S. Frost (eds.), *New Materialisms: Ontology, Agency, and Politics*, 70–91. Durham, NC: Duke University Press.
Guarnizo, L. E. 1997. "The Emergence of Transnational Social Formation and the Miracle of Return Migration Among Dominican Transmigrants." *Identities* 4 (2): 281–322.
Guo, S. 2013. "Economic Integration of Recent Chinese Immigrants in Canada's Second-Tier Cities: The Triple Glass Effect and Immigrants' Downward Social Mobility." *Canadian Ethnic Studies* 45 (3): 95–115.
Hari, A. 2018. "'Someone Kept Sacrificing': Disentangling Gender Ideology in Immigrant Narratives of Social Reproduction." *Signs: Journal of Women in Culture and Society* 43 (3): 539–562.
Kapur, M. 2008. *The Immigrant*. New Delhi: Random House.
Knox, P., and L. McCarthy. 2011. *Urbanization: An Introduction to Urban Geography*. 3rd rev. ed. Upper Saddle River, NJ: Pearson Prentice-Hall.
Lahiri, J. 2004. *The Namesake*. New York, NY: Mariner Books.
Lehrer, U. A., and R. Keil. 2006. "From Possible Urban Worlds to the Contested Metropolis: Urban Research and Activism in the Age of Neoliberalism." In *Contested Urban Futures*, edited by H. Leitner, J. Peck, and E. Sheppard, 291–310. New York, NY: Guilford Press.
Livingston, M., N. Bailey, and A. Kearns. 2010. "Neighbourhood Attachment in Deprived Areas: Evidence from the North of England." *Journal of Housing and the Built Environment* 24 (4): 409–427.
Long, J. C. 2013. "Diasporic Dwelling: The Poetics of Domestic Space." *Gender, Place and Culture* 20 (3): 329–345.
Maitra, S. 2018. "The Making of the 'Precarious': Examining Indian Immigrant IT Workers in Canada and Their Transnational Networks with Body Shops in India." *Globalisation, Societies and Education* 13 (2): 194–209. DOI 10.1080/14767724.2014.934070.
Mallett, S. 2004. "Understanding Home: A Critical Review of the Literature." *The Sociological Review* 52 (1): 62–89.
McDowell, L. (1999). *Gender Identity and Place: Understanding Feminist Geographies*. Minneapolis, MN: University of Minnesota Press.
Mukherjee, B. 2002. *Desirable Daughters*. New York, NY: Theia.

Power, E. R. 2009. "Domestic Temporalities: Nature Times in the House-as-Home." *Geoforum* 40 (6): 1024–1032.

Pradhan, M. 2007. *The Hindi-Bindi Club*. New York, NY: Bantam Books.

Pratt, G., and B. Yeoh. 2003. "Transnational (Counter) Topographies." *Gender, Place and Culture* 10 (2): 159–166.

Purkayastha, B. 2004. "Skilled Migration and Cumulative Disadvantage: The Case of Highly Qualified Asian Indian Immigrant Women in the U.S." *Geoforum* 36: 181–196.

Purakayastha, B. 2010. "Interrogating Intersectionality: Contemporary Globalization and Racialized Gendering in the Lives of Highly Educated South Asian Americans and their Children." *Journal of Intercultural Studies* 31: 29–47.

Razack. S. 2002. *Race, Space and the Law: Unmapping a White Settler Society*. Toronto: Between the Lines.

Rose, D. 1993. "On Feminism, Method and Methods in Human Geography: An Idiosyncratic Overview." *The Canadian Geographer* 37 (1): 57–61.

Sangha, J. K., and T. Gonsalves. 2013. *South Asian Mothering: Negotiating Culture, Family and Selfhood*. Bradford, ON: Demeter Press.

Sheel, R. 2005. "Marriage, Money and Gender: A Case Study of the Migrant Indian Community in Canada." *Indian Journal of Gender Studies* 12 (2–3): 335–356.

Silvey, R. 2004. "Power Difference and Mobility: Feminist Advances in Migration Studies." *Progress in Human Geography* 28 (1): 1–17.

Turner, Victor W. 1969. *The Ritual Process: Structure and Anti-Structure*. London: Routledge & Kegan Paul.

Valentine, G. 2007. "Theorizing and Researching Intersectionality: A Challenge for Feminist Geography." *The Professional Geographer* 59 (1): 10–21.

Walton-Roberts, M., and G. Pratt. 2005. "Mobile Modernities: A South Asian Family Negotiates Immigration, Gender and Class in Canada." *Gender, Place and Culture* 12 (2): 173–196.

Walton-Roberts, M., and J. Hennebry. 2012. *Indirect Pathways into Practice: A Comparative Examination of Indian and Philippine Internationally Educated Nurses and Their Entry into Ontario's Nursing Profession*. CERIS Working Paper No. 92. Toronto: CERIS–The Ontario Metropolis Centre.

Young, I. M. 2005. "House and Home: Feminist Variations on a Theme." In *On Female Body Experience: "Throwing Like A Girl" and Other Essays*, edited by I. M. Young, 123–154. New York, NY: Oxford University Press.

17
MIDDLING TAMIL MIGRANTS IN SINGAPORE AND THE TRANSLOCAL VILLAGE

Selvaraj Velayutham

In 2013, while browsing the internet, I came across a website dedicated to the Musuguntha Vellalar village of Soorappallam, located in the district of Thanjavur in the Southern Indian state of Tamil Nadu. Further electronic search revealed that there were several dedicated websites for a number of other fellow caste villages. I was pleasantly surprised to see these developments because some of the villages now had a digital presence and the websites served as a new communication platform linking villagers between the village and its overseas communities. I contacted Chandran, the creator of the Soorappallam village website, to find out more about it. Chandran, who was in his early 20s, was in fact on a temporary employment visa working as an electronic engineer in a software firm in Singapore. He said that he set up the website so that news about the village and the diasporic community in Singapore and elsewhere in Australia, the United States, the UK and Middle-East can be disseminated quickly and so that members can stay in touch with the latest happenings. He added that the web platform enabled posting of announcements accompanied by images and films-clips as well as other relevant internet links useful to the villagers and readily accessible to all. More than a decade earlier, I had co-authored an article on the Musuguntha Vellalar caste members based in Singapore and their transnational ties with their villages in India, and the caste and kin relations among villagers from Soorappallam in particular featured prominently in our discussion (Velayutham and Wise 2005; Wise and Velayutham 2008).[1] The villagers reproduced the *translocal village*, a particular form of moral community based around village-scale, pace-oriented familial and neighbourly ties that have subsequently expanded across extended space, that is, between Soorappallam and Singapore. This was a major development compared to how information sharing took place in the past, mostly via telephone calls, return visits and gossip. The eyes and ears of the translocal village have been further enhanced by this website, which provided up-to-date news on birth, death, marriage, graduation and other festivities in Singapore and Soorappallam. Significantly, Chandran and the users of the Soorappallam website, unlike their predecessors, are a generation of young, educated, tech-savvy and mobile Musuguntha Vellalar caste members participating in the reproduction of the translocal village. They represent what Conradson and Latham (2005a) refer to as 'middling transnationals'.

In a journal special issue on transnational urbanism, guest editors Conradson and Latham (2005a) suggest a new term, 'middling' forms of transnationalism, so as to re-orientate the focus of transnational research from exclusively concerned with transnational elites and migrants from the South to include people who fall between these two categories. According to Smith (2005: 8) these 'middling transnational actors are those who [occupy] more or less middle class or status position' in both their home country and immigration country. Examples of such migrants include skilled workers on gap years or people taking career sabbaticals overseas. Conradson and Latham (2005b) conducted research with young New Zealanders who left well-paid skilled positions in their home country in order to come to London for personal development. This points to a specific set of motivations for migration that do not necessarily centre on economic gains. Although they can be classified as economic migrants, this group have migrated to the United Kingdom not only in order to earn money but also to try life abroad, see the world or learn English. Conradson and Latham's idea of 'middling transnationals' has been further explored by Ho (2011) and Parutis (2014), but both were concerned with migration trajectories and migrants' decision-making and strategies they deploy to achieve successful migration outcomes. These narratives help to explain why and how migration takes place and how migrants deal with opportunities and challenges presented to them in the migration context. Working with the concept of middling transnational actors as it fits the category of migrants in my study, I am interested in examining both the motivations for migration and how this relatively mobile and educated group experiences work and negotiates cultural difference in the workplace. The strategies that migrants employ and the capacities they build to deal with situations in the migration context have been well researched (Levitt and Schiller 2004). In this paper, I want to focus my attention on how middling transnational Musuguntha Vellalar negotiate the conditions of their migrant and work status and consider the ways in which they maintain links with their home village. I argue that both social media and budget air travel have completely revolutionised transnational relations by enabling a real presence with their village.

Workplaces are sites of enforced proximity to difference, and for many, one of the few contexts where difference is encountered on a sustained basis. In Ash Amin's most recent work (2013), he places a great deal more emphasis on the factors that mediate through situations of interethnic encounter. He suggests a focus on habits of everyday engagement, which, he suggests, are often deeply sedimented through rhythms of situated experience, yet always mediated by localised legacies of difference, and the local reception of national and international framings of difference. He argues that situated behaviour is the product of dwelling in many relational worlds, with intensities of kinship towards others profoundly affected, for example, by representations of diversity and difference in the public sphere. Thus the challenge, he suggests, is not so much to see how cosmopolitans are 'made' through interethnic encounter but in developing an awareness of how the world at large shapes local habits of social encounter. Amin's work highlights the fact that not all multicultural micro-publics are the same, and all are mediated by factors internal and external to the situation and the immediate individuals involved (Wise and Velayutham 2008). For example, a diverse school, a football team and a blue-collar workplace all have their own internal and external dynamics. To take one example, previous research in the sociology of work has focused on the ways in which broader social economic and political contexts such as neo-liberalism interact with micro workplace processes and practices to produce and constrain particular types of social relationships at work (Vogl 2009). These findings are supported by Sennett, who argues that some of the changes that have occurred in the neo-liberal workplace such as casualisation, job insecurity and increased competition have diminished the sense of mutual dependency and reciprocity among workers (Sennett 1998; Komter 2005: 173). Again, what we know less about is how these dynamics inflect inter-ethnic relationships at work. The central research problem for this study is whether meaningful everyday intercultural 'contact' leads, as some have claimed (Amin 2002; Pettigrew 1998), to more positive relationships across difference? If so, what practices, ideas and structures underpin these emergent convivialities (Gilroy 2004)? How are cultural identities transformed in the process? And under what circumstances do more negative inter-ethnic and race relationships occur in these everyday settings?

Through the course of this research (2012–2014) on everyday diversity at the workplace, we conducted interviews (90) with blue-collar workers in manufacturing, construction, health, hospitality, security, IT, transport, cleaning and administration in Sydney and Singapore. It was during the fieldwork phase of this study that I came across a number of recently arrived Musuguntha Vellalar caste members, including Chandran, in their late 20s to early 30s working in Singapore. They were all men – although I was informed that there were a handful of women in the group – trained in various technical degrees such as electronic, electrical and civil engineering, and a majority were employed in the IT sector, specialising in programming, software development, system analysis, network administration, technical support and web design. IT is an interesting example of a highly transnational skilled occupation that has become associated with workers from India. It is argued that IT has emerged as a quintessential post-industrial service industry characterised by highly precarious sub-contracting forms of transnational labour supply stemming from India. Yet this occupational category has enabled the movement of hundreds of thousands of Indians across the globe.

Part 1: Middling Musuguntha Vellalar transnational migrants

Singapore has accepted immigrants (under the professional and business migration scheme) from overseas since the late 1980s, with a special emphasis on attracting and recruiting so called 'foreign talent'. The policy of attracting 'talent', especially from other Asian countries, was first spelt out in The Next Lap policy vision document unveiled in 1991. The policy was part of the government's strategy to offset the problem of migrant outflows, recurring labour shortages, declining fertility and an aging population. The term 'talent' was used officially to refer to foreigners with highly specialised technical, business and intellectual skills who can do jobs that Singaporeans cannot do or provide additional human resources where there simply were not enough Singaporeans to fulfil a task. As highlighted in the Next Lap policy vision (The Next Lap 1991: 15),

> Singapore is what it is today because we have been able to attract talent from all over the world to work and live here. We must attract more world talent, especially Asian talent. Our city can accommodate them, and we will be the richer for it.

The term 'foreign talents became synonymous with Western expatriates. At the same time, Singapore began recruiting low-skill temporary migrant workers – officially termed 'foreign workers' – from Bangladesh, India, Sri Lanka, Thailand, China and the Philippines to work in various manual and labour-intensive occupations. These include construction, manufacturing, shipbuilding, and cleaning and domestic work. The Indian low-waged and low-skilled migrant workers were entirely from Tamil Nadu. They are generally seen as indispensable labour undertaking dirty, dangerous and difficult jobs which Singaporeans were unlikely to take on. Since the late 1990s there has been an influx of a middling migrant labour force from China, India, Burma, Indonesia and the Philippines (employment pass – skilled category 2 and S-Pass holders) employed in hospitality, marketing, low-to-mid-level technical positions, business service, education, retail, health, public service, IT and so forth). These migrant workers were neither in the top income bracket and enjoying the perks of expatriate lifestyle nor in precarious low-paid occupations like the foreign workers.

Singapore immigration work/employment scheme – characterised by 'racialised' hierarchy:

1) Employment Pass –
   a) Professional class (I & II) – monthly salary of more than SGD8000 and SGD4500–8000.
   b) Skilled workers on a fixed monthly salary of more than SGD3300. A degree holder from reputable university (no quota). Eligible to apply for PR in due course.
2) S-Pass – mid-skilled on a fixed monthly salary of SGD2200. Technical diploma acceptable (quota system). Eligible to apply for PR after 4–5 years and have a stable job.
3) Work permit – is generally issued to foreign unskilled workers. The duration of a work permit is generally two years.

Unlike the foreign talents and foreign workers – who are at the opposite end of the spectrum in terms of employment, pay, work and living conditions and visa status and generally do not mingle or come into contact with ordinary Singaporeans – the middling migrant workers compete directly with Singaporeans for jobs, housing, education, public infrastructure and public spaces. Many have taken up permanent residency after 4 years in Singapore. Remarkably, in-depth qualitative research into temporary work visas (employment and S-Passes) in Singapore is rare. This is quite contrary to trends in scholarly research of labour migrants in other parts of the world, where anthropologists and sociologists have been extremely active in this field. Important influences on our study include Datta et al. (2009) and Osella and Osella (2000) and their work on masculinities and labour migrants from Kerala in the Middle East and Xiang Biao's work on Indian IT workers in Australia, especially his reflections on gender and dowry and their role framing the experiences of male IT professionals (Biao, 2005).As a general estimate there are around 1200–1500 Musuguntha Vellalar caste members (including children) living in Singapore. Of these, some 400 have arrived in the last 5–10 years; with an estimated 50 becoming Permanent Residents, 100 on Employment/S-Pass and the remainder being Work Permit holders/worker.

Senthil arrived in Singapore in 2007. He is working as a programme analyst in a computer company in Bishan in the central part of Singapore. He has a degree in electronical engineering from a college in Thanjavur, and on the recommendation of his uncle in Singapore applied for the current position. He got the job and arrived in Singapore on a S-Pass visa. In 2012 he became a Singapore permanent resident and in the same year returned to the village for an arranged marriage. He has bought a new flat in Sembawang and lives with his wife and two children. This has been the same narrative for most of the recently arrived Musuguntha Vellalar caste members. Many of these young men left their villages for the first time in search of employment and settled in Singapore with their new families. The precedent for a continuous flow of Musuguntha Vellalar caste members to Singapore was set in the 1950s. For this largely farming community, a combination of long and dry seasons, water shortage for irrigation and dwindling supply of farm labour forced many to travel overseas for work. Farming as an occupation has become less attractive. Remittances from overseas have served this community well and have been productively deployed in education. By the 1990s a majority in the community had a qualification. According to the 2011 Indian census, the literacy rate of Thanjavur district was 82.64 percent compared to the Tamil Nadu state and national averages of 80.3 percent and 74 percent respectively. Increasingly, young and educated Musuguntha Vellalars travelled to nearby cities such as Chennai, Bangalore, Hyderabad and Delhi and afar to places like Singapore, Australia, the US, Middle-East and the UK in search of employment.

Kumar and Siva are in their early 30s, on an Employment Pass, employed as IT consultants in a Singapore bank. Kumar has been working for more than 5 years, first with an aircraft manufacturing company, then another bank, and he took up his current position about 3 months ago. Siva only arrived about a year ago. Like other middling transnational migrant workers, they indicated that there were plenty of job opportunities in the related sector in Singapore, better salary, a good lifestyle, and it was a safe and good place to a raise a family. As Shiva noted, 'I like Singapore because the way of working here is nice. I like the country because [. . .] it is the safest country. I came here to better good [myself] as well, for my family'. Kumar and Siva, though coming from different villages, have become close work colleagues. Both also already had relatives in Singapore who were part of the extended Musuguntha Vellalar kinship network. When asked about their work arrangements, they said that they worked in teams in the bank's IT department and handled several projects. While the composition of the IT department was, according to Kumar, '50 percent Singaporeans, 10 percent will be Indians, other 10 to 30 (percent) will be Philippines, Malaysians, those neighbour countries, five to 10 (percent) will be Australians and US'; their project team consisted mainly of Indians and was overseen by Singaporean Chinese project team leaders. When asked about their experience of encountering and working with culturally different colleagues, both felt that it has been relatively positive. They particularly got along well with Singaporean Chinese co-workers through their enthusiasm to learn some words in Chinese and also to teach them a few Tamil words. Kumar observed,

> I like to learn very basic Chinese . . . That is good, actually, can talk to people. [. . .] At least can say thanks sometimes. We cannot learn too many things. At least it is good to learn so that we can interact very happily.

Their effort to learn a word or two in Chinese so as to maintain positive relations with colleagues has worked well. As Siva noted,

> so the Chinese they also learn Tamil. So can speak (a few words) in Tamil. When they do something good response or something, they will tell 'nandri'. It means 'thanks'. They will tell something, which is like, I like more because they are telling in Tamil, like me.

On a personal level both found that working in a culturally diverse environment is an important life experience. Siva highlighted that

> hmm . . . the good thing is we must learn a new language. Chinese or Malay. Another one is, we meet people in the different regions. So we know how the people lives like. So just learn new things from them. That is the good thing.

Kumar went further to say,

> ya, to me is also, of course, I feel happy about it. Cos we live and work in a city with people (who are so different). Second thing, it is also a life experience. So when we talk to, I can know about their language. I can learn from them. A kind of learning. Multicultural . . . how they are like. It is good actually, in terms of working.

Such positive interactions tend to be overlaid by particular anxieties that come with being in the IT profession, visa status and maintaining convivial workplace relationships. IT is an interesting example of a highly transnational skilled occupation that has become associated with workers from India. It is argued that IT has emerged as a quintessential post-industrial service industry characterised by highly precarious sub-contracting forms of transnational labour supply stemming from India. Most of the major IT companies are located in the South Indian cities of Bangalore, Hyderabad and Chennai, and there is huge competition for jobs from applicants from all over India. Most of the Musuguntha Vellalar young men we interviewed in Singapore, though English literate, lacked fluency speaking the language. This was a major impediment to finding employment with companies like TATA, Infosys and Sathyam. Kumar and Siva had applied for positions in India but were not successful and thus turned their attention towards Singapore simply because there were more IT jobs advertised. The IT profession is fundamentally fragmented and categorised into areas of specialisation and levels of priorities. At any given time a large organisation like a financial institution require IT specialists attending to maintenance and trouble–shooting; developing new software and programs; client services; and so forth. The bank has both in-house IT staff (consisting of Singaporeans, Employment Pass and S-Pass holders) and sub-contractors. According to Kumar, within the IT department some jobs like IT programming are outsourced. Streams of Indian IT workers deployed by their parent company come to Singapore on 3- or 6-month contracts and return to India. Kumar and Siva, though, had directly applied for their positions in Singapore and, being on Employment Pass, can stay up to three years in Singapore with the possibility of finding a new job if they are no longer required in their current position.

The working conditions for IT workers were generally good; however, many of the key issues among this cohort had to do with their contract status as 'employees' and a sense of uncertainty this caused in terms of day-to-day life, relationships with permanent colleagues and who to turn to in difficulty or for complaints. The uncertainty of tenure was highlighted by many of our interviewees as always hovering in their minds. This uncertainty of tenure also made it difficult for these workers to feel settled, especially those who had brought family. Kumar, for instance, spoke about being employed on a contract basis:

> Because for contract, okay, I just came here to work, I don't care about it. Contract means like when the project is over, they will ask us to go. So I am worried. If I'm married, and have to consider contract, it's very difficult. But in terms of permanent, okay, even though I don't have a job, I can stay back . . .
>
> So when I keep in mind, even though my job is good or something, automatically I feel scared, I think. Even I get in touch with the manager (and ask), okay, if I lose my job, what to do. If I'm a permanent, they cannot ask me to do this. At the same time, another (issue) is the visa. If I'm a PR or a citizen, at least I can find another job.

A key aspect of labour hire that has been discussed in non-migration-related literature is the precarious nature of contract-based employment, and the ambiguous, both in legal and moral terms, relationship 'triad' between the labour hire firm, the employee and the employer/ day-to-day workplace. Despite many of these IT workers working in one company for long periods – in some cases running into years – the ambiguous nature of their employment status – as contracted staff, rather than direct employees – had a negative impact on their everyday life as a worker. For example, relationships with local colleagues were minimal. It appeared that local employees of the client company were reluctant to 'invest time' in establishing friendships with these workers who were understood to be temporary and not 'real colleagues'. Furthermore, the temporary status of Employment or S-Pass holders meant that they themselves were reluctant to engage with Singaporeans regarding pay or work conditions and personal issues. As Shiva noted, 'the one is physically different. If we like to share some things we can just share. Personal things, we cannot share because each different people will tell to anyone . . . so we don't tell'. And Kumar added, 'makes us worried all the time. Sometimes . . . how can I trust you? So we will tell our friends, but not tell our colleagues. Because friends will try to help you. Colleagues not so sure'. In occupations like IT services where there are turn-overs, characterised by casual and contract labour and project-based tasks which atomises workplace interaction to a handful of people, the conditions for developing enduring ties with other colleagues are weak. The fear of gossip and limited trust make workplace relationships bounded to the routines of work, especially for Kumar and Siva.

The middling transnational migrants in the works of Conradson and Latham (2005a and 2005b), Ho (2011) and Parutis (2014) were middle-class and had travelled overseas for personal development rather than economic gain. As Conradon and Latham (2005b: 288) point out for middling transnationals, 'mobility emerges from a complex set of personal motivations, amongst which financial considerations are not necessarily primary'. It has to be emphasized that Singapore has long been a destination for Indian, especially Tamil, immigrants. Further, the mobility and settlement of Musuguntha Vellalar caste members in Singapore since the 1950s have resulted in the production of small-scale, village-level social relationships that span across national borders. Singapore therefore is an attractive place for employment and maintaining tightly based caste and kin relationships and networks. The middling Tamil migrant workers were educated and thus less constrained by what jobs they could do, length of stay and so forth. In addition to better salaries compared India, our participants, like the Poles and Lithuanians in Parutis' (2014) study, expected their jobs to 'provide them with personal and professional development'. However, as Employment and S-Pass temporary visa holders, they were restricted by the specific visa conditions from moving freely to other jobs or employers and advocating for better work conditions and pay. Nonetheless, the opportunity for these visa holders to apply for permanent residency after spending several years on the job meant that there was potential to advance their future prospects of better and meaningful employment.

At the level of everyday interactions in the workplace, it can be argued that Singapore has a relatively simple racial landscape and so many Singaporeans are aware of and act in respectful ways towards the cultural and religious codes and practices of the other groups. This is particularly so around everyday codes surrounding cross-cultural communication, banter, food and religious observance (Wise and Velayutham 2014: 408). Singapore's racial composition of Chinese, Malays and Indians and the cultural affinities and knowledge each group has with one another means that the presence of middling Tamil migrant workers in the work place does not pose any threat or disruption to everyday interactions. The migrant workers, despite language barriers, were able to maintain convivial relationship with their fellow Singaporean colleagues. At the same time, as Employment and/or S-Pass visa holders, they were acutely aware that they were on temporary and insecure work contracts and that building long-term and deep workplace friendship was unviable unless they have been granted permanent residence in Singapore.

Outside of work, the steady arrival of these new middling transnational migrants has helped to grow Singapore's Musuguntha Vellalar population. These young Musuguntha Vellalars are educated, tech savvy and navigate mobile technologies and electronic and social media applications with ease. In the next section, I explore how the migrants maintain their transnational relationship with digital and social technologies.

Part 2: The translocal village goes live!

The Musuguntha Vellalar community consists of 32 villages located in the district of Thanjavur and quite a number surrounding the town of Pattoukkotai. It is a relatively closed community because of endogamous and cross-cousin marriages. Even as many Musuguntha Vellalars ventured overseas since the 1950s, the practice of arranged marriages within the caste community has meant that the villages have remained a tightly knit social unit bounded at once by place and extended family caste-relations (Velayutham and Wise 2014). The first generation Musuguntha Vellalars caste members in Singapore replicated a particular form of moral community which we describe as the 'translocal village' based around village-scale, place-oriented familial and neighbourly ties that have subsequently expanded across extended space. The moral order of the translocal village was underpinned by a sense of reciprocal obligation and responsibility to fellow caste-members and policed by an affective regime of guilt, shame and fear of ostracism. Collectively, through the power of gossip and the panoptic gaze of the *villagers* in India and Singapore, a self-regulating and self-generating transnational moral community was maintained. At that time the villagers in our study were primarily linked with their village in Tamil Nadu via landlines and regular return visits.

The immediacy and intensity of this transnational network have been further transformed since young Musuguntha Vellalars embarked on creating an online presence of the community and the arrival of low-cost and shorter air travel time. A young generation of tech savvy and relatively mobile Musuguntha Vellalars especially based in Singapore have now created a seamless connection, barring internet connection failure, to their villages. Introduction of daily flights between Singapore and Tiruchirappalli has meant that, with the time difference, villagers can now depart from Singapore in the morning (3-hour flight) and arrive (2-hour drive) in the village for lunch. This route is offered by budget airlines such as Tiger and Air India Express at very low cost. The frequency of villagers' movement between Singapore and the villages has multiplied, with up to 8 daily flights between Singapore and Tiruchirappalli.

Since the founding of the Soorappallam village website, scores of others of the Musuguntha Vellalar community have sprung up. In 2010 Mani, a civil engineer working in Singapore, setup the Soorappallam Facebook and WhatsApp group. Unlike the static features of standard website, social media such as Facetime, Skype, Facebook, WhatsApp and other online communication tools with their interactive features have intensified the transnational social field and relationships. News and information now circulate in real time between villagers located in different places. In 2015 the Musuguntha community organised its first Family Day via WhatsApp messaging. A total of 400 people – which included Singapore citizens, permanent residents and Employment, S-Pass and Work Permit holders and their children – attended the event. The family day is now held annually during the June school holidays, and there are plans to organise other activities to build stronger relationships between caste members.

The work of the translocal village discussed in my earlier study (Velayutham and Wise 2005) still continues with a younger generation of Musuguntha Vellalar migrants now at the helm. Regular monetary contributions are made to support the educational needs of poorer villagers, and funds are raised for fellow caste members contesting in elections as Member of the Legislative Assembly or Member of Parliament in India. The villagers also raise funds for the construction of buildings and the restoration of temples and schools.

On the 18th of June, Rajendran's elderly mother passed away in the village. Within minutes, mobile text messages about the death were sent to relatives far and wide. Even before the customary landline phone call was made to close relatives outside of the village and in the diaspora, news of the death had gone viral via the Soorappallam Facebook and WhatsApp messaging. This was shortly followed by information on the funeral and prayer services. By the end of the day, some 100 relatives started gathering at Rajendran's Aunt Mani's house in Singapore to pay their respects. Eleven days later, Mani's family conducted Atma Shanthi pooja (prayers for the departed) at the Sri Veeramakaliamman Temple located in the middle of Little India in Singapore. Some 15 close relatives attended the temple ceremony – mostly young men on S-Pass and recent Permanent Residents. Before the commencement of the prayers, a fellow villager was showing Mani and her husband, in their late 70s, a video on his mobile phone that he had received just an hour ago of a gas-bottle explosion that rocked Pattukkottai (closest town to Soorappallam). The video clip was already uploaded on the Soorappallam Facebook page. The young men who had not seen each other in months were exchanging gossip, news and messages posted on the Facebook page. All of them were multi-tasking – participating in the conversation and scrolling through the Facebook page on their mobile phones. One villager commented that they should ask *so and so* to sign up to the Facebook page so that he is up to date with the happenings in the village. Another person said that because he was on many Facebook groups he has been careful not to randomly post personal/family pictures on his Facebook page, as he was worried that he was giving away too much information.

I queried what has become of the Soorappallam webpage? One person replied that the number of visits to the website has substantially dropped since a Singapore-based villager started the Soorappallam group on Facebook. The interactive nature of Facebook and regular updates has made it extremely popular with well over 200 followers (in the village and the diaspora in Singapore, UK and the USA). Furthermore, villagers also send text messages and audio/video files via their mobile devices, factoring time-zone difference, immediately as significant events unfold or trivial chatters. Four of the older villagers who were listening to the conversation started shaking their heads, and one person said these days they instantly know what is happening in the village on their mobile phone!

Pioneering studies on transnational migrants' use of mobile phones (as opposed to landlines) suggest that transnational communication has shifted from an intermittent event to a part of daily life (Vertovec 2004, 2009; Horst 2006; Thompson 2009). Gone are the days of prepaid telephone cards and costly mobile phones and international call charges. We have reached a point where owning and use of a mobile phone with a data package has become relatively inexpensive. Mobile phones now connect far and near, here and now, old and younger generations and different genders and class backgrounds. They enable the transnational production of communities and the reproduction of an extensive kinship network between Singapore and the Musuguntha villages and within these localities themselves.

The low cost of text messaging (especially via hotspots and free wifi) has completely reshaped distance and presence. As Bacigalupe and Camara (2012: 1428) observe:

> Texting can create an ambient virtual co-presence in which people have an ongoing awareness of others. Text messaging allows for communication of insignificant or non-urgent updates 'predicated on the sense of ambient accessibility, a shared virtual space that is generally available between a few friends or with a loved ones' (Ito and Okabe 2005: 264). The texts create a space between direct interaction and non-interaction. Transnational migrants can use technologies like texting to cultivate this 'ambient co-presence' among family members who are in other countries and share information that would typically be inaccessible across geographic distances.

The cultivation of the *ambient co-presence* is especially interesting because, up until the arrival of mobile technologies, the Musuguntha Vellalars reproduced their kinship relationships in the context of immigration through occasional return visits and sporadic phone calls. The villagers in Singapore met regularly to catch up on news updates and partake in gossip. Now the 'daily virtual communications that characterise their present exchanges' (Bacigalupe and Camara 2012: 1431) have created the capacity to maintain connections continuously and unhindered. The circulation of images through text-message services has also expanded the repertoire of information tools available to this transnational migrant community, thus amplifying and cementing the Musuguntha Vellalar community bond and identity across the transnational social field. Moreover, as Dekker and Engbersen (2014) have argued, social media, in general, have enabled users to primarily generate their own content and participate in an open (or semi-open) network infrastructure enabling networking.

As a close-knit kinship and caste-based community, the Musuguntha Vellalars have continuously been back and forth between their home villages and Singapore since the 1950s. This city-state still remains an attractive destination because of its relative proximity to India, multiracial population, employment and lifestyle opportunities and importantly the presence of an existing Musuguntha Vellalar community. Many have settled in Singapore, others come for temporary work and the better educated young caste members seeking employment opportunities and work experience hope to settle permanently. The latter are able to return regularly to the villages on budget air carrier services, marry and bring their families to Singapore. These face-to-face meetings or offline contacts combined with mobile phone, internet and social media technologies have enabled the reproduction of strong ties between older and new/younger transnational migrant community members. Unlike the previous generation, the young Musuguntha Vellalars exchange information and resources more readily, quickly and actively assist fellow caste members to migrate to Singapore. In this paper I have shown that the changing characteristics of migrants and contours of migration pattern have strengthened transnational social ties and that mobile technologies and social media now play a central role in connecting and replicating the translocal village in Singapore.

Note

1 The Musuguntha Vellalar caste community members also identify themselves as Veerakodi Vellalars and reside in 32 villages collectively termed as Musuguntha Nadu, named after a Chola king. The 32 villages are Aaladikkumulai, Alampalam, Alathur, Andami, Athikkottai, Eanathi, Karuppur, Kasangadu, Keerathur, Mannangadu, Mathukkur, Mattankal, Moothakuruchi, Musiri, Nattuchalai, Paalamuthi, Palaya Madukkur, Pallathur, Pattikkadu, Pulavanchi, Pudukkotai, Sembalur, Sengapaduthankadu, Seventhanpatti, Silambavelankadu, Soorapallam, Sundampatti, Thamarankottai, Thittakkudi, Ulloor, Vendakkottai, and Vattukudi.

References

Amin, A. 2013. *Land of Strangers*. London: Polity Press.
Amin, A 2002. 'Ethnicity and the multicultural city: Living with diversity'. *Environment & Planning A* (34) 959–980.
Bacigalupe, G. and Camara, M. 2012. 'Transnational families and social technologies: Reassessing immigration psychology'. *Journal of Ethnic and Migration Studies* 38(9): 1425–1438.
Biao, X. 2005. 'Gender, dowry and the migration system of Indian information technology professional'. *Indian Journal of Gender Studies* 12(2–3): 357–380.
Conradson, D. and Latham, A. 2005a. 'Transnational urbanism: Attending to everyday practices and mobilities'. *Journal of Ethnic and Migration Studies* 31(2): 227–233.
Conradson, D. and Latham, A. 2005b. 'Friendship, networks and transnationality in a world city: Antipodean transmigrants in London'. *Journal of Ethnic and Migration Studies* 31(2): 287–305.

Datta, K., McIlwaine, C., Herbert, J., Evans, Y., May, J. and Wills, J. (2009) 'Men on the move: Narratives of migration and work among low-paid migrant men in London'. *Social & Cultural Geography* 10(8): 853–873.

Dekker, R. and Engbersen, G. 2014. 'How social media transform migrant networks and facilitate migration'. *Global Networks* 14(4): 1470–2266.

Gilroy, P. 2004. *After Empire: Melancholia or Convivial Culture?* London: Routledge.

Government of Singapore. 1991. *The Next Lap*. Singapore: Times Editions.

Ho, L.E.E. 2011. 'Migration trajectories of 'highly skilled' middling transnationals: Singaporean transmigrants in London'. *Population, Space and Place* 17 (1): 116–129.

Horst, H. 2006. 'The blessings and burdens of communication: Cell phones in Jamaican transnational social fields'. *Global Networks* 6(2): 143–159.

Ito, M. and Okabe, B. 2005. 'Technosocial situations: Emergent structuring of mobile e-mail use'. In Ito, M., Okabe, B., and Matsuda, M. (eds), *Personal, portable, pedestrian: Mobile phones in Japanese life*, 257–76. Cambridge, MA: MIT Press.

Komter, A. 2005. *Social solidarity & the gift*. New York: Cambridge University Press.

Levitt, P. and Schiller, N. 2004. 'Conceptualizing simultaneity: A transnational social field perspective on society'. *International Migration Review* 38(3): 1002–1039.

Osella, F. and Osella C. 2000. 'Migration, money and masculinity in Kerala'. *The Journal of the Royal Anthropological Institute* 6(1): 117–133.

Parutis, V. 2014. '"Economic migrants" or "middling transnationals"? East European migrants' experiences of work in the UK'. *International Migration* 52(1): 36–55.

Pettigrew, T.F. 1998. 'Intergroup contact theory'. *Annual Review of Psychology* 49: 65–85.

Sennett, R. 1998, *The corrosion of character*. New York: W.W. Norton.

Smith, M.P. 2005. 'Transnational urbanism revisited'. *Journal of Ethnic and Migration Studies* 31(2): 235–244.

Thompson, E. 2009. 'Mobile phones, communities and social networks among foreign workers in Singapore'. *Global Networks* 9(3): 359–380.

Wise, A. and Velayutham, S. 2014. Conviviality in everyday multiculturalism: Some brief comparisons between Singapore and Sydney'. *European Journal of Cultural Studies* 17(4): 406–430.

Wise, A. and Velayutham, S. 2008. 'Second generation Tamils & a cross cultural marriage: Managing the translocal village in a moment of cultural rupture'. *Journal of Ethnic and Migration Studies* 34(1): 113–131.

Velayutham, S. and Wise, A. 2005. 'Moral economies of a translocal village: Obligations and shame among South Indian transnational migrants'. *Global Networks* 5(1): 27–47.

Vertovec, S. 2009. *Transnationalism*. London: Routledge.

Vertovec, S. 2004. 'Cheap calls: The social glue of migrant transnationalism'. *Global Networks* 4(2): 219–224.

Vogl, G. 2009. Work as community: Narratives of solidarity and teamwork in the contemporary workplace, who owns them? *Sociological Research Online* 14(4): 1–4).

PART V

On historic and contemporary networks in transnational spaces

18

THE TRANSNATIONAL MOBILITY OF INDIANS IN THE TIME OF THE BRITISH EMPIRE

Sumita Mukherjee

Transnational approaches to migration history allow us to 'examine the impact and reasons for migration at both the point of departure and that of arrival' (Bayly et al. 2006). During formal British crown control of India, 1858–1947, Indian men, women and children were extremely mobile. They migrated, travelled and moved both within the Indian subcontinent and to nearly all other parts of the world. Their mobility had social, economic and political impacts upon the Indian subcontinent, especially shaping and influencing nationalist politics in the lead up to independence. Indians were also shaping new communities outside of the subcontinent, which were determining the identities and outlook of the nations they were becoming a part of, as well as influencing the nature of modern transnational links India had with the rest of the world.

In this chapter I will be outlining the ways in which historians have considered the movement of professional adult Indians between 1858 and 1947 and the ways in which these mobile Indians created and were involved in transnational ties and associations, which were influential in shaping understandings of the nation and empire. It is during this period of imperial rule that nationalism, anti-colonialism and new ideas of the international and global grew. Indian men and women left the subcontinent to pursue economic and political independence as individuals, but also engaged in a breadth of organisations, associations and debates around nationalism, citizenship and socialism, among other topics. Despite their mobility, much of their travel and their associations were shaped by the predicament of being colonial subjects. Their experiences and networks were also inflected by issues of caste, class, religion and gender.

The focus of this chapter will mainly be on educated, urban Indians, who had the wealth, or access to wealth, that enabled them to travel freely in this period – forming the emergent middle class in India from the nineteenth century onwards.[1] There were millions of other Indians who were forced to leave the subcontinent, usually through some form of economic necessity. Following the official abolition of the slave trade in 1833, millions of men, women and children were sold into bondage labour, largely on plantations in the Caribbean and Pacific, until indenture was officially abolished in 1917. Other Indians were engaged in labour on the African continent or tried to find work in the Americas or Australasia. Often these journeys were treacherous, exemplified by incidents such as the Komagata Maru incident of 1914. The ship arrived in Vancouver in May 1914, holding 376 passengers from India (mainly Punjabis).

Canadian authorities refused entry to the majority; only 20 were allowed to disembark. The SS Komagata Maru was eventually forced to return to India, via Japan, with many Indian passengers killed or jailed when they disembarked in Calcutta (Johnston 1989).

Much of this chapter focuses on Britain. The long-lasting trade routes between India and Britain, solidified by the East India Company, made travel to Britain a well-worn route for ship-workers, peddlers, and traders for centuries: the first known baptism of an Indian in Britain occurred in 1616 (Visram 2002). During this time of formal imperial rule, Indian men and women strengthened their transnational ties with Britain. Much of this was inevitable because of the structures of imperial governance. India was ruled by the British Crown. Although representative assemblies, limited in nature, were introduced in 1920 in India, major political decisions relating to the constitution, trade and foreign policy were determined through the Secretary of State for India's office in London and the British Parliament. Political petitioners often had to travel to Britain and form associations in Britain in order to gain political leverage in India. The Indian education system was also based upon the British one, and many Indians were compelled to pursue educational and professional training in Britain in subjects such as law and medicine to enhance their career opportunities in India. Admission to the higher levels of the Indian Civil Service was also determined by examinations that took place in Britain, until 1922.

The history of nineteenth- and twentieth-century British imperialism is as much about anti-colonial nationalism as it is about imperial dominance. As Indians became increasingly educated in British systems, as they gained promotions within the imperial bureaucracy and as they had opportunities to travel and gain a better sense of India as a nation and Britain as an imperial ruler, they began to demand more political representation and eventually to campaign for full independence. This was not a straightforward struggle. Indian nationalist politics was characterised by splits between left and right, between religious and regional factions, and culminated in the bloody partition of the subcontinent.[2] Resistance against imperial rule was not solely characterised by violence, nor did it only take place in the Indian subcontinent. As Rehana Ahmed and I showed in a collection we edited in 2012, Indians were engaged in a varied range of resistances in Britain in this time period, from violent acts of 'terrorism' and riots, to boycotts, literary critiques and challenges to ideas of racial and class hierarchies through their very presence in other parts of the world (Ahmed and Mukherjee 2012, introduction).

Yet, the relationship between Britons and Indians was not all about conflict and resistance. The British Crown had relied on Indian 'collaborators' to govern their empire, and many Indians were loyal to the imperial hierarchy. Aside from the public sphere, many friendships and networks were forged privately between Indians and British people. Collaborations across the arts, for example, were evident by the twentieth century, such as through the India Society, which was set up in 1910 by British artists in London. Indian writers and poets from India and other countries published alongside each other.[3] Ayahs (nursemaids) accompanied British families on their travels, looking after their children. Indians were also engaging in a range of intimate relationships, creating new families and communities through their migration.

In this chapter I will draw attention to some trends in the historiography of mobility, networks and exchange. Much of the focus will be on Britain and the Anglo-world, as I discuss the ways in which Indians navigated transnational associations at the heart of the empire. Most of the attention of this chapter will also be on nationalism and the ways in which Indians used transnational links at the height of empire as a way to challenge a range of social and political hierarchies. This is an area of history that has been influenced by the works of geographers, sociologists and post-colonial theorists but is heavily reliant on the types of archives and archival material we use when trying to give voice to itinerant Indians, from different vernacular and cultural backgrounds and levels of literacy. At a time of empire, much of their movement and connections can be found by reading colonial archives, surveillance records and ship lists. Personal memoirs, accounts, writings, photos and other materials do exist and can be used by historians looking for the perspectives of educated, elite Indians, but we must always be conscious of whose privileged voices emerge more forcefully in these archives and whose perspectives continue to be silenced, obscured or inaccessible.

Transnational mobility and networks

As Mary Louise Pratt has argued, empire provided 'contact zones' where disparate cultures could meet, collaborate and clash, often in asymmetric relations of domination and subordination (Pratt 2008, 7, passim). These were not merely created by colonisers in colonised spaces; mobile Indians as well were creating new 'contact zones' and engaging in them in various sites around the world. In them they were collaborating and clashing, reasserting and challenging various hierarchies that had been solidified by empire. As Ann Stoler has argued, the production of knowledge may have been uneven during the time of empire, but the circuits of exchange were not just abstract; they were peopled. People moved, changed identities, and borrowed or reinvented categories, identities and cultures (Stoler 2006, 6). We see this in the case of Indians.

Antoinette Burton and Tony Ballantyne (2016) have hugely shaped the study of mobility and networks in the field of the British Empire and World History. They have emphasised the importance of considering gender and embodiment when studying mobile subjects, as well as the range of nodes that networks had. Transnational relationships were not just binary ones between coloniser and colonised, or between Britain and India, but incorporated influences, networks and contacts with a range of cultures and people across the world. Burton and Ballantyne have emphasised how mobility was at the root of much of the agitation, rebellion and insurgence from below:

> These folks were radical not simply because they were rising up from below or striking at the root of power, but because they were more often than not mobile – literally, on the move. That rootless energy made them cosmopolitan in their repertoires and ready to appropriate forms and images across a range of movements and causes . . .[4]

Mobility, therefore, gave Indians agency during a time when they were subject peoples and offered new ways of networking and organising in radical fashions to challenge hierarchies of empire, race, class and gender.

Tony Ballantyne has encouraged historians to think more deeply about the webbed connections of the empire, and of the ways disparate parts of the empire were brought together in new relations. These networks did not solely emanate from Britain. These connections were not permanent. They were constantly being constructed and shifting, growing and declining, during the time of empire (Ballantyne 2014). As Alan Lester has emphasised, imperial networks were nodal, and there were multiple centres of connection (Lester 2006). Another geographer, David Featherstone, has explained how transnational solidarity could be shaped by marginal groups despite uneven relations across space. It was not merely elites who used these networks for political action. Studying these historical transnational networks can reveal subaltern identity and agency and can reveal how subaltern resistances were not confined to particular places but embraced transnational spaces (Featherstone 2007). Clearly, the British Empire was not the only structure in which Indians were engaging, moving and networking in during this period. However, for the purposes of this chapter, my focus is on the spaces and forms of empire.

Travel and travel-writing

Understanding of space and place is very important in assessing the effects of mobility and analysing the networks, connections and solidarities that form during the time of empire. Elleke Boehmer's research on 'Indian Arrivals' to Britain between 1870 and 1915 highlights the importance of the destination for Indian travellers and also the journey itself. The Suez passage, for example, held symbolic importance for many Indians, as it was seen as border between 'East' and 'West'. Arrival in Britain gave these Indians a sense of achievement, but this was one 'of welcome and incursion, of encountering an ostensibly strange new world that was, however, in many ways foreseen and charted in advance' (Boehmer 2015, 16).

But it was the journey as well that was incredibly important for mobile Indians in shaping their cosmopolitan outlook, that allowed them to see more of the world and to become modern imperial citizens. The journey emphasised the shifting nature of their position in the world, the cultural transitions between spaces, and it taught mobile Indians how to adapt and navigate new thoughts and identities. Travel writing was a powerful way of 'dramatizing and consolidating these mobile new Indian identities' (Boehmer 2015, 63). It was a specific genre of writing, adapted from Western models of 'exploration' and travel. By adopting this genre, Indian travellers were able to demonstrate their modernity and the modernity of the emerging Indian nation.

Indian travel writers in this period were reversing the 'gaze' of European travel writers who had 'explored' and written about the subcontinent and the 'East' for centuries; who in their accounts and attempts to 'map' the subcontinent had imposed their own ideas, borders and hierarchies upon 'India'. Examples of such Indian travel writers include T. N. Mukharji, Lala Baijnath and Jhinda Ram, whose accounts of their visits to Britain and Europe were all published in India in the late nineteenth century. For mobile Indians, especially those travelling to Europe and Britain, their journeys were a process of awakening on several fronts. Literate Indians were well versed in European history and literature and had strong ideas about what Europe and Britain would look like. Their travels showed them the difference between their expectations and reality, but in their writings they often repurposed and reiterated tropes around the 'West' in an Occidentalist gaze. Their journeys, especially in the nineteenth century, were also important in showing them new modern technologies, different social customs, and encouraging them to consider what elements of modernity they might wish to learn and bring back to India (Burton 1996; Sen 2005).

Travel itself was a form of modernity. The ways in which middle- and upper-class Indians engaged with discourses of travel show how Indians were grappling with issues of modernity and colonialism at the same time. Indians utilised travel in specific ways according to their caste, class and gender. As Inderpal Grewal has argued, analysis of this travel and the discourse around it, in the comparisons Indian men and women made between the binaries of 'East' and 'West', reveal the ways in which colonial modernity was a gendered discourse. Indian men and women had different opportunities for travel, different experiences and were constructed differently by the people they met (Grewal 1996, 15). As Burton has explained further, the home and domestic spaces were important figurations for Indian women, even mobile Indian women such as Cornelia Sorabji, Sarojini Naidu or Janaki Bonnerjee. During the high nationalist period of the interwar years, nationalists were keen to depict India as a modern nation, but it was also depicted as motherland, home and a domestic space – an arena that Indian women had to preserve, including mobile Indian women (Burton 2003, 9–11).

Indian travellers were not just passive tourists; they were the object of interest too in the West – their skin colour, clothing and accents were remarked upon and objectified.

Through the process of being observers, but also being observed at the same time, Indian travel writers were reconceptualising their sense of 'self' and 'Indianness' through their presentation of the 'Indian gaze'. As Burton puts it: 'Thus they did not simply return the gaze, but demonstrated how readily available its disciplinary regimes were for contest and refiguration – especially by Indian men, whose pretensions to nationhood and its cultural corollary, Victorian masculinity, were under scrutiny at this particular historical moment' (Burton 1996, 128).

Britain and the imperial metropolis

In this section I want to focus on Britain, and specifically London, as a key site of metropolitan encounter for Indians to engage in transnational networks and collaboration, following the discussion above. Michael Fisher has explained how Indians living in London after 1857 had their understanding of the British and themselves reshaped, through awareness of the degrading effects of colonialism, and how the shared condition they held with Indians from other regions often overcame traditional cultural or political distinctions (Fisher 2008, 430). Fisher has pointed out that it was those who came in the later nineteenth and twentieth centuries who better understood British culture, politics and law. They had many more compatriots to associate with and with whom to share the experience, and it was they who discovered the discrepancies between the British image of liberal humanism and the practice of British colonialism in India (Fisher 2008, 438).

Indian views of Britain shaped Indian identities. Their admiration for Britain often played out in the form of an inferiority complex, which was related to issues of race, class and culture. Comparisons between India and Britain led to tensions because of the different values upon which societies can be judged (Nandy 1983). Lakshmi Subramaniam has argued that Western-educated Indians searched for self-esteem but could never be satisfied when they imposed alien, Western standards upon themselves. Subramaniam has highlighted the 'concealed sense of injury, the need for approval by Englishmen, the yearning to visit England, the craving for recognition and acceptance within white social circles in India' and 'the exhausting attempt at imitation' as signs of an aggressive 'inferiority complex' that had arisen from colonial subjugation (Subramanian 1995, 451). At the same time, some Hindus, including Mohandas Gandhi, had had caste objections to travelling overseas, which remained relevant for some regional caste communities into the early twentieth century (Carroll 1979). Thus many Indians had exaggerated fears about the effects of going abroad, including fears of contamination and dilution of their culture and traditions (Markandaya 1976). As a result, travel and stay in Britain brought up a range of emotions and responses.

Admiration for British culture was demonstrated by those Indians who adopted British habits and characteristics, notably Indians (from all regions) who had studied at British universities. However, this created further tensions, as they were sometimes mocked by both the British and Indians for their mimicry. They had become 'Brown Englishmen' as desired by Macaulay in 1835, but this only served to increase their alienation. Mimicry was pursued by some Indians who had been educated in Britain because of the way the colonial power in India had accentuated difference and measured success by British standards. This included adoption of 'Western' dress and other material goods, eating habits and other leisure activities when abroad but also upon their return. Examples included the family of W. C. Bonnerjee, whose wife adopted English dress and whose children were educated in England and were given mixtures of 'Indian' and 'English' names (Bhabha 1984; Majumdar 2013). This widened divisions within Indian society and entrenched stereotypes about Britain and the West. However,

Indians could adopt these manners without travelling to Britain. Western tastes permeated Indian society widely, and Indian admiration implied an understanding of the superiority of European ways (Raychaudhuri 1992).

The influence of British customs on mobile Indians is best exemplified through the example of Indian students at British universities in this period. As I have shown elsewhere, despite the heterogenous experience of thousands of Indian students in Britain, in the first few decades of the twentieth century, there are certain trends that emerge. This group of Indians were known as the 'England-Returned', a term which demonstrates the social significance British education and experience was given in Indian elite society at the time. As students, many young Indians adopted Anglicised manners and clothing, including the well-known figure Mohandas Gandhi. Anglicisation was often equated with 'superiority'. However, with growing political consciousness, and growing criticism of 'deracinated' Indians, many of these students felt torn by their 'loyalties' and a growing sense of their racial and national identity. D. F. Karaka, for example, who studied at Oxford and became President of the Oxford Union, explained: 'Intellectually I felt I belonged to the West, emotionally to the East' (Karaka 1938, 81).

Many Indian students became politicised by their experiences in Britain, particularly influenced by the associations and societies they joined, and it is notable that so many leaders of the Indian nationalist movement – including Jawaharlal Nehru, Subhas Chandra Bose, Muhammad Ali Jinnah and Sarojini Naidu – were educated in Britain. Some university societies were exclusively formed for Indian students only, such as the Majlis societies in London, Cambridge and Oxford. Other students, such as Mulk Raj Anand, Jyoti Basu and Renuka Ray, engaged with more transnational groups such as various Communist societies, reading clubs and the Communist Party of Great Britain itself (Mukherjee 2010, 110). Outside of the student milieu, many other Indians were engaging with British politics. Britain had elected three men of Indian descent in this period into the British parliament – Dadabhai Naoroji (Liberal Party, 1892), Mancherjee Bhownaggree (Conservative Party, 1895 and 1900), and Shapurji Saklatvala (Labour Party, 1922; Communist Party, 1924). These men were engaged in transnational political associations beyond Britain but also demonstrated the roles that Indians could have at the heart of the empire.

As Michael Goebel argues, the social history of migration is an integral root of the intellectual history of anti-imperialism: 'Migration rendered injustices, inequalities, and the juridical pitfalls of colonialism much more palpable' (Goebel 2015, 4). Goebel and I have drawn similar conclusions about the ways in which colonial subjects became politicised during their stay in imperial centres; where I have written about Indian students in Britain, Goebel has discussed colonial subjects in Paris. However, Goebel has warned that much of the literature on non-European migrant groups tends to focus on one particular group and one country of destination, whereas historians need to pay more attention to cross-cultural linkage between different groups and places (Goebel 2015, 7). Britain and Europe were not the only destinations for Indian students. In 1906–1907, the Industrial and Scientific Association of Calcutta sent 99 scholars abroad for technical training. Twelve were sent to Britain, and two to France, but 36 to Japan and 48 to the USA (Sarkar 1973, 114).

The experience of travelling to, and living in, Britain, however, sharpened the identities of Indians, who became more aware of their subject positions within the empire but were also able to take advantage of life in Britain to further their careers. In Britain, Indians from across the subcontinent could meet fellow-Indian subjects from other parts of the subcontinent, often for the first time, drawing into sharp relief the commonalities between the diverse Indian regions and allowing these educated Indians to articulate how an Indian nationalism could be understood. This facilitated the growth and strength of organisations such as the India League and Indian National Congress, who worked to fight for Indian nationalism in the early twentieth century.

Political networks/ transnational campaigning/anti-colonialism

Indian transnational activism during this period often brought together diverse groups united by a common cause. Political groups such as the Indian National Congress and India League attracted an array of people with sympathies for the Indian nationalist cause, and the Indian Freedom Association, for example, included Egyptians, Somalis, West Indians and Malaysians among its members (Fisher, Lahiri and Thandi 2007, 137). Indians were also involved in political activities that were not of direct 'nationalist' concern. Shapuri Saklatvala and V. K. Krishna Menon, for example, were sympathetic to the Irish Home Rule movement, which worked in tandem on issues of independence from British imperialist control (O'Malley 2012). Indians involved in transnational mobility were engaging with debates around empire, nationhood and citizenship outside of Britain as well. Political discussions did not have to take place just in London, and the benefits of the metropolis in bringing together students, activists and exiled people were replicated in other Western cities such as Paris and New York.

Kris Manjapra has written extensively about the activities of Indians in Europe and elsewhere in the early twentieth century. As he explains, during anticolonial struggles from the end of the nineteenth century, Indians were engaging with shared transnational public spaces, in 'cosmopolitan thought zones' (Bose and Manjapra 2010, 1). Specific examples of mobile Indians involved in the circulation of ideas include the scientists P. C. Ray and B. N. Dasgupta, or the artist Benoy Kumar Sarkar. But it was the anti-colonial, and usually socialist activities of many Indians who spent some time in Europe in this period that is pertinent here. Indians were attending specific conferences and Congresses such as the Comintern International 4th Congress in Moscow 1921 (attended by M. N. Roy, Virendranath "Chatto" Chattopadhyaya, Bhupendranath Datta and Muhammad Barakatullah). Datta also spent time in New York, where he met African-American thinker W. E. B. Du Bois and was involved in the Bronx Socialist Club. Chatto was also a huge influence on a range of Indians who came through Europe, including Abinash Chandra Bhattacharya (Manjapra 2014, 53, 54, 179, 248). Subhas Chandra Bose spent a formative period in Austria in the mid-1930s, meeting Indian students and Benito Mussolini in Rome. Another key transnational anticolonial organisation was the Ghadar party, formed by Lal Har Dayal, a former Oxford student, in San Francisco from 1913. This party had strong links with the radical India House group in London and the 'revolutionaries' V. S. Savarkar and Shyamaji Krishnavarma. Meanwhile, Mohandas Gandhi had honed much of his political acumen while working in South Africa as a lawyer between 1893 and 1914.

Although European powers continued to hold empires and subject peoples around the world to colonial oppression in this era, imperialism was becoming internationalised and decentralised in this period. This new outlook, as Daniel Gorman has argued, was exemplified by the foundation of the League of Nations but also evident in the increased number of international NGOs and the expansion of transnational civil society (Gorman 2012, esp. 3; Davies 2013). Simultaneously, many men and women looked to form new alliances that decentred global networks away from the West. Mobility and travel abroad had facilitated these alliances. Distance away from India allowed activists to gain some perspective on India's position in the world, on the common fights for freedom and human rights around the world. Political leaders such as Lala Har Dayal and Sohan Singh Bhakna of the Ghadar Party in the US, and Mohandas Gandhi in Natal, South Africa, were also able to galvanise the growing Indian diaspora into political activity, both for their rights as diasporic citizens and also in connection to the ongoing struggle for independence in India.

The concept of 'Asia' was also becoming very important to Indian elite thinkers. For example, the Japanese Pan-Asian Society convened a Pan-Asian Conference in 1920, and there was an Afro-Asian Conference held in Delhi in 1929 (Davies 2013, 98–99). The Indian poet Rabindranath Tagore forged close intellectual links with Japan and China in this period, keen to discuss the ways a Pan-Asian unity and 'Eastern' civilisation would 'regenerate' the world against the inevitable decline that would come through Western modernity. His critique of imperialism extended to Japanese rule in Korea, so he embraced a cultural rather than political pan-Asianism (Saaler and Szpilman 2011, 1–41). Inspired by the success of Meiji Japan, a number of Indian men travelled to Japan for further education and technological training, while other Indians looked to South-East Asia, where a high proportion of ethnically Indian men and women had migrated for work, to find unity across bonds of Islamism (Stolte and Fischer-Tiné 2012). Influenced by the organisational reach of the Comintern, Jawaharlal Nehru and the Indian National Congress attempted to cement Asian bonds through the League Against Imperialism, and Indian trade unions organised together through associations such as the Pan-Pacific Trade Union and the Asiatic Labour Congress, while ideas about an all-Asian army were put forward by men such as the revolutionary nationalist Raja Mahendra Pratap (Stolte and Fischer-Tiné 2012; Stolte 2012). Yet, as Indians conceptualised and grappled with the 'nation' and nationalism in this period, complicated by the regional, ethnic, religious and caste diversity within the subcontinent itself, and as the Hindu right wing focused its attentions on the 'motherland', visions of pan-Asian unity did not gain much traction. Carolien Stolte and Harald Fischer-Tiné, citing John Steadman, have argued that 'Asia' had no clear definition in this period and that it came out of a continuum of various collective identities (Stolte and Fischer-Tiné 2012, 91).

Exemplified by the foundation of the Greater India Society in 1925, visions of a 'greater India' became the basis for much of the pan-Asian ideology in this period. In the face of British imperialism, Indian nationalists looked to assert themselves intellectually. They attempted to reclaim past glories of Indian civilisation and looked beyond its territorial boundaries to argue that India had given birth to various Asian philosophies. The Indian proponents of a 'greater India' celebrated notions of Indian cultural imperialism and made a claim to Indian cultural superiority over their neighbours, failing to recognise diverse subaltern perspectives from the region. Buoyed by these beliefs, they felt confident to assert the need for Indian leadership in the region (Tankha 2011). As Prasenjit Duara has explained, pan-Asianism in this period was not only based upon abstract and essentialised notions of culture and civilisation, rather than drawing upon the actual encounters Asian people had, it also had a 'lethally close relationship' with nationalism (Duara 2010, 973). It was part of an ideological growth that had seen mobile Indians first use and then reject British experiences and connections in favour of nationalism and other productive collaborations.

Indian women, gender and transnational mobility

As discussed at the outset of this chapter, in considering mobility we need to consider the gendered embodiment of mobility – the different physical experiences of travel that women and men experienced through different quarters on ships and the differences of social contact with host communities as regulated by gendered norms. Discourses around travel, study, nationalism and exploration were also usually gendered in masculine terms, even though images of the emerging Indian nation were often codified as 'female' and 'maternal'. Indian women who travelled in this period were useful to the ongoing Indian nationalist project because they were able to project modern ideas of womanhood and the emerging nation through their education, travel and networking.

For example, it was not just men who were inspired by Chatto and other European revolutionaries. Kamaladevi Chattopadhyaya was inspired by her brother-in-law and visited Berlin in 1921. She became enraged by British authorities when she was (initially) refused a passport to visit Berlin again in 1929, because of her connections to Chatto, even though her visit this time was for an international women's conference (Mukherjee 2018, 134). In contrast, Noor-un-nisa Inayat Khan is an example of someone who engaged in subversive political activities under the sanction of the British state. Khan had lived much of her life in France and had to flee in 1940 when German forces occupied Paris. However, she returned in 1943 as a Special Operations Executive – an undercover wireless operator assisting with communications for Allied forces (Lahiri 2010, ch. 5).

Educated middle-class urban Indian women were also engaging in broader discussions around citizenship and political rights. The notion of citizenship was gendered, and female suffrage was a key concern for many Indian reformers in this period. Mobility had brought this issue into sharp relief as women around the world were campaigning for female suffrage across the early twentieth century. Indian women travelled to and engaged with a range of transnational associations on this issue. These included the British Dominion's Women's Suffrage Union, which brought together women from Australia, New Zealand, Canada, South Africa and India, with its headquarters in London. Indian suffrage activists also engaged with the National Woman's Party in the USA but had a particularly close link with British suffrage groups and activists. Herabai and Mithan Tata, for example, visited London in 1919 to petition the government on the suffrage issue and toured England and Scotland holding meetings in order to win over British public opinion. In 1933, Rajkumari Amrit Kaur, Shareefah Hamid Ali and Muthulakshmi Reddi visited London to meet with a Joint Parliamentary Committee to urge the government to grant full adult suffrage in India, and Kaur set up links between the All-India Women's Conference (one of the main national women's organisations in India) and women's groups in Britain, which led to the publication of a regular bulletin and appointment of liaison officer (Mukherjee 2018, 227).

The main international women's organization involved with female suffrage was the International Woman Suffrage Alliance (IWSA), founded in 1904, which met every three years. Indian women started attending IWSA conferences from 1920, after the end of the First World War. They also contributed, and were regularly reported upon, in the IWSA's journal, *Jus Suffragii: International Woman Suffrage News*, which was published in London. By attending these international women's conferences, Indian women were able to share political strategies, learn about political organisation and demonstrate they ways in which Indian women were 'becoming modern'. In 1935 the IWSA conference was held in Istanbul, marking a sea-change in the organization, which was led by European and American women. This conference was the first time a woman of African descent (Una Marson) was invited to attend, and Indian women attendees formed strong links with the Turkish women there. At this conference Shareefah Hamid Ali gave a speech on 'East and West in Co-operation', in which she spoke about the solidarity of the 'women of the East' and also warned European and American women against any 'arrogant assumption of superiority or patronage' (Mukherjee 2018, 185). Hamid Ali was challenging the ways in which the broader women's movement assumed a perspective from a white European or American standpoint and gave more strength to Indian women activists who started to turn away from British and American women's groups after 1935.

Indian nationalists were able to use these examples of the mobility and engagement of Indian women with international groups (including the League of Nations) in the 1920s and 1930s to demonstrate the alleged progressiveness of Indian society. In so doing they were able to argue that India was able to succeed as modern nation-state. The British Empire had facilitated economic and military networks, but now individuals were creating their own social, cultural and political connections around the world, which acted as a precursor to the more expansive globalisation that took place after the end of the Second World War.

Conclusion

This chapter has offered a snapshot of a few of the ways historians and social scientists have been studying and writing about mobile Indians and their transnational networks at the time of empire. In this chapter I have focused on some of the ways Indians have been the agents of change and creation, not merely subjects of contemporary transnational associations and networks. One might have discussed other issues and networks such as those relating to sex and prostitution, merchant trade and labour at more length, especially those engaging 'lascars'. More could be said about Indian interactions and migration to the United States. There is also a strong area of study around the Indian Ocean, and other chapters in this collection highlight how bright and vibrant the field of transnational studies is.

The history of migration and mobility is a global history. Going forward, writing these kinds of histories may require more collaboration (including more interdisciplinary conversations) and more thought into the process of archival research for this kind of topic. The Afro-Asian Networks Research Collective have offered some reflections on how we can write a more inclusive history around subjected peoples, transnational affinity and complex international networks, such as by collaborative real-time research in archives and in emphasising the importance of translingual research (Afro-Asian Networks 2018).

Clearly, Indian men and women were engaging with a range of transnational conversations at the time of empire. Politicised Indians were engaging with multiple causes; however, their movement, networks and activities were all shaped by their subject position and imperial politics, whatever their political affiliation. As India was moving towards becoming an independent nation, these mobile Indians were demonstrating the ways in which India was already modern and already able to engage in international debates. This included demonstrating the ways in which they were educated, how they were able to travel and the freedom accorded to women travellers. For many of these elite Indians, this process was important for growing a sense of an 'Indian identity' and for cementing links with diasporic communities around the world that would grow further after 1947. The impact of this migration was not just at the point of departure from the Indian subcontinent, nor just at the point of arrival in their destination, but was an ongoing transnational dialogue, which continues to have effects on the travel routes South Asian people take today and the ways in which they imagine their relationship with the rest of the world.

Notes

I would like to thank Stephen Mawdsley for his comments on an earlier version of this piece, and Ajaya Sahoo for his editorial guidance and interventions.

1 For more on the definition and emergence of the Indian 'middle class', see Joshi 2017.
2 It should be noted that I use the term 'Indians' throughout this chapter. I am referring to people who lived in 'India' before 1947 and incorporate modern-day Indians, Pakistanis and Bangladeshis.

3 See Making Britain website, http://www.open.ac.uk/makingbritain/, for more on the connections and networks between South Asians and the British.
4 Burton and Ballantyne 2016, 5, 'Keyword: "World History," "Below," and "Dissent and Disruption"'.

References

Afro-Asian Networks Research Collective. 'Manifesto: Networks of Decolonization in Asia and Africa', *Radical History Review* 131 (May 2018): 176–82.
Ahmed, Rehana and Sumita Mukherjee. *South Asian Resistances in Britain 1858–1947*. London: Continuum, 2012.
Ballantyne, Tony. 'Mobility, Empire, Colonisation', *History Australia* 11, 2 (August 2014): 7–37.
Bayly, C. A., Sven Beckert, Matthew Connelly, Isabel Hofmeyr, Wendy Kozol, and Patricia Seed. 'AHR Conversation: On Transnational History', *American History Review* 111, 5 (Dec. 2006): 1440–64.
Bhabha, Homi. 'Of Mimicry and Man: The Ambivalence of Colonial Discourse', *October* 28 (Spring 1984): 125–33.
Boehmer, Elleke. *Indian Arrivals 1870–1915: Networks of British Empire*. Oxford: Oxford University Press, 2015.
Bose, Sugata and Kris Manjapra, eds. *Cosmopolitan Thought Zones: South Asia and the Global Circulation of Ideas*. Basingstoke: Palgrave Macmillan, 2010.
Burton, Antoinette. *Dwelling in the Archive: Women Writing House, Home, and History in Late Colonial India*. Oxford: Oxford University Press, 2003.
———. 'London and Paris through Indian Spectacles. Making a Spectacle of Empire: Indian Travellers in Fin-de-Siècle London', *History Workshop Journal* 42 (1996): 127–46. https://doi.org/10.1093/hwj/1996.42.127.
Burton, Antoinette and Tony Ballantyne. *World Histories from Below: Disruption and Dissent, 1750 to the Present*. London: Bloomsbury, 2016.
Carroll, Lucy. 'The Seavoyage Controversy and the Kayasthas of North India, 1901–1909', *Modern Asian Studies* 13, 2 (1979): 265–99.
Davies, Thomas. *NGOs: A New History of Transnational Civil Society*. London: Hurst & Company, 2013.
Duara, Prasenjit. 'Asia Redux: Conceptualizing a Region for our Times', *The Journal of Asian Studies* 69, 4 (2010): 963–83.
Featherstone, David. 'The Spatial Politics of the Past Unbound: Transnational Networks and the Making of Political Identities', *Global Networks* 7, 4 (2007): 430–52.
Fisher, Michael H. *Counterflows to Colonialism: Indian Travellers and Settlers in Britain 1600–1857*. Delhi: Permanent Black, 2008.
Fisher, Michael H., Shompa Lahiri and Shinder Thandi. *A South-Asian History of Britain: Four Centuries of Peoples from the Indian Sub-Continent*. Oxford: Greenwood Press, 2007.
Goebel, Michael. *Anti-Imperial Metropolis: Interwar Paris and the Seeds of Third World Nationalism*. New York, NY: Cambridge University Press, 2015.
Gorman, Daniel. *The Emergence of International Society in the 1920s*. Cambridge: Cambridge University Press, 2012.
Grewal, Inderpal. *Home and Harem: Nation, Gender, Empire, and the Cultures of Travel*. London: Leicester University Press, 1996.
Johnston, Hugh. *The Voyage of the Komagata Maru: The Sikh Challenge to Canada's Colour Bar*. Vancouver: University of British Columbia Press, 1989.
Joshi, Sanjay. 'India's Middle Class', *Oxford Research Encyclopedia of Asian History* (April 2017), DOI:10.1093/acrefore/9780190277727.013.17.
Karaka, D. F. *I Go West*. London: Michael Joseph, 1938.
Lahiri, Shompa. *Indian Mobilities in the West 1900–1947: Gender, Performance, Embodiment*. New York, NY: Palgrave Macmillan, 2010.
Lester, Alan. 'Imperial Circuits and Networks: Geographies of the British Empire', *History Compass* 4, 1 (2006): 124–41.
Majumdar, Janaki Agnes Penelope. *Family History*. Edited by Antoinette Burton. New Delhi: Oxford University Press, 2013.
Manjapra, Kris. *Age of Entanglement: German and Indian Intellectuals Across Empire*. Cambridge, MA: Harvard University Press, 2014.

Markandaya, Kamala. 'One Pair of Eyes: Some Random Reflections', in A. Niven (ed.), *The Commonwealth Writer Overseas: Themes of Exile and Expatriation*, 23–32. Brussels: M. Didier, 1976.

Mukherjee, Sumita. *Indian Suffragettes: Female Identities and Transnational Networks*. New Delhi: Oxford University Press, 2018.

———. *Nationalism, Education and Migrant Identities: The England-Returned*. Abingdon: Routledge, 2010.

Nandy, Ashis. *The Intimate Enemy: Loss and Recovery of Self under Colonialism*. New Delhi: Oxford University Press, 1983.

O'Malley, Kate. 'Metropolitan Resistance: Indo-Irish Connections in the Inter-War Period', in R. Ahmed and S. Mukherjee (eds), *South Asian Resistances*, 125–39. London: Continuum, 2012.

Pratt, Mary Louise. *Imperial Eyes: Travel Writing and Transculturation*, 2nd edition. Abingdon: Routledge, 2008.

Raychaudhuri, Tapan. 'Europe in India's Xenology: The Nineteenth Century Record', *Past and Present* 137 (Nov. 1992), 156–82.

Saaler, Sven and Christopher W. A. Szpilman (eds). *Pan-Asianism: A Documentary History, Volume 2: 1920–Present*. Lanham, MD: Rowman & Littlefield Publishers, 2011.

Sarkar, Sumit. *The Swadeshi Movement in Bengal, 1903–1908*. New Delhi: People's Publishing House, 1973.

Sen, Simonti. *Travels to Europe: Self and Other in Bengali Travel Narratives 1870–1910*. New Delhi: Orient Longman, 2005.

Stoler, Ann Laura. *Haunted by Empire: Geographies of Intimacy in North American History*. Durham, NC: Duke University Press, 2006.

Stolte, Carolien. '"Enough of the Great Napoleons!" Raja Mahendra Pratap's Pan-Asian Projects (1929–1939)', *Modern Asian Studies* 46, 2 (2012): 403–23.

Stolte, Carolien and Harald Fischer-Tiné. 'Imagining Asia in India: Nationalism and Internationalism (ca. 1905–1940)', *Comparative Studies in Society and History* 5, 1 (2012): 65–92.

Subramanian, Lakshmi. 'Rabindranath Tagore and the Problem of Self-Esteem in Colonial India', in R. K. Ray (ed.), *Mind Body and Society: Life and Mentality in Colonial Bengal*. Calcutta: Oxford University Press, 1995.

Tankha, Brij. 'The Greater India Society: Indian Culture and an Asian Federation', in S. Saaler and C. Szpilman (eds), *Pan-Asianism*, 93–6. Plymouth, UK: Rowman & Littlefield, 2011.

Visram, Rozina. *Asians in Britain: 400 Years of History*. London: Pluto Press, 2002.

19
LAYERED CITIES, SHARED HISTORIES
Gold, mobility and urbanity between Dubai and Malabar

Nisha Mathew

Introduction

A remarkably intriguing phenomenon with its nucleus in Dubai, a hitherto little-known city-state in the oil-rich Persian Gulf, came to light in the mid-twentieth century. Gold smuggling, as it was referred to, made regular headlines in the international press. Through the following decades, smuggling became synonymous with Dubai, perceived as a way of life and an art form perfected under the freewheeling ways of its ruling elite and their laissez-faire attitudes towards trade.[1] Triggering it, many reports observed, was the insatiable demand for gold in India, where its trade was prohibited by the newly independent state infamous for its policy of import substitution. Bombay on the west coast was the centre of this lucrative trade, while Gujarat and Malabar, to the city's north and south respectively, supplemented it on a much smaller scale. A key aspect of smuggling featuring in editorials and press reports published out of Bombay was the figure of the smuggler. Embodied in such men as Haji Mastan and Dawood Ibrahim, the smuggler was at the node of illicit logistic networks relaying contraband arriving from Dubai across the maritime borders of the country and into cities such as Bombay and Calicut. An economically and politically subversive category detrimental to the interests of the nation, the figure of the smuggler has mostly dominated narratives and popular perceptions on smuggling in India. Dubai did matter, but only insofar as it served as a safe haven for smugglers and other kinds of criminals.

By the mid 1990s Dubai had begun to reinvent itself, transforming from an entrepôt and a smuggling capital to, as it has since then represented itself, the 'City of Gold.' Not unlike its earlier phase, the new cast too was a response to the radical shift in India's economic policy revolving around the import of gold. As India threw open its borders to trade, the intractable problem of smuggling abated, even as gold continued to flow in steadily rising volumes into the country. There was, however, much more to Dubai's transition than a switch of labels signifying a phenomenon that alternated between smuggling and legitimate trade as India's economy opened or shut its doors to gold. The manner in which it was implemented on the ground revealed a connection between Dubai, Bombay and Malabar that was much deeper than what could be made from an economic perspective on smuggling. This transition, the effects of which were visible across the Arabian Sea from the creek in Dubai to Malabar in the southwestern India, constitutes the focus of this chapter. It addresses this transition from the frame of reference of Malabar, both through its connections with Bombay as an intermediary space in the 1960s and 1970s and in terms of its immediate relationship with Dubai, then and in the 1990s.

Malabar affords a perspective on Dubai's transition as well as on gold smuggling that Bombay does not. In Bombay, where the smuggler figure and the sheer scale of the activity spearheaded by him dominate the narrative on smuggling, the social and cultural aspects underlying the phenomenon remain obscure. A predominantly economic view taints the question of demand for gold—it has been addressed almost exclusively in terms of profit or as a mode of primitive accumulation, such as arbitrage among merchants, entrepreneurs and criminal syndicates in cities, and hoarding among rich peasants in rural areas. Even the ritual of dowry becomes either an economic transaction, as the transfer of the bride's wealth, or a categorically non-economic one, as gift (Mehrotra 1998, 2004). Bankers, journalists and writers attempting to make sense of Dubai's rapid urban expansion in the 1960s and 1970s espouse an economic view too, arguing for revenues from smuggling as having provided the initial capital for commercial and infrastructure projects in the city. While this certainly needs to be taken into account, what may be lost in leaning excessively on such narratives are the social and cultural aspects of material practices that have built Dubai from below, making it a contemporary Indian Ocean city. It is in terms of an intervention along such lines that Malabar and its connections with Dubai merit critical attention here.

The chapter maps the social context driving the mobility of gold between Dubai and Malabar through the changing legal regimes of trade in the 20th century (Appadurai 1986; Gregory 1997). In restoring a cultural dimension to the economy and a calculative dimension to cultural practices defining the exchange of gold within this geography in the western Indian Ocean, it analyses the constitution of a particular kind of a social space and the different spatial relations reinforcing it. This social space, contesting the territorial economy of the state in India and spilling out of its political boundaries, becomes the basis of Dubai's urban growth and transition from a smuggling capital to the City of Gold.

Malayalis in Dubai: multiple regimes of mobility

The centuries-old circulations in the western Indian Ocean gave way to what we today understand as international migration regulated by states in the 1960s and 1970s in the Persian Gulf (Birks and Sinclair 1979).[2] Redefining the earlier regime of mobility in which men, mostly merchants and traders from the western coast of India, undertook periodic visits to Bahrain, Dubai, Sharjah and other parts of the Gulf, was the new wave of labour migration spurred by oil.[3] Facilitated by the acquisition of passports and work permits, the new migration brought Malayalis from across the newly formed state of Kerala in southwestern India in massive numbers to the Gulf (Weiner 1982: 4–5). What started in the 1960s with Bombay as the centre of recruitment of a workforce required to man the industrial and service sectors of oil economies in the Gulf continued through the late 1970s and 1980s, with labour recruitment agencies extending their operations to Kerala. Many of those who migrated in the 1950s and 1960s, mostly to Kuwait, Bahrain and Saudi Arabia, were recruited by British shipping agents such as Gray Mackenzie as well as subsidiaries of oil companies such as British Petroleum to work for different firms and in an entire range of professions.[4] Some, as they revealed during interviews, were already employed in the railways, hospitals, the port, customs, shipping firms, banks and other institutions in Bombay and were highly solicited for their skills, which the British, the

Americans and the Arabs required to recreate and run similar institutions in Bahrain, Dubai, Kuwait and other burgeoning cities in the Gulf.[5] A report published by the *Times of India* points to an interesting incident where 16 of the 62 mechanics operating mobile cranes in the docks of Bombay had migrated to the Gulf, leaving them idle and the docks they were meant to clear, congested.[6]

The new wave of migration did much to supplement and expand an already thriving urban economy built on gold smuggling and spatially configured across Dubai, Bombay and Malabar in the western Indian Ocean. In fact, by the time the majority of the Malayalis arrived in the city and other emirates in the Persian Gulf, smuggling, in the words of Yusuf Pathan, a well-known smuggler, had become an overcrowded profession in India. The Gold Control Act was already in place, and any kind of exchange of gold between dealers was made illegal. Malabar had by the late 1950s been well entrenched in the gold smuggling circuit and produced its own regional versions of a Haji Mastan in the figures of men like Kallatra Abdul Kadir Haji, K.S. Abdulla, A. Karthikeyan and Muhammad Bafaki.[7] Prominent business magnates, they operated out of ports such as Calicut, Beypore and Kasargod, where they owned hotels, cinemas, timber export firms, had stakes in the fishing industry and were on friendly terms with customs and police officials, thus earning the tag 'Kerala's gentleman smugglers.' Some among these – Kallatra Haji for instance – had started out as young men in Bombay, where they made contacts with Arabs and worked on commissions for them, but later branched out on their own with Calicut as their base and with many of their Arab connections intact. Gold thereafter found its way directly into Malabar, where it sank as hoards in the homes and warehouses of businessmen evading taxes, politicians, corrupt officials and bureaucrats, became the raw material for jewellers or was transferred overland in trucks to places in neighbouring Tamil Nadu or as far as Delhi and Calcutta.[8] In the course of less than two decades, a smuggling geography evolving as an offshoot of Bombay had fanned out from Calicut to other parts of Malabar, creating new commercial nodes within the region and arteries penetrating inland as far as the country's capital.

Such was the state of affairs in the 1970s on the gold smuggling front, when new labour recruitment agencies appeared on the scene in Kerala. Some of these were initiatives of the government, for instance the Overseas Development and Employment Promotion Consultants (ODEPC), while quite a few employment agencies were run illegally.[9] With the demand for workers rising consistently, Gulf migration had become a money-making enterprise for everyone involved in it, either directly as professional and labour recruits or indirectly as agents drawing commissions on visas and travel documents issued to potential migrants (Weiner 1982). The Indian state, earning foreign exchange through remittances made by migrants, had a vested interest in sustaining it and did practically little to protect these workers, even as incidents of abuse, particularly in menial jobs, came to its attention. This lethargy on the part of the state created new opportunities for labour recruitment agencies, hawala agents and smugglers alike. As they spread their net from Bombay to other parts of Maharashtra, Goa and Kerala on the west coast, these agencies provided a fillip to gold smuggling by entering new terrains in labour recruitment that blurred the boundaries between the legal and the illegal (Kodoth and Varghese 2012). Maid-runners and smugglers made a bid for profits as they sourced foreign currency from the salaries paid to maids, cooks and men and women either legally recruited or smuggled as human cargoes on dhows to parts of the Gulf.[10] This currency, meant to have been transferred home in the form of remittances, was used by agents of smugglers and hawala dealers in Dubai to buy gold, freely available in the city's banks by the early 1970s. While the dinars, dirhams and dollars that were to fill the state's foreign exchange reserves flowed in the form of contraband gold into the hands of an array of players in India, the families of these maids, cooks and others were paid the stipulated amount in Indian rupees at rates higher than the official exchange rate.

The dhow in many ways constituted the lifeline of organised smuggling (Martin 1979, 1982). If the cash collected from maids, menial workers and other migrants pooled together went into buying the necessary gold, a different set of dhow passengers, mostly drawn from Malabar, contributed to the actual labour involved in smuggling. This included the task of physically transferring the gold on dhows sailing from Dubai and other ports in the Gulf to agents in Bombay or Malabar. The illegal migration by dhows, launches or the *uru*, as they are called in Malayalam, is today celebrated in cultural stereotypes of heroic daring and adventure of the men who risked their lives in voyages on an open sea and braved many odds to make a living in the Gulf.[11] Yet we know little of the lives of these men as they were roped in as one-time couriers in random smuggling operations spearheaded by Arab, Gujarati and Sindhi merchants in Dubai in the 1960s and 1970s. Many of these men, now in their seventies and eighties, recounted how the Arabian Sea and the dhow coming down from Dutch and Kathiawar in Gujarat had been an integral part of their lives for generations and how their fathers and uncles were associated in different capacities with the timber and coir trades, keeping this traffic to the Gulf alive even in times of oil. Several dhows that had dotted the Arabian Sea for centuries were built at Beypore, which was a flourishing dhow-building centre, especially during the pearl boom of the 19th century. In such capacity Beypore was well known to the Omanis, Kuwaitis and other Arabs in the Persian Gulf as well as to Parsis and Gujaratis in Bombay, all of whom had had their ships built here. Beypore may have fallen out of the circuit as a key ship-building centre in the new scheme of things, but the social relationships of an earlier regime of mobility would not fade away so quickly. It was in such relationships that the key to unlocking some of the social division of labour in Dubai's smuggling lies.

Koya, a gentleman now in his late seventies who lives in Beypore, remembered how he had paid 200 rupees to a Kutchi whom he had known on the latter's regular visits to Malabar during the early 1970s so that he could be "smuggled" to somewhere in the Gulf, Dubai.[12] He was fortunate, he sighed as we spoke, that he could eventually reach Dubai from Khor Fakkan, a port on the northern shores of the United Arab Emirates, and find work with a Sindhi textile merchant known to his *Kutchinakhuda*.[13] Some others, he said, died of thirst, heat and disease during the voyage. Conversations with others like him revealed Koya's life as a pattern that dovetailed with the social landscape of smuggling in Dubai during the period and filled the gaps in press reports on couriers among Malabar Muslims, who alongside Arabs and Pakistanis were considered enemies of the state in India. Moideen, younger to Koya by a year or two and hailing from *Nadapuram* in Calicut, put the pieces of the puzzle together with his narrative, highlighting yet another strand of Malabar's connections with Dubai, woven through the Sindhis.[14] Arabia was the land of gold, of plenty and promise, but not for those like him who remained in a part of the world which had not caught up to the changing times. An imagination that had multiple temporal dimensions to it—reinforced by centuries of diasporic connections and the pilgrimage as well as the more recent, yet very visible, signs of success spelt out by the *Kutchi nakhudas* and Malabar's own smugglers—did not, in other words, translate into easy success for those who were led by it. Unlike their fellow Malayalis migrating from Bombay and those with a similar profile beginning to travel form Kerala itself by the mid-1970s, these dhow passengers were illegal migrants with hardly any education or skills to find them regular employment in oil companies or other prestigious institutions in a rapidly changing Persian Gulf.[15] Nor were they like the Sindhis, who, despite having lost their homeland to Pakistan in the partition of 1947, were able to start afresh in Bombay and Dubai with a social capital and connections grounded in mercantile connections dating back to centuries (Vora 2011).

Dubai however, was not entirely representative of the oil economies of the Persian Gulf. In fact, oil had become a reality in Dubai only in the late 1960s. What this meant for men like

Koya, Moideen and the Sindhi and Arab merchants who employed them was that it had room for what the rest of the Persian Gulf used to be until oil had changed them to the point of almost no return. A part of Dubai may have moved onto a different temporality with an oil economy in the seventies and incorporated the other Malayalis we came across at the beginning of this section as guest workers on permits that were renewable. Their professional and technical expertise may have contributed much to its making as a modern city and was in stark contrast to the commercial pursuits of the Sindhis and Gujaratis, which continued to define Dubai as part of an earlier and a much older world in the Indian Ocean of movements and exchanges. Yet such contributions could not supplant those of the latter, whose presence as merchants, bankers and pearl financiers in the region through the 18th and 19th centuries was at the core of Dubai's economic and political configuration as an Indian Ocean city-state (Al-Sayegh 1998). In fact, Dubai only accelerated this earlier temporality and its Indian Ocean-ness by further reinforcing its logic and bringing it to pace with the oil modernity in the region, perhaps even outpacing it, through smuggling. Men like Koya and Moideen were integral to such a project, and Dubai pushed more and more of them into it over the years in ways that changed its own destiny as well as those of places like Beypore in Malabar linked to it.

A thriving Indian Ocean logic of trade and politics in Dubai amidst an oil modernity in the region opened up new paths to mobility for many in Malabar. Men like Koya, Moideen and others found themselves enveloped within the mutually intersecting worlds of the two, the interface given immediate contours by the dhow. New relations between Sindhis and Malayalis—now deeply entrenched and perceived as ethnic bias and social hierarchy in Dubai and other parts of the Gulf—began to evolve as the dhows of the *Kutchis* and the *Kathiawaris* carried these men, mostly but not entirely Muslims, from Malabar to the shores of the Gulf. Often it was the dhow crews that passed their passengers on as personal contacts to Sindhi and Iranian merchants in whose textile shops and construction businesses they found occasional employment as shop assistants, porters and labourers. In such capacity these men from Malabar served the commercial interests of an entire spectrum of players and 'investors' in the gold business, working as couriers alongside Arabs and Pakistanis on actual smuggling trips undertaken by dhows laden with gold for Bombay, Gujarat and Calicut.[16] In return for the risks involved of interception by customs and imprisonment if convicted in court, they were paid a reasonable amount as fee, often in Indian rupees at home. The Hawala agents through whom the money was routed also brought them return tickets and a visa valid for employment, or some form of entrepreneurship in Dubai. The courier deal in smuggling was thus, for the men from Malabar, a means to legalising their status as migrant workers in Dubai and the other emirates. Many who chose this path found in it an impetus and did not take long to start out on their own as entrepreneurs in a range of small trades from provisions, textiles and electronics in the city and elsewhere in the emirates. The cafeteria business, or the *Nadapuram* cafeteria business as it is more popularly known in Dubai and the other emirates, is an unmistakable offshoot of this trajectory of dhow migration and its links with the world of smuggling.[17] Later in the 1990s, many of these men from Malabar, including Koya, who owned a readymade garments shop in Dubai, diversified and scaled up their commercial interests and expanded into Malabar, setting up similar businesses in many towns. Others, like Moideen, have ventured into real-estate business as property agents working on commissions from buyers and sellers. The dhow, thus, was a route to legitimacy and acceptance in a society that values a fluid and easy mobility between Arabia, the land of plenty, and Malabar, its outpost, as a virtue above all else. Gold, as we shall see in what follows, was the material on which this mobility as virtue was etched in Malayali society. It was also a key site on which social and cultural codes, as well as the laws of the state, were inscribed as contestations over differential interpretations of value.

Malayali, gold and the mobility complex

In March 1963, a fierce debate broke out in India's Parliament on the prevailing gold-control policies of the government, which, among other things, prohibited the manufacture of gold jewellery above 14 carats for domestic use. The preferred purity of gold jewellery the world over was 22 carat, and it could be manufactured under the new scheme only for export to other countries.[18] What was interesting about the debate was that it brought to the fore distinct views on the use of gold in India and the value regimes within which it remained implicated. As the opposition parties presented the case of those agitating against the Gold Control Order across the country, they highlighted the social and religious dimensions of gold, insisting that the state respect the sentiments of the people and withdraw the order. However, as Morarji Desai, the Finance Minister, saw it, the lure for gold in India was part of a mindset that required social reform which could only be achieved by means of legal intervention such as the Gold Control Order. He pointed to hoarding by the wealthy and dowry involving the exchange of gold as social and cultural practices that deserved to be rooted out completely. Equally troublesome for the state and some of the members of the opposition were the consumption habits and fashion trends around gold developing among Indian women. Desai considered the 14-carat jewellery a panacea to all such evils, whether traditional, customary or contemporary. Nobody would hoard it as dead investment. It would very well supplant 22-carat jewellery in fashion and social transactions such as dowry and gift-giving. None of these theories worked, and by 1968, a revised Gold Control Act was implemented. Again, contrary to its desired effects, an illegal trade and an underground economy in gold emerged in the following years.

What the state could not see was that most people—merchants and smuggler-figures were exceptions—did not operate with a notion of economy, culture and religion as distinct realms into which social life and the use of gold itself could be compartmentalised. Neither could social life be rendered territorial in ways that reflected the categorical authority of the state over its people; nor could value be restricted to commodities, including gold, circulating within an economic system. A view from Kerala, where by the late 1970s Gulf migration had gained much currency, offers a clearer picture. It reveals how, in the context of a temporary and contractual Gulf migration, gold and the values it embodied consolidated social life and pushed into circulation men, women and commodities as cultural markers of a certain Malayali-ness lived within and across the territorial borders of India. This circulation and the ways in which it defined being Malayali I call the 'mobility complex' of the Malayali. The mobility complex of the Malayali had significant material, social and urban implications for Dubai, as we will see in the section that follows.

Young men with a successful career in the Gulf returning home on vacation created a new economy of circulation centred primarily but not exclusively in marriage. Not only were these 'successful' men themselves greatly sought after as bridegrooms in a society where a marriage arranged by the family was the norm. Their sisters, cousins and nieces too were prized as brides simply by virtue of their proximity to these men and the prospect of social mobility it brought along in the form of a visa to the Gulf for the prospective groom, apart from the dowry in gold, cash and household as well as personal goods (Osella and Osella 1999). It was, as Appadurai argues in his seminal essay, a case of reciprocal construction of value between gold and men, like that between shells and men in *kula* exchanges (Appadurai 1986: 20). For instance, in the late 1970s the sister's dowry could go up to 35 sovereigns or more, while he was expected to give a cousin at least 10 sovereigns depending upon the caste and class they hailed from.[19] In return he could claim from the family of his bride an equal or even greater number of sovereigns as part of the many exchanges and transfers constituting the marriage. It was no irony,

Layered cities, shared histories

then, that the migrant's bride often came from a higher class, occasionally even a higher caste than his own, culminating in a marriage of material wealth, mobility and social capital and the advantages entailed by the coalescence of the two for subsequent generations. The flow of gold did not end with the wedding. On the contrary, a wedding only initiated an entire series of life-cycle rituals revolving around gold, including baby showers, christening, ear piercing, baptism and house-warming ceremonies and carried through to the betrothal and marriage of the next generation. Gold as money, measure of value and store of wealth at multiple scales of the economy, from the global and the national to the local, met gold as property, gift and ritual object in a moral economy of exchanges among families and communities. As long as Dubai and access to gold through migration, smuggling and marriage existed among Malayalis, gold could switch between these different value regimes and men could jump scales to their advantage as individuals and social beings.

The mobility complex was an attribute not of individuals alone. Jewellers, as well as merchants specialised in local manufacturing and other small trades in parts of Malabar, joined their fellow migrants to set up jewellery stores in Dubai in the 1980s. Desai's Gold Control Act had provided for the manufacture of 22-carat jewellery for export, but for jewellers based in Kerala, this was not something to be achieved without direct access to Dubai and its gold. Their business in Malabar had come from the young men who brought their quotas for sale, redesign and exchange, as well as smugglers and couriers. However, the demand far exceeded what they could offer with the gold available via these sources. A commercial presence in Dubai they realised, could both address inadequacies and bring greater profits in business. Thus, instead of catering to migrants arriving in Malabar, these jewellers began to offer in Dubai their stipulated quotas for a journey back home.

An interesting paradox of Dubai, despite its tainted international image as a smuggling capital, was its credibility in terms of the quality and purity of its gold. This was particularly so for Indian consumers, who before 22-carat jewellery or 916-hallmarked gold became a reality in the 1990s, had no means to detect the actual volume of gold they received for the price they paid for a gram or sovereign of the metal. The *Sonis* who pioneered gold jewellery retailing in Dubai in the 1950s had worked within a bazaar economy, the logic of which was completely different to that brought in by the Malayali jewellers. The *Sonis* are an artisanal community of goldsmiths hailing from Gujarat and Sindh. Following the Partition of India and the loss of Sindh to Pakistan, many of them relocated to Dubai and other parts of the Persian Gulf, where they rose to prominence as jewellers catering to the newly rich Arabs and the Indian expatriates. Most of them had operated the way traditional and family jewellers did in India, making ornaments to orders from clients with whom they had long-term relations of 'calculative trust.' As in hawala transfers offering varying exchange rates to clients based on their commercial and business proximity to the hawaldar, these *Sonis* offered gold of different purities to different buyers. As some of the early Malayali migrants interpreted it, they were subject to the tactics of the *Soni* jeweller who, operating between legal restrictions in India and the mechanisms of profiteering, toyed with the alloy content of jewellery, bringing down its gold content by a carat or two. With Malayali retailers entering the scene in Dubai and transacting on the basis of an international gold price displayed at the counter as well as certifications of purity, the methods of retail trade in gold had changed, offering consumers greater options to choose from. Every purchase of ready-made jewellery was considered a one-off transaction and a terminal relationship between the store and the buyer, leaving no obligations behind on either side. That the reconfiguration of the retail trade along, in the words of Joy Alukkas, a prominent Malayali jeweller, "modern lines" evolved its own mechanisms of building long-term relationships is another matter altogether. What remains significant, however, is how such reconfiguration translated into a culture of trust and a larger customer base not just among Malayalis but from among other Indians as well as the Arabs themselves, and how it created a niche for the Malayali jewellers in a gold market hitherto dominated by the *Sonis*. As we will see in the following section, it was partly this trust and the politics of purity and value defining it that shaped in many ways Dubai's trajectory towards its avatar in the 1990s as the City of Gold.

Liberalisation in India, brand-building in Dubai

The 1990s in India was a time of epochal transformation on the political as well as the economic front. With the shift in state policy from import substitution towards trade liberalisation, the stage was set for the deregulation of markets, reduction of import tariffs and private foreign investment in key manufacturing and service sectors. In the domain of gold, direct and immediate legislation lifting the ban on import was passed, thus bringing the curtain down on almost half a century of smuggling between India and Dubai. Special import and open-license schemes were introduced through the decade, allowing jewellers and banks to import bullion in tonnes both for consumption at home and for export production of jewellery. More importantly, a set of schemes was introduced specifically with the Non-Resident Indian or the NRI in view as part of the policy regime on gold imports. Periodically revised, the regulations, launched for the first time in 1992, permitted NRIs returning to India every six months to bring in up to 10 kilograms of gold on payment of duties amounting to a meagre 220 rupees per 10 grams in foreign exchange (Tcha 2003: 84–85; Bhattacharya 2004). These schemes were juxtaposed alongside the revoked Gold Control Act of 1968 and the Foreign Exchange Regulation Act of 1973, as immediate measures to increase the flow of gold through official channels and to curb smuggling.[20] Since gold bullion could now be imported at a modest tariff of 6 per cent and held legally in the private possession of individuals, rich Indians were beginning to chose gold over foreign currency in investment portfolios and private reserves of capital.

For Dubai itself, the new policy developments across the Arabian Sea raised new challenges as well as prospects. Given that gold prices in India were brought on par with prices in the international market, and its legal landscape altered to revive an official economy in the metal, smuggling was no longer a feasible option. Dubai as a modern city had evolved around India's appetite for gold. It had to continue in the same vein if it were to grow and sustain itself, regardless of whether such growth came through smuggling or legal trade. In other words, Dubai had to adapt and play around India's changing gold laws to enter a new phase in its own urbanity. With a history spanning more than half a century of gold imports involving Indian merchants, international banks and bullion dealers on the one hand, and a logistics of transfer developed by traders, workers and smugglers on the other, the infrastructure to effect the implementation on the ground of India's gold import liberalisation scheme was in place in the city. How did it translate these possibilities into action? I argue that Dubai began redefining its urban and social spaces on the one hand and strategically working on its migration and visa regimes on the other, in order to attract greater numbers of consumers of gold and other commodities to the city.

Central to the new migration regime in Dubai was the relaxation of visa regulations. Visas for transit and tourism were made more accessible and easily disbursable through a bureaucratic machinery of citizens as well as travel and ticketing agencies, many of which were owned by Indians. In 1993 alone, the number of people arriving at the Dubai International Airport was 426,723—of these 278,718 were on 96-hour transit visas and 148,005 on 90-day visit visas.[21] Greater numbers of short-term visas issued meant an economy whose wheels were well oiled to run with a circulating population of migrants that carried back home or elsewhere gold and other consumer goods purchased in Dubai. Besides, these migrants were also instrumental to absorbing the social and political pressure of a growing population of citizens who continued to demand welfare and social security from the state despite declining revenues from oil. The bureaucracy built as a redistributive mechanism in the wake of oil had begun to come under strain by the 1990s everywhere in the Persian Gulf. This was more blatantly so in Dubai, where oil concessions yielded far fewer returns as compared to its neighbouring states.

The new legal conduit opened for gold trade in India and the relaxed visa regulations in Dubai revived an existing practice of short-term migration in Malabar. In the late 1970s and 1980s, when voyages by dhows and steamers gave way to air travel, a new kind of figure began to make an appearance on the Gulf migration stage. The 'passenger,'" as he was referred to, was marked somewhere between a smuggler and a legal migrant, carrying gold in ways that were generally invisible to customs authorities at airports, sometimes in false bottoms of suitcases, at other times hidden in shoes or under a belt etc.[22] These passengers could be 'normal' or 'hired' as mules by smuggling syndicates[23] or they could simply be individuals undertaking a journey to buy some gold for themselves. These developments came in the wake of the Customs department in India introducing a system of green-channel clearance to enable smooth clearance of passengers and cargo at airports. It was only if one aroused suspicion that one could be pulled out of a green-channel queue for a check by authorities. This green-channel clearance come in as handy for those wanting to transfer gold legally into India in the age of liberalisation, including jewellers themselves. While some of those undertaking such trips were businessmen who sought to evade taxes by having a part of their commercial revenues and export earnings stashed away in gold, many others were agents working on commissions for them. A practice, more or less taken for granted for more than two decades now, drew attention in the wake of the recent demonetisation in India, when news of gold sales in Dubai's gold souk having been on a steady decline, broke.[24] In Malabar, where many ambitious entrepreneurs sought to establish themselves in the jewellery trade and where already-established jewellery groups looked to expand business, this unbroken circuit of 'passengers' spelt out new possibilities, emerging as the most effective means of transfer of duty-free gold on a regular basis. This was particularly true since the physical process of transferring the metal via channels of trade stipulated by the state was a tortuous one, despite the law, and was subject to the whims of bureaucrats, politicians and others involved in the game.

It was not enough for Dubai in the 1990s to merely pack gold off to India. People had to be brought to Dubai in a reverse flow, and other than as smugglers, workers, traders, businessmen and passengers. A new category, most dominant on the streets and in the malls in 21st-century Dubai, was invented in the 1990s from the pool of casual tourists, businessmen and families travelling from India and frequenting the city's gold souk and malls in the quest for gold and other consumer goods. This was the 'shopper.' The event marking the arrival of the shopper on Dubai's urban stage was the Dubai Shopping Festival, or the DSF as it is popularly known, in 1996. Malayali gold retail chains were key players, partnering with the state and its ministerial departments to establish the Dubai Gold and Jewellery Group (DGJG) and launch the first edition of the DSF.[25] Gold remains the key attraction of the DSF as city-based wholesalers, refiners and bullion-dealers come together every season to sponsor and give away prizes in gold amounting to thousands of kilograms as part of several commercial events held as part of the festival. The institutionalisation of the state–merchant relationship around Dubai's booming trade in gold, true to its constitution as an Indian Ocean city-state, not only redefined the city's international image but also offered a metaphor to capture its transition from a smugglers' cove into the 'City of Gold.' Launched during the first edition of the DSF in 1996, the punch line has added significant brand value to the city and its urban projects in the 21st century.

Concurrently, the category of the shopper began to espouse and resonate with ethnicities across the world, visibly obscuring its origins in the spatial and cultural politics of Dubai's gold trade around India in the 1990s and becoming a cultural marker for its global city status.

Dubai, Malabar and cities of gold

As the 'City of Gold,' Dubai has multiple dimensions to it. In its literal and territorial sense, it points to an urban space which has the largest density or concentration of gold-trading establishments anywhere in the world, as well as the entrepôt through which a large quantity of the physical gold traded across the world transits. In its metaphorical sense, it signifies Dubai as the ultimate city, be it in terms of lifestyle, leisure or the pace of development; a benchmark for urban standards and a model for other cities to emulate. Looked at from Malabar, Dubai is a city that is all of these and much more. True to what it claims to be, Dubai is for Malabar where the ultimate is constantly made and remade in the everyday engagement of its migrant communities with the city; a ubiquitous presence in the form of gold, commodities and people moving in a circuit of relentless flows between the two geographies. Dubai pushes the limits of their physical and social mobility as individuals, as members and stakeholders in society and as economic players defined by this realm of flows. What they could not achieve in Malabar as Malabar, or more precisely from within the confines of the geographic region of Malabar, they have achieved in and through a Dubai coalescing socially and spatially with Malabar for more than half a century now.

In order to make sense of these achievements, we need to return to the Dubai Shopping Festival. If Dubai stood to gain in brand value from the marketing strategy around gold and the DSF, retailers who were at the core of these initiatives drew on Dubai itself in mutually beneficial ways to expand their commercial base. As more shoppers began to throng to the city, boosting its revenues from tourism and trade, these retailers took Dubai and their own jewellery brands to geographies beyond its territorial limits. They opened multiple branches in Saudi Arabia, Kuwait, Qatar and Muscat, where sizeable populations of Indians, particularly Malayalis, live and work. Gold kiosks in shopping malls and airports became popular in Dubai and other cities in the Gulf. Following in the trail of these traders, many other Dubai-based businesses, particularly electronics and consumer-goods chains, set up shop in other cities and began to claim a regional presence in the Persian Gulf. Conversely, many traders in other parts of the Gulf with the ambition to scale up their businesses took cues from these gold retailers and began to establish themselves in Dubai.

Through all of these criss-crossings in the regional commercial landscape of the Persian Gulf, our jewellers began to look back to Malabar, where they began their trajectory as traders and entrepreneurs. They drew on Dubai's brand value, and the trust they had secured among their clientele in the city and the Gulf at large, to break into the retail market in gold in India. In ways reminiscent of Malabar's Roman past, when, in exchange for pepper, gold entered peninsular India through its entrepôts, they began to operate as leading businesses and retail chains in major south Indian cities such as Chennai, Coimbatore, Mangalore, Bangalore and Hyderabad. The trust that they had earned in the 1980s as reliable traders offering gold of higher purity did help the process in many ways.

Dubai was made part of not merely a commercial continuum but also a social and cultural one with Malabar through the interventions of these retail chains. Cultural events and festivals – in which popular actors, musicians, singers, theatre and folk artists were flown in from Kerala for performances in Dubai – had been sponsored by these groups since at least the 1980s. The Gulf tours of celebrities often involved transactions in gold as gifts from different

Gulf-based sponsors, creating an imagination of the city and gold as an intertwined duality among a cultural elite that on its own terms had very little to do with migration to the Gulf.[26] By the 1990s, this practice was extended to Kerala, Chennai, Bangalore and Hyderabad, where celebrity shows and film award functions began to be staged and broadcast live on television in India and the Gulf. Likewise, events around the releases of many Malayalam films were staged in Dubai. For the Malayali, regardless of where he or she was based, Dubai was part of the popular cultural landscape of Malayalam, existing in a relationship of financial and cultural symbiosis with cities and spaces of its production in Kerala. A relationship that had been deeply entrenched in the everyday lives of the people began to take on a newer dimension within wider institutional settings. This relationship equipped a number of Malayali traders, besides the gold retailers, to extend the gold and real-estate corridor to cities in Kerala, including Calicut, Kannur, Tellicherry, Thrissur and Cochin. A supermarket and mall culture celebrated in the form of shopping festivals, created in Dubai but revolving around cultural practices and life-cycle rituals in Malayali society, began to be imported into these emerging cities of gold in Kerala. With brand names made in the process of mobility and circulation within this corridor, many of these jewellers have been able to expand into places such as Singapore, Kuala Lumpur, New York, New Jersey and London. They have become, like Dubai itself, global brands.

Conclusion

What we observe in the historical geography of the gold corridor between Dubai and Malabar is a shared social formation. At the heart of Dubai's transition from a smuggling capital to a city of gold, it is the social space where the material practices that have built the city from the bottom evolve and consolidate themselves in time. This social space has generated its own hierarchies that crisscross class, region (region within the nation) and caste as we have seen in the case of the Sindhis and Malayalis in the dhow traffic of contraband gold flowing from Dubai into Bombay, but also to a lesser extent Malabar. Communities that are otherwise part of different territorial, political and legal orders function as part of a broad spectrum of related activity that brings mutual advantages to all, although such advantages may be of different degrees, depending on the power relations between the players involved. States who are guardians of these territorial, legal and political orders respond to this social formation, even intersect with the players contouring it in significant ways. With its fluidity and its perpetually moving urban parts, it calls for a method and a set of concepts radically different from the territorial ones we are accustomed to, such as class, caste and region, to bring it into sharp focus. Following the mobility of gold in the western Indian Ocean has been a method pursued here to illuminate the moving parts of this social engine from different angles and frames of reference. Likewise the concepts of the smuggler, the passenger and of the Malayali mobility-complex are all in some sense importations from the everyday perceptions of those located within and outside this social formation struggling to get at the material practices that reinforce and add value to this social formation.

The story of Dubai's growth and transformation not only illuminates the varied social functions of gold and the diverse value regimes they feed into in the modern world. It also shows how Malabar and its urban spaces have grown in tandem with Dubai, deepening their spatial connections through an array of commercial strategies and regimes of labour as well as other forms of mobility. In the early part of the 20th century, these connections were mediated by Bombay as the centre of a post-imperial economy in the western Indian Ocean. Over the decades and as air travel became the norm, Bombay fell out of the immediate circuit drawn between Dubai and Malabar. Yet it continues to direct the energies within this space in ways that impact the two, and sustain relationships between all three, but that discussion has been beyond the scope of this essay. Urban scholars have shown how Dubai is looked at, particularly by cities in the developing world aspiring to its global city status, as a unique entity, a manufactured brand, a model to be emulated or what may be visibly "inter-referenced in the urbanscapes and emergent lifestyles of people" (Haines 2011: 160–81). While this view of Dubai as a model focuses on its scores in real estate, luxury and consumption, I take it a bit further and pursue the Dubai model as a method in urban historiography. It is not Dubai as intertext in the history of Bombay and urban spaces in Malabar that I approach the model, but Dubai as a constitutive space and aspect of their urban careers and vice-versa. On the one hand, I restore to Malabar and its players a narrative voice in the history of Dubai which has been remarkably silent about it. On the other, I also reinforce the cross-territorial nature of social institutions and practices that we are used to thinking and analysing from within the containers afforded by categories. Methodologically, therefore, we are moving from a linear process of writing the history of a particular place to a circular one of simultaneously writing the connected histories of different places that are constantly making and remaking each other in what Doreen Massey refers to as a "dynamic simultaneity" (Massey 2005: 55).

Notes

1 "Dubai's golden fleece," *The Guardian*, January 13, 1971
2 For a historical account of Indian traders and merchants in the Persian Gulf, see Markovits 2000.
3 For details on labour migration, see Birks and Sinclair 1979.
4 National Archives of India, New Delhi: File No. F13-17/53 (Emi) of 1953.
5 These interviews, around 35 in number, were conducted over a period of 6 years between 20111 and 2016 in different parts of Kerala, as well in Dubai, Sharjah and Abu Dhabi among nurses, and employees of different international firms and ministerial departments in Bahrain, Kuwait and the United Arab Emirates.
6 "Gulf jobs leave cranes idle at city port," *Times of India*, July 31, 1977.
7 "Wanted nan in Kerala surrenders," *Times of India*, September 25, 1974; "5 more Malabar "top smugglers" held under MISA," *Times of India*, October 2, 1974.
8 "Kerala's gentleman smugglers," *Times of India* September 29, 1974
9 For details on the functions of the ODEPC, see http://www.odepc.org.
10 "Gulf trade in Indian maids," *Times of India*, August 28, 1972
11 The 2015 Malayalam film *Pathemaari* offers a picture of this illegal migration by dhows from Malabar.
12 Interview with author in October 2011 at Beypore.
13 'Nakhuda' is the term used for the captain of the dhow in the Indian Ocean. Mr. Koya, Interview by the author, Beypore, Calicut, May 1, 2011.
14 Mr. Moideen, Interview by the author, Nadapuram, Calicut, December 15, 2012.
15 On illegal migrants, see Martin 1978.
16 Mr. Moideen, Interview by the author, Nadapuram, December 15, 2012.
17 Cafeterias are a genre of eateries unto themselves in the Gulf. Between a restaurant and a hotel, they serve cheap food, mostly consisting of bread with meat and vegetables and fruit juices.
18 "Further steps if needed to halt smuggling," *Times of India*, March 7, 1963.
19 A sovereign weighs 8 grams and is a standard measure used in gold stores and personal transactions, including in dowry and gift exchange, in India and by Indians generally. It does not actually relate to the purity of gold, although in principle it ought to be 22 carats.
20 See the entry for Gold under the section on India in International Monetary Fund Monetary and Capital Markets Department, Annual Report on Exchange Arrangements and Exchange Restrictions 1991 (International Monetary Fund, 1991). The Gold Control Act of 1968 was repealed in 1990 For details on the Foreign Exchange Regulation Act repealed in 1993, see the Reserve Bank of India's Exchange Control Manual, https://www.rbi.org.in/scripts/ECMUserView.aspx?Id=21&CatID=12.

21 "An Accessible Destination," *Times of India*, May 27, 1994.
22 "2 held at airport on smuggling charge," Times of India, November 3, 1982.
23 "Anti-smuggling steps," *Times of India*, January 29, 1983.
24 "Dubai's Gold Souk feels Indian demonetisation heat," *Gulf News*, February 1, 2017, http://gulfnews.com/business/sectors/retail/dubai-s-gold-souq-feels-indian-demonetisation-heat-1.1951418 (accessed February 1, 2017).
25 "Dubai gearing up for the gala mall," *Times of India*, October 19, 1995; "The Gold Corridor," *The Times of India*, March 14, 1998.
26 It must be noted, however, that although these artists and actors were not migrants themselves, the Malayalam cinema industry they were a part of owed much of its financial base to Dubai and the Persian Gulf. Many film producers in the 1980s and 1990s were Gulf-based businessmen and merchants. For details, see Radhakrishnan 2009. Dubai was also a significant black market for Malayalam, Hindi, Tamil and other regional films, the reels of which were smuggled from Bombay, Calicut and Mangalore by passengers, air crew and shipping staff. The contents of the reels were then transferred to video cassettes for viewing at home in Dubai and elsewhere in the Persian Gulf. A reverse traffic also took place, with families carrying these video cassettes back home on vacation to India.

References

Al-Sayegh, Fatma. "Merchants' Role in a Changing Society: The Case of Dubai, 1900–90." *Middle Eastern Studies* 34, no. 1 (January 1, 1998): 87–102.
Appadurai, Arjun. *The Social Life of Things: Commodities in Cultural Perspective*. London: Cambridge University Press, 1986.
Bhattacharya, Himadri. *Deregulation of Gold in India: A Case Study in Deregulation of the Gold Market*. World Gold Council, Research Study No. 27 (2004): 1–28.
Birks, J. S. and C. A. Sinclair. "International Labour Migration in the Arab Middle East." *Third World Quarterly* 1, no. 2 (1979): 87–99.
Haines, Chad. "Cracks in the Façade: Landscapes of Hope and Desire in Dubai." In *Worlding Cities: Asian Experiments and the Art of Being Global*, edited by Ananya Roy and Aihwa Ong, 160–81. Malden, MA: Blackwell, 2011.
Kodoth, Praveena and V. J. Varghese. "Protecting Women or Endangering the Emigration Process: Emigrant Women Domestic Workers, Gender and State Policy." *Economic and Political Weekly* 47, no. 43 (October 27, 2012): 56–66.
Martin, Esmond Bradley. *Cargoes of the East: The Ports, Trade and Culture of the Arabian Seas and Western Indian Ocean*. London: Elm Tree Books, 1978.
Martin, Esmond Bradley. "The Geography of Present-Day Smuggling in the Western Indian Ocean: The Case of the Dhow." *The Great Circle* 1, no. 2 (1979): 18–35.
Martin, Esmond Bradley. "The Present-Day Dhow Trade of India." *The Great Circle* 4, no. 2 (1982): 105–18.
Massey, Doreen. *For Space*. London: Sage, 2005.
Mehrotra, Nilika. "Cultural Value of Gold." *Eastern Anthropologist* 51, no. 4 (1998): 333–49.
Mehrotra, Nilika. "Gold and Gender in India: Some Observations from South Orissa." *Indian Anthropologist* 34, no. 1 (2004): 27–39.
Osella, Filippo and Caroline Osella. "From Transience to Immanence: Consumption, Life-Cycle and Social Mobility in Kerala, South India." *Modern Asian Studies* 33, no. 4 (1999): 989–1020.
Radhakrishnan, Ratheesh. "The Gulf in the Imagination: Migration, Malayalam Cinema and Regional Identity." *Contributions to Indian Sociology* 43, no. 2 (2009): 217–45.
Sassen, Saskia. *The Global City*. 2nd ed. New York, London, Tokyo: Princeton University Press, 2001.
Sassen, Saskia. *Global Networks, Linked Cities*. 1st ed. New York: Routledge, 2002.
Tcha, Moon Joong. *Gold and the Modern World Economy*. London: Routledge, 2003.
Vora, Neha. "From Golden Frontier to Global City: Shifting Forms of Belonging, 'Freedom,' and Governance among Indian Businessmen in Dubai." *American Anthropologist* 113, no. 2 (2011): 306–18.
Weiner, Myron. "Migration and Development: Indians in the Persian Gulf." *Population and Development Review* 8, no. 1 (March 1982): 1–36.

20
EMERGENCE OF SINGAPORE AS A PIVOT FOR INDIAN DIASPORIC AND TRANSNATIONAL NETWORKS

Jayati Bhattacharya

The idea of the 'transnational communities' and the 'diaspora' are often used in close relation to each other or even substituted one for the other in popular discourses. Though familiar, they are distinct concepts and not necessarily reflective of each other, though there may be considerable overlaps. Both concepts generate ideas of flows, fluidity and transience and thus are often substituted for one another. Certain layers in the broad category of the diaspora can be part of transnational networks; however, all in the diaspora are not necessarily transnational. These differences in perspectives make the study of the diaspora more complex, challenging and dynamic. The Indian diaspora is the largest group of people across the globe at present (*World Migration Report*, 2018), and Singapore is well positioned to explore an evolving and a complex Indian diaspora within the city-state, with generations of movements of the Indian people through different periods of history. The new millennium has ushered in new frameworks of globalization, technological advancements and pro-diaspora policies of states to reduce the distance between the homeland and the host country, thus transforming the sentiments of 'nostalgia' and 'melancholy' to that which is 'celebratory' and 'progressive'. Thus globalization meets transnationalism in one of the 'dominant cities in the world urban hierarchy' (Yeoh and Chang 2001: 1025) in Singapore. The new age has extended its arms of kinship, religion, labour and business networks to like-minded groups of people beyond the borders of the nation states in different geographies, creating diverse transnational identity and groups that shared ethnic and cultural rooting, but may be difficult to categorize as homogenous national groups.

Singapore has become an important node for connecting different strands of migratory movements, either forming circulatory journeys to and from the Indian sub-continent and South Asian region or extending their movements further eastwards into other parts of Southeast Asia, China, the U.S.A., Australia or Canada, thus connecting first-time migrants with those of earlier generations and also giving rise to a new generation of 'twice-migrants'. The 'twice-migrants' may be categorized as ones making an onward movement from Singapore to other places in the West as descendents of earlier migrants. They may also comprise of an inward flow of descendants of earlier migrants from other parts of the world. Singapore has been a reconnector to the homebound 'brain-drain' diaspora, and /or accommodating migrants from the West in the face of a 'Rising Asia' or the economic downturn of the West. It provides space for those Indians who are apprehensive of living in India after years of residence in the Western world but are more comfortable with First-World living conditions and other conveniences available in Singapore, bringing them in close proximity to the 'home'. With a structural framework of Singapore as an effective pivot of economic, political and cultural convergences, Indian transnational networks have taken a sound footing in the city-state. This chapter will explore some of the examples of Indian transnational networks through different layers of the diaspora and will show how Indians have become an inevitable part of global connectivity, stretching their arms from Singapore to different geographies transcending the boundaries of the nation-state.

Positing Singapore as a 'node' and 'space' for Indian transnational networks

The surging academic interest on transnationalism is a direct departure from state-centric discourses of the post-colonial and the Cold War period. Post-Cold War globalization trends have resulted in two apparently opposing forces of state centricism and transnationalism working hand in hand. Strange bed fellows as they may have been, this convergence has brought about new paradigms within the study of social sciences, presenting new ways of looking at social phenomena through mobilities, transnational networks, diasporic identities and how the state facilitates it with policies and incentives. Some scholars have attempted to separate the studies on transnationalism from that of globalization and diaspora studies (Ozkul 2012). However, formation and characterization of Indian transnational networks are intimately connected with the wave of globalization and transformation in the diaspora. It also incorporates and problematizes the differences in the layers and different generations of the diaspora in the formations of the transnational spaces. In fact, the concept of diaspora now has assumed a much broader meaning. Vertovec argues that diaspora at present is used to 'describe practically any population that is considered "deterritorialized" or "transnational"' (Vertovec 1997: 277).

Among the many drivers of flows of people, finances, knowledge and networks, economic considerations have played one of the most important factors for a long time in history. In the case of the Singaporean economy, it has been made progressive, vibrant and attractive with relevant state policies as a space for networking, business opportunities, skilled labour and commodity markets – all to fit into the 'increasingly globalized capitalism of the late twentieth century' that has 'produced the space of flows with global cities as nodal points' (Voigt-Graf 2004: 27). Singapore, in the league of these global cities, has created unique space of its own that not only forms an effective node of connectivity but also represents a lived space where social, cultural and economic fabric is both 'woven of local elements' and 'involves a high density of transnational relationships' (Yeoh & Chang 2001: 1026). An island city-state, comprising a migrant population as an inevitable part of their demography and long historical links with the Indian sub-continent, Singapore has been ideally posited as an important node of outward-bound human flows from India and an important transit point for onward migration. It is also ideally posited to receive the inflow of people, ideas, information and knowledge from other Asian states and the West. Substantial scholarship, both historical and contemporary, is available on the Indian migrant communities between India and Singapore (Sandhu 1969; Arasaratnam 1970; Brown 1994; Sandhu and Mani 2006; Bhattacharya 2011). The Indian diaspora that has flourished in Singapore is very different from the 'Silicon Valley' links, but not necessarily disconnected from it. The formation of this global node of inter-connectivities may not essentially be free from the fetters of nation-centric discourses. Rather, it has emerged as a transformed space by the effective and assertive state driven policies that have been supported by a strategic geographical location, but it has been limited by territorial extent and scanty natural resources (even drinking water). With its politically stable governance, state-driven economic incentives and vigorous planning for the future, Singapore has been able to maintain an edge over the other Asian metropoles and has emerged as one of the more favourable transnational space (in terms of economic opportunities, educational standards, urban conveniences, environmental concerns, tourism activities etc.) in popular and public discourses.

The formation of transnational nodes and circulation of mobilities led to formation of dynamic spaces, both physical and virtual. Voigt-Graft brings to our attention the importance of geography in the spatial metaphor of transnational networks (Voigt-Graf 2004). The argument is based on the understanding that the "spatial organization of transnationalism provides another powerful tool for comparisons between different communities" (Voigt-Graf 2004: 25). Thus the production of space then reflects upon the action of people at different moments of history. In Singapore, the architectural landscapes and lived-spaces of the colonial times reflected the colonial strategy of segregating people on the basis of their ethnicity. This was overturned during the post-independent PAP (People's Action Party) governance, which placed emphasis on the different races living together and the development of an integrated Singaporean identity through their public-housing policy, the Housing Development Board (HDB) project. The legacy of the colonial architectural plan remains preserved as heritage spaces and places of tourist interests at present. However, the growth of private housing remained more organic, without directives of ethnic ratio and balance, and it resulted in formation of dynamic spaces outside the government-controlled HDB area with the influx of highly skilled and affluent entrepreneurial Indians who have carved out their own spaces in different districts in the city state (Barman 2009). Thus Singapore presents two different dimensions of the development of Indian transnational space – one that shifted internally from the past to the present, which involves the negotiation and accommodation within different layers of the Diaspora; and the other: transition of Singapore as a centre for inbound and outbound mobilities of Indians within Asia and beyond. Thus, instead of thinking of a space as one with defined boundaries, it can be imagined, as Massey points out, 'articulated moments in networks of social relations and understandings' (Massey 1991: 28). Massey's argument of power-geometry that implies different levels of power that are associated with the global flows of networks, nodes and position in the networks (Massey 1993) can also be quite strongly reflected in the transnational space of Singapore.

Transition of Indian transnational spaces in Singapore

Historically, the growth and development of Singapore was quite intimately connected to the Indian sub-continent through British colonial administration, their economic projects and migration policies. Thus, while it was administratively connected to the Indian sub-continent and all of South Asia during the colonial period, Singapore was also suitably connected to other parts of Southeast Asia (intra-regional trade and ethnic networks) and China (China trade) in the same period, enabling the smooth flow of human mobilities in different directions from the ideal node of the connectivity that the British created.

Indian migration to Singapore and the Malaya Peninsula in the colonial period has been mostly studied as labour history narratives (Sandhu 1969; Arasaratnam 1970; Siddique and Purushotam 1982; Mani 2006 to name a few scholars), categorized either as plantation, coolie or convict labourers brought into the region from the Indian sub-continent, particularly the southern region of India. The migrants served different necessities of the colonial masters, whether infrastructure-building for the development of Singapore as a transit point in the China trade or catering to the plantation economy in the Malayan Peninsula under the indenture/*kangany* system of labour. The migrants were mostly lured, coerced or forced by colonial strategies and can be largely described as part of an involuntary migration. However, there were also voluntary migrants who travelled to different parts of Southeast Asia as merchants, traders, sojourners, professionals, nationalists and social, religious and political activists; these have not been studied with adequate attention, except very few exceptions (Bhattacharya 2011). The period witnessed a large movement of Indians to and from the sub-continent facilitated by colonial strategies and new technologies. Singapore was also administered from the Bengal Presidency between 1826 and 1867 (Yong and Major 1995: 4). Between 1850 and 1930 there was a movement of around 30 million people from India to Ceylon, Burma and the Malaya Peninsula, and about 19 million from China to Southeast Asia (Amrith 2011: 18–19). From 1930s onwards, there were also reverse flows, making the patterns of human mobilities (also commodities, ideas and information, trade networks) circulatory in nature (Bose 2006; Bhattacharya 2011; Amrith 2013) and making it more transnational. However, there was a seeming paradox in positing the Indian communities in the social architecture of Singapore during this period. On the one hand, their circulatory movements across the Bay of Bengal made them part of transnational networks; on the other hand, they remained as ethnically divided communities situated in demarcated lived spaces (Makepeace 1991: 345) in a local context, where 'each group retained an unchallenged claim to defining the identity of various areas allotted to them' (Siddique and Purushotam 1982: 7). This was a part of Raffles' town planning, where each ethnic group was confined to a definite space in the Singapore landscape that ensured that they were closely connected with their linguistic and regional groups but also hindered formation of a local identity and unity.

In the post-independence era, the political situation changed for both India and Singapore, as did their policy decisions. Singapore declared multiethnicity, multiculturalism and meritocracy as driving principles of its state policies, thus incorporating the diverse migrant groups within its national fold. It embarked upon a complete infrastructural overhaul since the 1960s. Rapid industrialization led to the conversion of the enclave structures into Housing Development Board (HDB) flats, with more integrated living for all ethnic groups together. Education was made compulsory for all. National Service became mandatory for boys, and urban-renewal schemes totally restructured the city's landscapes. The older Indian living spaces almost disappeared (Bhattacharya 2016), with the shining exception of Serangoon Road, which was later named Little India in the 1980s. It remains as the representative space for the Indian communities and has been preserved as a heritage space, also serving as a major tourist attraction. On the economic front, Singapore remained a free-market economy with rapid industrialization targets and participation of multinational corporations in its economic growth process. Starting from the import substitution of 1960s, Singapore moved towards export orientation policies of the 1970s and 1980s (Bhattacharya 2011: 93–94) and soon emerged as one of the Tiger Economies of Asia.

India started on a very different note, having had to deal with unabated violence and the irrevocable trauma of the Partition along with receiving its independence in 1947. It transformed into an inward-looking economy, restricting market interactions with other states and promoting rapid industrialization through huge investments in public-sector undertakings. In spite of their radical differences in economic trajectories, both Singapore and India declared similar stringent immigration policies and citizenship laws restricting human flows. India, under its first Prime Minister, Jawaharlal Nehru, decided that the Indian diaspora should choose to be loyal to their host country or the country of their residence (*Indian Foreign Policy* 1961).[1] Singapore also restricted immigration of people, thus directly affecting those Indians those who have had regular communication links with their homeland under the British rule. The ethnic Indians now had to choose citizenship of either of the nation-states. Thus there was new creation of national and ethnic identities. The nation-building ideology of Lee Kuan Yew, the first Prime Minister of Singapore, was guided by pragmatism to make a young, vulnerable and diverse city-state survive, and he carried out his task as a 'constructivist' and an 'instrumentalist' (Han 2016: 205). Another important policy for managing the polyethnic Singapore population was to make the CMIO factor as the 'building blocks of Singapore's "multiculturalism"' (Siddique and Purushotam 1982: 3). This is based on the acceptance of four major ethnicities of Singapore (Chinese, Malay, Indians and Others [CMIO]) to ensure social harmony and continue to remain as prominent identity markers. However, the homogenization of the different ethnic groups remains problematic.

The Indian communities in Singapore went through various negotiations of their identity in the post-independence period, and by the late 1970s, three major groups emerged with distinct ideas of Indianness: (a) working-class Tamils promoting bilingualism in their children, more receptive to the socio-economic changes and believing in being more secular; (b) the category of Indians who interpreted loss of link language to Indian culture; and (c) those who embraced religion as the most important cultural identifier and lineage (Mani 2006: 800–801). Thus one could envisage the Indian diasporic formation taking deeper roots in Singapore in this period. The transnational connection remained mostly as cultural and ideological links[2] rather than regular physical interactions.

The decade of the 1990s brought about a lot of changes for Singaporeans in general, and also Singaporean Indians in particular. Goh Chok Tong became the second Prime Minister of Singapore after 25 years of Lee Kuan Yew's political leadership. Goh's period ushered in many political, economic and structural changes that had immense impact on the Indian community in the years to come. Among other things, Goh initiated the formation of the Indian self-help group SINDA (Singapore Indian Development Association) with government support and patronage in 1991, primarily to address falling educational achievements of Indian students, which gradually assumed an important symbol of community development and participation. Another very significant step taken was to re-invigorate the bilateral relations between Singapore and India and start what has been famously known as the 'mild India fever' (Mani 2009; Bhattacharya 2011; See et al. 2015). For India, the decade was a watershed in the history of its growth, when the market reforms were initiated, economic liberalization began, Look East Policy was declared and efforts to reconnect with its diaspora across the globe was undertaken – initiated under the leadership of the then Prime Minister Narasimha Rao and continued by his successor with similar enthusiasm. This convergence of interests, as I have discussed in an earlier work (Bhattacharya 2011), brought about enormous changes within the Indian diaspora in Singapore (both in terms of composition and numbers, as the table below shows), reconnected the diaspora with an emerging India and created suitable platform for networking and transnational interactions from the pivot of Singapore. The new generation of migrants consisted of highly skilled professionals, entrepreneurs, researchers, scientists and financiers who fitted well into the demand of Singapore's new economic trajectory of a knowledge economy. Increasing positivism and interactions in the bilateral relations led to increase in trade, investments and mobilities of people. The CECA[3] that was signed between the two states in 2005 became the corner stone of spiraling bilateral economic relations.

Table 20.1 Increasing Indian residents in Singapore

Year	Total residents (Citizens & PRs)	Indian residents
1970	2,133,724	144,622
1980	2,500,765	151,254
1990	3,091,550	213,293
2000	3,776,092	295,860
2010	4,540,322	393,420
2016	4,994,232	418,233
2017	5,089,716	423,433

Source: Calculated as SUM from dataset: Singapore Residents by Age Group, Ethnic Group and Gender, End June, Annual (URL: https://data.gov.sg/dataset/resident-population-by-ethnicity-gender-and-age-group accessed 14.5.2018).

The transformation that the Indian communities went through in terms of re-imagination of their identity, lived-spaces and professional and entrepreneurial trends requires a separate and in-depth research in itself. In this chapter I have tried to discuss some of the contemporary strands of the diasporic interactions that are both local and global and share overlaps and characteristics facilitated by global market interactions, state initiatives and a rising Asia.

Indian economic networks and platforms

Economic opportunities have long been main drivers of migration flows, and the present period is no exception. The choice of economic opportunities that worked in permutation and combination with other factors in present-day Singapore – safe, secure, environmentally friendly, geographical proximity to India, First-World infrastructure facilities, cultural familiarities – are all great pull factors for global, tech-savvy and upwardly mobile Indians who have been seeking further opportunities from different locations, either from the Indian sub-continent or from other parts of the Western world.

Indian business communities have always had a transnational presence in Singapore, right from colonial times. They had institutionalized their presence with different regional- and linguistic-based organizations like the Sindhi Association (1921), Gujarati Society, Chettiar Chamber of Commerce (1928)[4] and Sikh Moneylenders and Businessmen's Association (little is known about this organization). They were also quite closely associated with the homeland through kinship networks, financial transactions (*hundi* or bills of exchange, etc.), sourcing for commodities, manufacturing or distribution of finished goods, and manpower resources from their respective regions and ethnicities (Bhattacharya 2011). Some groups, such as the Sindhis and the Parsis, also used Singapore as their transit point in making an onward journey to other parts of Southeast Asia, Hong Kong and China, while other Gujarati merchants and traders, such as the Jumabhoys, linked Southeast Asia to the Middle East and Africa through Singapore (Jumabhoy 1990). Many of these associations initially started out as platforms of business networking, taking up other issues of trading interest later, however, transforming themselves into more socio-cultural organizations (as discussed later) and using the Indian Chamber of Commerce (ICC established in 1935, later became SICCI-Singapore Indian Chamber of Commerce and Industry) as a platform for business interactions between themselves or with the government (Bhattacharya 2011: 212–230) or with other Chambers of Commerce.

The scenario changed in the post-independence period, as did many other aspects of life. The changes led to a struggle for survival, where many of the smaller firms petered out of existence. The rest diversified into electronics, tourism, real estate and hospitality sectors, though trading still remained the primary occupation for many business firms. New enterprises also emerged and flourished. Some of the prominent names were the Thakrals, Tolaram group, Kewalrai Chanrai group and Royal Sporting House (Bhattacharya 2011: 97–119). Others popular names of the period, such as the Mustafa and Govindasamy Pillai, were mostly in the retail sectors. This period witnessed major disruptions from the earlier established networks. The Indian regional associations gradually re-oriented towards upholding cultural values and practices (in the face of the homeland disconnection) rather than focusing on economic networks, which, however, continued within the folds of social networking.[5] Economic interests of the Indian community found manifestations in the platform of the Indian Chamber of Commerce, SICCI. SICCI joined in various trade delegations to different nation-states, participated in meetings with the Chinese Chamber, supported social activities and educational initiatives with bursaries and scholarships and also hosted Indian business delegations (*The SICCI Journey* 2014). The Chamber largely represented Indian transnational networking during this period in initiating and chairing ASEAN-CCI meetings in 1984 and 1985 (*The SICCI Journey* 2014: 37–38, 43–44) along with other government representations such as the Singapore Trade Development Board (TDB). There were also initiatives to boost trade with India. On an individual level, Indian business firms remained connected to the region (limited by Singapore's market size) and beyond.

During the 1990s, transnational business links with India started with renewed vigour with the growing relationship between the two states that revived their dormant politico-economic relations to a new level of partnership. In the decade of Indian economic liberalization, Look East Policy, 'India fever' and ASEAN partnership, SICCI took the initiative, along with government organizations, to venture into the Indian markets. Apart from heading and hosting several delegations to and from India, SICCI also set up the Parameswara Holdings Ltd. in 1993, an investment company to spearhead investments in India (*The SICCI Journey* 2014: 58). An Indian Business Interaction Group (IBIG) was also set up by TDB to provide networking facilities and make informative business proposals in 1993[6] (PhuaKok 1993). Soon the first Global Indian Entrepreneur's Conference was organized in 1996 by SICCI, TDB, EDB (Economic Development Board) and STB (Singapore Tourism Board). Thus SICCI became a major conduit between government organizations and entrepreneurs for both India and Singapore.

The Indian business Chambers like the CII (Confederation of Indian Industries) and ASSOCHAM (Associated Chambers of Commerce) were also making their way into Singapore, initially through participation in business delegations headed by the government and later through their Chamber's initiatives to create networking platforms as well. The CII Southeast Asia Region office was established in 1994 to broaden relationship with ASEAN and to work with both corporations and the government in Singapore. CII has been very active in Singapore and the region in promoting business interests and collaborations.[7]

The turn of the century witnessed a dramatic change in the outreach and transnational activities of the Indian business communities. The opportunities for highly skilled professionals (particularly in the IT and finance sectors), entrepreneurs, research scientists and academicians had already opened up since Singapore's ambitious target of a knowledge economy since the 1990s. The signing of CECA in 2005[8] opened doors for these professionals since 2005. The momentum of the earlier decade not only increased rapidly but also witnessed greater participation by the Indian corporate sector from India as well as beyond the region. The number of Indian residents in Singapore (citizens and Permanent Residents) increased phenomenally, from 13,261 to more than 30,000 between 2000 and 2015. The figures for the Indian professionals have grown from 13,490 to over 41,000 in the same period (Singapore Census 2000 and General Household Survey, 2015). Many of these professionals have turned into first generation of entrepreneurs as well. Another trend that quickly caught up with the Indian entrepreneurs following the success of the Silicon Valley was that of the 'start-up' culture. Singapore, with all the ingredients and favourable conditions for such a change, started to actively participate in the start-up scene. Indians comprise a considerable number in this sector, and a shift from an Indian location to Singapore is also a significant feature, thus making their companies and products more transnational, while using brand name of Singapore. Flipkart was registered as e-commerce company in Singapore by Indians Sachin and Binny Bansal, while Mobikon (founder, Sameer Khadepaun) shifted its base from Pune to Singapore in 2012 (Khan 2013), the security software Appknox moved to Singapore and AdNear, a mobile advertisement network, also shifted from Bangalore to Singapore in November 2012. Pranoti and Rishi Israni, National University of Singapore (NUS) students who started their company, Zimplistic in 2008, launched Rotimatic, the popular robotic roti-making machine (Quek 2016). Dexecure was also started by NUS graduates, Parameshwaran and Srirangam (Kaur 2017). An example of a crowd-sourcing platform similarly launched as a start-up is Milaap (Ganesan and Ghosh 2016: 107).

To facilitate transnational networking amongst such entrepreneurs and start-ups, the platform of TiE (The Indus Entrepreneurs) has been very useful. TiE was initially started in the Silicon Valley by a group of successful South Asian corporate executives and senior professionals. It stared its Singapore Chapter in 2002 to create a 'vibrant eco-system of Asian entrepreneurs, angel investors, global capitalists and industry professionals'.[9] With mentorship, education and funding opportunities, TiE Global has been able to connect investors, entrepreneurs and professionals bringing about digital transformation and borderless growth across the globe. In Singapore, TiE partners with SMART (Singapore-MIT Alliance for Research and Technology), SP Jain School of Management and Tata Communications, thus creating an important agency to connect India, Singapore and the world on a transnational platform.

Indian socio-cultural networks

Indians in Singapore have had the trend of forming associations and grouping based on regions of their origin and linguistic affiliations. The same had been true for original business associations as well, which later changed into more of social and cultural organizations.[10] Caste, region, religion and language were determinants of associations and groupings among the Indians, so though Tamil became a dominant language of the people, Indians could not be grouped as a homogenous lot. Celebration of festivities such as Deepavali or Pongal brought them closer, although regional and caste group identities were quite pronounced. (For example, Thendayuthapani Temple was closely associated with and managed by the Chettiars.) The more visible differences were between the North Indians and the South Indians, speaking Tamil being the most common difference identified easily. Tamil had been recognized as one of the official languages since the 1950s and continues to be one of the four languages recognized by the state ("Singapore Committed" 2018). The Arya Samaj introduced the Hindi classes from 1930s onwards, which remained confined to the lesser North Indian population. Eventually the ethnic walls began to crumble after 1959 (Mani 2006:796), largely due to the introduction of the new educational policy, and later, after 1965, with new housing development schemes and integrated living.

In the colonial period, the Indian communities in Malaya were directly affected by the course of events in the sub-continent, thus maintaining their ideological and physical transnational connections across different geographies, not only with the circulation of migrants but also with the visits of social reformers, political activists, poets and thinkers. The Self-Respect movement in 1920s, aimed at defying the upper-caste domination, had immense impact in the region. The leader, E.V Ramasamy, toured Malaya in 1929, spreading the message of reform aimed at amelioration of the backward castes in the society (Amrith 2011: 86–87). Similarly, the Indian National Army that was headquartered in Singapore under the charismatic freedom fighter S.C. Bose created a huge impact in arousing consciousness about rights and liberties, nationalism and patriotism, and was a significant unifier in the background of different social and economic boundaries. The 1947 Partition was another event that brought about many socio-economic changes when large groups of people, especially Punjabis and Sindhis, fled to Malaya, creating linguistic complexities in a dominant Tamil-speaking community, which in turn accelerated differences between the perceptions of the North and South Indian communities more markedly. Further separatist identity formations were mobilized by the breakup of the Madras Presidency along linguistic lines, creating the states of Tamil Nadu, Andhra Pradesh, Kerala and Karnataka. These events had diverse effects on the social identity and formation of organizations. The Tamil Representative Council (TRC) was formed in 1952 to promote Malayan Tamil identity and incorporated 56 Tamil social organizations in the region (Mani 2006: 796). The Singapore Malayalee Association, one of the oldest of the regional associations, started centenary celebrations in 2017. In the post-independence years, Britain's withdrawal of military bases reduced the Malayalees from 16.8 percent of the population in 1957 to 8.1 percent in 1980 (Mani 2006: 796), making them similar in number to Punjabis in the demography. Gujarati Yuvak Mandal (1956),[11] which later became the Singapore Gujarati Society, and Bengali Association of Singapore (BAS), established in 1956, were some examples of other older regional organizations in Singapore.

Holding on to the identity of language seems to be a major focus of Indian communities, particularly for Tamils, Malayalees and Punjabis. Tamil had already been recognized as one of Singapore's official languages in the 1950s and remains the dominant spoken language even at present, though the percentage of Tamil speakers among Indians has reduced quite significantly and other languages have also been recognized in Singapore's bilingual educational system. Apart from TRC, there are other Tamil organizations like the Tamil Language and Cultural Society and the Association of Tamil Writers that promote the language.

With the changes in the bilateral relations and increased human mobility since the 1990s, a number of new regional associations have been established, such as the Marwari Mitra Mandal (MMM) that was formed in 2005 though there were Marwaris residing in Singapore since 1970s and 1980s.[12] Other organizations, such as Maharashtra Mandal (1994), Kannada Sangha and Singapore (1996) have also been established. Some regional identities, for example the Assamese, have not yet been able to form organizations but organize periodical gatherings on the occasion of Bihu festival informally (Kaur 2018: 10). There are also smaller groups formed with sub-caste and spatial identities, such as the Mathurs in Singapore[13] (Aggarwal 2018: 10). Thus the global convergences of different Indian communities in Singapore has led to a lesser emphasis on building up of homogenous national identity but upholding regional festivals, culture and cuisine in the production of consumption.

Indian transnational alumni networks

The trend of the alumni networks is also an outcome of the globalization trends and the revised diaspora policies, which has reversed the earlier imagination of 'brain drain' into 'brain bank' and ultimately into 'brain gain'. The popular educational, management and technology institutes of India have sought to maintain connections amongst their alumni, creating a global chain of connectivities of (mostly) successful entrepreneurs, professionals, technologists, academicians, performers and practitioners in fine arts, etc. Singapore provides an ideal platform for these transnational links. One of the most prominent among these networks is the Pan-IIM Alumni Association in Singapore. It was formed in 2005 to 'promote better integration amongst the various IIM communities, to enable the exchange of thoughts and ideas with the Singapore business community and drive pan-IIM events and initiatives'.[14] About 1,800 IIM alumni present at Singapore, thus making the Singapore chapter one of the largest of the global platforms for their alumni network. They have organized successful forums and conferences since 2005 and have also received the recognition of the Singapore government. The other very popular alumni network is the IIT[15] Alumni Association Singapore (IITAAS), which started much earlier, in 1994. Singapore has the second largest IIT community in the world, with some 3,500 IITians and 100 entrepreneurs as its residents.[16] The Harvard Club of Singapore is another alumni networking body that works closely with the IIMPACT and other IIM alumni events.[17] TiE has also had collaborations with IIM alumni networks. In fact, there are strong possibilities of overlaps of members between the different alumni networks, where interactions are carried out on in a global scale and not confined within any geographical or political boundaries. Singapore provides the ideal platform of such networking forums.

Much lesser known and publicized is the Singapore Chapter of Jamal Mohamed College (a religious minority institution in Tamil Nadu) Alumni Association, formed in 2010. Members comprise mainly professionals and are involved in providing education-related social and community services (*JMC Souvenir Magazine* 2015).

Conclusion

The euphoria around mobile networks and transnational connections bring us to the question as to whether the 'nation-state' is then being marginalized in the geopolitical frameworks of a rising globalization. While apparently it may seem so at one level, it may not be actually true. In the expressions and formation of various interest groups, a strong aspect is to revisit the nation from outside with different strands of emotions and sentiment of the soil. In fact, the state and its leaders are promoting these forms of national identity and consciousness for further outreach and incorporate broad categories of ethnic Indians to propagate inclusiveness and encourage participation of the diaspora in the nation's development.

The Indian transnational networks have gone through different transformations over the years, and they are still evolving. The fluid characteristic of migration and diasporic formation is intimately associated with development of transnational imagination. They have been characterized as 'fleeting and flexible' (Bhattacharya 2011) groups who are open to better transnational opportunities and networks, thus much less inclined to nourish deep-rooted local identity in many cases. The online interactive practices help to maintain their connectivity (Sahoo and De Kruijf 2014) despite their changing locations, thus the sense of loss of 'home' or 'relations' are not felt in the same way as they were in past generations. It is also significantly affected by the globalization flows, market trends and state-driven policies and initiatives to interact with the diaspora and global citizens.

In Singapore, the focus on language as an identity marker for the Indian communities has disseminated to celebration of culture, festivities and sports in the region, bringing about greater visibility and diversity. It facilitates the establishment of a consciousness that is more regional, accommodative and fluid rather than a homogenous ethnic/racial identity. Several religious and cultural organizations in different parts of the globe are now connected with technology quite easily. Keeping to the legacy of the British strategy of developing it as an effective connector, Singapore remains an important node and platform for linking different interest groups, institutions and like-minded people in the region, across the world and for Indians, also back to the homeland.

Notes

1. For detailed reference, see Nehru's debates on foreign policy in Lok Sabha in 1957.
2. Indian communities were affected by developments in the Indian sub-continent, whether it was the anti-British struggle, the Partition of 1947, or the Dravidian movement, separation of the Madras Presidency, etc., as has been discussed by many scholars (Mani 2006; Amrith 2010)
3. The Comprehensive Economic Cooperation Agreement (CECA) brought about significant changes in the economic collaborations between Singapore and India. It is commonly known as the FTA+ agreement and was the first of its kind to be signed between India and any of the Southeast Asians states. For Singapore too, it was the first such trade agreement signed with any of the states of South Asia and served as a guiding example to be emulated in many such future agreements in the region. For further details of the agreement and the consequences, see See 2006; Bhattacharya 2011: 157–161.
4. The Chettiars, who were predominantly financiers and moneylenders, were an extremely close-knit group from South India who had strong ties with their homeland villages in South India. Their activities mainly centred around the *kittangis* or shop houses that were centres of their business transactions and also served as residences. The Nattukottai Chettiars were present in the Southeast Asian region almost as early as the British arrival, following British footsteps into the region. However, their chamber of commerce was only established in 1928.
5. The Sindhi community, for example, arranged match-making sessions for marriage alliances within the community. These alliances were mostly motivated by and facilitated business alliances.
6. About 50 local companies expressed their enthusiasm about proposals of networking.
7. In one of the recent news updates, five states of India (Andhra Pradesh, Madhya Pradesh, Bihar, Chattisgarh, Odisha) have signed MOU with CII and LKY School of Public Policy of Singapore for building a master plan on Ease of Doing Business: Vision 2020. This information is taken from "CII News Update" in CII website, http://www.cii.in/Country.aspx?enc=7pte/yD9Tk2p+488+KK4zYrF4OMQiE0jz7y3rVWNtjYtMTUbp5cISPMorETBsCbf accessed on 10.5.2018
8. The Comprehensive Economic Cooperation Agreement (CECA) was signed between India and Singapore in 2005. This was a FTA+ agreement and a first of its kind to be signed by India with any of the Southeast Asian states. It formed the basis of many future bilateral agreements between Indian and other states.
9. This information is quoted from the TiE website, https://singapore.tie.org/about/ accessed on 12 May 2018.
10. The Sindhi Merchants Association formed in 1921 was one of the earliest of the organizations formed by the merchants and traders of the same region from the Indian sub-continent. However, with changing circumstances, it later changed its name to Singapore Sindhi Association in 2003 and became more of an association associated with spiritual, cultural and sport activities.
11. Gujarati merchants were among the earliest of the migrants to Southeast Asia, much before the colonial times. Thus circulation of the Gujarati merchants and traders in Southeast Asia was not introduced in colonial times. The Hindu Paropkari Fund was started in 1908 and a Gujarati School in 1947. The Gujarati Yuvak Mandal initially comprised of employees from the Gujarati business community. The Singapore Gujarati Society (SGS, as it is popularly known) has a membership of 550 at present and has transformed into a more socio-cultural organization ("About SGS – History," http://mysgs.sgs.org.sg/History accessed on 14 May 2018).
12. This has been shared by the President of the MMM in his message in 2015 in the Souvenir volume. He mentioned that the Marwaris kept meeting informally on the occasion of Holi and Diwali and when their number reached to about 100, decided to formally register their organization.
13. The Mathurs in Singapore comprise about 400 people, mostly professionals. They origin from Mathura in Uttar Pradesh, North India and belong to the sub-caste of the kayastha community.
14. The PIIMA website gives the details of its events and its vision, http://www.deideaz.com/Pan-Indian-Institute-of-Management-Alumni.php accessed 14 May 2018.

15 The Indian Institutes of Technology are the premier institutes in India for imparting higher education in technology and is quite a popular brand name across the globe.
16 Details of the Singapore network and events of IITAAS is found in their website, https://www.iitaas.org accessed on 14 May 2018.
17 For details refer to their website, http://harvardclubsg.blogspot.sg accessed 14 May 2018.

References

Aggarwal, Vandana, "Meet the Mathurs," *Tabla!* 7 September 2018.
Amrith, Sunil S., "Mobile City and the Coromandel Coast: Tamil Journeys to Singapore, 1920–1960," *Mobilities*, Vol. 5, No. 2, 2010, pp. 237–255.
Amrith, Sunil S., *Migration and Diaspora in Modern Asia* (Cambridge: Cambridge University Press, 2011).
Amrith, Sunil S., *Crossing the Bay of Bengal: The Furies of Nature and Fortunes of Migrants* (Cambridge, Mass.: Harvard University Press, 2013).
Arasaratnam, Sinnappah, *Indians in Malaya and Singapore* (London: Institute of Race Relations, 1970).
Barman, Amrit, "The Orchard Road Indian," *Tabla!* 21 August 2009.
Bhattacharya, Jayati, *Beyond the Myth: Indian Business Communities in Singapore* (Singapore: Institute of Southeast Asian Studies, 2011).
Bhattacharya, Jayati, "Less Remembered Spaces and Interactions in a Changing Singapore: Indian Business Communities in the Post-Independence Period." In Pillai, Gopinath and Kesavapany. K., eds. *50 Years of Indian Community* (Singapore: World Scientific Publishing Co., 2016).
Bose, Sugata, *A Hundred Horizons: The Indian Ocean in the Age of the Global Empire* (Cambridge, Mass.: Harvard University Press, 2006).
Brown, Rajeswary Ampalavanar, *Capital and Entrepreneurship in Southeast Asia* (Houndmills, Basingstoke, Hampshire, London: The Macmillan Press Ltd.; New York, N.Y.: St. Martin's Press, Inc., 1994).
Ganesan, Karthik and Ghosh, Arunabha, "A Three-Point Agenda for Two Brands of Entrepreneurship." In Tan, Tai Yong and Bhattacharya, A.K., eds. *Looking Ahead: India, Singapore in the New Millennium* (Singapore, New Delhi: Institute of South Asian Studies, Ananta Aspen Centre, 2016), 101–114.
General Household Survey (GHS), Department of Statistics, Ministry of Tarde and Industry, Republic of Singapore, 2015.
Han, Christine, "Citizenship Education: 50 Years of Constructing and Promoting National Identity in Schools." In Lim, Jason and Lee, Terence, eds. *Singapore: Negotiating State and Society, 1965–2015* (London, New York, N.Y.: Routledge, 2016).
Indian Foreign Policy: Selected Speeches, September 1946- April 1961 (New Delhi: Government of India, 1961).
Jamal Mohamed College Alumni Association (Singapore Chapter), 5th Anniversary Souvenir Magazine (Singapore, 2015).
Jumabhoy, Rajabali, *Multiracial Singapore: On to the Nineties* (Singapore: Chopman Publishers, 1990, revised edition).
Kaur, Amrita, "Want to Speed Up Your Website?" *Tabla!*, 31 March 2017.
Kaur, Amrita, "Keeping Colourful Culture Alive," *Tabla!*, 4 May 2018.
Khan, Taslima, "Look East Policy," *Business Today*, 31 March 2013, http://www.businesstoday.in/magazine/features/why-many-indian-start-ups-are-moeving-to-singapore/story/193222.html retrieved 13 May 2017.
Makepeace, Walter, Brooke Gilbert, E., and Braddell, Roland St. J., *One Hundred Years of Singapore* (Singapore and New York: Oxford University Press, 1991).
Mani, A., "Indians in Singapore Society." In Sandhu, K.S. and Mani, A., eds. *Indian Communities in Southeast Asia* (Singapore: ISEAS, reprint 2006), pp. 788–809.
Mani A., "The Man Who Nurtured Indians and Started the India Fever." In Welsh, Bridget, et al, eds. *Impressions of the Goh Chok Tong Years in Singapore* (Singapore: NUS Press, 2009), pp. 375–386.
Massey, Doreen, "A Global Sense of Space," *Marxism Today*, June 1991, pp. 24–29.
Massey, Doreen, "Power-Geometry and a Progressive Sense of Place." In Bird, Jon, Curtis, Barry, Putnam, Tim, Robertson, George, and Tickner, Lisa, eds. *Mapping the Futures: Local Cultures, Global Change* (London: Routledge, 1993), pp. 59–69.

Ozkul, Derya, "Transnational Migration Research," *Sociopedia.isa*, 2012, pp. 1–12.
PhuaKok, Kim, "TDB To Set Up Informal Business Grouping of Indian and S'pore Firms," *The Straits Times*, 18 August 1993.
Quek, Eunice. "Singaporean Couple Invests Roti-Making Robot Rotimatic," *The Straits Times*, 28 August 2016, http://www.straitstimes.com/lifestyle/food/easy-roti-in-a-jiffy retrieved 13 May 2017.
Sahoo, Ajaya Kumar and Johannes G. De Kruijf, *Indian Transnational Online: New Perspective on Diaspora* (Surrey, Burlington: Ashgate, 2014).
Sandhu, Kernial Singh, *Indians in Malaya: Some Aspects of their Immigration and Settlement (1786–1957)* (London: Cambridge University Press, 1969).
Sandhu, K.S. and A. Mani, eds. *Indian Communities in Southeast Asia* (Singapore: ISEAS, 2006).
See, Chak Mun, "The Comprehensive Economic Cooperation Agreement: The Strategic Imperatives," *Singapore Year Book of International Law and Contributors (SYBIL)*, Volume 10, 2006, pp. 233–242.
See, Chak Mun, Tan, Li-Jen, Advani, Rahul and Dutt, Rinisha eds. *Singapore and India: Towards a Shared Future* (Singapore: ISAS, 2015).
The SICCI Journey: The Singapore Indian Chamber of Commerce and Industry, 1924–2014, SICCI, 90th Anniversary (Singapore: SICCI, 2014).
Siddique, Sharon and Purushotam, Nirmala, *Singapore's Little India: Past, Present and Future*, (Singapore: ISEAS, 1982).
Singapore Census of Population 2000, Department of Statistics, Ministry of Trade and Industry, Republic of Singapore.
"Singapore Committed to Keeping Tamil as an Official Language, Says Cabinet Minister," *Business Standard*, 13 May 2018, http://www.business-standard.com/article/pti-stories/singapore-committed-to-keeping-tamil-as-an-official-language-says-cabinet-minister-118051300277_1.html accessed on 13 May 2018.
Vertovec, Steven, "Three Meanings of 'Diaspora' Exemplified among South Asian Religions," *Diaspora: A Journal of Transnational Studies*, Vol. 6, No. 3, 1997, pp. 277–299.
Voigt-Graf, Carmen, "Towards a Geography of Transnational Spaces: Indian Transnational Communities in Australia," *Global Networks*, Vol. 4, No. 1, 2004, pp. 25–49.
World Migration Report 2018, UN Migration Agency (Geneva: International Organization for Migration).
Yeoh, Brenda S.A. and Chang, T.C., "Globalising Singapore: Debating Transnational Flows in the City," *Urban Studies*, Vol. 38, No. 7, 2001, pp. 1025–1044.
Yong, Tan Tai and Major, Andrew J., "India and Indians in the Making of Singapore." In Yong, Mun Cheong and Rao, V.V. Bhanoji, eds. *Singapore-India Relations: A Primer* (Singapore: Singapore University Press, 1995).

GLOSSARY

Arangetram The debut on-stage performance of a former student of Indian classical dance and music.

Baul *Baul* or *Bauls* are a group of mystic minstrels from Bengal.

Bhangra A type of popular music combining Punjabi folk traditions with Western pop music.

Cappella Meaning unaccompanied vocal.

Chamars One of the untouchable communities, or dalits in India.

Chettiars *Chettiar* or Chetti is a title used by various mercantile, agricultural and land-owning castes in South India, especially in the states of Tamil Nadu and Kerala.

Chowtal The name of a "taal"/ "tala" or meter in Hindustani classical music and also a form of folksong of North India's Bhojpuri region, sung by amateurs during the vernal Phagwa or Holi festival.

Dandiyas Sticks used for Raas or *Dandiya*. Raas is the traditional folk-dance form of Gujarat and Rajasthan in India.

Dangdut Indian-style rhythms and instrumental idioms with international pop and rock sounds.

Devadasi A girl dedicated to worship and service of a deity or a temple for the rest of her life.

Dhrupad A genre in Hindustani classical music.

Ghazal A lyric poem with a fixed number of verses and a repeated rhyme, typically on the theme of love, and normally set to music.

Hawankund Site of the ritual fire.

Kritis A format of musical composition typical to Carnatic music.

Mrdangam A barrel-shaped double-headed drum with one head larger than the other, used in South Indian music.

NātyaŚāstra A Sanskrit Hindu text on the performing art.

Glossary

Navaratri A nine-night (and ten-day) Hindu festival.

Pandit/pujari Priest in the temple performing religious duties and activities.

Phagwa Colours used in the Holi festival in India.

Rāgs A *raga* is a melodic framework for improvisation akin to a melodic mode in Indian classical music.

Tatkars The stamped rhythmic footwork of Kathak.

Thang-ta "The Art of the Sword and Spear", the traditional martial art exclusive to the Meitei people of Manipur in northeast India.

Vina An Indian stringed instrument with four main and three auxiliary strings.

Vinayakacaturtti/ganesacaturthi The Ganesha Festival, held in the month of September in India, is one of the most famous Hindu religious festivals.

INDEX

Abdulla, K. S. 255
Abrams, Kerry 46
activism 2–3, 6, 13; *see also* Dalit transnational activism today; Indian/American foreign policy
Adivasis 161
Adur, Shweta 5–6
African National Congress 194; Women's League 194, 197
Afro-Asian Networks Research Collective 250
Agarwala, R. 29
Ahmed, Attiya 44
Ahmed, Rehana 242
Ahmed, Syed Jamil 100
Ajai, M. 162–163
Ali, S. 123, 125
Ali, Shareefah Hamid 249
All-India Women's Conference 249
Alukkas, Joy 259
Alvarez, Sonia 3
Ambedkar, B.R. 159, 160, 162–163, 166
American Association of Physicians of Indian Origin (AAPI) 137
American Israel Public Affairs Committee (AIPAC) 137
American Jewish Committee (AJC) 137
Amin, Ash 228
Amrute, Sareeta 45
Anand, Mulk Raj 246
Aneesh, A. 6
Anti Caste Discrimination Alliance (ACDA) 166, 167
apartheid *see* Indian origin women in South Africa
Appadurai, Arjun 1, 3, 120–121, 258
Arabian Gulf 119, 122–123
Asia Dalit Rights Forum 166, 167

Asian-American Hotel Owners Association (AAHOA) 137–138
Asiatic Labour Congress 248
Azmat, Fara 186

Bacigalupe, G. 235, 236
Bafaka, Muhammad 255
Bahaud-din Dagar, Mohi 97
Bahrain 119
Bai, Manorama 43
Baijnath, Lala 244
Ballantyne, Tony 243
Banerjee, Pallavi 6
Bangladesh 3, 135
Bansal, Sachin and Binny 273
Barakatullah, Muhammad 247
Bassett, Ross 43
Basu, Jyoti 246
baul 95, 279
Baul, Parvati 95–96
Bauman, Chad M. 145
Bayly, C. A. S. 241
Belarmino, Vanini 98, 100, 101
Bengali Association of Singapore (BAS) 274
Benhabib, Seyla 162
Bergson, Henri 214
Besant, Annie 79
Bhaba, H. 213
Bhakna, Sohan Singh 247
bhangra 9, 82, 83, 86, 87, 88, 89, 279
bharatanatyam 79, 80, 81, 84, 85
Bharatiya Janata Party (BJP) 137, 139, 161, 166
Bharucha, Rustom 94
Bhatt, Amy 48
Bhattacharya, A. 35
Bhattacharya, Abinash Chandra 247

Index

Bhattacharya, Jayati 275
Bhownaggree, Mancherjee 246
Biao, Xiang 230
Binder, J. 35
Blackwill, Robert 138
Blunt, A. 215, 218, 224n12
Boehmer, Elleke 244
Bollywood 6, 9, 81, 83, 85, 86, 87, 88
Bombay *see* layered cities, shared histories
Bonacich, Edna 173
Bonnerjee, Janaki 244
Bonnerjee, W. C. 245
borders 4
Bose, Subhas Chandra 246, 247, 274
Bourdieu, Pierre 89, 177–178, 214, 224n9
Bourrier, Ani 149
Bozeman, B. 64
Brah, A. 120, 121, 127–128
brain drain, defined 32; *see also* return migration of scientists and engineers; skill gap and brain drain for the U.S.
Brar, B. 23
Brickell, Katherine 74
British Dominion Women's Suffrage Union 249
British Empire transnational mobility of Indians 14, 241–243; Britain and the imperial metropolis 245–247; Indian women, gender and transnational mobility 248–250; Komagata Maru incident (1914) 203, 241–242; nationalism 242; political networks/transnational campaigning/anti-colonialism 247–248; transnational mobility and networks 243; travel and travel-writing 244–245; conclusion 250
Broadwater, T. 34
Brook, Peter 93–94
Brooklyn Raga Massive (BRM) 85, 86
Browning, Robert 84
Burke, Richard 38
Burton, Antoinette 243, 244, 245
Burton, Dan 135
Bush, Michael L. 5

Cabrera, Luis 165
Cachalia, Amina 191, 194, 195
Calder 14 135
call-center workers 6, 7, 24–25, 26, 27–28
Camara, M. 235, 236
Canada: workers, families, and households 13, 201–202; Chinese Immigration Act (1885) 203; Continuous Journey Regulation (1908) 203; gendered, classed, raced negotiations 205–208; gendered negotiations of childcare 206–208; Immigration Act (1906) 203; Immigration Refugees and Citizenship Canada (IRCC) 37; Indian hi-tech migrants 201–202, 204; racist history of Indian migration to Canada 202–204; scaling-back/restructuring career commitments 205–206; White Paper on Immigration (1966) 203; concluding remarks and future directions 208–209; *see also* Indian women in Toronto; second-generation South Asians in Canada
Carnatic Music Association of North America (CMANA) 84–85
Carrim, Nasima 192, 193
caste 158–160, 163, 166–168, 193; *see also* Dalit transnational activism today
Castells, Manuel 1
CBS Interactive 33
Centre for the Study of Developing Societies and Konrad Adenauer Stiftung (CSDS-KAS) 48
Cerase, F. P. 64
Chakravorty, Sanjoy 175
Chamars 83, 279
Chan, Raymond 204
Chandra, Ram 134
Chang, T. C. 267
Chattopadhyaya, Kamaladevi 249
Chattopadhyaya, Vierndranath "Chatto" 247, 249
Chettiars 271, 273, 276n4, 279
Chhandayan 85
Chile: zones of exception 25
China: residents in U.S. 57; scientists and engineers 54; Thousand Talents Programme 56
Chowdhury, Ashna 98–99, 100
Chowdhury, Elora 3
chowtāl 79, 87, 89, 279
Chretien, Jean 204
CII *see* Confederation of Indian Industry
circular migration theory 55
circular transnational migrants 54–55
citizenship 2, 56
class formation 178
Cleveland Thyagaraja Festival 89
Clinton, Hillary 138
CMANA (Carnatic Music Association of North America) 84–85
Colas, Nick 151
Cold War 135–136
collaborations by Indian dancers 9–10, 92–94; Contemporary Indian Dance 92; hegemonic intercultural theatre (HIT) 94; India–Bangladesh collaboration 98–102; India–Korea collaboration 94–98; interculturalism 93
Collins, R. 213
Colombo, Enzo 108, 114
colonialism 4, 5, 6
Communist Party South Africa 194
Confederation of Indian Industry (CII) 138, 272
Conradson, D. 227–228, 233
Contemporary Legend Theatre of Taiwan 94
Cooper, S. 197

Corbyn, Jeremy 167, 168
Corley, E. 64
cross-border flows and movements 3, 177
Cross, J. 22
Crowley, Daniel 6
cultural capital 177
culture and identities 6; collaborations by Indian dancers 92–102; Indian music and transnationalism 9, 78–90; second-generation Indian residents in Oman 10, 119–129; second-generation South Asians in Canada 10, 104–115; translocal puja in Guyanese Hindu communities 8–9, 69–76

Dadoo, Yusuf 191
Daily News and Analysis 151
Dalit transnational activism today 11–12, 158–159; Dalit diaspora and the United Nations 163–164; impact of neoliberal globalization on India 160–161; internationalizing the Dalit movement 162–163; transnationalization of Dalit women's movement 164–165; WCAR and Dalit human rights 165; who are the Dalits? 159–160; World Social Forum 165–167; conclusion 167–168
dalits 6, 83
Dall, Caroline Wells Healey 42–43
dance *see* collaborations by Indian dancers; Indian music and transnationalism
Das Dasgupta, S. 212
Das, Taraknath 134
Dasgupta, B. N. 247
Datta, Ayona 74
Datta, Bhupendranath 247
Datta, K. 230
Dauvillier, Sylvie 145
Dayal, Lal Har 247
Deb, Sandipan 43
Deboo, Astad 92–93, 94–95, 96–98, 100, 102
Deffner, V. 122, 128n4
Dekker, R. 236
Desai, Ashwin 5, 192, 195
Desai, Manisha 158
Desai, Morarji 258
Desai, N. P. 194
Dhaka Tribune 98
Dhaliwal, Spinder 173, 186
diaspora 6, 133–134, 137, 175–176, 266, 267
displacements 4
Divakar, N. Paul 162–163
Diwali 87
domestic work abroad 43–44
Dornan, Robert 136
Dowling, R. 215, 218, 224n12
Dreyfuss, Joel 151
Drori, Israel 178

Drucker, P.F. 40n1
Du Bois, W. E. B 247
Duara, Prasenjit 248
Dubai *see* layered cities, shared histories
Dutta, Debalina 43, 45

Ebaugh, Helen Rose 147
Economic Times 37
Edwards, B. H. 23
Engbersen, G. 236
engineers *see* return migration of scientists and engineers
English Vinglish (film) 212, 215
Erel, Umut 178
ethnic enclaves 187, 188n8
ethnicities 1–2; *see also* translocal *puja* in Guyanese Hindu communities
European Parliament 167
exceptional spaces 23–24

Faist, Thomas 2, 188n5
Featherstone, David 243
feminism 2–3
Ferguson, J. 1
festivals 87–88
field 178, 188n5
Finn, Rachel L. 108
Fisher, Michael 245
Fix, M. 32–33
flexible citizenship 56
forced migrations 4
Foreign Contribution Regulation Act (FCRA) 166
France *see* Hindu identities in France and the U.S.
France 24 151
Fraser, N. 162

Gandhi, Ela 191
Gandhi, Mahatma 191, 193, 196, 245, 246, 247–248
garba 86, 87, 88, 89
Gardner, A. 123
Gatina, Liliya 6
gender and Indian transnationalism 3; in British Empire 248–250; Canada: workers, families, and households 13, 201–209; Indian origin women in South Africa 12–13, 191–199; Indian women in Toronto 13, 212–223; middling Tamil migrants in Singapore 13, 227–236; transnational Indian women entrepreneurs 12, 173–188; in the United States 146–147
gender and labor in Indian transnationalism 8, 42; anchors and displacements 50–51; domestic work abroad 43–44; family reunification and gendered labor 46, 47; global IT workers 45; migration and gendered employment 42–43;

nursing and caring labor 44–45; professional volunteers 49–50; temporary worker programs 46–47; transnational housewives 47–49; conclusion 51
George, Sheba Mariam 45
German Federal Cultural Foundation 98
Ghadar party 247
Ghosh, Jayati 161
Ghosh, Sutama 205
Ginwala, Frene 191
Glick-Schiller, Nina 1, 2, 89, 104
Global Organization of People of Indian Origin (GOPIO) 137
globality and globalization 23, 160–161, 164, 267
Goebel, Michael 246
Goethe Institute of Bangladesh 98
Goh Chok Tong 270
gold *see* layered cities, shared histories
Gold, Steve J. 177, 178, 181, 182, 187
Goonam, Dr. Kesaveloo 191, 193, 194, 196
Goreau-Ponceaud, Anthony 149
Gorman, Daniel 247
Gorringe, Hugo 160
Govinden, D. 192, 194, 196
Greater India Society (1925) 248
Greenfeld, Liah 144
Greiner, Clemens 74
Grewal, Inderpal 244
Grosz, Elizabeth 214, 222
Grotowski, Jerzy 93
Guarnizo, L. E. 215
Gujarati Yuvak Mandal 274
Gulf Cooperation Council (GCC) countries 43–44, 119; *see also* second-generation Indian residents in Oman
Guo, S. 220
Gupta, Akhil 1
Gupta, Namrata 45
Guyanese Hindu communities *see* translocal puja in Guyanese Hindu communities

habitus 177–178, 214–215, 224n9
Hague International Conference on the Human Rights of Dalit Women (2006) 167
Haines, Chad 264
Hamid Ali, Shareefah 249
Hamilton, Lee 135
Han, Christine 270
Har, Lala 134
Harada, Keiko 97
Hardill, Irenen 44
Hardtmann, Eva-Maria 163
Harrison, George 80
Hays, Sharon 49
Hebert, Yvonne 106, 107
Hegde, Radha 6, 139

hegemonic intercultural theatre (HIT) 94
Hewitson, Gillian 48
Himanshu 161
The Hindu 97
Hindu identities in France and the U.S. 11, 143; conceptions of nationhood and religion 143–144; construction of Hinduism in France 148–152; construction of Hinduism in the U.S. 136, 139, 143, 145–148; Hindu migration histories and population growth 144–145; conclusion: rethinking transnationalism 152–153; *see also* translocal puja in Guyanese Hindu communities
Hindu Swayamsevak Sangh 136
Hiralal, Kalpana 5, 6
historic and contemporary networks in transnational spaces: British Empire transnational mobility of Indians 14, 241–251; layered cities, shared histories 14, 253–265; Singapore as pivot for diasporic and transnational networks 14, 266–277
Ho, L. E. E. 228, 233
Holi 87
Hollande, François 151
homemaking and transnationalism 47–49, 111, 121–122, 123, 124–125, 127–128
housekeepers 24–27
human rights 46, 158, 159, 162, 163, 165, 193
Human Rights Watch 163, 165, 166
humanitarian organizations 3

IAA (Indian Association of America) 135
IACPA (India Abroad Center for Political Action) 137
IAFC (Indian American Friendship Council) 139
IAFPE *see* Indian American Forum for Political Education
IASLC (Indian American Security Leadership Council) 138
Ibrahim, Dawood 253
ICC (India Chamber of Commerce) 134
identity *see* second-generation Indian residents in Oman; second-generation South Asians in Canada
IDRF (India Development and Relief Fund) 136
IDSN *see* International Dalit Solidarity Network
IIT Alumni Association Singapore (IITAAS) 275
IITs *see* Indian Institutes of Technology
ILA *see* India League of America
ILO (International Labor Organization) 44
immigration market model 55
IMRC (Indian Muslim Relief Committee) 136
indentured migration 5
India: diaspora policy 137; independence 11, 87, 134, 135, 145, 203; interventionism 175, 188n2; Look East Policy 270; remittances 83,

Index

120, 147, 176; soft power 56; University Grant Commission 56; *see also* Indian/American foreign policy
India Abroad Center for Political Action (IACPA) 137
India Chamber of Commerce (ICC) 134
India Development and Relief Fund (IDRF) 136
India League 247
India League of America (ILA) 134, 135
India Society 242
India Today (magazine) 24
India-US migration 5
Indian/American foreign policy 10–11; current issues and road forward 138–140; early political activism and Cold War 134–136; Ghadar Party 134; Indian American lobby 136–138; Indian diaspora in the U.S. 133–134, 175–176; nuclear deal 137–138; conclusion 140–141
Indian American Forum for Political Education (IAFPE) 136, 140
Indian American Friendship Council (IAFC) 139
Indian American Security Leadership Council (IASLC) 138
Indian Association of America (IAA) 135
Indian Emigration Act (1983) 44
Indian Freedom Association 247
Indian Institutes of Technology (IITs) 43, 275, 277n15
Indian music and transnationalism 9, 78; commercial popular music and dance 81–83; international connections prior to independence 78–79; transnationalization of Indian classical music 80–81; concluding perspectives 88–90
Indian music in greater New York City region 83–84; classical music in the metropolis 84–86; high school in the South Asian diaspora 88; holidays and festivals 87–88; universities and regional musics 86–87
Indian Muslim Relief Committee (IMRC) 136
Indian National Army 274
Indian National Congress 247, 248
Indian Ocean 119
Indian origin women in South Africa 12–13, 191; diasporic/hybrid identity 195–196; Durban and District Women's League 197; gendered identity 196; historical perspective 192–193; identity work 196–197; Indian Education Act 193; Job Reservations Act 193; Mixed Marriages Act (1949) 193; negotiating a hybrid identity 195; Population Registration Act (1950) 193; South African Indians: contemporary hurdles 197–199; Women's March (1956) 194; women's solidarity 194; Zenzele club 194
Indian transnationalism: defined 4–5; literature review 5; in this book 6–14

Indian women in Toronto 13, 212–214; freedom and the transnational habitus 214–215, 224n9; freedom: inside and/or outside? 215–216; geography of freedom 218–222; research design 216–217; research findings 217–222; what is freedom? 217–218; discussion and conclusions 222–223
Indian Women's Movement 164
inequality 2
Information Technology-Business Process Outsourcing (ITBPO) industries 174
Infosys 35
InKo Centre 93, 94–95
INSEE (Institut national de la statistique et des études économiques) 145
interculturalism 93
internal migrations 3, 15n3
International Convention to Eliminate All Forms of Racial Discrimination 163–164
International Dalit Solidarity Network (IDSN) 165, 166, 168
International Labor Organization (ILO) 44
International Woman Suffrage Alliance (IWSA) 249
internationalism 1, 2
Israni, Pranoti and Rishi 273
IT/ITES/ICT sector: Canada 201–202, 204; Dalits 161; in India's transnational economy 21, 22–23, 24, 25–26, 34–35, 45; in Singapore 229, 231, 232–233, 275; in United States 34–35, 175, 176; women 44–45, 48, 50
ITBPO (Information Technology-Business Process Outsourcing) industries 174
IWSA (International Woman Suffrage Alliance) 249
Iyengar, Vikram 92, 98, 99, 100, 101–102

Jafer, Rathi 93, 95, 96, 100
Jaffrelot, Christophe 159, 161
Jain, Sonali 6
Janmohamed, Z. 38
Jinnah, Muhammad Ali 246
Johari, Aarefa 100
Johnson, Lyndon B. 135
Johnson, Sonali 44
Joseph, Helen 194
Joseph, May 6
Joshee, Anandibai 42–43
Juhongman 96
Juster, Kenneth 140

Kallatra Abdul Kadir Haji 255
Kane, Shyam 84
Kapadia, Karin 159, 161
Kaplan, R. 39
Kapur, Deepak 43

Kapur, Steve 82
Karaka, D. F. 246
Karnad, Bharat 140
Karodia, Farida 192
Karthikeyan, A. 255
kathak 80, 85, 94, 95, 98, 99, 100–101, 102
Kaur, Rajkumari Amrit 249
Kaushal, N. 32–33
Kavilanz, P. 37
Kearney, Michael 1
Kelly, Philip 178
Khadepaun, Sameer 273
Khadria, B. 40n1
Khan, Noor-un-nisa Inayat 249
Khan, Nusrat Fateh Ali 78
King, R. 55
Kirkpatrick, Dr. Maynard 96
knowledge workers, defined 40n1; *see also* skill gap and brain drain for the U.S.
Kodoth, Praveena 44
Kohli, Atul 160, 188n2
Krishnavarma, Shyamaji 247
kritis 84, 85, 279
Kurien, Prema 146
Kuwait 44, 119

La Guerre, John 5
labor *see* gender and labor in Indian transnationalism
Landolt, Patricia 187
Lang, Iain 49
Lappin, Sonali 140
Latham, A. 227–228, 233
layered cities, shared histories 14, 253–254; Dubai, Malabar and cities of gold 262–263; Dubai Shopping Festival (DSF) 261, 262; Foreign Exchange Regulation Act (1973) 260; Gold Control Act 255, 258, 259, 260; gold smuggling 253–254, 255–257; liberalisation in India, brand-building in Dubai 260–262; Malayali, gold and the mobility complex 258–260; Malayalis in Dubai 254–257; *Sonis* 259; conclusion 263–264
Le Pen, Jean-Marie 150
League Against Imperialism 248
League of Nations 247, 250
Lee Kuan Yew 270
Lei, Daphne P. 94
Les Bronzés (film) 150
Lester, Alan 243
Levitt, Peggy 2, 89, 104, 107, 147
Light, Ivan 173, 177, 178, 182, 187
Limb, Hyoung-Taek 94, 95
Loi de 9 décembre (1905; France) 148
Long, J. C. 216
Lusis, Torn 178

Macaulay, Thomas Babington 245
MacClarenin, Roy 204
MacDonald, Sandra 44
McDowell, L. 216
Made in Bangladesh (dance) 98–102
Maharaj, B. 193, 198
Mahatma Gandhi National Rural Employment Guarantee Act (MGNREGA) 161, 168
Mahdavi, Pardis 44
Majumdar, T. 40n1
Malabar *see* layered cities, shared histories
Man, Guida 48
Mandela, Nelson 196
Mandela, Winnie 197, 198, 199
Mani, A. 270
Manjapra, Kris 247
Manjunath, C. 96
Manohar, Namita 6
Manoharan, Vincent 165
Manorama, Ruth 164, 167, 168
Manuel, Peter 89
Marson, Una 249
Martin-i-Pardo, Meritxell 149, 150
Marwari Mitra Mandal (MMM) 274
Massey, Doreen 264, 268
Mastan, Haji 253
Mathurs 274
Mayet, Khatija 194
Meer, Fatima 191, 192, 194, 195, 196–197, 198, 199
Meer, Ismail 197
Meer, Zohra 194
Mehta, Purvi 164
Mehta, S. R. 122, 128n4
Menon, V. K. Krishna 247
MGNREGA *see* Mahatma Gandhi National Rural Employment Guarantee Act
Middle East 43–44
middling Tamil migrants in Singapore 13, 227–229; middling transnationals 227–228; Musuguntha Vellalar transnational migrants 227, 228, 229–233, 236n1; The Next Lap policy 229; translocal village 227, 234–236
Mies, Maria 48
migrants'/workers' lives: gender and labor 8, 42–51; return migration of scientists and engineers 8, 54–64; service workers in India's transnational economy 7, 21–30; skill gap and brain drain for the U.S. 7–8, 31–40
migration 2, 3–4, 5–6
Migration Policy Institute 32–33, 174
Mitra, Subrata K. 161
Mkhize, Bertha 194, 197
MMM (Marwari Mitra Mandal) 275
Mnouchkine, Ariane 94
Modi, Narendra 139, 141, 151, 152, 161, 166
Mok Chin 97

Moore, Dorothy Perrin 184
Morrison, Bruce 33
Mukharji, T. N. 244
Mukherjee, Madhushree 5
Mukherjee, P. 23
Mukherjee, Sumita 249
music *see* Indian music and transnationalism; Indian music in greater New York City region
Mussolini, Benito 247

Nagengast, Carole 1
Naicker, Dr. Gangathura Mohambry Naicker 191
Naidoo, Phyllis 191, 192, 194
Naidu, Sarojini 244, 246
Naoroji, Dadabhai 246
Narayan, Anjana 146
NASSCOM (National Association of Software & Service Companies) 174
Natal Indian Congress 193
National Campaign on Dalit Human Rights (NCDHR) 159, 164, 165, 166, 167
National Committee for India's Freedom (NCIF) 134, 135
National Council of Applied Research 159
National Federation of Dalit Women (NFDW) 159, 164, 165, 166
National Foundation for American Policy 34
National Woman's Party (USA) 249
NātyaŚāstra 94, 279
Naujoks, Daniel 139
Navaratri 87, 88, 280
Navatman Inc. 85
Nehru, Jawaharlal 134, 160, 246, 248, 269–270
New Zealand migrants 55
Ngema, Mbongeni 195
Ngoyi, Lillian 194
Nixon, Richard 135
Noiriel, Gérard 143, 144
Non-Resident Indians (NRI) 175–176, 180–181, 260; *see also* Indian/American foreign policy
Noreum Machi 96
Nowicka, Magdalena 178
Nurnberger, Ralph 137
nursing and caring labor 44–45
Nye, J. 56

Obama, Barack 38, 40n2, 47, 59
O'Brien, S. A. 38
OECD (Organization for Economic Cooperation and Development) countries 32
Oman *see* second-generation Indian residents in Oman
Ong, A. 22, 56
Ong Keng Sen 94
Onley, J. 122
Osella, C. 230
Osella, F. 230

Overseas Citizenship of India (OCI) 139, 175–176
Overseas Friends of the BJP (OFBJP) 139
Ozden, C. 32

Padamjee, Dadi 97
Palmer Josie 194
Pan-Asian Conference (1920) 248
Pan-IIM Alumni Association (Singapore) 275
Pan-Pacific Trade Union 248
Pandurang Munow 14 6
Pant, Harsh V. 139
Parutis, V. 228, 233
Patel, Suriakala 194
Pathan, Yusuf 255
Pather, Veeramah 194
Pavlova, Anna 92
Penn Masala 86–87
Percot, Marie 44
Pew Research Center 145, 174
Pfaffenbach, C. 122
Phule, Mahatma Jotirao 159
The Pickle Factory 98
Pillai, Shanti 81
Pillayk, Navi 166–167
Poggesi, Sara 186
Polanyi, Karl 159, 162
political engagement in transnational spaces: Dalit transnational activism today 11–12, 158–168; Hindu identities in France and the U.S. 11, 143–153; Indian/American foreign policy 10–11, 133–141
Pollock, Sheldon 78
Portes, Alejandro 2
Power, E. R. 215
Prameswran 273
Prashad, Vijay 137
Pratap, Raja Mahendra 248
Pratt, Mary Louise 243
puja *see* translocal puja in Guyanese Hindu communities
Puri, Sanjay 137, 140
Purkayastha, Bandana 3, 4, 48, 108, 146
Purushotam, Nirmala 270

Qatar 43–44, 119

Radhakrishnan, Smitha 45
Raghuram, Parvati 45, 48
Raghuram, Shobba 164
Rahman, Manjulika 99, 100
Rai, Lajpat 134
Raj, Y. 37
Rajan, S. Irudaya 43
Raju, Gopal 137, 141
Ram, Jhinda 244
Ramabai, Pandita 42, 43
Ramasamy, E. V. 274

Index

Rao, Nirupama Menon 138, 140
Rao, Praveen D. 96
Rashtriya Swayamsevak Sangh (RSS) 152
Ray, P. C. 247
Ray, Renuka 246
Rebughini, Paola 108, 114
Reddi, Muthulakshmi 249
Reddy, Sujani 44
Reitz, Jeffrey G. 105
religious transnationalism 120; *see also* Hindu identities in France and the U.S.; translocal puja in Guyanese Hindu communities
The Renan Performance Collective 98
repeated migration 4
resources 5
return migration of scientists and engineers 8, 54–55; circular migration theory 55; conceptual framework 61, *61*; economic factors 56, 58–59; family factors 57, 60–61; findings 58–61; immigration market model 55; literature review 55–56; methodology 57–58; political factors 56–57, 59–60; post-return transnationalism 61–63; social/cultural factors 57, 60; conclusion 63–64
Rischer-Tiné, Harald 248
Roma refugees 150–151
Rose, D. 215–216
Roy, M. N. 247
RSS (Rashtriya Swayamsevak Sangh) 152
Rubinoff, Arthur G. 136, 138
Ruiz, R. G. 34
Rutgers New Brunswick (RU), New Jersey 86

Sahoo, Ajaya 6, 106, 121, 275,
SAIC *see* South African Indian Congress
Saklatvala, Shapurji 246, 247
Salkever, Alex 181
Samaddar, Ranabir 3, 5
Same-Same but Different 96
Sampat, P. 21, 22
Sangh Parivar 136
Saran, Rupam 114
Sarkar, Benoy Kumar 247
Sarvarkar, Veer 152
Saudi Arabia 119
Saund, Dalip Singh 135, 141
Saunders, Jennifer 145
Savarkar, V. S. 247
Saxenian, A. L. 55
Schäfer, W. 23
Schechner, Richard 93, 94
Schiller, N. 55
Schöttli, Jivanta 161
scientists *see* return migration of scientists and engineers
second-generation Indian residents in Oman 10, 119–120, 128n1; case study 122–128; education 123–124, 126, 128n6; framing the transnational 120–121; homemaking and transnationalism 121–122, 123, 124–125, 127–128; kafala system 119, 122, 128n2–5; women 126, 127, 129n9–11
second-generation South Asians in Canada 104, 105–106; methods 108–109; multiculturalism 106; negotiated belonging in a transnational social field 109; (understanding belonging through physical border flows 109–112; understanding imagined belonging 112–114); South Asians in Canada 105; transnational identity formation 107–108; transnationalism: literature review 106–107; conclusion 114–115
Seedat-Khan, Mariam 5, 192, 198
Sen, Kunal 161
Sennett, R. 228
Seoul Factory 94
service workers in India's transnational economy 7, 21–22; call-center workers 24–25, 27–28; class and experience of globality 28–29; exceptional spaces 22–23; globality within exceptional spaces 23–24; housekeepers 24–27; IT/ITES sector 21, 22–23, 24, 25–26, 34–35; pride and subservience 24–28; special economic zones (SEZs) 21–22; study methods 24
Shadhona 98
Shaffer, Robert 134
Shakespeare, William 94–95
Shankar, Ravi 78, 80, 84
Shankar, Uday 92
Sharma, Ashok 138
Shaw, M. 23
Sheng, E. 39
Shinde, Gauri 212
Sholte, Jan Aart 23
Short, E. 38
Siddique, Sharon 270
Sindhi Merchants Association 276n10
Singapore as pivot for diasporic and transnational networks 14, 266–267; CECA (Comprehensive Economic Cooperation Agreement) 270, 272, 276n3; Indian economic networks and platforms 271–273; Indian socio-cultural networks 273–274; Indian transnational alumni networks 274–275; language 270, 273, 274; multiculturalism 270; Self-Respect movement 274; Singapore as 'node' and 'space' for Indian transnational networks 267–268; transition of Indian transnational spaces in Singapore 268–275; conclusion 275–276; *see also* middling Tamil migrants in Singapore
Singapore Gujarati Society 274
Singapore Indian Chamber of Commerce and Industry (SICCI) 271, 272
Singapore Indian Development Association (SINDA) 270

Index

Singapore Malayalee Association 274
Singapore Sindhi Association 276n10
Singh, J.J. 134–135, 141
Singh, Prerna 160
Singh, Supriya 6
skill gap and brain drain for the U.S. 7–8, 31–32; H-1B and India 35, **35**, *36*, 47–48, 59–60, 175, 188n3; H-1B and tech companies 34–35; H-1B visa system 33–34, *36*, 39, 46–47, 56–57; H-4 visa holders 38, 40n2, 47–48, 49–50, 57, 59; impact on India as sending country 37–38, 40n2; impact on US-based companies 38–39; migration of knowledge workers and the H1B 32–33; skill gap in US and reverse brain drain 39; Trump executive order and impact 31, 35–37; conclusion 39–40
Smith, M. P. 228
social capital 177, 181
social networks 55, 177
Society for the Promotion of Indian Classical Music and Culture Amongst Youth (SPIC-MACAY) 86
soldiers 5
Somayya, Votti Veeramah 195
Somerville, Kara 108
Soni, Punit 38–39
Sorabji, Cornelia 244
South Africa *see* Indian origin women in South Africa
South African Indian Congress (SAIC) 193, 194
South Asia Parliamentarians Forum for Social Justice 166
South–South interactions 6, 7, 121; *see also* collaborations by Indian dancers
special economic zones (SEZs) 21–22
Sri Lankans: in Canada 105, 108–109, 112, 113, 115; in France 145
Srinivasan, T. 93
Srinivasan, Vasanthi 45
Srirangam 273
Sriskandarajah, Anuppiriya 106
Steadman, John 248
Stevens, M. 37
Stoler, Ann 243
Stolte, Carolien 248
Stone, Pamela 49
Subramaniam, Lakshmi 245
supra-national blocks 4
Swaminathan, Chitra 97

Tadashi, Suzuki 94
Tagore, Rabindranth 248
Taiwan: Ministry of Education 56; National Science Council 56; National Youth Council 56
Tamaris, William de 151
Tamil Representative Council (TRC) 274
Tamils *see* middling Tamil migrants in Singapore; Singapore as pivot for diasporic and transnational networks
Tan, Justin 181
tāssa 79, 87, 89
Tata Consultancy Services (TCS) 35
Tata, Herabai 249
Tata, Mithan 249
Tellis, Ashley 138
Teltumbde, Anand 161
temporary workers 5–6, 46–47
Tharamangalam, Joseph 160
Thiollet, Hélène 123
Thorat, Vimal 164
Thotakura, Prasad 139–140
Thrush, G. 31
TiE (The Indus Entrepreneurs) 273, 275
Times of India 32, 255
The Times of Oman 128n6
Tokyo Wonder Site 97
Tomic, P. 25, 27
transgender transnationalism 14n1
transitional spaces 188n5
translocal puja in Guyanese Hindu communities 8–9, 69; ethnic groups 69–70, 75n2; Hinduism 70–71, 75n4; locality and puja 73–75; puja and transnational gift exchange 71–73; conclusion 75
transnational communities 266
transnational housewives *see* homemaking and transnationalism
transnational Indian women entrepreneurs 12, 173–174; immigration from India to the U.S. 175–176; inheritors 182–183; lone crusaders 183–185; methods 174–175; migrant entrepreneurs 188n1; power couples 179–181; returnees 188n1; survivalists 185–187; theory 176–178; conclusion 187
transnationalism 1–4; defined 1, 158; Global North 3, 4, 6, 14n2; Indian transnationalism 4–6, 7–14; South–South 6, 7, 121
travel and travel-writing 244–245
TRC (Tamil Representative Council) 274
Trouillet, Pierre-Yves 149
Trudeau, Pierre 203
Trump, Donald 31–32, 39, 47

UNESCO 120
United Arab Emirates 43–44, 119
United Kingdom: Anti Caste Discrimination Alliance (ACDA) 166, 167; Commonwealth Immigrants Act (1962) 46; Dalit Solidarity Network 167; Equality Act (2017) 167; Immigration Act (1971) 46; migrants to Canada 55
United Nations 3, 163; Committee on the Elimination of Discrimination Against Women 167; Committee on the Elimination of Racial

Discrimination (CERD) 163–164, 165; Fourth Women's World Conference (1995) 164; Human Rights Commission 166; International Covenant on Economic, Social and Cultural Rights 46; Universal Declaration of Human Rights (1948) 46, 163; WCAR (2001) 163, 164–165, 166, 168

United States: Burton Amendment 136; Chinese Exclusion Acts (1882) 43, 46; Citizenship and Immigration Services (USCIS) 32, 36, 37, 38; Civil Rights Act (1964) 33; Congressional Caucus on India and Indian Americans 136; Hinduism 136, 139, 143, 145–148; Immigration Act (1990) 33, 34, 46, 175; Immigration and Nationality Act (Hart-Celler Act,1965) 33, 46, 84, 133, 175; immigration laws 33, 46; Luce-Celler Act (1946) 84, 134; National Academy of Sciences (NAS) 54; National Science Foundation (NSF) 54; Office of Immigration Statistics (OIS) 174; Senate Caucus "Friends of India" 138; *see also* Hindu identities in France and the U.S.; Indian/American foreign policy; Indian music in greater New York City region; return migration of scientists and engineers; skill gap and brain drain for the U.S.; transnational Indian women entrepreneurs

United States India Political Action Committee (USINPAC) 137, 138, 140

untouchables *see* Chamars; Dalit transnational activism today

Upadhya, Carol 45, 48

U.S.-India Business Council (USIBC) 138

Vahed, Goolam 5, 192, 195
Valk, Reimara 45
Vally, R. 196
Van der Veer, Peter 70
Varadarajan, Latha 141
Varijashree 96
Varma, Roli 43
Vasavi, A. R. 45
Veda Federation of France 152
Verhade, Yogesh 163
Vertovec, Steven 2, 70, 75n4, 120, 121, 267

Vishwa Hindu Parishad of America (VHPA) 136
Vogel, Ann 49
Voigt-Graf, Carmen 267, 268
Vora, N. 123

Wacquant, Loïc 177
Wadhwa, Vivek 181
Wajid, A. 197
Waldmann, Helena 98, 99–100, 101, 102
Wall Street Journal 37
Weibel, Nadine 149
Weinbaum, A. E. 23
Wells, J. 194
Willis, Katie 48
Wilson, Robert 94
women 2–3, 5, 6; in British Empire 248–250; citizenship and suffrage 249; domestic work abroad 43–44; Hindu women 146–147; nursing and caring labor 44–45; Oman 126, 127, 129n9–11; transnational housewives 47–49, 111, 121–122, 123, 124–125, 127–128; U.S. H-4 visa holders 47–48, 49–50, 51, 57; in work 161; *see also* Indian origin women in South Africa; Indian women in Toronto; transnational Indian women entrepreneurs
World Bank 32
World Conference Against Racism, Racial Discrimination, Xenophobia and Related Intolerance (WCAR) 163, 164–165, 166, 168
World Music Institute 84
World Social Forum (WSF) 158, 163, 165–167

Xuma, Madie-Hall 194

Y Space 97
Yang, Fenggang 147
Yeoh, Brenda 48, 267
Yung, Danny 97

Zachariah, K.C. 43
Zed, Rajan 151
Zhou, Min 173
Zondo, Andrew 196
Zuckerberg, Mark 35
Zuni Icosacherdron 97